Sam Moskowitz

THE IMMORTAL STORM

A HISTORY OF SCIENCE FICTION FANDOM

BY

SAM MOSKOWITZ

Illustrated with photographs from
the collections of Sam Moskowitz
and Robert A. Madle

PREFACE by A. Langley Searles

Including an INDEX compiled by
Jerry Burge and Carson Jacks

HYPERION PRESS, INC.
WESTPORT, CONNECTICUT

Library of Congress Cataloging in Publication Data

Moskowitz, Samuel.
    The immortal storm.

    Reprint of the ed. published by Atlanta Science
Fiction Organization Press, Atlanta.
        1. Science fiction--Periodicals--History and
criticism. 2. Science fiction societies. I. Title.
[PN3383.S4M6 1973]   809.3'876   73-15069
ISBN 0-88355-131-4
ISBN 0-88355-160-8 (pbk.)

Published in 1954
by The Alanta Science Fiction Organization Press, Atlanta, Georgia

Hyperion reprint edition 1974

Library of Congress Catalogue Number 73-15069

ISBN 0-88355-131-4 (cloth ed.)

ISBN 0-88355-160-8 (paper ed.)

Printed in the United States of America

To SCIENCE FICTION FANDOM

PREFACE

Editorial note by A. Langley Searles, editor of
Fantasy Commentator, *prefacing the first instal-
ment of* The Immortal Storm *in that magazine.*

FOR SOME REASON unknown to this writer, it is usually customary to
preface a work of this length and scope with a tedious editorial
discussion of its intrinsic importance and the qualifications of its
author. To me, it seems unnecessarily redundant to indulge in a sym-
posium concerning either. Like any other historical ducument, "The
Immortal Storm" will be judged on its own merits and on these also
will the reputation of the author rest; they and they alone are the
criteria. Lest this give the impression that I purposely refrain
from giving a positive opinion in advance, however, let it be positively stated that I believe this to be one of the most important
works ever to have sprung from the ranks of fantasy fandom—and did
I not consider it outstanding you would not now find it in these
pages. More need not be said; for, as Johnson once remarked, those
of the reading public are the ultimate judges: if they are pleased,
all is well; if they are not, there is no point in telling them why
they should have been.

ACKNOWLEDGEMENTS

TO Dr. A. Langley Searles who inspired and carried forth the serial publication of this History; to Henry Burwell who successfully put the History into one mimeographed package and conceived its present form; to Dr. D. C. Montgomery whose interest extended beyond moral support; to Ian Macauley who kept the project alive during transition, and finally to Carson Jacks and Jerry Burge who carried it through to its successful completion.

CONTENTS

LIST OF PHOTOGRAPHS

All photographs are from the collections of
Sam Moskowitz and Robert A. Madle

THE IMMORTAL STORM

Chapter I

INTRODUCTION

FOLLOWERS and glorifiers of the fantastic tale like to think that they are different, that they represent something new on the face of the earth; mutants born with an intelligence and a sense of farseeing appreciation just a bit higher than the norm. They like to believe that their counterpart has never before existed, that they have no predecessors. "No one," they say, "has ever seen our visions, dreamed our dreams. Never before has man's brain reached out so far into the limitless stretches of the cosmos about him."

But facts belie this assertion of newness. Since the dawn of time man has woven his fantasies, fabricated his gods and their imaginative origins, told tales of things beyond the range of his senses. The Old Testament contains not only the fantasy of Adam and Eve, But more than one out-and-out ghost story as well. *The Iliad* and *The Odyssey*, two of the greatest of ancient works, are forthright unblushing fantasies. So is *Beowulf*, the oldest written saga in English.

For ages man lived in a world where he was a slave to the elements. His own achievements were by comparison crude and immature; his every living moment was subject to the blind caprices of fate. Not unnaturally, he dreamt of greater things. At first his achievements were limited to dreams, and to dreams only. And in fantasy he created wonder-lands of magic carpets, healing potions, and all the other requirements of a luxurious existence. He held little hope of ever encountering such a life, but in these visions he found escape from his mean, primitive world. It was not until man found himself capable of transforming dreams into prophesy that he wrote science fiction. For science fiction was prophesy. And, being based on extrapolations of known theories, its possibilities were subject only to the degrees of factuality in its groundwork. The only difference between the science fiction fan of today and the Homer of yesteryear is that the fan of today knows there is a sufficiently large kernel of truth in his dreams to make them possible of realization—that the fantastic fiction of today may well become the fact of tomorrow.

When one sees his sketches of flying machines, parachutes, submarines, tanks and guns, and realizes that he knew the distant stars to be suns and postulated the existence of other earths, it is difficult to believe that Leonardo da Vinci was not a science fiction fan. Nor is one inclined to doubt that Galileo, constructor of the first astronomical telescope and promulgator of the heliocentric principle, was also a devoted follower of extrapolated science. For then, as now, every great new discovery posed a hundred more unanswered riddles. And there came the day when not only scientists, but writers of fiction suggested possible explanations. Some of these read like fantasies—yet at the core they were but extrapolations from a basis of fact. They were science fiction.

Collectors of fantasy books point proudly to this, battered volumes

1

in archaic type dealing with such plots as imaginary voyages to
the moon. The earliest use of this theme that we know of dates back
two thousand years—but who can say with certainty that Lucian of
Samasota was the first to write of it? And since his day many hundreds of books, now old, have seen the light of day—fantastic
flights of fiction now all but forgotten, many, possibly, recorded in
no biographical list. What numbers have been ground up in the pass-
age of time? Somebody must have read them, collected them even——
followers of science fiction you and I will never know.

Great authors could no more help being impressed by the forward
rush of science than could the man in the street. Science fiction
and fantasy are liberally sprinkled through their works, and scarcely a single comprehensive anthology of short stories will be found
to lack one having such a theme. Notables of no less a stature than
Edgar Allen Poe, Rudyard Kipling, H. G. Wells, Washington Irving,
Mark Twain, Fitz-James O'Brien, Guy de Maupassant, Stephen Vincent
Benet and Nathaniel Hawthorne have found this medium far from un-
satisfying, nor have their readers been overly critical of their
writings in this vein.

And yet today, with many of the past's basic story-conjectures being realized, it is feared that there will soon be nothing left to
write about. This is the creed of hide-bound, conservative hack-
worshippers. Many science fiction publications have fostered such a
belief by sacrificing their product on an alter of sensational commercialism. They have banned all but two of the stereotyped plots,
they reject every new idea and novel twist as too radical. The fantastic complaints they utter would never have been voiced in the
"new policy" days of *Wonder Stories* or in the heyday of *Astounding's*
"thought-variant" issues. In those times, the trouble was not in
obtaining enough new ideas, but in choosing the best from those
which were submitted for publication. When man can no longer think
ahead, when he has reached the limits of his imagination, he is
through. Yet each new discovery opens up greater vistas for science
to explore, and since each new discovery is the springboard from
which more, not less, science fiction is launched, we reach the obvious conclusion that the end is nowhere in sight.

Another delusion that many apparently suffer from is that science
fiction is the virtual monopoly of America and England—that the
people of no other country have ever cared for such reading matter.
But again the facts easily disprove such an allegation. Books of
science fiction have appeared in every nation where a publishing industry exists, and have ever found a wide and appreciative audience.
Germany has produced literally thousands of them. Japan has reprinted many of the tales of the popular fantasy author Ray Cummings, and
recently a Japanese edition of *Amazing Stories* has appeared. Science
fiction magazines printed in Spanish have come into the hands of
collectors. Willy Ley has spoken of a Russian magazine similar to
the American *Argosy* using science fiction as a matter of policy,
that originated in 1907, which is supposedly still in existence.
Science fiction magazines have been published in Holland, Mexico,
Canada and Australia. The popularity of A. Merritt's writings is an
excellent example of fantasy's international appeal: they have been
translated into French, Spanish, German, Norwegian and Russian, always meeting with enthusiastic response. Indeed, there is no questioning science fiction's universal popularity.

The middle and late Nineteenth Century saw fiction of this type appear with ever increasing frequency. *Harper's Magazine, The Atlantic Monthly, Godey's Ladies' Book* and other magazines featured it consistently, and Jules Verne wrote many novels having fantastic themes—some of which, at the present time, have already become realized prophesies. H. G. Wells capitalized on the taste which had been thus created with a long series of excellent science fiction novels beginning with the popular *Time Machine* (1895). From then on these tales followed on one another's heels with amazing rapidity. The number of periodicals printing them during the following quarter century was startlingly high. In America alone *Argosy, All-Story, Munsey's, The Cavalier, Modern Electrics, Popular, The Black Cat, Everybody's, The Blue Book, People's Favorite, MacClure's, Living Age, Cosmopolitan, Pearson's* and numerous others presented such fiction with the utmost regularity.

Just how much science fiction fans shaped the policies of those magazines is problematical; possibly their influence was greater than has been realized. However that may be, it is certain that the demand for their specialized product caused Street & Smith to issue *The Thrill Book* magazine—the first to be devoted in large part to the fantastic—early in 1919. Under the editorship of Harold Hershey and Eugene A. Clancy it ran for sixteen issues. Nevertheless, it seemingly produced but a negligable effect on the trend of science fiction; but as an initial ground-breaker in this country it is undeniably of interest and importance.

Of far more importance, however, was the advent of *Weird Tales* magazine in March, 1923. Despite the fact that its early days were rocky and hazardous it was a real crucible of fantasy. Never before, and possibly never again, were so many Simon-pure fantasy addicts united in a single reader-audience. *Weird* catered to them all: the supernatural, fantasy and science fiction tale, each was there. But the task of satisfying everyone was no easy one. From its earliest days those who wanted it to be predominently supernatural and those who would have it mainly scientific waged a bitter struggle for supremacy. It is perhaps fortunate that the former clique, supporting the more literate school of writers including H. P. Lovecraft and Clark Ashton Smith, eventually won out. But the win was by a fluke: Having committed itself to the title *Weird Tales,* little else was possible; to adopt a 100% science fiction policy in this guise would have been sheer suicide. So voluminous were the ranks of the latter, however, that a concession had to be made them—and thus it came about that in addition to the few (but regularly appearing) out-and-out science fiction tales, there appeared in those pages that fiction binding the supernatural with the scientific—the combination so well mastered by the late H. P. Lovecraft and used to a lesser extent by Clark Ashton Smith and Nictzin Dyalhis. Such stories as "When the Green Star Waned" and "The Dunwich Horror" —representing this school—came closest to satisfying all factions.

In the early 1920's, then, simply the reading of a magazine like *Weird Tales* was sufficient to characterize a man as a fantasy fan, a rule which held true until at least 1930.

Chapter II

GERNSBACK AND THE FIRST ALL-SCIENCE FICTION PUBLICATION

SINCE THE TURN of the century Hugo Gernsback had featured science fiction in all his published magazines. He was, moreover, the leading advocate of science fiction with the accent on science. Not scientific romances, fantasies, or "different" stories, but *science* fiction. From the time of his earliest periodical, *Modern Electrics,* through the *Electrical Experimenter,* into the days of *Science and Invention* he featured his own favorite brand, and won a following for it. He even introduced this type of fiction into such of his lesser lights as *Radio News.*

Hugo Gernsback did something for the science fiction fan that had never been attempted before: he gave him self-respect. He preached that those who followed this sort of reading-matter avidly were not possessed of a queer taste, but actually represented a higher type of intellect. And he tried to lay down rules for science fiction. Primary among these was plausibility: nothing was to appear in the stories he published that could not be given a logical, scientific explanation. To bolster this, ingenious photographs and related news paper columns surrounded the tales, until after a time it became difficult to differentiate between the fact and the fiction in *Science and Invention.*

One number of this magazine (August, 1923) was boldly labelled: "Scientifiction Issue," and featured half a dozen of these tales. The results of this experiment must have been gratifying, for Gernsback soon after circularized his readers with an announcement forecasting the appearance of a magazine entitled *Scientifiction*—wherein stories of the type popularized by his other publications were to appear. But the response was evidently not strong enough to warrant going through with the venture, and it was temporarily abandoned. A year later, however, deciding that his coined title had frightened many likely prospects away, Gernsback took a chance and brought out *Amazing Stories.*

The magazine skyrocketed to success overnight. The reasons for this have never been adequately explained, but what seems most plausible is that Gernsback had been carefully building up an audience for this venture, one which, on recognizing a 100% science fiction periodical for what it was, eagerly flocked to its support.

Had the science fiction fan of 1926 been less greedy *Weird Tales* might have been seriously hampered by this turn of events. Many read it solely for the occasional science fiction it printed and nothing else. But because of their insatiable appetite they did not desert *Weird Tales,* but rather began a strenuous effort to swing it away from the supernatural. And although as a result the magazine did veer in the science fiction direction during the next year, the change was only a temporary one. The appearance of *Amazing Stories,* however, had driven a wedge very deeply between the fantasy and science fiction groups. Heretofore, though differences had existed, both groups had pretty much occupied the same boat. But now each had its own magazine. And the fact that the latter clique was by far the most powerful was shown by comparison of the two periodicals' circulations.

The appearance of readers' letters in the "Discussions" column of *Amazing Stories* marked the beginning of science fiction fandom as we know it today. The volume and quality of mail received by the average science fiction magazine (both then and now) has always been a source of wonder, especially to those outside of the field. And in the old *Amazing* fans were ready and willing to discuss anything. The eagerness with which they prattled scientific talk was directly traceable to some scientific fact which had aroused their interest in its extrapolated counterpart in fiction. Be it astronomy, biology, physics or chemistry, they broached some query which coeval science could not answer, but which science fiction tried to. And the readers expressed their opinions on how logically it had been answered.

Nowadays, of course, fans are more interested in discussing trends in past fiction. But in those days, since a common background of reading was the exception rather than the rule, this was out of the question. They had no magazines, authors, traditions and fanwide happenings to talk about. If two fans had read a dozen of the same tales before becoming acquainted through correspondence brought about through "Discussions," it was highly unusual, and something to comment on with surprise. And thus having little ground for an exchange of likes and dislikes, fans of that decade naturally reverted to scientific discussions as a matter of course.

Amazing Stories' editor was Hugo Gernsback himself, if anything a more avid and widely-read fan than the majority of his readers. He constantly introduced into the magazine features dealing with his readers themselves, or those in which they might take part—pictures of the oldest and youngest readers, a prize story contest, slogan and emblem awards. Most important of all from a historical standpoint was the regular appearance of the already-mentioned "Discussions" column; since readers' letters to the editor were accompanied by the writers' full addresses, communication between interested fans was greatly facilitated.

It was in this manner that Jerome Siegel and Joseph Shuster, now famed as the originators of the character "Superman" became acquainted. Enthused by *Amazing Stories*, they presently produced *Cosmic Stories* and *Cosmic Stories Quarterly*, amateur, carbon-copied publications; these are the earliest—and rarest—fan-published "magazines." Such later-active fans as Raymond A. Palmer and Jack Williamson (to cite two other examples) also contacted one another through this same medium.

Then occurred an event whose details are shrouded in mystery. One day Gernsback was prosperous. The next he had lost completely his magazine chain and his radio station, and found himself in receivership. Though many have speculated on the causes of his financial crisis, naming frozen assets, family hardships and dishonest employees as the core of the trouble, the complete story has never been made clear. But everyone knew the man was not a failure. Their confidence was justified, for it did not take him long to regain a sound financial footing. Gernsback did so by one of the most remarkable stunts seen in the publishing game—an authentic example of a man pulling himself up by his own bootstraps. Early in 1929, then, he mailed

circulars to readers, informing them of his intention to publish a
magazine along the lines of the now-defunct *Science and Invention* to
be titled *Everyday Mechanics*. Advance Subscriptions were asked for.
And so fine was Gernsback's reputation at that time as a producer of
excellent scientific journals that 20,000 two-dollar subscriptions
poured in it is claimed. (Hugo Gernsback later claimed that this
figure was exaggerated, that 8,000 might be closer to the truth.)
With this intake, then, Hugo Gernsback again set himself up in business.

A spate of science fiction magazines followed. *Amazing Stories,*
which had been taken over by Teck Publications in this interim,
found itself competing with Gernsback's newly-founded *Science Wonder
Stories, Air Wonder Stories* and *Scientific Detective Stories.*
Amazing and *Science Wonder* issued quarterlies in addition to their
regular monthly numbers. Clayton Publications followed with *Astounding Stories* late in the same year. In 1930 Harold Hershey, former
editor of *Thrill Book* published two issues of *Miracle, Science and
Fantasy Stories,* edited by the blind Douglas M. Dold and illustrated
by his brother Elliot Dold. Hershey abandoned the publication when
Douglas Dold died suddenly. Elliot Dold later achieved reknown when
F. Orlin Tremaine brought him to Street & Smith to illustrate for
Astounding Stories. And to add to the flood Gernsback issued a series of paper-bound pamphlets of the same fiction. For the first time
science fiction fans were surfeited!

It did not take long for equilibrium to establish itself. *Scientific Detective Stories* soon ceased publication, and *Air Wonder* combined with *Science Wonder* under the latter title. *Astounding,* favoring a blood-and-thunder action policy as opposed to the more sedate
offerings of her older competitors, appealed to a new class of readers and managed to hang on.

Most interesting was the effect of these events on *Weird Tales.*
Never independent of those readers who bought the magazine solely
for the few science fiction tales it published, the sudden influx of
new periodicals all but ruined her. Surfeited elsewhere, readers de-
serted in droves, and by 1931 the diminishing circulation had forced
a bi-monthly schedule of appearance into effect. In casting about
for some means to avert disaster, Editor Farnsworth Wright hit upon
the plan of advertising current science fiction of *Weird Tales* in
Science Wonder and *Amazing Stories.* Tales having an interplanetary
theme were very popular in those times, and by procuring as many as
possible, and by printing the work of popular authors, *Weird Tales*
managed to return to its monthly schedule once more. It should be
borne in mind that a science fiction fan of that time was primarily
concerned with scientific plausibility, and had little or no penchant for stories dealing with ghosts or werewolves. This is shown today by the great rarity of complete copies of early *Weird Tales* numbers—while sets of excerpted and bound science fiction stories from
these same numbers are far more common. Having removed the stories
that interested them, science fiction fans of that time threw the
remainder of the magazines away, as it held no interest for them.

It is no wonder, therefore, that the early followers of the fantastic were called science fiction fans. Organization of the fans
was an outgrowth of the professional publications they followed, and
these were predominantly of the science fiction variety. It is quite

true that followers of the weird were also in evidence; but, perhaps because of personal inclination as well as their smaller numbers, they rarely organized themselves into any official or unofficial body. Indeed, they remain both unorganized and in the minority to this day. Yet because they and their media have much in common with that of the majority they may be considered as a part of a larger organic whole. This group will henceforth be referred to *in toto* in this work as "science fiction fandom"—or more simply "fandom"; and it should be understood to include within its ranks followers of supernatural and fantasy fiction generally as well as those who insist that every story be "scientifically plausible."

Chapter III

THE BEGINNING OF ORGANIZED FANDOM

LET IT AGAIN BE STRESSED that the very first organized groups consisted of *science* fiction fans. They were one in mind with Hugo Gernsback in believing that every one of their number was a potential scientist, and that the aim of every fan should not be a collection of fantastic fiction, but a home laboratory where fictional dreams might attain reality. Such a frame of mind laid the basis for the Science Correspondence Club, an organization which later evolved into the International Scientific Association (ISA). Such fans as Raymond A. Palmer (later editor of *Amazing Stories,* and presently editor and publisher of his own magazine, *Universe*), P. Schuyler Miller (well-known author), Frank B. Eason, Aubrey McDermott, Robert A. Wait and others had struck up a mutual correspondence. This prompted Palmer to suggest the encouragement of such correspondence among fans on a larger scale. Thus was the Science Correspondence Club organized. The members issued a club organ called *The Comet,* the first number of which was dated May, 1930; later numbers bore the title *Cosmology.* The club declared itself to be devoted to "the furtherance of science and its dissemination among the laymen of the world and the final betterment of humanity"; and the third issue of *The Comet* stated the organ's purpose: "This issue is dedicated to the furtherance of science through scientific articles printed in its pages and contributed by its more learned members." The Science Correspondence Club's president was Frank B. Eason; Raymond A. Palmer was editor of its publication, and Roy C. Palmer the assistant editor and distributor. Honorary members included such notables as Dr. T. O'Conor Sloane, Hugo Gernsback, Dr. Miles J. Breuer, H. V. Schoepflin, David Lasser, Jack Williamson, Ed Earl Repp, Harry Bates, Dr. Clyde Fisher, and others.

Love of science fiction was the basic bond that united these fans. Yet discussions in *The Comet* were a far cry to discussions of fiction —articles such as "The Psychology of Anger," "Chemistry and the Atomic Theory," "Recent Advancements in Television," "What Can Be Observed with a Small Telescope" and "Psychoanalysis" abounded. As time passed, however, the non-scientific note increased in volume somewhat. Articles based on science fiction stories appeared occasionally. Professionally known authors such as P. Schuyler Miller and A. W. Bernal contributed fiction. Accurate information on German rocketry was printed under the name of Willy Ley. Such luminaries as Miles J. Breuer, Jack Williamson, R. F. Starzl and Lilith Lorraine were also represented.

But after a dozen issues had appeared at regular monthly intervals the magazine came out more and more infrequently. At about this same time, too, a series of frantic appeals to members asked for stronger support in the form of regular payment of dues, contribution of more material and campaigning to introduce *Cosmology* to friends. In January, 1932, Palmer turned his editorial post over to Aubrey McDermott and Clifton Amsbury. They in turn attempted to inject new life into the publication. The news that P. Schuyler Miller had purchased a life membership in the club for $17.50 was offered as bait to those who hesitated to renew their memberships or who believed the organization to be shaky. Despite all these efforts, however, the club drifted into a period of greater and greater lethargy, until finally publication of the official organ was discontinued altogether.

Heretofore, *Cosmology* had been a mimeographed publication. In 1933 as a last effort at revival, the seventeenth (and last) issue was printed. Coincidentally, the club was thoroughly reorganized. Raymond A. Palmer occupied the president's and treasurer's posts, Clifton Amsbury became secretary, and McDermott remained as *Cosmology's* editor. A few "name" positions were also assigned: Willy Ley became director of rocketry, Philip G. Ackerman, director of theoretical chemistry, and Clifton Amsbury, director of anthropology. A new constitution was published, and the magazine was packed with scientific articles. Once lost, however, interest could not be brought back; and within a short time the club passed quietly away into oblivion. A few years later many fans had forgotten it completely.

Yet by science fictional standards the organization was far from being a failure. Its three-year life had set a mark in club longevity, and its seventeen consecutive issues of *Cosmology* would be considered a fine record even today. Its membership was said to have neared 150—nearly tops, as fan organizations go. By every standard we have for comparison today the Science Correspondence Club was an eminently successful group that died a natural death when its members grew tired of it.

The reason for their tiring of it is not hard to discern. Midway in its life a new group of fans had arisen and entered the amateur publishing field with their *Time Traveller* and *Science Fiction Digest*. These publications talked about science fiction itself rather than the minute details of science involved in it. And these, apparently, won the fans' preference. Nevertheless, interest did not shift either completely or immediately in this direction: it was a gradual change, and those who preferred to discuss science still remained. Indeed, several years later there were enough of them to reaffirm their views by forming the International Scientific Association. But more of this in coming chapters.

Almost concurrently with the Science Correspondence Club there existed an organization known as the Scienceers, which claimed affiliation with the YOSIAN Society, a world-wide nature study group. It is this organization to which we must give credit for forming the first true science fiction club and publishing the first true science fiction fan magazine.

In New York, the world's greatest city, fans flourished in such abundance that it was inevitable that personal contact among them be sooner or later made through the media of magazines' readers' columns and chance acquaintances. And so, learning of one another's existence, this new group sprang up. At that point, too, there was evidenced for the first time that strange camaraderie which binds those interested in this hobby. For some odd reason they seem friends before they even have met. By some strange chemistry their mutual interest in fantasy binds them together as kindred souls. This one-ness of mind has been the topic of much speculation ever

since. Events have destroyed the allegation that science fiction
followers are superior to other men, showing them to be well represented in the congress of human faults and failings, but their severest critics have been forced to recognize this mental similarity,
as well as grudgingly admit the group to possess at least the normal
quota of intelligence and literary ability.

Like the Science Correspondence Club, the excuse given by the Scienceers for forming their club was the intelligent discussion of the
science arising from science fiction. Unlike the former organization
however, this turned out to be patent camouflage—for all the science they extrapolated upon in their rocky three-year existence
would make an exceedingly slim volume indeed. Science *fiction* was
their forte, and they not only talked about it but wrote and published it as well as obtaining lectures for it.

The first president of the club was a colored fan whose hobby was
rocketry, and the Scienceers met at his Harlem home. The willingness
of the other members to accede to his leadership, regardless of rac-
ial difference, has never had an opportunity for duplication, for
James Fitzgerald was the first and last colored man ever actively to
engage in the activities of science fiction fandom. It is an established fact that colored science fiction readers number in the thousands, but with the exception of Fitzgerald, the lone Negro who attended the first national science fiction convention in 1938 and the
single Negro members of the later groups, the Eastern Science Fiction Association and the Philadelphia Science Fantasy Society, they
play no part in this history.

Members of the original Scienceers included Allen Glasser, the
club's librarian, a leading fan and a beginning author of that period; Maurice Z. Ingher, soon to become editor of the now-legendary
Science Fiction Digest; Julius Unger, the well known fan and dealer
of today; Nathan Greenfield, staff member of *The Time Traveller;* and
Mortimer Weisinger and Julius Schwartz, both of whom were to make
their professions in the field.

The idea for publishing *The Planet,* the club's organ, probably
stemmed from the mimeographing of its membership list. The choice
for editor was almost uncontested: Allen Glasser was *the* fan of the
day. His letters had been published in virtually every fantasy magazine. He had sold stories professionally. He was regarded, consequently, as "the writer" of the group; and he was generally looked
up to as having opinions that merited respect. His accession to editorship was therefore the most natural thing in the world. And so,
with Glasser at the helm, the first issue of *The Planet* appeared in
July, 1930. In content it presaged the balanced generality that was
to characterize the later *Time Traveller*—reviews of current pro-
fessionally-published fantastic fiction in both magazines and books,
reviews of fantasy films, and miscellaneous chatter and news about
the fans themselves. This policy, too, remained for the most part
unchanged during the remaining five monthly numbers of the magazine
that appeared.

At about this time Hugo Gernsback ran a contest in *Wonder Stories,*
offering prizes for the best reports on the question "What am I doing to popularize science fiction?". A prize-winning entry by Allen
Glasser mentioned his work in the Scienceers, and, impressed by the
concept of enthusiasts forming clubs, Gernsback requested that the

organization send a representative to visit him. For obvious reasons
Glasser was chosen to act in this capacity, and he returned with the
startling news that Gernsback had arranged for a group of authors to
address the club at New York City's Museum of Natural History, all
expenses paid.

When the day arrived no less than thirty-five members had mustered
out for the occasion. When one reflects on the fact that fandom was
not then well knit on a national scale, and that years later the
same number was considered a good showing at the Philadelphia Conference, thirty-five seems a copious attendance indeed. Gernsback
himself was unable to attend, but he had sent in his place David
Lasser, then editor of *Wonder Stories,* a man who was later to
achieve national prominence as head of the Workers' Alliance. With
Lasser was Gawain Edwards Pendray, author and rocketry expert, Dr.
William Lemkin, also a well-known author, as well as lesser lights
of the Gernsback staff. They lectured eruditely to the Scienceers on
their individual specialties, and finally departed amid much pomp
and ceremony. The day had been a heady one for most of the neophyte
fans, and they wandered to their homes in a happy daze.

At the club's next meeting they were rudely awakened, however, for
they were then presented with a bill for use of the room at the museum; through some misunderstanding Gernsback had not paid the museum
rental. And to add insult to injury Glasser himself billed the
club for the cost of his time spent in contacting Gernsback. The ensuing bitter debate as to the legitimacy of these debts was more
than the conventional tempest in a teapot, for controversy reached
such a pitch that it led to dissolution of the Scienceers.

It is probably true, however, that this incident was not the only
bone of contention present. Throughout the club's existence minor
strife had been occasionally precipitated by that minority of the
membership which was composed of science-hobbyists. It was the old
story of the Gernsback ideal—all science fiction lovers were potential scientists, and should aim at something more than mere entertainment. But to the majority of the Scienceers entertainment was an
end in itself, and they revelled in a frank enjoyment of discussing
their hobby with kindred spirits. Nevertheless, this difference added fuel to the already-kindled fire, and did its part in producing
the conflagration.

Yet so enjoyable had been these informal club discussions that by
twos and threes many members of like tastes drifted together frequently, and although the old-time strength was never again achieved
two individual sections, one in Brooklyn and another in the Bronx,
met irregularly as late as 1933. The fate of a branch in Clearwater,
Florida, is unknown; this, the first branch of the Scienceers, was
founded by Carlton Abernathy as a result of correspondence with the
secretary of the main organization in New York. Its first official
meeting was held August 5, 1930, and Carlton Abernathy was elected
president, Wallace Dort vice president and Stanley Dort secretary-
treasurer. There were eight other initial members and the club had
a library of 125 science fiction magazines and several books. Like
the parent organization, meetings were held weekly. It published at
least one, possible more, issues of a four-paged bulletin titled *The
Planetoid.* The magazine contained articles, fiction and humor. Gab-
riel Kirschner made an earnest attempt to form another branch of the
Scienceers in Temple, Texas, but met with failure.

In the October, 1930, issue of *The Planet,* mention is given to an organization named the Bay State Science Club which published a bulletin titled *The Asterotd.* There is a possibility that this may have been, at least partially, an early science fiction group.

Chapter IV

THE EMERGENCE OF THE TRUE FAN MAGAZINE

AMONG THOSE FANS who had met and cultivated friendships at the gatherings of the Scienceers were Julius Schwartz and Mortimer Weisinger. As time was to prove, they had much in common and many latent capabilities. Weisinger was a jovial, rotund fellow, possessed of a slight lisp, who was later to make his mark as a columnist, author, literary agent and editor. By contrast Schwartz seemed sober, and was a steady person with a good sense of perspective. Between them they conceived the idea of remedying fans' apathy since the Scienceers' dissolution by initiating a fan magazine. Enlisting the aid of Allen Glasser—for they apparently doubted their abilities to accomplish something creatively successful alone—who edited their brain-child, they circulated an announcement predicting the early appearance of a publication of interest to the science fiction fan, editor and author which was to feature descriptive and biographical articles, news, bibliographical material and occasional fiction. The response—as hundreds of would-be publishers have since discovered—was far from sensational; but it was sufficient encouragement for the magazine to be issued. It was called *The Time Traveller*.

The first two numbers of *The Time Traveller,* like its announcing circular, were mimeographed. The main feature of the initial issue was a complete list of extant fantastic moving pictures (or, as they have come to be known, "scientifilms") contributed by Forrest J. Ackerman of California. Like many others in the early days of fandom Ackerman had become well known in the field through his many letters printed in science fiction magazines' readers' departments. And as there was no other criteria at the time to utilize, the gauge of someone's interest and activity in the field was how often he wrote to the professional science fiction magazines. Editors vigorously urged their readers to write each month, and Ackerman's production as a rule exceeded this editorial quota. Jack Darrow and Bob Tucker are two other prominent examples of readers who won their fame in the letter columns and found that it followed them into the fan field. Though this remained an easy road into fandom for some years, it was eventually considered an excessive display of egotism to appear month in and month out there; fan indulgence in this once-accepted must became less and less frequent, so that if a well known fan's letters not written in self-advertisement appeared at all regularly in these columns he soon found them quoted in the fan press and satirically commented on. Indeed, by 1938, letter columns were well representative of the opinions of the average reader—as opposed to the active fan—although editors to this day delude themselves into believing that this is not the case.

But we have digressed. Good as they were, *The Time Traveller*'s future was not to be judged by its first two numbers. For at this time Weisinger and Schwartz became acquainted with Conrad H. Ruppert, an avid fan whose interest in amateur journalism had led him to acquire a printing press. Overnight *The Time Traveller* metamorphozed into a printed journal and an upward spiral of progress was begun.

To most present-day fans Conrad H. Ruppert is an all but unknown name, but his part in creating for fandom the finest set of periodicals it has ever produced is a story of unbelievable devotion to science fiction. He painstakingly set by hand every issue of *The Time Traveller* from then on, and every number of *Science Fiction Digest* and *Fantasy Magazine* up until the latter's third anniversary number. The fact that each of these rarely were less than 30,000 words in length and appeared on a regularly monthly schedule gives the reader a rough notion of the amount of work involved. during this time, too, Ruppert hand-set Hornig's *Fantasy Fan* and the "Cosmos" supplements to *Fantasy Magazine*—and all at below-production cost, out of the sheer love of science fiction. Later he was to appear as printer of the weekly *Fantasy News*, the "Nycon" program and *Dawn of Flame*, the Weinbaum Memorial volume. Ruppert's contribution to the field would be difficult to estimate.

Meanwhile, the standards of *The Time Traveller* were constantly raised. An index of *Amazing Stories* was completed, and one of *Weird Tales* begun. Gossip and news of fans, authors, editors, magazines and allied topics found an eager audience, and the material published aroused interest to a peak never before attained. Exhilirated by this success, the staff organized science fiction fandom's first publishing company, the Arra Publishers. It is remembered today for three pamphlets: Allen Glasser's *Cavemen of Venus*, Mort Weisinger's *Price of Peace*, and *Through the Dragon Glass* by A. Merritt, the first two being original short stories and the third a reprint.

Precisely how important the work of Glasser in these publishing enterprises was has never been made clear. However, the later success of Schwartz, Weisinger and Ruppert as a trio leaves no question of their abilities to carry on without him. Those who have known Glasser say that above and beyond an unmistakable superiority complex he was intelligent almost to the point of brilliance. He had made himself well known through letters in readers' columns, he was looked up to as a leading fan, and generally regarded as an amateur author about to be graduated to the status of a professional.

But Glasser's fall from fame proved to be even more meteoric than had been his rise. *Wonder Stories* at about this time offered prizes for the best science fiction story plots submitted by its readers. Allen Glasser's prize-winning submission was of such excellence that A. Rowley Hilliard's inspired writing turned it into a classic. Older fans today still remember the poignant little tale, "The Martian." But what many do not know is that the plot was actually Weisinger's. Mort Weisinger maintained he told Glasser the plot in confidence, and, realizing its worth, Glasser hastened to mail it in to *Wonder Stories'* contest. Close upon the heels of this alleged breach of ethics followed another, more serious one. The August, 1933, issue of *Amazing Stories* published, under Glasser's name, "Across the Ages." It was made common knowledge, however, that this story was a plagiarism of an earlier tale entitled "The Haze of Heat." And, although the evidence involved was never published, it was alleged at the time that further investigations showed Glasser to be guilty of numerous other plagiarisms in non-science-fictional circles.

These events produced the expected results, Glasser running afoul of legal consequences, losing the respect of fandom, and finding his

friendship with Schwartz and Weisinger completely broken. They also
resulted in the demise of *The Time Traveller*. The ninth and last
number of this publication was a small-sized, four-page affair wherein the names of Schwartz and Weisinger were nowhere to be found, and
which carried the announcement that it was to merge with *Science-
Fiction Digest*, a magazine that was to fill all unexpired subscriptions. And so was terminated the first true fan magazine as we
recognize such today.

But *The Time Traveller* had left its mark behind. It had been the
first sizeable central rallying-point in the science fiction world,
and this had given the more active fans opportunity to segregate and
come into mutual contact. The seeds had been sown, and they proved
to be far more prepotent than anyone then would have thought possible.

In Cleveland, Ohio, Jerome Siegel and Joseph Shuster surveyed *The
Time Traveller* and one of the seeds sprouted. The magazine's policy
was a mistake, they decided. What fandom really needed was a publication devoted mainly to fiction and having a minimum of fan-chatter.
After all, the main thing people were interested in was science fiction itself. And so was produced another amateur periodical—*aptly*-
titled *Science Fiction*. It started in October, 1932, and ran for
five numbers. It was mimeographed, and rather poorly, too, but its
contents were of reasonably good quality. The editors managed to get
material from such well known writers as Raymond A. Palmer and Clare
Winger Harris, and Siegel himself wrote fiction under the *nom de
plume* of Bernard J. Kenton. Shuster's artistic abilities were in
evidence also, and turned out well despite the limited medium of the
stencil with which he contended. Today *Science Fiction* is a collect-
or's item of extreme rarity; few fans possess copies of it, and
these are rarely known to change hands.

In California, meanwhile, Forrest J. Ackerman, together with a fan
named Norman Caldwell, had founded a minor clique known as the Fantasy Fans' Fraternity. Meetings were held in San Francisco, then
Ackerman's home town. Although this organization had little or no
influence in fandom at the time it is notable in that it was the
fore-runner of a series of California clubs that terminated in the
world-famous Los Angeles chapter of the Science Fiction League.

Meanwhile, further activity was taking place in New York City.
After the break with Glasser, Schwartz and Weisinger, together with
Conrad Ruppert, Forrest J. Ackerman and Maurice Z. Ingher, formed
Science Fiction Digest, a corporation in which each had a share and
to which each contributed a specified sum of money. This corporation
then issued a magazine under this title, its first number appearing
in September, 1932. Because of default in payment, Weisinger was
later dropped from the organization, and Ruppert eventually bought
Ingher's share; but with these changes the corporation continued in
force, making a profit, in fact, during its latter days.

The initial issues of *Science Fiction Digest* were almost identical
in format and content with the large printed numbers of *The Time
Traveller*. Except for the title and the staff the two would be difficult to tell apart. Maurice Ingher was editor, and Weisinger, Palmer, Schwartz, Ackerman and Schalansky· also held editorial posts.
After Ingher left the group Ruppert assumed editorial directorship
in April, 1933, a position which he held until mid-1934, when vocational duties forced him to relinquish it for the less time-consum-

ing one of business manager. From this time until the magazine's demise Julius Schwartz carried the editorial reins.

For all-around quality *Science Fiction Digest* has never been surpassed in the history of fandom. Its regular columns became famous; these included "The Science Fiction Eye" which Julius Unger devoted to information for the collector; "The Ether Vibrates," a gossip column of news sidelights conducted by Mortimer Weisinger; Raymond A. Palmer's "Spilling the Atoms," which also concerned chatter of current topics; "The Scientifilms," devoted to reviews of current and past fantasy moving pictures by Forrest Ackerman; Schwartz's "Science Fiction Scrap Book," featuring thumbnail reviews of fantasy fiction books; and "The Service Department," which listed valuable bibliographical data. Excellent original fiction by such authors as A. Merritt, Raymond Palmer, P. Schuyler Miller, Clark Ashton Smith, Dr. David H. Keller, C. L. Moore, Mortimer Weisinger, Donald Wandrei and Arthur J. Burks appeared regularly. A biography or autobiography of a famous author, artist or editor connected with the field was included in almost every issue. The outstanding authors in the field —among them Lovecraft, Weinbaum, Leinster, Smith and Howard—combined their talents on a cooperative basis to produce two popular tales, "The Challenge from Beyond" and "The Great Illustration." Most legendary of all, however, was the novel "Cosmos," written by eighteen authors and issued with the magazine in supplementary serial form. Each part ran from five to ten thousand words, and the author line-up was as follows: A. Merritt, Dr. E. E. Smith, Ralph Milne Farley, Dr. David H. Keller, Otis Adelbert Kline, Arthur J. Burks, E. Hoffman Price, P. Schuyler Miller, Rae Winters, John W. Campbell, Jr., Edmond Hamilton, Francis Flagg, Bob Olsen, J. Harvey Haggard, Raymond A. Palmer, Lloyd A. Eshbach, Abner J. Gelula and Eando Binder. Besides such special features, *Science Fiction Digest* printed solid, interesting, factual articles in every number. Up until the end of its life it remained the undisputed leader in the field, and its influence on the varied currents of fan history was profound indeed.

It became obvious to Raymond Palmer early in 1933 that even the elaborate printed number of *Cosmology* which Ruppert had been kind enough to print for him was not enough to reawaken a fanwide interest in the International Scientific Association. He therefore abandoned the ISA and its club organ and cast about for something else. Inspired in all probability by "The Best Science-Fiction of 1932," filler in the Winter, 1933, issue of *The Time Traveller* which listed the readers' choices of the outstanding fantasy of that year, Palmer hit upon the Jules Verne Prize Club. Its aims are perhaps best expressed by quoting an advertisement printed in the January, 1933, *Science Fiction Digest:*

> Help select the three best stf stories of 1933. Join the JVPC and do your part in carrying forward the torch ignited by the immortal Jules Verne. Help make the world "Science-Fiction Conscious."
> The Jules Verne Prize Club is non profit-making, all receipts going to the selection of the stories and the awarding of suitable cups to the winners.

Dues were set at twenty-five cents, and Palmer was the organization's chairman. Moribund from the start, however, the club soon expired completely when members failed to pay dues. For this reason, too, no loving cups were awarded the winning stories' authors. After announcing these facts in the February, 1934, issue of *Fantasy Magazine*, Palmer stated that the club would revert to an inactive status for the year 1934, and promised its revival in 1935; not surprisingly, this suspension of animation proved permanent.

In Europe, meanwhile, the most active group was to be found in the membership of the German Rocket Society, a large percentage of which were science fiction enthusiasts—this being regarded, however, as mere coincidence. Hermann Oberth and Max Valier, known in this country because of the generous publicity furnished them by Hugo Gernsback, belonged to the society, and together with Willy Ley they conducted a series of experiments that (unknown to them) presaged the German "buzz-bombs" of the Second World War. Ley, as is generally known, eventually emigrated to America, where he has since acquired an enviable reputation in his vocational field. A long and excellent history of the German Rocket Society may be found in his book *Rockets*.

An organization known as the British Science Fiction Association had sprung up in England in the meantime. This was predominantly a correspondence club, and by 1933 had linked itself to the American ISA.

Chapter V

THE FANTASY FAN

THE GREAT DEPRESSION was now at its peak, and there was scarcely any activity or industry in the United States which did not feel its effects. The science fiction magazines, selling at prices above the average "pulp" level, were particularly hard hit. Probably the keen loyalty of their followers was the only factor which saved them from swift extinction. As it was they were badly shaken. *Astounding Stories* began to appear bi-monthly instead of monthly, and finally ceased publication altogether with its March,1933, number. After futuristic cover designs did not perk up lagging sales, *Amazing Stories* reduced its size after a single bi-monthly issue. *Wonder Stories* experimented with a slimmer magazine at a reduced price, and after a time reverted to small size and the original 25¢ figure. The quarterly companions to the latter two periodicals eventually gave up the ghost altogether when metamorphoses of price, thickness and schedule failed to keep production out of the red. Under the stress of such changing conditions staff heads began to fly, and for reasons never accurately ascertained, David Lasser, then editor of many of Gernsback's magazines, left his post there. In dire need of someone to fill the vacant post, Gernsback cast about for a competent editor. His eye caught the title of a pamphlet on his desk—*The Fantasy Fan*. He glanced through it, at first casually and then with studied interest. A short time later, on the strength of the impression gained from the first issue of this amateur publication, he hired its seventeen-year-old fan editor, Charles Derwin Hornig, to edit *Wonder Stories!*

Truly, this is a Cinderella story of science fiction fandom. But what was this publication of such promise? What of the man who produced it?

Its editor, Charles D. Hornig, was born in 1916 in Jersey City, New Jersey. Next to Mortimer Weisinger he was the second fan of importance to come from this area. By nature he was—and is—friendly, genial and idealistic. This latter trait, whence stem his alleged pacifistic beliefs, caused him some trouble with draft authorities in recent times when he refused to undergo combat training.

Young as he was, Hornig in 1933 possessed a fine collection of science fiction as well as a near-complete set of *Weird Tales* magazine. The idea of publishing a fan magazine sprang from sight of a copy of *The Time Traveller*. Subsequently he became a regular contributor to *Science Fiction Digest,* and eventually struck an agreement with Ruppert to print *The Fantasy Fan.*

Even to day many fans believe that Hornig's effort was created for the sole purpose of giving the follower of weird fiction his medium in the fan press. This is a grave error. *The Fantasy Fan* was founded as a general type fan magazine, styled along the pattern set by *Science Fiction Digest* and *The Time Traveller.* It was even advertised as such. More, its initial issue articles dealt with nothing but science fiction subjects. With the second number an abrupt change of policy occurred, the editorial stating:

> Starting with this issue, we will present a story every month (maybe more than one) by Clark Ashton Smith, H. P. Lovecraft, August W. Derleth, and other top-notchers in the field of weird fiction. You science fiction fans are probably wondering by the import of the last sentence why we will not print science fiction. Well, here's the reason. In the *Science Fiction Digest* we have a fan magazine for those scientifictionally inclined.... We feel that the weird fan should also have a magazine for themselves—hence *The Fantasy Fan.*

More factors than this actually brought about this change, however. First, Hornig had obtained unexpectedly several excellent contributions from Lovecraft, Smith, Howard and Derleth. Secondly, despite the statement in *The Fantasy Fan*'s first issue that it was not a competitor of *Science Fiction Digest,* it was inevitable that the two publications would compete if their policies were not changed. In the third place, Hornig's recent elevation to the post of a professional editor doubtless made him feel it was incumbent upon him to show more literate taste. Lastly, he had a wide knowledge of the field of supernatural fiction. Ease of policy-shift was likewise favored by the very name of his magazine, it being realized that he could ill afford to alienate science fiction readers, Hornig cannily continued to print features designed to win their support.

Allen Glasser returned to some activity in *The Fantasy Fan,* possibly feeling that any aid given the magazine would help it show the rival *Science Fiction Digest* in a bad light. He even plugged the Fantasy Fan Federation now that one faction of the Scienceers had affiliated with it. His sporadic contributions to Hornig's sheet was not a true index of continued interest in fan activities, however; as a matter of fact, the true state of affairs was expressed by an advertisement in the very first number, where Glasser offered his science fiction collection for sale. Nevertheless, it was not until 1938, when his personal file of *The Time Traveller* was put up for sale, that most people felt that Glasser was retiring from fandom permanently.

Bob Tucker commenced journalistic activity in the first (September, 1933) number of *The Fantasy Fan.* His initial contributions concerned "scientifilms," which he was well acquainted with, and British science fiction. In those days Tucker was a strait-laced bibliophile; a year later, however, with his "How to Write a Weird Tale" he had launched upon a campaign of tomfoolery as "Hoy Ping Pong" that was to earn him his present reputation as a humorist.

In a department entitled "The Boiling Point" *The Fantasy Fan* provided a medium of expression for readers wishing to air their pet gripes. This department ran for six issues, being discontinued because of the ill-feeling aroused. As might therefore be guessed, debate waxed hot and furious throughout the half-year period. Forrest J. Ackerman initiated the verbal hubbub by claiming Clark Ashton Smith's "Light From Beyond" to be a sorry example of science fiction, although he at the same time expressed admiration for the author's "Flight Through Super-Time" and "The Master of the Asteroid." He was promptly pounced upon by both Smith and Lovecraft, who, with verbal pyrotechnics and glorified name-calling proceeded to pummel him soundly. It is the opinion of this writer that their actions were unbecoming to their statures as intellects and authors; Ackerman was definitely entitled to his opinion, which he expressed intelligently. It happened to be his misfortune, however, to be defending science fiction as preferential to weird fiction in a magazine catering to supporters of the latter, and also to be labelling as poor the work of a then very popular writer. One of the very few readers to come to his support summed up the situation as follows:

> It seems to me that young Forrest J. Ackerman is by far the most sensible of the lot. Instead of intelligently answering his arguments, Mssrs. Smith, Lovecraft, Barlow, etc., have made fools of themselves descending to personalities.

As a real help to the lover of weird and fantasy fiction Hornig's magazine reigned supreme in the field at that time. Superb fiction and excellent poetry by H. P. Lovecraft, Clark Ashton Smith, August Derleth, Eando Binder, Dr. David H. Keller, Robert W. Chambers, H. Rider Haggard and Charles Williams appeared in its pages. (Indeed, it was in *The Fantasy Fan* that H. C. Koenig began his twelve-year-long campaign to gain recognition for Hodgson that has proved to be so successful in recent years.) Lovecraft's scholarly essay, "Supernatural Horror in Literature," was published serially, but unfortunately was never completed. There were fine regular columns on many phases of fantasy, too, the best of which—"Weird Whisperings" by Weisinger and Schwartz—claimed credit for doubling the magazine's slim circulation. Almost every weirdist of importance in fandom was at one time or another represented in its pages. And as a love-feast for such fans it has never again been equalled.

Much of Hornig's salary went into publishing the magazine, But despite its sterling contents and attractive format no more than a pitiful circulation was ever attained. Finally, when well-paying jobs began to monopolize more and more of Ruppert's time, he was forced to discontinue printing it at the reduced rate he had been charging. And with genuine regret Hornig discontinued *The Fantasy Fan* with its February, 1935, number, after eighteen consecutive monthly issues. It is indeed fortunate that many readers took out their remaining subscription money in back numbers; that is why so many leading fans today possess complete sets of *The Fantasy Fan*. In vivid contrast is *The Time Traveller,* of which few fans own single copies—let alone intact files.

Chapter VI

WILLIAM H. CRAWFORD AND HIS CONTEMPORARIES

THOSE WHO OWN COPIES of *Fantasy Magazine, The Time Traveller, The Fantasy Fan,* "Cosmos," the final *Cosmology* and the Arra Publishers' pamphlets can gain some idea of the great contribution made to fandom by Conrad H. Ruppert. Had it not been for him its embryonic days would have been a sorry story indeed. His well-printed copy lured professionals who would scarcely have lingered long otherwise into taking active part in these journalistic endeavors. There is no question but that many professional authors took great delight in their fan activities, and entered into them with the same enthusiasm as did the neophyte fans. It is also not to be questioned that Ruppert's inability to continue the below-cost printing of fan magazines was a major factor in the deterioration and eventual eclipse of the old-time fandom centering about *Fantasy Magazine* and a shifting toward the foreground of secondary publications which theretofore had been of little importance. This change was rendered an even more gradual one than the reader has been led to expect by the presence of another publisher who operated in the field at almost the same time as Ruppert, and whose productions were of almost equal importance. This publisher was William H. Crawford.

Crawford's position in an impoverished field was unique in that he had a certain amount of ready capital. This he intended to invest in a science fiction magazine designed to feature a more literary grade of prose than that being currently offered by corresponding newstand publications. In late 1933 prominent fans received a neatly printed circular announcing the magazine—titled *Unusual Stories*—and reproducing its first page, which embodied the beginning of "The Titan" by P. Schuyler Miller. Material by H. P. Lovecraft, Ralph Milne Farley, Dr. Miles J. Breuer, Robert E. Howard, Stanton A. Coblentz and Dr. David H. Keller was also scheduled for this and future issues. The magazine was labelled a monthly, the subscription price being twenty cents or one-fifty by the year.

It has been said that science fiction as an art is undergoing a period of slow and painful evolution, from which it will eventually emerge as the literature of tomorrow. Though this is undoubtedly true it has been our conviction that science fiction should have a place in the literature of today. It does not occupy that position now, we believe, because of the restrictions placed upon it by short-sighted editors and publishers. They use only tales which follow certain stereotyped forms. They avoid the "off-trail" story because if violates one or another of their editorial taboos, with the result that science fiction has been sinking into the mire of the commonplace.

So ran the context of the announcement circular. Dissatisfaction with the current newstand fare was, of course, nothing new—but this was the first instance of any action crystallizing out of such dissatisfaction. It is worthy of note also that *Unusual Stories* was not,

as the above quotation might lead one to believe, to feature science
fiction only: Crawford planned to include tales of fantasy and the
supernatural as well, realizing that only by appealing to all factions in the field could he hope to accumulate a modicum of support.

Months passed, and nothing more was heard from Crawford. Finally,
advance subscribers received a circular wherein Crawford explained
the delay had been caused by the printer, who had contracted for a
job considerably bigger than he proved able to handle. What Crawford
did not explain was that he himself was the printer involved, and
that consequently all blame was his alone. This so-called "Advance
Issue" was dated March, 1934, and was mailed in the preceeding January. It contained an editorial, a short biography of author Richard
Tooker, and nearly all the pages of Cyril G. Wates' story "When the
Waker Sleeps," which was illustrated by Guy L. Huey. Pulp paper was
used (contradicting Crawford's promise of fine book-paper stock) and
the type-size was large and readable. Some time after, an additional
fragment of the magazine was mailed; this contained pages finishing
Wates' tale and beginning "Tharda, Queen of the Vampires" by Richard
Tooker. For some reason, this portion was apparently not sent to all
subscribers. Both of these advance sections are today among the rarest of fantasy fans' collectors' items. Cajoling, pleas and threats
alike proved of no avail: Crawford never did complete this initial
issue of *Unusual Stories*.

Instead, he bent his efforts toward the production of another title entirely: *Marvel Tales*. This was a *Readers Digest*-sized magazine
whose first number was dated May, 1934, and whose contents included
Lovecraft's "Celephais" and Keller's "Binding De Luxe" both of
which had been originally scheduled to appear in the ill-fated
Unusual Stories.

Crawford's makeshift plans and press make *Marvel Tales* a difficult
item to collect. The second number, dated July-August, 1934, appeared with no less than three different covers on different colors
and grades of paper, with even the wording of the story-titles and
authors shifted about. Fortunately the contents did not vary. Of the
fiction presented, Howard's "Garden of Fear," which probably comes
closer to pure science fiction than anything he has written, was
easily the best. A prize contest for the best stories written around
titles the editor named was also announced in this issue.

It required Crawford six months to bring out the third *Marvel
Tales*. In that issue appeared P. Schuyler Miller's superb novel "The
Titan" as a serial; disappointingly, however, it was never completed.
Outstanding also was Keller's "Golden Bough," and Robert Bloch was
represented in print for the first time with "Lilies." Winners of
the contest described in the second number were announced; they were
W. Anders Drake, R. DeWitt Miller, Richard Tooker and Forrest J.
Ackerman. Drake's tale was the only one of these that Crawford ever
published, although for the sake of completeness it should be noted
that Miller's ("The Shapes") was eventually accepted and printed by
Astounding Stories (February, 1935).

With the fourth number Crawford at last presented a reasonable
facsimile of his ideals. This neat, enlarged issue would have shamed
no editor or publisher. Clay Ferguson, Jr., whose work had previously appeared in *Fantasy Magazine,* had added his talents to the magazine with excellent effect, holding down the art editor's post. A

column of readers' letters made its appearance. Along with fiction by Miller, Lovecraft, Amelia Raynolds Long and John Beynon Harris, there was the initial installment of George Allan England's lengthy novel, "The Nebula of Death," this being a reprint from *The People's Favorite Magazine* of fifteen years before. "The Creator" by Clifford D. Simak appeared in entirety, and was very favorably received, many fans terming it a classic. Despite some crudities of construction it is yet a memorable story, and epitomized to perfection Crawford's policy of publishing stories having too controversial a theme to be used by the average professional fantasy magazine.

But, apparently elated by his success, Crawford propounded further grandiose plans, announcing in the fourth *Marvel Tales* that *Unusual Stories* would materialize after all in a modified form, and that Fantasy Publications (the name his publishing enterprises now carried) would enter the book-publishing field. The first volume announced was Eugene George Key's "Mars Mountain"; this was to be followed by Andrew North's "People of the Crater" and "The Missing Link" by Ralph Milne Farley. As if all this were not enough, a series of paper-bound pamphlets were planned as well.

Only one of the pamphlets actually appeared. This was a neat booklet bound in stiff white cover stock that contained two short stories: "The White Sybil" by Clark Ashton Smith and David H. Keller's "Men of Avalon." Its selling price was a modest fifteen cents per copy.

Two numbers of *Unusual Stories* materialized as well. They contained forty-eight small-sized pages apiece, and were dated May-June, 1935, and Winter, 1935. Material by P. Schuyler Miller, Robert A. Wait, Lowell Howard Morrow, Robert Bloch and others appeared. The second number printed "Derelict," Robert W. Lowndes' first essay into fan journalism; Donald A. Wollheim and Forrest J. Ackerman likewise contributed poetry to the magazine, although it was not for them their first important appearance. As a whole *Unusual Stories* was an invertebrate affair which never packed the punch of Crawford's *Marvel Tales*. And though it sold for but ten cents a copy it never attained even the meagre circulation of its sister publication.

Crawford finally managed to issue "Mars Mountain," which emerged as a tiny board-bound volume of 142 pages. In addition to the title story two others were included, "Earth Sees Mars" and "Lake Tempest," both authored by Eugene Key. They were of little merit, and amateurishly illustrated besides, though the book is a rare and sought-after item in collecting circles today. It was not well received in 1935, however, and this probably discouraged Crawford from issuing the North and Farley titles he had contemplated. His second attempt in the field was far more pretentious and important—but equally unsuccessful. It was the production of the first book by H. P. Lovecraft: *The Shadow over Innsmouth*. This boasted high quality paper, strong black linen binding, and four illustrations by Frank Utpatel; it was an exceptional bargain at the selling-price of a dollar. Nevertheless, scarcely a hundred copies were bought. Crawford's third (and final) effort was the non-fantasy "Facts Behind the Evidence," which proved also to be a failure from the standpoint of sales. Had his book-publishing been a success, he planned to print E. E. Smith's "Skylark of Space" and a collection of C. L. Moore's fiction; fandom was not yet ready for this early version of Arkham House, However.

In the meantime the final issue of *Marvel Tales* was distributed. this fifth number was enlarged in size, and with this change all the atmosphere of compact, balanced professionalism that had character- ized the fourth was lost completely. But despite the ungainly, ama- teurish appearance the quality of the contents did not suffer. Apart from serials, the outstanding story was "Mars Colonizes" by Dr. Miles J. Breuer, which virtually rates the designation of classic, as it is the finest fantasy the author wrote except for his "Paradise and Iron."

After the circulation of many hints and suggestions subscribers to *Fantasy Magazine* were electrified upon reading in the fourth anniver- sary issue of that periodical that *Marvel Tales,* the most ambitious of amateur science fiction magazines up until that time, was finally to appear on the newstands. The publication was to resume as Vol. 1, No. 1, sell for fifteen cents and have sixty-four large sized pages. The initial newstand number was to feature material by H. P. Love- craft, Edward E. Smith, Stanley G. Weinbaum, Donald Wandrei, Harl Vincent, Murray Leinster, Francis Flagg, David H. Keller, M. D., and others.

After a time notices of "insurmountable" obstacles began to appear in the fan journals in relation to this publication, and finally, years later, when the first issue of Red Circle's *Marvel Science Stories* appeared on the stands, fans at first thought that Crawford had achieved his ambition. Actually, the use of the same title, by another company, was the final evidence that his cause was hopeless.

Partial proofs of the "newstand" issue found their way into the hands of Julius Schwartz and thence to James V. Taurasi. From them it could be gleaned that the magazine indeed would have been large size, printed on cheap pulp paper, printed in two sizes of type, partially in 11 point and partially in 8 point. The fourth and final installment of "The Titan" by P. Schuyler Miller was to have been included along with a synopsis of preceding installments; "The Shadow Over Insmouth" by H. P. Lovecraft was to appear complete; re- printed from the third anniversary issue of *Fantasy Magazine* would have been the round-robin story "The Challenge From Beyond," both stories under that title being included, the science fiction one jointly composed by Stanley G. Weinbaum, Donald Wandrei, Edward E. Smith, Murray Leinster and Harl Vincent, and the fantasy one by A. Merritt, C. L. Moore, H. P. Lovecraft, Robert E. Howard and Frank Belknap Long in cooperation. In addition there were short stories scheduled by Stanton A. Coblentz, Francis Flagg, Miles J. Breuer and Raymond Z. Gallun. Illustrations were by Clay Ferguson, Jr., and Frank Utpatel. Crawford never quite made the grade, but if his maga- zine had appeared as presented above, he might well have given the competition something to think about.

In 1946 science fiction readers received a taste of some of the stories of the old *Marvel Tales* when William Crawford managed to put out a reprint selection in pocket-book form under the title of "The Garden of Fear" by Robert E. Howard. In addition to the title story the volume contained fiction by Miles J. Breuer, M. D., L. A. Eshbach, H. P. Lovecraft, David H. Keller, and others. This pocket-book received spotty newstand circulation in many parts of the country and sold roughly fifty percent of its printing. And in 1953, William Crawford finally succeeded in putting a professional science fiction magazine, *Spaceway,* in general distribution on national newstands.

A further signal contribution of Crawford to fandom was his printing of *Fantasy Magazine* after Ruppert was no longer able to do so. Had he not undertaken this task the periodical would have folded with the September, 1935, number instead of the January, 1937, one—so that its life was thus prolonged by a full year's time.

In analyzing the man's contribution to the fan world of his time we find that it ranks second only to that of Conrad H. Ruppert. At their poorest and sloppiest, Crawford's handiworks were a credit to the field; and his idealistic principles were unquestionably exemplary. But he was damned to failure by the crushing fact of being forever unable to reach his potential audience. Professional magazines would not run advertisements of an obvious competitor—indeed, *Weird Tales* turned down one proffered by *The Fantasy Fan*—and, barring newsstand distribution (which Crawford could not afford), it was only through such a medium that he could hope to obtain adequate support.

Aside from this, Crawford's publications are of interest as being the most ambitious of those created by fan dissatisfaction with the degenerating product of professional fantastic fiction extant during 1932-4. All such publications stemmed from the unwavering conviction of the fans that they were capable of doing a better job than the professionals; and their failure to achieve a permanent measure of success was due not to the fact that they were mistaken, but rather to an inability to master the mechanics of the productive medium.

(Lloyd Arthur Eshbach, one of the associate editors of *Marvel Tales*, a prominent author in his own right, and a science fiction fan and collector, is worthy of parenthetical note here because of his position as editor of an elite amateur journal, *The Galleon*. It is unfortunate that this journal was of a general type, for Eshbach showed good taste and excellent business acumen in its handling, and had it been devoted entirely to fantasy, history might have been different. However that may be, *The Galleon* is important from the viewpoint of fans by reason of two fantastic stories it printed: "The Quest of Iranon" (in the July-August, 1935, number) and "The Mist" (in the September, 1935, number). The second was written by David H. Keller, and the former, of H. P. Lovecraft authorship, is the most beautiful story Lovecraft ever wrote; Eshbach's publication undoubtedly rescued both from complete obscurity.)

Operating behind the scenes during these times were private literary organizations of whose existence fandom at large was scarcely aware. One such group was the Calem Club of New York City, whose members included H. C. Koenig, H. P. Lovecraft, Frank Belknap Long, Jr., F. Morton, Samuel Loveman and others, all drawn together through a mutual interest in fantasy. This was actually the nucleus of the Lovecraft circle with an ever-widening number of adherents throughout the country in the persons of such men as E. Hoffman Price, Farnsworth Wright, Robert Bloch, Henry Kuttner and August Derleth, becoming intimates who knew Lovecraft best. For a long time this circle held its meetings, somewhat aloof from fandom at large, and yet, possessing common cause with it, working in much the same manner. It was not until 1939, in fact, that its existence was expressly revealed. A similar organization calling itself The Outsiders Club was subsequently discovered to have been operating in Washington, D. C. A few of their meetings were attended by Jack Speer, who made the discovery; according to him, the members' interest was so strongly for supernatural fiction that they were prone to belittle and ridicule science fiction as a whole. Because of this attitude it is to be doubted that they could ever have been smoothly assimilated by fandom in general.

At a somewhat later date in Milwaukee, Wisconsin, there sprang into existence a group titling itself the Milwaukee Fictioneers. It was in the main composed of professional authors, formed for mutual exchange of ideas as well as for social reasons. By the time that its membership included Raymond A. Palmer, Stanley G. Weinbaum, Ralph Milne Farley, Robert Bloch and Lawrence Keating, however, a specialization slant became perceptible above the basis of generality. After Weinbaum's death, and more especially after Palmer's ascension to the editorial staff of the Ziff-Davis Publishing Company as custodian of *Amazing Stories,* less and less was heard from the group. One suspects that this double loss extracted all the spirit of vitality from it.

It may be felt by some readers that this professed history of fandom is too bibliographical in nature. If so, let them reflect upon the fact that the early fan publications were not only the pride but the very foundation of the field; more, they were the existent proofs that the fans were capable of more than criticizing the professionals and quarreling among themselves, that they possessed the ability to think and act constructively. The lives of these publications is consequently more important than ninety percent of the rest of fandom's history. For, since history is essentially a systematic record of man's progress, we turn to their magazines to discern the story of science fiction fans' progress—and progress it was. The outgrowths of the publications all too often bore the stamp of degeneracy and decadence.

Chapter VII

SECONDARY FAN PUBLICATIONS: THE TFG AND ITS FOLLOWERS

ABOUT MIDWAY THROUGH 1934 a new, secondary group of fans began to make itself evident. They were those fans who, either through lack of contacts, tender years or non-possession of pronounced journalistic abilities, did not fit into the elite circles dominated by *Science Fiction Digest, The Fantasy Fan* or *Marvel Tales*. They admired and respected the work of these top fan journals, considering them ideals worthy of emulating; but at the same time they were a little envious and felt hurt at being excluded from what almost amounted to a closed *entente*. Often they were fans whose very natures made cooperation with an existent group impossible. But individualistic or no, they found no welcome mat upon the doorstep, and were forced to progress on their initiative.

From out of Oakman, Alabama, there appeared full-blown an organization bearing the unwieldy title of The International Science Fiction Guild. The only member listed by name was Wilson Shepard. This group issued a four-paged hektographed bulletin (the first time, incidentally, that hektography as a method of duplication had appeared on the scene) entitled *The International Science Fiction Guild's Bulletin* and dated May-June, 1934. Disconcertingly, it gave no clue as to the type of organization it represented, and nebulously stated itself to be the magazine "we have promised you." The bulk of its first number was taken up with a gossip column "Odds 'n' Ends" by one Willis W. Woe, and began a continued story "The Murder by Long Distance" by "Noname." The entire contents were obviously written by Shepard himself, and smacked of humorous juvenility.

The second number, together with a letter printed in the readers' column of *Amazing Stories,* cleared up some of the mystery. Some of the members were named and the club's aims were given as doing "everything to boost science and weird fiction" (note the all-inclusive appeal!) and to publish "real" news "not covered with sugar." This was the first published hint of reaction against *Fantasy Magazine's* carefully censored news reports which strictly avoided the controversial slant. And while it might be an admission by Shepard that he felt incapable of competing with the latter magazine in her own field it was certainly an indication of his willingness to publish anything it was afraid to.

The ISFG swung into activity by instituting a campaign against back-number magazine dealers who charged "crooked prices." Members were warned not to pay more than ten cents for older second-hand copies of fantasy magazines, not more than cover price for recent ones. Further, Shepard threatened to publish names of those dealers who were guilty of excessive overcharging. This was an amazing tack for a fan journal to take—indeed, an unprecedented one for that time. By open blacklisting, a sheet boasting of but a few dozen recipients at most was attempting to control something national in scope. And surprisingly enough, a certain measure of success attended these efforts. A later number of the *Bulletin* reported that Isadore Manzin, a dealer well known at that period, had reduced his prices to the point where his name was being removed from the blacklist; he was cautioned, however, against further offences.

It would seem highly unlikely that any such actions as these would have as their basis an isolated fan circle in rural Alabama—and such indeed was justified suspicion. Shepard had, through a letter in the *Amazing Stories* "Discussions" column, come into contact with the New York fan Donald A. Wollheim; and it was Wollheim who had suggested to him the anti-dealer campaign, Furnishing the names and addresses which the *Bulletin* published. As time progressed Wollheim began to assume a continuously increased importance in the club, influencing Shepard's most important decisions from behind the scenes and shaping the course of the organization as a whole.

In its fourth number the ISFG's *Bulletin* announced its first inde- pendantly published "book," which was also the first of a series of stories promised members in the initial issue. It was far from a book, being a four-paged, hektographed leaflet on cheap yellow paper titled "I Was a Passenger In My Own Body" by Capt. N. E. P. North and crudely illustrated by one Ivan Nepolis. Despite the pseudonyms the entire sheet was quite obviously the work of Shepard himself.

From the beginning there had been strong emphasis on the fact that the ISFG was not a club in the usual sense of that term, but simply a voluntary union of science fiction lovers. Early in 1935, however, an effort was made to bring about more unified centralization, a number of proposals leading in this direction being put before the membership for a vote. As a result, a number of changes occurred. First of all, the organization adopted the title of the Terrestrial Fantascience Guild, the club organ being rechristened accordingly. Local organizations of members were forbidden. Each member was to be assessed twenty-five cents a year for "maintenance of Guild Facili- ties." All important matters were to be submitted for voting before the membership through the medium of the *Bulletin,* and the magazine itself was to be devoted to topics of general interest rather than to the strict agenda of business. The club was further to produce an emblem that was to be its official insignia. This set of working rules was the closest thing to a constitution the Guild ever achieved.

By this time the TFG *Bulletin* was appearing with monthly regulari- ty, and was increasing rapidly in quality. Its articles were inter- esting and frequently informative. Wollheim himself was represented with contributions of letters, articles and columns; one of the lat- ter, "Sun Spots," proved of sufficient fanwide appeal to outlast the life of the sheet and continue on elsewhere years later. Wollheim also designed the official emblem, which was subsequently first printed in the TFG *Bulletin's* April, 1935, issue.

Strong as the anti-dealer campaign had been, the one which the Terrestrial Fantascience Guild next began made it seem but the mild- est of issues. Wollheim had some time back sold to *Wonder Stories* magazine a story entitled "The Man From Ariel." But he claimed no amount of urging could prompt the publication to disgorge the stag- gering sum of ten dollars which therefore became due at the low word- rate in force at that time. Ignoring payment in lieu of his career, Wollheim sent them a second story (which was rejected) and then a third, whose plot they offered to buy for development by one of their staff writers. Feeling that if he could not collect payment for an entire story his chances for doing so on a mere plot were even slimmer, Wollheim turned down the offer. He next initiated a systematic survey of *Wonder's* treatment of their other authors. He alleged to have received letters from Arthur K. Barnes, Henry Hasse, W. Varick Nevins, Chester D. Cuthbert and Russel Blaiklock stating that they too had not received payment for stories. Barnes, in fact, was owed for fiction that had been printed as far back as 1932. Clifton B. Kruse was said to have claimed that he did not know that his "Heat Destroyer" had ever been published. He had submitted it years before to a contest sponsored by the magazine, and later received from them an empty envelope torn open at one end; believing the story to have been returned and lost in the mails, he had not pursued the matter further.

This matter was aired in detail by the TFG *Bulletin*. Moral support was received from Stanley G. Weinbaum and Henry Hasse, the latter referring his grievance to the literary agent he patronized. Aid was also lent by the International Cosmos Scientific Association, a group which had but recently sprung into existence, and concerning which we will learn more in later chapters. This aid involved the mimeographing by the ICSA of the April, 1935, *Bulletin* that carried the major story of the matter. This particular number received wide distribution, and the adverse effect it had on *Wonder Stories* may have been considerable. The upshot of the whole affair was that Nevins, Cuthbert and Barnes pooled their claims with Wollheim; a lawyer was hired and a settlement with *Wonder Stories* finally arrived at.

As is often the case in matters such as these, only one side—Wollheim's—was heard and *Wonder Stories* was tried and convicted without defence or jury. The truth was that *Wonder Stories'* payment policies were in the main little worse than those of other publications of the period, but they had been unfortunate enough to tangle with a wild-cat of a fan. *Amazing Stories,* another leading magazine of that time, paid on publication, at rates no better than *Wonder Stories,* and were known to have held manuscripts five years or more before publishing them! This actually amounted to the same as *Wonder Stories'* paying after publication when the money situation was tough and this historian knows of science fiction magazines as recently as *1952* that paid after publication! Wollheim, his indignation aroused, made it a point deliberately to have it appear that slow payment was the practice of only one publication. It has further been heard that during the period immediately preceding and after Wollheim's difficulty with *Wonder Stories,* the publication in question had difficulty with dishonest employees, and it is not beyond the point of credibility that their actions may have contributed to embarrassing the publication.

With fantastic irony, Wollheim's own exposé backfired on him when in 1941 his science fiction antagonists of that period, William S. Sykora and James V. Taurasi, ran a series of editorials in *Fantasy News,* alleging that *Stirring Science Stories* and *Cosmic Stories,* two magazines edited by Wollheim, had not been paying for many of their stories. Unlike Wollheim's treatment of *Wonder Stories,* the two magazines in question were permitted to give their defence. Its publisher, Mr. Jerry Albert, claimed that stories had been "donated" by authors to help the magazines get started. To add a touch of chagrin

to the situation, however, one author came forward and denied that
he ever had any intention of "donating" his story.

Raymond A. Palmer, then editor of *Amazing Stories* and *Fantastic
Adventures,* cudgeled Jerry Albert unmercifully for his policy of accepting "donations," but in 1949 he himself had to get up before an
audience at the Cincinnati World Science Fiction Convention to
announce that he was starting a new magazine titled *Other Worlds* and
that stories for the first issue were being "donated" by authors.

Mention of the last issue of the TFG *Bulletin* need be made but to
cite a few minor matters. First, probably as reward for being an
open ally in the above campaign, the ICSA was accorded official
recommendation. Second, the formation of local TFG groups received
sanction. And lastly, there appeared an account of an "Impossible
Story Club," which was allegedly founded in the *Argosy-Allstory* days
before the advent of science fiction magazines, and which included
such members as N. E. P. North, Ivan Nepolis, B. Murdock, etc. As
far as this historian can determine, no such club ever existed, its
name and membership list being a fabrication from the whole cloth by
Wilson Shepard.

One of the TFG's objectives had been the publication of a magazine
devoted entirely to science fiction. This was realized when in May,
1935, there appeared *Astonishing Stories,* an eleven-paged, small-
sized, hektographed affair which sold for ten cents. Stories by
Wollheim, Evert, Shepard and North were included. The almost ludi-
crous attempt of the sheet to pass itself off as a competitor to the
professional magazines doomed it from the start, and the greatest
success it ever attained was being considered a rare item by fan
collectors of 1937-38.

Wollheim assumed the editorship of the TFG organ, and promptly
changed its title to *The Phantagraph.* And after a single hektographed
number it metamorphosed in format. The first printed number (for
whose production W. L. Crawford was responsible) appeared in the
summer of 1935. It had large-sized pages and featured an excellent
array of material; encouragement from such notables as F. Orlin Tremaine (then editor of *Astounding Stories*) and H. P. Lovecraft also
materialized. Shortly afterward Shepard obtained access to a printing outfit and took over production himself.

Encouraged by the excellent material being received from Smith,
Lovecraft and others, Wollheim decided to pattern the publication
after the now-defunct *Fantasy Fan.* Simultaneously *The Phantagraph*
was standardized on a monthly schedule and small format. The quality
of material used was very high, and in this respect the magazine
easily equaled its ideal. Short stories, poems and essays by H. P.
Lovecraft, Clark Ashton Smith, Henry Kuttner, Robert E. Howard,
William Lumley, Duane W. Rimel, Robert Nelson, H. C. Koenig, Emil
Petaja and August W. Derleth were featured. Some of this material
had been intended for publication in *The Fantasy Fan,* as might be
suspected. Collectors who have overlooked this periodical have
missed much indeed.

Wollheim distributed *The Phantagraph* through the mailings of three
amateur press associations simultaneously. For a few numbers it kept
the heading "published by the Terrestrial Fantascience Guild," but
its July, 1936, issue abandoned what had become a mythical byline.
(Wollheim's association with these associations during this period

greatly influenced his thinking, and while active among them probably conceived the Fantasy Amateur Press Association.) In April, 1937,
when Wollheim discontinued the publication as a subscription magazine and initiated an exclusive press association distribution, fandom lost a worthwhile journalistic effort, for *The Phantagraph* quickly degenerated into its near-valueless form of today, when it is being produced solely to maintain the reputation of the oldest fan
magazine still appearing regularly.

The last effort of the Wollheim-Shepard combination was the magazine *Fanciful Tales of Time and Space*. This neat, printed publication
appeared in the fall of 1936. It boasted a fine cover by Clay Ferguson, Jr., and featured "The Nameless City" of H. P. Lovecraft, along
with other excellent material by, Keller, Wollheim, Howard, Derleth
and others. Yet, although fan response to it was fair, and although
it was in every way a production of which the publishers had every
reason to be proud, mechanical difficulties prevented a second number from ever being issued.

The failure of *Fanciful Tales* ended the coalition of Wollheim and
Shepard permanently. Shepard on his own tack produced "The History
of the Necronomicon" of Lovecraft, and issued three numbers of a
little fan magazine *The Rebel* which he planned to fill with hotly
controversial material. However, it never showed any promise and
went to its deserved death, dragging with it into oblivion Shepard
himself, whose only appearance thereafter was due to material left
in the hands of the Moskowitz Manuscript Bureau. The Terrestrial
Fantascience Guild itself expired quietly, too, dying as it had been
born with an utter lack of fanfare, and being quickly forgotten by
all concerned.

Chapter VIII

THE SCIENCE FICTION LEAGUE

THE BIRTH of the TFG coincided almost exactly with that of an even
more important organization, the Science Fiction League. Credit for
conceiving the league idea is generally given to Charles D. Hornig,
editor of *Wonder Stories* at the time and the first managing-secretary
of the group. However, in an autobiography printed in *Fantasy Magazine,* Hornig states that Gernsback broached the idea originally.
While this might be simple diplomacy of a subordinate, it will be
remembered that Gernsback initiated a Short Wave League in one of
his chain of radio magazines some years earlier, so that Hornig may
be relating no more than the simple truth.

Announcement of the SFL was made in the May, 1934, *Wonder Stories,*
and on the magazine's cover there appeared the league's emblem of a
soaring rocket. Gernsback himself had written a four-page editorial
introduction describing the plan. Certificates of membership, emblem-
atic lapel buttons and club stationary were ready for distribution.
It was obvious that more than trifling preparation had gone into the
creation of this, the first professionally sponsored club for fantasy
fans. A board of directors, largely composed of professional authors,
but with the most prominent letter-writers of the day (Ackerman and
Darrow) also represented, had been chosen. Gernsback was listed as
the executive secretary, and Hornig held the assistant secretary's
post.

Gernsback summed up the league as "a non-commercial membership organization for the furtherance and betterment of the art of science
fiction." No one realized at the time that in so doing he had re-
nounced his belief that science fictionists must be science-hobbyists, that he had founded an organization which specifically stipulated its aim to be the furtherance of science fiction—science—his
former idol—not even being listed secondarily. At this point it
should be realized that those who in their later battles against
Wonder Stories, the SFL and their representatives used "the Gernsback delusion" as a rallying-cry were actually crying down a conception long since discarded. A man of intelligence, Gernsback recognized that while science-hobbyists did exist, they were nevertheless greatly outnumbered by fans of the fiction stemming from it—
and recognizing this fact, acted accordingly.

League rules were few and liquid, their flexibility admittedly not
designed to cope with situations brought about by fan-feuding. Indirectly the organization would benefit *Wonder Stories* in building
up a stable reading audience, and thus increasing its circulation;
however, this in itself could be regarded as furthering the cause of
science fiction. Even if it were granted that the SFL's basis was a
wholly commercial one, therefore, fanwide benefits which accrued as
a result were of necessity independant of this. Looking back from
the vantage of a decade's perspective, we are forced in fact to admit that the Science Fiction League was more beneficial and important
to fandom than any organization which preceeded or followed it. Not

only did it actually create the fan field as we know the latter today, but it gave the field something that it had never possessed
before: realization of its own existence.

From every part of the country there emerged through local chapters those fans who were most interested in their hobby, those who
would form the backbone of a national structure. Communication between individual members was facilitated by the SFL columns that
appeared in each issue of *Wonder Stories,* and which carried fan
names and addresses. League-sponsored quizzes, compiled by leading
fans of the day, called for an encyclopedic science fictional knowledge if one were to obtain a high score, and through this medium
too were reputations gained in the field. The sections in these quizzes devoted to pure science were relatively small—an additional indication of the trend toward ever weightier emphasis upon fiction at
science's expense. Of the many other activities coming to light in
this column that of J. O. Bailey's compiling information for a bibliography of science fiction holds perhaps the most topical interest
at this writing, with the publication of his *Pilgrims Through Space
and Time* in the offing (one hopes!) after years of postponements.*

And slowly, frequently after a laborious gestation, individual
chapters began to appear. Some, of course, were of no lasting importance, being virtually no more than the three members' names required
for official recognition. Others were destined to leave a permanent
mark on fandom's history.

George Gordon Clark, who held the honor of being the SFL's first
member, was unique also in forming its first chapter, that of Brooklyn. The very fact that he had received membership card number one
was the determining factor in convincing Clark that he should make
himself a leading fan; and, after organizing local number one, there
was no holding him back. He quickly accumulated a large science fiction collection, purchased a mimeograph machine, and engaged in a
whirlwind flurry of activity that persisted at a high pitch for the
duration of his stay in the field.

Chapter number two was formed in Lewiston by Stuart Ayers, and never
attained much prominence, though Ayers was a sincere and interested
fan. Jack Schaller formed the third (Erie) chapter. The Los Angeles
chapter, one of the most important, was organized soon after (October, 1934) by E. C. Reynolds, about whom little is unfortunately known; two other important fans, Roy Test and W. Pofford, were on
the initial roster. Ackerman put in an appearance at this time too,
apologizing for his inability to create a chapter in San Francisco.
Soon the League was spreading like wildfire, with locals being sponsored by such names as Robert W. Lowndes, Arthur L. Widner, Olon F.
Wiggins, Lewis F. Torrence, D. R. Welch, Robert A. Ward, L. M. Jen-
son, Paul Freehafer, Clarence J. Wilhelm, Vernon H. Jones, Bob Tucker, Day Gee, H. W. Kirschemblit, Allen R. Charpentier, Thomas S.
Gardner, Henry Hasse, Joseph Hatch, Leslie Johnson, Raymond A.
Palmer, Lionel Dilbeck and Alvin Earl Perry. From this list one can
gain some idea of the number of fans urged into activity by the concept of the Science Fiction League. Today many fans are still well
known in the field, though until their appearance in SFL columns
they had never been heard from.

Pilgrims Through Space and Time was published, of course, in
1947, shortly after the above was written.—*Publisher*

As has been remarked, the greater part of the League roster was deadwood. Typical of many such short-lived locals was the Newark branch, organized in May, 1934, by Robert Gahr, Charles Purcell and Sam Moskowitz, and later augmented by John Maderas, William Weiner and Otto Schuck. Little of consequence was accomplished in the three or four meeting held, and the group finally broke up because of a controversy as to what type of activity to engage in. At no time did the members think of contacting the nearby New York or Jersey City chapters, oddly enough, and thus attain some share of mutual progress.

Undoubtedly the outstanding chapter of the time was that of Chicago. Authors and fans alike were represented on its roster, names such as Walter Dennis, Jack Darrow, William Dillenback, Harry Boosel, Florence Reider, Paul McDermott, Milton J. Latzer, Howard Funk, Neil de Jack, Al Fedor and the three Binder brothers being prominent. The reports of their meetings printed in *Wonder Stories* eclipsed in interest those of all others. Moreover, they published an official organ called *The Fourteen Leaflet* which appeared regularly from November, 1935, to the spring of 1937.

The Chicago chapter planned, during the summer of 1935, to send delegates to the national SFL headquarters in New York—a meeting which would, had it materialized as planned, have been in effect the first national convention in fandom. Charles D. Hornig was informed that Jack Darrow, William Dillenback and Otto Binder would arrive in New York on the evening of June 28, 1935. In honor of the occasion a meeting was arranged at the *Wonder Stories* offices, to which Hornig invited many of the most important local science fictionists of the day. At the eleventh hour word was received that the Chicago delegation had been delayed, and could not arrive as planned; Hornig decided to hold the meeting despite this fact—a wise decision, since it proved to be far and away the finest held up to that date. Present were Philip J. Bartel, Frank Belknap Long, Jr., Theodore Lutwin, Lawrence Manning, George G. Clark, Irving Kosow, Herman Leventman, A. L. Selikowitz, Conrad H. Ruppert, Julius Schwartz, John B. Michel, Donald A. Wollheim, Herbert Goudket, Kenneth Sterling and Julius Unger. The Chicago trio arrived the next day, which they spent in company with Hornig, Weisinger and Schwartz; their thousand-mile trip was one of the most interesting news tidbits to circulate in fandom at the time, and went well with the chapter's reputation as the leading SFL group of its day.

As leading members moved from the Chicago area, however, the chapter gradually lost the nucleus of its activity, and when the Gernsback regime collapsed in 1936 the beginning of its end was marked. Dissatisfaction with the rejuvenated league under Standard Publications' banner was a possible cause of severance of all SFL ties in 1937, when the club announced themselves as the Chicago Science-Fiction Club in the final number of *The Fourteen Leaflet*. Soon meetings were abandoned entirely, and members were heard from only on an individual basis thereafter.

The Brooklyn chapter, meanwhile, though boasting less than ten members, blossomed forth smartly under Clark's live-wire guidance. Together, these fans produced *The Brooklyn Reporter,* whose first issue was mimeographed in February, 1935. In all-around interest it had more appeal than any extant publication in the field save *Fantasy Magazine*. Basically it was a primer for the neophyte fan, and truly to the uninitiated an object of fascination, though at the time Wollheim and other comparitive veterans pooh-poohed its "stale news." The *Reporter* featured biographies of science fiction celebraties, reviews of current fantastic stories, quiz columns, hints to collectors, etc.; to those were later added reviews of books, news items and longer articles. Before the magazine's five-issue life was over it had added Selikowitz, Widner and Wollheim to its staff, sent copies to the heads of every Science Fiction League chapter, and undoubtedly converted many fans to real activity in the field.

The only other league organ of importance was *Lincoln SFL Doings,* published by the Lincoln, Illinois, chapter which was headed by P. H. Thompson. This group soon faded into inactivity, however, without having made any substantial contribution to the fan world.

Two other locals are worthy of passing mention. In England Douglas F. Mayer headed the league's first foreign branch at Leeds, a chapter which was to include many of the most important science fictionists in the area and prove a rallying-point for British fans generally. In Philadelphia the chapter of Milton A. Rothman was likewise destined to have a long and active life.

A second SFL quiz had been published, and the organization presented a placid surface mirroring national cooperation. But beneath this calm were beginning to flow currents that were to wreck the league's efficient functioning completely. The sources of these were not only the Terrestrial Fantascience Guild and the International Scientific Association, but the Greater New York chapters of the Science Fiction League itself. Development and interdependence of the latter will now be considered in detail.

William S. Sykora, who had entered fandom when he attended a few of the later Scienceer meetings, was director of the New York City chapter, whose roster also included Julius Schwartz, Conrad H. Ruppert, Donald A. Wollheim and John B. Michel. Here for the first time the first and second fandom groups were meeting on common ground, and the close contact only emphasized the rift dividing them. The younger members, justly or no, felt that the attitude of veterans toward them was patronizing and at times antagonistic, and these mutual differences were unquestionably involved in the genesis of the trouble into which the chapter quickly drifted. Meetings were held alternately at the homes of Sykora and Ruppert. From the first this was the group for which Hornig held the highest hopes. His dream of making it the SFL showplace was doomed never to be realized however. The membership never exceeded the original five, and since these five promptly split into two factions having little in common Hornig in desparation finally issued a plea for someone to take the job of reorganizing the chapter and putting it on its feet. But no offers were forthcoming.

In Brooklyn, meanwhile, more trouble was afoot. At a well-attended meeting with Hornig himself present, member Harold Kirshenblit was voted out of the secretary's office on charges of gross inefficiency. Disgruntled by this, Kirshenblit later wrote to Hornig, saying that there was no reason why a borough the size of Brooklyn could not have two SFL chapters; Hornig consenting, a group of fans was rounded up and Kirshenblit applied for a charter. This was granted and in June, 1935, he was appointed director of the Eastern New York SFL, subsidiary 1A of the Brooklyn chapter. By making it a subsidiary

club Hornig hoped to maintain greater measure of control over it, as
Clark, head of the parent chapter, was quite friendly to him.

Harold   Kirshenblit   had   not   shown   any outstanding abilities at
leadership prior to this time, but the new group he headed blossomed
forth remarkably. This was due not only to his own native ability,
but to a rapid decline of the parent Brooklyn chapter as well. There
are several reasons for this decline. First of all, its activities
fell off in interest. Aside from publication of *The Brooklyn Reporter*
the only serious pursuit undertaken was a weak attempt to catalog
fantasy cartoons; and in a day when the groundwork of fandom was in
the process of being laid this was idle luxury at best. More important, however, was Kirshenblit's favorable location; unlike Clark,
he headed a chapter which met near members' homes. And with these
factors in his favor, he soon had such active fans as Frederick Pohl,
Irving Kosow, Herman Leventman and Marvin Miller attending meetings
regularly; frequent visitors being Wollheim and Sykora, with Hornig,
Schwartz, Michel and even Clark himself being present occasionally.
The editorial in the first *Arcturus,* official organ of the Eastern
New York SFL, summed up the situation quite aptly:

> The ENYSFL, the   largest   in New York City to date, has
> grown from the modest role of the first sub-chapter, to its
> present commanding position on the SFL horizon. It has far
> outgrown its parent chapter, the Brooklyn SFL, and is still
> growing rapidly. Scarcely a meeting goes by without the
> addition to our rolls of at least one new member. Charles D.
> Hornig...agreed at a recent meeting that hereafter the ENY
> SFL would be in complete command of the SFL activities in
> Brooklyn, the Brooklyn chapter to become dormant.

This was an almost sensational turn of events. And it was now evident to Hornig that he had failed in his attempt to keep the local
chapters strongly under his control. Here the Brooklyn stronghold had
quickly melted away and the New York group, having shown virtually no
activity, required reorganization. In an attempt to reaffirm leadership, Hornig took over directorship of the latter himself. The result
of his action was an explosion which rocked the Science Fiction
League to its very foundations, one which for showmanship has yet to
be surpassed in the fan world.

Chapter IX

THE NEW ISA AND *THE INTERNATIONAL OBSERVER*

IN 1932, as a result of letters interchanged in the readers' column of *Amazing Stories,* a correspondence had sprung up among Carl Johnson, E. C. Love and Walter Kubilius. The three decided to form an organization for the benefit of science fiction advocates, and, formulating it on the basis of Gernsback's ideal that fans should be science hobbyists (a genesis similar to that of the old Science Correspondence Club), they founded the Edison Science Club. Coincident with this action, *The Edison Science Correspondence Club Journal* was issued. Elections held in September, 1932, elevated Love to the presidency, and gave the posts of vice-president and secretary-treasurer to Johnson and William Palmer respectively. At first the group prospered, but all too soon many felt hampered by the lack of facilities for expansion. So, believing that the organization was simply becoming enmired ever more deeply in a hopeless rut, members Kubilius and Gervais left the parent body and formulated plans for the Cosmos Science Club. When John B. Michel entered the scene he suggested the addition of the word "international" to the new club's title. And he, together with the other two, published a fan magazine *Radiogram,* which published a miscellaneous assortment of odds and ends and ran for but two issues. Failing in his attempts to strengthen the Edison Science Club after the defection of Kubilius and Gervais, Love ceded all its rights to the two for their International Cosmos Science Club and publicly announced the fact in a bulletin titled *The Ediogram.*

Upon learning of the ICSC, William S. Sykora felt that it was an excellent beginning for a type of club he had in mind. He became a member, and noting that progress was at a virtual standstill because of abandonment of its publication and inefficient campaigning for new recruits—the latter reason, ironically enough, having been the main one for its secession from the parent ESC—he arranged with Michel for his own appointment to the chairmanship to a committee possessing virtually dictatorial powers, being even entrusted with the authority to interpret the club's constitution to the membership.

But before describing the first important events of Sykora's fan career, let us consider briefly the man's background. Sykora first appeared on the scene during the latter days of the Scienceers. Indeed, after the dissolution of this group he approached Glasser and Unger early in 1934 in an unsuccessful attempt to bring about its revival. To understand him best, it must be realized that William Sykora was an old-time science fictionist. He epitomized the Gernsback ideal that all readers of the genre should consider the advancement of science their serious aim. He had amassed a solid scientific background, and his cellar boasted a well-equipped laboratory. Beside an excellent science fiction collection rested an imposing assemblage of scientific tomes. Several short articles by him had appeared in *Science and Mechanics,* including "A Scientific Paradox," a prize-winning entry in a contest sponsored by this magazine. He

garnered yet another prize in a similar contest published in *Mechan-
tcs and Handtcraft*. Undoubtedly he was a person of intelligence and
capability. The old ISA and its *Cosmology* had always fascinated him;
to his mind, this was the type of organization fandom needed. And
when all efforts to revive the Scienceers came to naught, he therefore cast about for means whereby a new group conforming to these
ideals might be found. In so doing he contacted the International
Cosmos Science Club through Michel, his friend.

Realizing immediately the ICSC's potentialities, Sykora lost no
time in utilizing his newly-won powers in that organization. On the
strength of Michel's association with *The Radtogram,* he was entrusted with the editorship of *The Internattonal Observer,* the revital-
ized club's organ. Perhaps unexpectedly, Michel seemed to have a
flair for this type of work. He created for *The Internattonal Observer* the first silk-screened cover ever seen in the fan world. From
the first issue these covers, astoundingly well done for an amateur,
lent to the magazine a distinctive, pleasing appearance unlike that
found in the majority of its fan competitors. This enviable standard
was maintained throughout its entire life.

The second issue of this publication presented a constitution, as
drawn up by a committee composed of Edward Gervais, Day Gee and Michel. (Gervais will be remembered as an outstanding member of the
Terrestrial Fantascience Guild and Gee had been on the roster of
Palmer's International Scientific Association.) This constitution
was unique in that it represented the first effort of a science
fiction fan club to establish anything resembling the mechanics of a
democracy. And although democracy often limped badly during the
ICSC's history, there was evident at all times some semblance of its
presence.

In theory, the club was designed to embrace both science hobbyists
and science fiction fans; this was borne out, furthermore, by the
Internattonal Observer's byline, "of science and science fiction."
As long as the first president, Edward Gervais, was in office, however, the emphasis was on science, and fiction was almost completely
crowded out of the club's periodical. The latter was divided into
such sectional headings as "Chemistry," "Physics," "Astronomy," and
"Biology," and its articles bore such staid titles as "Neutronium,"
"Color-Waves," "Diamonds," "A Visit to the Adler Planetarium," etc.
Nevertheless, some topics of fictional interest were introduced from
the very first. Michel wrote an interesting column titled "The Science Fiction Critic." A contest for the best original story was announced in the second number of *The Internattonal Observer,* this being open to all members who had paid their dues in full. (This contest was won by Florence Reider, an active member of the Chicago SFL
chapter.) A second contest of different nature was announced later.

Sykora's influence was also evident in the inception of a club
library, composed of both scientific and fictional volumes, which
was kept at his home. It was due in no small measure to him as well
that the club's publication maintained a regular, monthly schedule
of appearance, and that its membership grew steadily larger.

The International Cosmos Science Club was, of course, no local
group. Nevertheless many of its adherents lived in the greater New
York area, and so it was hardly surprising that they should affirm
their presence by designating themselves a local chapter. This was

done on February 3, 1935, at a meeting attended by Sykora, Wollheim, Michel and Herbert Goudket. Thereafter the group met regularly at Sykora's home, and these gatherings often reached peaks of interest that surpassed many of the best SFL chapter meetings.

Aside from the social benefits involved, the chapter undertook many worthwhile activities. The first of these was a series of experiments in amateur rocketry. Four rockets constructed by Sykora were launched on March 10, 1935, in the presence of the New York chapter of the ICSC and representatives of several SFL chapters. While none of these rockets achieved startling success, the subsequent account of the experiments written by Sykora were extremely well done, and drew forth profound respect from all quarters. Motion pictures of these experiments were taken, and were later shown at Queens SFL meetings among other places. It is obvious that despite the club's comparatively small roster it was very active and possessed of great potentialities because of alert leadership.

Attempts were made to get publicity for the organization through the SFL. Gervais' letter to Hornig met, however, with a curt rebuff.

> ...we are not going to ask our readers to join another science fiction organization when the S.F.L. gives and will give everything that can be asked for and is open to all— even those who cannot afford the $1.50 dues of your organization (which makes the ICSC look a bit commercial in nature).
> We can see absolutely no advantage in your organization over the S.F.L. If you can show us anything that the ICSC can do that the league cannot, we would be willing to go into this further.

This reply was printed above Hornig's signature in the *International Observer;* it was not commented upon editorially, and the matter was dropped. But it was the genesis of later discord with the SFL. The ICSC quickly and decisively showed that it could indeed accomplish things that the SFL could not—and the first of these was the rocketry experiment noted above. This achievement was begrudgingly acknowledged in the League's column in *Wonder Stories.* It became immediately obvious that Hornig had taken the wrong tack. The ICSC at this time was predominantly a scientific-minded organization, and could easily have been accorded an official blessing and recommendation as a haven for science hobbyists. Hornig's rough handling of the group, which he insisted on treating as a competing one, not only showed a lack of mature acumen but proved to have disastrous results.

The election of February 13, 1935, had raised Sykora to president, Gervais having been reduced to the vice president's post and Michel and Goudket being given the respective positions of secretary and treasurer. The leaders thus swept into power almost immediately transformed the ICSC into a militant group. As we have seen, Hornig's attitude had certainly not made relations with the SFL any more friendly. On top of this, personal arguments at local New York chapter meetings made them even less so. But they deteriorated into open animosity when Wollheim recounted to members in all its sordid detail the non-payment scandal he had recently uncovered.

The ICSC, which had previously lent but mildly passive aid to the Terrestrial Fantascience Guild, now cooperated completely in an all-out mutual effort to smash the Science Fiction League and *Wonder Stories* itself. ICSC members mimeographed on club equipment the April, 1935, number of the TFG *Bulletin,* which contained Wollheim's remarks concerning his payment difficulties with *Wonder Stories,* and helped distribute it as well. They emphasized their own democratic constitution with the slogan "the only members' club"—in contrast, of course, to the League, where members had no appeal from arbitrary decisions of the assistant secretary. They issued a fan magazine titled *Flabbergasting Stories,* an obvious burlesque of *Wonder Stories,* which bore the byline "a schrechlich publication." In this appeared humorous barbed allusions to the non-payment practices and references to a "Sexy Science Fiction Soviet Auxiliary" for frustrated fans, caricaturing the SFL.

Michel's "Science Fiction Critic" column in *The International Observer* printed decidedly unfavorable reviews of the fiction in *Wonder Stories.* Editorials urged readers to get the TFG *Bulletin* and learn of the *Wonder Stories* difficulty. A new column called "Sun Spots" was initiated by Wollheim, and blamed Gernsback for the dissolution of the old Scienceers, first by attempts to make them become the unwilling nucleus of the American Interplanetary Society and then by not paying for their meeting room at the Museum of Natural History—thus inferring that Gernsback spent most of his spare time in disrupting fan organizations. Simultaneously an attack was launched at the editors of *Fantasy Magazine,* who were labelled as traitors to the fan field for refusing to print in their magazine anything which reflected unfavorably upon *Wonder Stories.* The intolerance of the *Fantasy Magazine* group toward newcomers in the field was thus also reaping its harvest of opposition.

With each succeeding issue of *The International Observer* these attacks increased in volume and effectiveness. Those found in the "Sun Spots" column in particular left no line of fire untried. Wollheim showed a real talent for presenting legitimate news items in such a way that they reflected unfavorably upon Hornig, the Science Fiction League, *Wonder Stories* and *Fantasy Magazine.* He was an implacable foe, and had his column received wider circulation it seems quite likely that it could have brought the SFL to its knees without outside aid. Indeed, Wollheim boasted of his knowledge that copies of *The International Observer* were in the *Wonder Stories* editorial office, with all comments relevant to the situation circled. (These very copies are now in the possession of this historian, and have proved invaluable in compiling an account of the affair. Wollheim was not correct however in stating that such words as "untrue" and "scandalous" had been pencilled in the margins beside such comments. Moreover, interest had not been confined solely to this feud, for Schwartz had also encircled all statements relative to the Anthony Gilmore expose as well as Tucker's "death.") Michel's column, "The Science Fiction Critic," was likewise active in the battle. In it he once remarked:

> I believe fantasy saw its best days when it [*Fantasy Magazine*] was the *Science Fiction Digest* in purpose as well as name. Lately it has become the stamping ground for Charles D. Hornig, managing editor of *Wonder Stories,* who has taken it over (apparently) and is using it as a medium to advertise his magazine. I think this is an obvious fact.

Letters from an anonymous party terming himself "The Fantasist" began to circulate among SFL chapter heads, with effective propaganda against the League. At a meeting of the New York chapter Hornig himself was tricked into stating that the SFL's purpose was a commercial one.

For a while Hornig refrained from making any public statements. But the relentless pressure could not long be endured. His first defense was in the nature of vaguely phrased references to parties attempting to "undermine" the SFL, he hoped "would mend their ways." When this did no good, he threatened to "reorganize" the New York chapter, stating that the poor showing made by some of the top fans in the field there was shameful. The result being but to increase the activity of his opposition, Hornig resorted to a desperate and sensational expedient to quell this dangerous uprising. The September, 1935, number of *Wonder Stories* carried the following announcement:

THREE MEMBERS EXPELLED

It grieves us to announce that we have found the first disloyalty in our organization. We have discovered that three of our members, who run what they consider a competing club to the SFL, have done all within their power, through personal letters and published notices, to disrepute the League, *Wonder Stories,* and the Gernsback outfit by spreading gross untruths and libellous slander to other science fiction fans and authors. They joined the League only to be able to attack it better. We are extremely sorry that we cannot know every fan's intentions when applications are received, but we have proved only three-tenths of one percent wrong in our enrollment, so we hope that the other members will forgive us. These members we expelled on June 12th. Their names are Donald A. Wollheim, John B. Michel, and William S. Sykora—three active fans who just got themselves on the wrong road.

The attitude of fandom as a whole toward this expulsion was relatively passive. Most readers knew little, if anything, of the grim struggle between the SFL and the ICSC. Some had probably formed an unfavorable opinion of Wollheim through his extremely critical letters published in *Wonder Stories'* readers' column, and therefore dismissed the incident as an unpleasantly justified one. Only a handful was aware, through ICSC-distributed propaganda, of the other side of the matter. At least one important fan, however, Fred Anger, resigned in protest to the action. Among the active fans—outside of the *Fantasy Magazine* group—sympathy with the outcasts was general.

If the righteousness of their motives were disregarded, there would be no doubt that the three deserved to be expelled. But Hornig had blundered again. Wollheim, as we have noted, had made himself unpopular through publication of his letters criticizing (among other things) the magazine's policy of reprinting German science fiction; his unpopularity was not due to being wrong on these points, but rather to the man's habit of incorporating in each of his letters some personal slurs or innuendos entirely unnecessary to the success of his arguments. (This characteristic was apparent again and again in his later fan life, and often operated to cancel out an entire line of reasoning in the minds of readers, losing for Wollheim

debates he had easily won if simple logic alone were taken into
consideration.) Thus Wollheim could safely have been offered up as a
scapegoat, for beyond the publication and editing of the magazine
containing the bulk of his attacks Sykora had printed no attack of
his own, and Michel had been largely concereed with the *Fantasy
Magazine* group rather than with the SFL. When the comparatively passive Sykora and Michel found themselves in the same boat with
Wollheim they saw red, and thenceforward took an unqualifiedly
active role in the campaign. Hornig thus succeeded only in uniting a
vengeful opposition even more determinedly against him, and the
result was to be stark melodrama in the meeting halls of the SFL
chapters.

Chapter X

OTHER HAPPENINGS OF 1935

IN AUSTEN, Texas, an individual named D. R. Welch had gone into business buying and selling science fiction and fan magazines. This enterprise he conducted under the name of the Science Fiction Syndicate. In order to further his business by arousing interest in the lesser-known fan publications and such obscure professional efforts as the British *Scoops*, Welch compiled and William L. Crawford published the first list of amateur periodicals of fandom. It was entitled *Science Fiction Bibliography*, and its resumé omitted very few items of importance. It remains to this day a collectors' item of great interest.

In evaluating *The International Observer* and the TFG *Bulletin* Welch remarked that they were "not in themselves worthy of being collected." Learning of this, Wollheim contacted Welch, informing him of his campaign being waged by the TFG and the ICSC, asking him to examine recent issues of the organizations' official organs and to reconsider his opinion of their importance. Whether fear of the TFG's campaign boycotting unfair dealers had lent some weight to Wollheim's request is not known, but the fact remains that Welch shortly thereafter mimeographed and circulated with copies of his bibliography a one-paged circular which stated, among other things:

> The *Bulletin* is now a magazine in which all science fiction fans will be intensely interested. The April issue contains vital information about the failure of *Wonder Stories* to pay its authors.
> Fans should welcome this magazine which gives them honest and accurate information.
> Nor do we discourage fans from joining the International Cosmos Science Club or subscribing to its official publication, *The International Observer*. This magazine has shown consistant improvement with each issue. Under the guidance of William S. Sykora and Donald Wollheim it should make even greater strides in the future.

Arthur ("Bob") Tucker will be remembered as a contributor to the pages of *The Fantasy Fan* and *Fantasy Magazine*, both serious efforts and humorous ones coming from his pen. Of the latter (many of which bore the byline of his alter ego, "Hoy Ping Pong") such extrapolations on science fiction as his account of a future fan convention held on the planet Pluto proved most popular. His clowning spread to the magazines' reader-columns, where, hitting upon the notion of parodying readers' requests it reached its acme of notoriety— readers from time immemorial had complained about paper-quality, type-size, rough edges, quality of illustrations, the magazines' sizes, and so on. Tucker decided to show them how ridiculous and picayune all this was, and with characteristic mock seriousness wrote to the editor of *Astounding Stories*, demanding that the wire staples which bound the magazine together be removed, as they disgraced the field by indicting its originality. Flavored chewing-gum, he hinted, would be preferable; and for true dignity nothing could surpass the platinum fastener. To carry out his plan, Tucker appointed himself dictator of the Society for Prevention of Wire Staples in Scientifiction Magazines—or the SPWSSTFM for short.

The very absurdity of the movement caught the fickle juvenile fancy of the fans. A flood of letters pro and con poured in, the mock controversy giving rise to dozens of similar organizations, each and every one of them designating itself by a long set of initials. The primary opposing group was headed by High Cocolorum Donald A. Wollheim; it called itself the IAOPUMUMFSTFPUSA, which stood for International and Allied Organizations for the Purpose of Upholding and Maintaining the Use of Metallic Fasteners in Science Fiction Publications of the United States of America. Uncomplimentary remarks were exchanged between the rival groups in their official publications—these being Tucker's renowned *D'Journal* whose membership list alledgedly included many leading authors and editors, and Wollheim's *Polymorphanucleated Leucocyte*. The final rounds of the battle were unquestionably Wollheim's, for it was shown that *D'Journal* had, contrary to its ethical stand, used staples for binding.

Reader-reaction soon turned against the alphabetical societies as the more mature faction of the audience began to assert itself, however. But the horseplay was not destined to peter out ignominiously, being brought to an abrupt and dramatic conclusion by two letters printed in the January, 1936, issue of *Astounding Stories*. The first, a letter from one Anne Smidley, notified the magazine's readers of the death of Bob Tucker, who was operated upon and "never recovered consciousness." The second was from Tucker himself, ostensibly written before the operation, in which he requested all the alphabetical societies to combine into two opposing groups. Editor Tremaine in a footnote asked readers to "accept his challenge and work for unity."

The entire affair was so preposterous—imagine taking the organization of such groups seriously!—that readers did not know what to believe. Tucker, the perfect fan fool, dead? It was inconceivable. Some New York skeptics telegraphed Tucker's family, receiving a Twain-like reply from Tucker to the effect that reports of his death were greatly exaggerated. And slowly it became apparent to fandom that the entire affair had been a hoax. Tucker claimed that it was somebody's idea of a joke, and that he himself knew nothing of it; but Tremaine took an entirely different attitude. He had learned of the hoax before the copies of the magazine carrying it reached the newsstands, and, with the natural reaction of a man whose ready sympathy is made light of, he decided that as far as the readers of *Astounding Stories* were concerned, Tucker would stay dead. And indeed, it was a long, long time, as eras of fandom are reckoned, before letters bearing Tucker's name were published in *Astounding* again.

Although Tucker's *D'Journal* was not his initial entry into the amateur publishing field (he was responsible for *The Planetoid,* an evanescent periodical appearing in 1932) it remained for some time his most important one, for though Wollheim's "Sun Spots" spoke from time to time of projects he was allegedly planning, little or nothing further was heard of the man until late 1938.

Throughout all the strife of 1935 it is well to keep in mind that

Julius Schwartz and Mort Weisinger had kept *Fantasy Magazine* far in the front of the field, and that "the digest of imaginative literature" remained the dead center of science fiction fandom. The quality, variety and all-around interest of its features simply could not be matched. Its fiction was very good, and included stories by such top-notch authors as A. Merritt, stories that were obtained at no cost, while professional publications offering tempting word-rates could obtain from Merritt nary a line. The magazine's art work, done by the clever amateur Clay Ferguson, Jr., was likewise up to the same high standard, and compared favorably with that found in the professional fantasy magazines. With the change in title from *Science Fiction Digest* (made in January, 1934) the coverage of material had become broader than ever, and naturally had resulted in an even wider reader-appeal. After an elaborately fine second anniversary number, a series of issues increased *Fantasy Magazine's* popularity yet more. After three bimonthly numbers the periodical resumed monthly publication in April, 1935, and from then until the third anniversary issue its supremacy was impossible to challenge.

During the depression period jobs were extremely difficult to obtain, so Julius Schwartz and Mort Weisinger struck upon the idea of agenting fantasy stories as a means of earning a living. Weisinger, who had some abilities as an author, began by peddling his own yarns, some of which he eventually sold. The close contacts the two had with all the important authors and editors of the day (as a result of *Fantasy Magazine*) soon bore fruit, and it was not long before no less a personage than Stanley G. Weinbaum was a client of their Solar Sales Agency. Schwartz and Weisinger sold virtually all the stories that Weinbaum ever wrote, and the sheaf of correspondence concerning them is one of the most treasured items in Schwartz' files today. Henry Hasse was another author on their list, as were P. Schuyler Miller, J. Harvey Haggard, Dr. David H. Keller, Thomas S. Gardner and others. It was through the Solar Sales Agency that Weisinger first came into contact with Ned Pines' comparitively new magazine-chain, Standard Publications, which was managed by Leo Margulies. And later, when Standard purchased *Wonder Stories,* events showed that Margulies had not forgotten the young fellow who had continually tried to sell stories to him.

Schwartz took over the agency himself when Weisinger left in 1936, and several years later, when newstand fantasy titles were cropping up every month, his reputation as a "science fiction specialist" bore fruit, and his business became even more successful. At times, complete issues of science fiction magazines were composed of material purchased from the Schwartz agency. His early start in the field had eventually gained for him such popular writers as Eando Binder, John Russell Fearn, Manly Wade Wellman, Malcolm Jameson, Leigh Brackett, Ray Bradbury, David V. Reed and many, many others. (Later fans turned agent—such as Frederik Pohl, Robert W. Lowndes and Sam Moskowitz—found the pickings lean indeed, and theirs was the harder task of selling the work of many writers.)

Shortly after the inception of the Science Fiction League, Hornig created another new feature for *Wonder Stories,* "The Science Fiction Swap Column." This column was composed of advertisements of fans who had anything to buy, sell or exchange, and the rate charged (two cents a word) was eminently reasonable. It was through this medium

that many readers learned that fan magazines existed, and it was the
first important means whereby these fan magazines could reach the
attention of new converts.

The column also encouraged fans to issue their own amateur efforts,
and a number of such publications did spring up as a result. They
were mostly of a poor grade, however. One was *The Science-Fiction
Review,* edited and published by R. M. Holland, Jr., of Owensboro,
Kentucky. Holland's attempt was juvenile in almost every respect—
the format, method of duplication and type of material varying with
each issue. It can be imagined that the magazine did not have a very
large circulation as a result. Nevertheless, by the time Holland
reached a sixth number, *The Science-Fiction Review* was at least an
interesting commentary on current news, and boasted a single worthwhile column, E. H. Lichtig's "Science Fiction Film Comment."

However, in November, 1935, one Claire P. Beck of Reno, Nevada, advertised a publication of his own in the *Wonder Stories* column, this
also being entitled *The Science-Fiction Review.* This small-sized,
four-paged, mimeographed affair showed no virtue other than neatness,
and immediately incurred the wrath of Holland, who felt he had
enough trouble on his hands without the title of his magazine being
appropriated. Beck acceded to Holland's request that a change be
made, and thereby did himself one of the greatest favors of his fan
career, for he titled his second issue *The Science Fiction Critic,*
thus obligating himself to take a critical view of the field, which
he did with a vengeance. The provocative nature of the articles he
published made his magazine an immediate success, for there was at
that time no other periodical devoted exclusively to constructive or
destructive criticism. Beck's *Critic* quickly became noted for both.
The second number inaugurated a department conducted by the editor's
brother Clyde, who had won an honorable mention in an *Air Wonder
Stories* contest some six years back. This department was devoted to
"smashing idols and eyesores of science-fiction, and welding and
shaping the fragments into better form"; the four essays that resulted were lated compiled into a neat little pamphlet that carried the
column's heading, "Hammer and Tongs." Beck's impartiality to the
feuds of that time was characterized by a display of both the TFG
and the SFL emblems, side by side, on his magazine's cover. The Beck
brothers, who had acquired a hand press, turned out their next issue
in printed format, and a neatly executed job it was. Edward J.
Carnell's column, "Europe Calling," was added and an article by
C. Hamilton Bloomer appeared. Bloomer, as we shall see, was to play
an important part in fandom's history.

Holland, meanwhile, was becoming exceedingly dissatisfied with his
Science-Fiction Review, and was tiring also of his attempts to dab-
ble in fan feuds of the day, characterized by an attack on the SFL
made more out of friendship for Wollheim than because of personal
interest. The unfavorable manner in which his magazine compared with
Beck's printed one caused him to seek out means for having *The
Science-Fiction Review* printed also. The Becks were among those contacted in an effort to accomplish this; however, nothing ever came
of it, and, feeling he could accomplish little of benefit to fandom
in his present medium, Holland finally ceded all rights to *The
Science-Fiction Review* to Wollheim. Wollheim turned out a single
carbon-copied number, which is of interest only because it referred

to *The Canadian Science Fiction Fan,* produced "by a chap in Vancouver, B. C., where we least expected a fan to live! A fair little magazine." This constitutes the first and last mention of what appears to have been the first Canadian fan magazine, published in early 1936.

One day in late October, 1935, a number of fans received what is best termed a "thing" from East Orange, New Jersey. It was titled *The Planeteer,* and was perpetrated by a fifteen-year-old member of the ICSC, James Blish. The publication consisted of twelve small, readably hektographed pages, and was dated November, 1935. It featured a "complete novel" condensed to six pages and accompanied by some unbelievably crude illustrations. A single pin served as a binder. Just about the only encouragement Blish received was from Wollheim who had originally suggested the title to *Astounding Stories* as suitable for a companion magazine. Ackerman termed Blish's story as "comparable to an O'Leary yarn." (Dell Magazines issued during 1935 three issues of a fantastic story magazine titled *Terrence X. O'Leary's War Birds.*) And indeed, Blish did show an above-average—for his age—writing aptitude. Undaunted by the scanty praise coming his way, and though his finances were meager, Blish nevertheless continued to issue and improve his periodical. Its size was enlarged and a mimeograph was procured to duplicate it; William Miller, Jr., a fan who lived nearby, was added to the staff in the art editor's capacity, and several columns introduced. By its sixth monthly number *The Planeteer* was quite presentable, as fan publications go. Blish's error was similar to that of many other early fans. He, like them, attempted to emulate professional publications—and made a sorry farce of it. Indeed, Blish once went so far as to purchase from Laurence Manning (a professional science fiction author) a short story entitled "The Coal Thief," The less said about its quality the better, but Manning was paid for the tale at a similar rate as that dispensed by *Wonder Stories.* Such a policy was suicidal for a publication which never obtained sufficient subscriptions to pay even for its paper.

It was now obvious that in addition to the first stratum of fandom, prime examples of which were the producers of *Fantasy Magazine* and *Marvel Tales,* and the second stratum, which centered about the Terrestrial Fantascience Guild and the International Cosmos Science Club, yet a third fandom was forming. This ranked below the other two in power and importance, and was composed largely of very young fans, who, despite undeveloped talents and little support, were independantly minded enough to refuse to merge their identities with more experienced groups. Beck and Blish, with their *Science Fiction Critic* and *Planeteer,* were typical of the third fandom, and while they at first appeared to drift along with the tide, they and their fellows were soon to strike out on their own and become a major force in fan history.

Chapter XI

THE SFL-ISA SHOWDOWN

AS 1935 drew to a close, the tumultuous strife between the International Cosmos Science Club and the Science Fiction League entered its final stages following the expulsion of Sykora, Wollheim and Michel from the League roster.

Here it might be propitious to inquire how the ICSC was faring in its relationship with the professionals generally. Was it facing a solid bloc of professional antagonism? Was the SFL really the battleground for all the professionals against the fans? The answer to both questions is an emphatic *No*. Both F. Orlin Tremaine and T. O'Conor Sloane, editors of *Wonder Stories'* major competitors, had shown far greater wisdom than Hornig in their relations with the organization. When the ICSC asked Sloane for permission to use an emblem symbolizing science fiction that *Amazing Stories* had used as a cover illustration, Sloane could find "no objection." Early in its existence Tremaine acknowledged a complimentary copy of *The International Observer* sent him, saying, "I was really surprised at the pretentious presentation of your *International Observer*. It would seem to me that you're coming forward as a group. I wish you all the luck in the world." Thus, with a few simple words, Tremaine gained the undying gratitude and cooperation of the ICSC. Throughout its existence it maintained the most cordial relations with *Astounding Stories,* and in the latter magazine news and publicity of the club was occasionally published. Tremaine, editor of a magazine paying the highest rates in the field, had everything to gain by having the other science fiction magazines' payment practices contrasted with his own, but it is doubtful if this motivated his actions to any marked extent. It is obvious how easily and simply Hornig might have obtained cooperation from the ICSC instead of firing embers of hate. A few lines of publicity for the club in his letter column, a more tactful reply to its querying letter—and the entire history of the Science Fiction League might have been markedly changed.

In the meantime, Will Sykora, who had always cast envious eyes at Raymond A. Palmer's International Scientific Association, now wrote Palmer, urging him to sanction a consolidation of the old ISA with the ICSC, particularly since the ISA had never sounded an official death-knell, rather remaining in a state of suspended animation. By absorbing the older group Sykora saw an opportunity to gain for the ICSC a long, honorable history, a distinguished name, and unquestioned supremacy as the leading fan organization of the time. To Palmer it meant ridding himself of his obligations expeditiously and honorably. So, with its first anniversary issue *The International Observer* combined with *Cosmology* and printed a letter from Palmer, in which the latter announced handing over his club lock, stock and barrel to the ICSC. Although the International Cosmos Science Club did not officially change its title, it everywhere publicized itself as the ISA, becoming so well known by this abbreviation that most fans forgot that there had ever been an older version of the organization.

With this bit of business consummated, the new ISA prepared to launch a counterblow at the SFL for expelling three of its members. For this purpose they resurrected yet another old-time club organ, *The Planet,* official publication of the Scienceers. Its name was changed to *The Scienceer,* but continuity with the old volume number-ing was retained, so that the magazine proved eventually to be the final issue of *The Planet.* (Permission to use the old title, it might be noted, had long since been obtained by Sykora in his abort-ive attempt to revive the Scienceers prior to formation of the ISA.) It was quite out-spokenly termed "the first political fan magazine," and as a slap at the *Fantasy Magazine* group, was dedicated to Allan Glasser, "former editor, knifed in the back by his 'best friend'." The exact incident referred to is obscure, but probably is the plagiarism incident in which Glasser was involved.

The Scienceer featured an article titled "The Fall of the New York Science Fiction League," in which Sykora, Wollheim and Michel gave the reasons for the local chapter's lack of success, rehashed again the story of Gernsback's non-payment scandal, and denied that they had been guilty of actions treasonous to the SFL's ideals and purposes, claiming their activities in the field as evidence of their loyalty. To quote from the article—

> ...The SFL has only one purpose and that is to continually broaden the scope and popularize the art of science-fiction ...Is it treasonous and disloyal to *collect* from *Wonder Stories,* the backer of the SFL, what is justly owed? Perhaps it is against the advancement of science-fiction to permit authors to be paid for their work...

To these uncomfortable questions posed by the "outcasts" Charles D. Hornig's reply was not forthcoming. Readers were urged to shun the reshuffled chapter of the New York City SFL, emphasising its "dicta-torial aspects" by inviting them to join instead the local ISA group, titling it "a free man's club."

Had *The Scienceer* received wider distribution, and had its subject-matter been presented with a trifle more restraint, the results could have been more damaging to the League indeed. The magazine is of further interest in that there was published the first official announcement of the ICSC s changing its name to the Internation-al Scientific Association. This information was not even mentioned, strangely enough, in the current *International Observer*—possibly because the issue was stencilled some time in advance of publication.

All this time Sykora and Wollheim had been regular attendants at meetings of the East New York SFL chapter, phenominally successful offshoot of the dormant Brooklyn group and publishers of *Arcturus.* At one of these Hornig happened to be present; indignant at finding expelled members about, he asked that they be barred from attending future gatherings. But Sykora and Wollheim, quite popular with fans of the time, were defended by others present, who demanded that Hornig express his views on the matter more explicitly before they would consent to take any action. Realizing that he was edging into the non-payment angle, however, Hornig wisely did not press his point nor elaborate on his accusations.

But this was the last straw. The spark had reached the magazine, and the long-awaited explosion took place. It was without precedent in drama, and superceded in brute dictatorial force anything the ISA had hitherto resorted to. The second meeting of the reorganized New York chapter was in progress, with Hornig presiding, in a New York school room. Suddenly the clumping of many shoes was heard, and in burst Sykora and Wollheim at the head of eight other youths (not all science fiction fans) recruited from the streets for rough action if necessary. Sykora walked up to Julius Schwartz, a member of the audience, and shook a fist under his nose as a gesture of defiance to the *Fantasy Magazine* group. Then with the aid of his comrades he chased Hornig from the platform. Producing a gavel of his own (one which later became famous, being wielded at many conventions and fan gatherings), Sykora proceeded to call the meeting to order in the name of the New York branch of the International Scientific Association. Such brazen effrontery left the audience too flabbergasted to protest. Wollheim then ascended the platform and vividly outlined his grievances with *Wonder Stories,* which he was still in the process of detailing when the building superintendent—probably summoned by Hornig—arrived and broke up the gathering.

But the blaze was to leap still higher. The next meeting of the East New York chapter found all aggrieved parties present, in addition to numerous visitors. It was a banner assembly. Hornig seized upon this opportunity to expose the culprits. He dealt in detail with the campaign they had carried on against *Wonder Stories* through the TFG and the ISA, citing such incidents as the anonymous letters from "The Fantasist" sent to heads of many SFL chapters. He claimed that the ISA members were not fighting for democracy, but were actually attempting to seize control of the fan world themselves. But Wollheim's talk at the dramatic meeting mentioned above had evidently proved more effective than was believed possible. The audience scarcely gave Hornig's talk fair consideration. Members conversed among themselves, many not taking the slightest trouble to listen so firmly were they convinced that he was wrong.

Then William Sykora arose to give his side of the dispute. And in a flash of comprehension the New York fan world realized that the drive against the Science Fiction League had changed leadership. Previously neutral, Sykora was now in the driver's seat, and was forcing the bitter campaign to a short, hard-fought conclusion. Behind-the-scenes plotting, the grand strategy of the campaign against the League as expressed by the last few numbers of *The International Observer* and *The Scienceer,* the New York chapter fiasco—all of these were now traceable directly to him. He was the master-mind harnessing Donald Wollheim's fighting rhetoric, with his organizing and political abilities now plainly evident. Argument by argument, Sykora ripped the salient points of Hornig's appeal to shreds. And the audience, already leaning toward his views, now swung over *en masse*

There was but a single attempt to halt the shifting tide of opinion. George Gordon Clark, editor of *The Brooklyn Reporter* and organizer of the defunct Brooklyn chapter, rose to throw in his lot with Hornig's. The ISA had long suspected him of favoring the *Wonder Stories* clique, but until then Clark had expressed his views so cleverly that on one occasion an ISA reviewer had remarked in *The International Observer* that *The Brooklyn Reporter* did "not seem to show the slightest control by the SFL." Now, however, he sided openly with Hornig against the ISA. He slandered Sykora and Wollheim, his words being so strong that Wollheim threatened to file suit for slander if retraction were not made. Forced later to withdraw his statements, Clark with this action virtually resigned from fan activity. Though Wollheim probably received full credit for driving an opponent from the field, it should also be remembered that Clark was tiring of fandom anyway, so that loss of face was simply the deciding factor.

The forces of Hornig now were in utter rout, though how complete his defeat was was not apparent for yet another month. At that time Hornig was reduced to offering reinstatement to Sykora, Wollheim and Michel on condition they apologise for past offenses. Sykora at first seemed irreconcilable, though he had been less maligned than Wollheim, who, with Michel, gave serious consideration to the proposal. All three were reinstated at a later date, although it is extremely unlikely that they made amends for anything less flagrant than the breaking up of the New York SFL meeting.

Chapter XII

THE DECLINE OF THE SFL AND THE ISA'S BID FOR POWER

THE FEBRUARY, 1936, *Arcturus* announced the dissolution of the Eastern New York Science Fiction League chapter by a unanimous vote of the membership. In its place was to be a new organization, the Independant League for Science Fiction. Members listed the following reasons for their action, which was obviously an aftermath of the last SFL-ISA clash: First, they felt that the SFL was not altruistic, but purely commercial in nature. In the second place, it was a dictatorship headed by a single individual, with no machinery available for his removal or for the election of new officers, since there was no written constitution. Thirdly, they believed the reputation of *Wonder Stories* was detrimental to any organization it sponsored. Fourthly, such chapter organs as *Arcturus, The Fourteen Leaflet* and *The Brooklyn Reporter* gave fuller, more helpful information about the League than the latter's own column in *Wonder Stories*. And Lastly, because three members had been expelled before being given any opportunity to speak in their own defense. The Eastern New York chapter now termed itself the Brooklyn League for Science Fiction. Its members were Harold Kirshenblit, Donald A. Wollheim, Frederik Pohl, Herman Leventman, Milton White, Israel Brodsky, Morris Davis, R. Drucker, Morris Miller, Louis Heynick, Irving Kosow, William S. Sykora and Bernard Weldt.

The Science Fiction League had now lost control of the last important New York chapter. And in the Independant League for Science Fiction it had a bone permanently stuck in its throat; the newly formed group was a constant reminder to fans of a battle the SFL had lost, a sure guarantee that formation of any new local chapter would be frustrated. Despite this, however, progress continued to be reported from elsewhere in the country, and for a short while it appeared that the ISA's victory was local in character. But that this was far from the truth soon became evident.

In December, 1935, the SFL granted a charter to a group of Denver fans, all of active importance, Olon F. Wiggins, Fred J. Walsen and Mervyn Evans. When informed of the details behind the SFL-ISA fracas however, they rescinded all League ties, and applied for a local ILSF charter, which was granted. Similarly the Albany chapter headed by A. L. Selikowitz, which included P. Schuyler Miller in its retinue, and the Nassau chapter headed by A. J. Aisenstein also resigned from the Science Fiction League, though small memberships prevented their being given charters from the ILSF. What further progress the organization might have made against the SFL is debatable, but in any event strife was broken off, for with dramatic suddenness *Wonder Stories* was sold.

In an effort to counteract diminishing circulation, Hugo Gernsback had proposed a scheme whereby readers would receive copies of *Wonder Stories* directly from the company upon remitting the 15¢ cover price, thus eliminating the publisher's losses on useless unsold copies of the magazine that were returned from newstands. But the handful of readers who cooperated was insufficient to keep the periodical in existence, even at a slight profit. Disappointed, Gernsback cast about for a purchaser who would take *Wonder Stories* off his hands, finally completing arrangements with Ned Pines and Leo Margulies of Better Publications.

For four months during mid-1936 the future of the SFL was therefore in doubt, and the very presence of doubt was enough to sever the comparitively tenuous links that bound the scattered chapters to the home office. Most of the smaller ones disappeared permanently, and the larger groups—like the Los Angeles and Chicago chapters— marked time anxiously until their new status could be determined.

Then word came through that Mort Weisinger, veteran fan and co-editor of *Fantasy Magazine,* was to edit a rejuvenated *Wonder Stories.* Fans breathed a sigh of relief. Frowns creased their brows anew, however, when they learned that the new magazine was to be titled *Thrilling Wonder Stories*. Furthermore, Margulies was reported to have stated point-blank that he did not plan on catering to the fans who he claimed were "a loud minority." But the SFL would be continued, nevertheless.

Fans naturally wondered how this would effect the Independant League for Science Fiction. The answer was swift in appearing. Despite the fact that the ILSF had no personal argument with the new SFL sponsors, the same aura of commercialism and dictatorship surrounded the latter organization; therefore although the ILSF would remain ostensibly at peace with the SFL, it would continue its status of an active, independant body. And shortly thereafter it published its constitution. It appeared that fandom had a representative organization at last.

Pride of the greater New York fans was the monthly publication *Arcturus.* From the attractively artistic covers through the last-page advertisements it was a periodical of absorbing interest. "The Circle" by "The Ringmaster" kept fandom informed, in political commentary style, of late developments in the SFL-ISA strife, as well as on other topical items. The magazine carried a column of the most recent science fiction news of Britain, written by Edward J. Carnell. Articles on early fan magazines, interviews with professionals in the fantasy field, reviews of current science fiction and occasional fan-written stories were also regularly in evidence. Undoubtedly the most popular feature, however, was a column titled "13" conducted by "Willy the Wisp," a pseudonym of Donald Wollheim. "13" was composed of squibs on thirteen prominent characters or fans in science fiction—sometimes complimentary, always newsy, frequently barbed. It was the forerunner of a similar, but more detailed, column, "As Others See Us," published in *The Science Fiction Fan,* which proved equally popular.

In the January, 1936, installment of "13" Wollheim had this to say about Forrest J. Ackerman:

> He doesn't know it, but when his name is mentioned in stf circles, it causes considerable snickers and suppressed laughter. This obstreperous author-pester, silly-letter writer, and what-have-you, is now going off half-baked on Esperanto and Universal Languages, a subject which he really doesn't know any too much about. Recently he renounced citizenship in the United States by joining the World Society of Nationless People.

Ackerman could scarcely allow such slurs to remain uncommented upon,
and he dispatched a heated letter to the editor of *Arcturus,* condemning "Willy the Wisp" and denying some of the accusations. But in a
special two-page reply entitled "Sez You," Wollheim added insult to
injury by elaborating in humorous fashion on his previous remarks,
retracting only his statement that Ackerman was no longer a United
States citizen, though he added that he considered Ackerman hypocritical in joining the World Society of Nationless People if he did
not intend to renounce national citizenship. Through inability or
disinclination, Ackerman did not counter further, and the incident
was duly recorded in fan journals of the period as the Wollheim-
Ackerman feud despite the brief period of its duration. That Ackerman was not sufficiently embittered to bear any grudge is indicated
by his ready collaboration with Wollheim on several later occasions.

Finally, *Arcturus* is of historical interest because of the appearance in its pages of some of the earliest examples of "Ghughuism," a
mock religion of Wollheim's concoction that might well be relegated
to the same position as the previously mentioned SPWSSTFM affair.
Wollheim took the god's position in this parody of religion, gathering about him a lavishly titled circle of adherents. "Ghughuism"
endured a longer period than the alphabetical societies, but its
tenets were never clarified. In later years when his associates
appeared to follow his lead in fan affairs without question, many
wondered almost seriously if Wollheim were not actually regarded as
deity in truth.

The collapse of *Wonder Stories* and its resultant change of ownership was glad news to the ISA members, who had scarcely hoped to
have Gernsback and Hornig so completely disposed of. In their gloat-
ing they gave themselves the lion's share of credit for the over-
throw of the Gernsback crew, forgetting that in many respects their
relentless campaign possessed more nuisance value than lethal poten-
cy, and that *Wonder Stories'* failure was primarily due to economic
conditions of the time. And in their joy at winning their battle,
too, the ISA voiced little criticism of the comparatively inferior
policies of *Thrilling Wonder Stories,* overlooking entirely the
unwelcome assurances of editorial director Margulies that blood-and-
thunder juvenility was his functional aim. This attitude is also an
indication of the extent to which personal dislike of Gernsback and
Hornig—rather than their policies—played a part in the ISA campaign.

In the interim, however, attempts were made by the organization to
bid for control of many disintegrating SFL chapters. In the May,
1936, number of *The International Observer* was introduced "The SFL
Page," conducted by Alan J. Aisenstein, director of the Nassau SFL;
this column carried news of the League chapters (most of which were
sadly inactive) in the period when *Wonder Stories* had suspended
appearance, and the ISA hoped by this means to lure at least a small
percentage of the science-fictionists and -hobbyists from the ruins
of the SFL. Despite the fact that sample copies of *The International
Observer* were dispatched to many of the chapter heads the policy was
never particularly successful, and as soon as it was realized that
Thrilling Wonder Stories was to continue the SFL column the ISA
ceased its efforts altogether.

Not all the group's activities in this period were politically-
minded, however. Aware that it was science fiction's tenth anniver-

sary of appearance in magazine form, New York members of the ISA arranged a celebration in honor of the event. On Sunday, May 3, 1936, a party consisting of Michel, Goudket, Pohl, Aisenstein, Blish, Kirshenblit, Sykora and Wollheim attended a showing of the splendid film based on H. G. Wells' story, *Things To Come*. Despite the date, it was one of the first purely social gatherings seen in fandom, meetings being as a rule leavened by business activities.

At a meeting of the New York branch of the ISA, George Gordon Clark, no longer active in fandom, was given the final shove toward oblivion when it was unanimously voted to expel him from membership in the local group because of activities treasonous to its best interests. (These were characterized by the attack on the ISA at an ILSF meeting; his alleged Rosicrucianist beliefs, moreover, were never looked upon with favor by other fans thereabouts.) Clark rallied sufficiently to protest that such an action by the ISA smacked of the very procedure that had so embittered members expelled from the SFL, and that it was dictatorial in essence. Secretary Wollheim replied to the effect that ISA meetings were open to the accused, and that he could have been present to defend himself had he so desired. More, the vote had been taken in democratic fashion, and the expulsion was merely from the local branch, not from the ISA itself. As time showed, Clark was insufficiently interested in fandom to renew his membership in that organization when it presently expired.

By now the continued presence of Wollheim's name in fan controversy after fan controversy was becoming noticable, as was his tendency to take a few parting shots at opponents after their defeat was obvious. This latter was expecially in evidence in his "Sun Spots" column, whose very high news value was then and later impaired by items presented in such a fashion as to prick the hides of downed antagonists.

Throughout 1936 the ISA rode high. Its official organ, *The International Observer* continued to appear regularly and to improve in quality. John B. Michel's "Humanity Must Look to the Stars," which was published in the September number of that year has an expecial significance, for it revealed clearly Michel's leftist political beliefs, bedrock of the later Michelist movement, of which we will later have more to say. Also again and again in the pages of *The International Observer* Sykora kept requesting someone who could write as well as Wollheim to volunteer for the position of science-hobbyist reporter. The only answer was a slow but inevitable increase of the magazine's science fiction content; the great majority of newcomers to the ISA, moreover, were recruited from the ranks of active fandom, names of science-hobbyist members being few and far between.

Now that the battle with the SFL had ended, leaders of the ISA began to regard the Independent League for Science Fiction as a boulder in the path of their progress. Meetings of the latter's Brooklyn branch were better attended than were many of the ISA's, and the ILSF's very title sounded as though it were an organization created for science fiction purists (though in actuality it had many science hobbyists in its ranks) in contrast to that of the ISA, so that new fans as a rule drifted first into the orbit of the ILSF. Then, too, the ISA had been rather unsuccessful in recruiting members from ex-SFL chapters. Sykora not unnaturally would have very much liked to see his ISA absorb the newer group, and hit upon a plan that would accomplish this very feat. With the same thoroughness and flair for the dramatic that had marked the successful culmination of his plans against the SFL, he mapped out a line of action against the ILSF, keeping his supporters fully informed as to the particulars. The ILSF meeting of Friday, November 6, 1936, was the zero hour.

On that day when Sykora arose to deliver his carefully planned talk he found himself facing a nine-man group composed of Kosow, Drucker, Heynick, Hahn, Leventman, Wollheim, Kyle, Pohl and Kirshenblit. As he began to speak there was a note of sureness in his voice, a confidence that only the knowledge of a well-laid scheme and cooperating minions could inspire. In brief, he stated that members of the ISA (as well as some in the ILSF, including some who belonged to both organizations) believed that meetings of the ILSF were proving of scant value, that the club was drifting into lethargy, and that its only hopeful future required coalition with the ISA.

Dramatic as these words were, the members of the ILSF were not taken completely by surprise. Some propaganda to this effect had been circulated for some time, emanating from those who were also ISA members. And in discussion among themselves they had been forced to concede that ILSF meetings were not indeed all that could be desired; however, they were even more certain that merging with another group would not solve the problem.

At this juncture Kirshenblit asked Sykora why, as an ILSF member, he had not broached his opinion at a prior meeting. So imbued with self-confidence was Sykora that he abandoned all pretense of tact, replying bluntly that his sole reason for joining in the first place had been to induce its members to join the ISA, and that since the increasing lethargy of the club had fallen in with his plans he had seen no reason to remedy it. ILSF members were thunderstruck. For the past two years the ISA had come to personify a Sir Lancelot of fandom, striking out in righteous wrath at those who would enslave it. It represented every fan's resistence against blatant, heartless commercialism. But now it was evolving into a monster in its own right. And the unheeded words of Charles D. Hornig, spoken a short time ago in that very room, now seemed to echo out of the emptiness to haunt them—"The ISA is attempting to seize control of fandom itself!"

Now that Kirshenblit had given Sykora to understand that the ILSF was to refuse his offer—"demand" would probably be a better term— what was to happen? The answer was not long in coming. All members of the ILSF who were also members of the ISA resigned *en masse*. Those were Sykora, Kyle, Wollheim, Michel and Pohl. The loss of five prominent members of such a club as the ILSF, already lethargic, proved ultimately fatal.

Two days later a startling aftermath occurred. These five ex-members held a meeting (of which other ILSF followers were not informed) at which a new ILSF chapter constitution was adopted. (Five individuals not making up a majority of ILSF chapter membership, the adopted constitution was obviously illegal.) Backed up by this spurious constitution, a majority of the five voted to have Pohl—one of their number—refund them the dues they had paid to the organization's treasury, excepting monies remitted in each case for copies of the official organ, *Arcturus*. But Pohl Balked. Despite hot words, he refused to carry this travesty on legality to such lengths without the express consent of Kirshenblit (director of the club), who of course was not present. Later, indeed, he turned over the ILSF treasury to Kirshenblit intact, and even went so far as to announce his intention of retaining membership.

Kirshenblit, meanwhile, had viewed the mass resignations with anything but calm silence, having tagged the deserters as "cowardly." Wollheim promptly lashed back with a vitriolic answer to this and other epithets, requesting ballots for ISA members who had "resigned." Kirshenblit left it to the membership to decide whether or not the oral resignations constituted legal departures, and the group decided that they did. He further answered Wollheim's missive, clarifying some of his previous epithets but not retracting any, saying that his use of the word "cowardly" referred mainly to Wollheim's and Sykora's disrupting the New York SFL meeting at which Hornig presided. (This, we might note, was the first opposition Wollheim had yet encountered on his record, and it presaged the later general use of this record of controversies by the man's enemies—sometimes to devastating effect.)

Kirshenblit now claimed the chapter purged of its unwelcome adherents, and voiced the opinion that the action would produce a salutary effect. But when the dust had cleared he found himself heading an anemic organization of six members. They managed to issue two more inferior numbers of *Arcturus,* the last being dated January, 1937, before complete collapse. One of the last notes on the ILSF was carried in "Sun Spots" in the November, 1936, *International Observer:*

> ...The ILSF, which was carried on almost solely by its Brooklyn chapter, is now on the verge of dissolution. If information gathered by our correspondent is correct, the members plan one more issue of their organ, *Arcturus,* after which it will be dropped. The Brooklyn League will become merely a bunch of fellows engaged in science-experimenting (otherwise known as kidding around—in this writer's opinion.)

This brief battle had two important effects. Firstly, their victory over the ILSF was to prove pyrrhic to ISA members; in wantonly destroying what was essentially a friendly organization when its absorption failed the ISA inadvertantly had sown the seeds of its own destruction.

Secondly, Wollheim's parenthetical remark anent science-hobbyists that has been quoted above was—though probably neither man was conscious of it—the first seed that led from coolness to open, bitter enmity between him and Sykora. The effect of such sarcastic scoffing on Sykora can be well imagined; to him, who at that time held an unshaking belief in the worth and efficasy of science as a hobby, Wollheim's statement amounted to indirect sabotage of the International Scientific Association's very foundations. The trust he had reposed in the man now smacked of foolhardiness. So, from that time forward, Sykora took Wollheim less into his confidence. But Wollheim, despite his frequent callousness in wounding the feelings of others, was himself a sensitive person, easily susceptible to hurt; he recognized Sykora's change of attitude almost immediately, and felt at a loss to account for it. Sykora, on his part, met inquiries with evasions, asserting that his own attitude had undergone no change whatsoever. But to Michel he unburdened himself, confessing a distrust for Wollheim, and expressing the belief that his influence was harmful to the club—all this being precipitated by a long discussion with Michel concerning *The International Observer's* policy. (As might be guessed, it was the same bone of contention all over again—science fiction versus science-hobbying.) Sykora's views, not unnaturally, eventually reached Wollheim's ears, and Wollheim felt there was but one course open to him. This he took, publishing the following open letter to Sykora in the November, 1936, issue of *The International Observer:*

> Dear Sir:
>   Feeling that I no longer have the honor of your confidence, I hereby tender my resignation as Acting Treasurer of the International Scientific Association.

Accompanying this resignation was another one by John B. Michel, asking that he be relieved of his editorial duties because of poor health and business matters. Michel's reasons were legitimate, but there is little doubt but that his growing friendship for Wollheim prompted its simultaneous issuance.

Despite everything, Wollheim had unquestionably been a loyal and valuable member of the ISA. He had worked hand in hand with Sykora on previous club projects, had fought side by side with him during ISA battles. Consequently fans were surprised to learn of the apparent rift between the two men.

Sykora accepted Michel's resignation, but refused to accept Wollheim's, claiming his work for the ISA had been exemplary. Wollheim then withdrew his resignation, and there is no doubt that the strain had been alleviated to some extent. But the seeds of doubt had been sown.

Sykora then appointed Pohl editor of the club periodical in Michel's place. In retrospect this was both a very good and a very bad choice for him to make. It was good because Pohl had a definite talent for editorial work, and the interest of the magazine's contents swerved upward almost immediately. It was bad—from Sykora's point of view at least—because Pohl was at heart predominantly a science fictionist who cared little for science as a hobby. And soon, where fiction and derived topics never filled up more than a third of *The International Observer,* they now took up close to double that amount. The science-hobbyists began to voice faint, uneasy complaints and Sykora began to frown. On this unsteady note the ISA worked toward its greatly important concluding activities in early 1937.

Dr. A. Langley Searles, who inspired and published *The Immortal Storm* in its early phases

Robert A. Madle when he published *Fantascience Digest*

Hugo Gernsback (left), accepting the Hugo
Gernsback Testimonial Trophy from S. L.
Baraf, President of Radio Parts and Elec-
tronic Equipment Shows, Inc,, at the Radio
Industry Banquet in Chicago, May 18, 1953.

Left to right: Mort Weisinger, Raymond A. Palmer, Edward Weisinger and Julius Schwartz 1938

William S. Sykora at the Portland World Convention, 1950

Below, left to right: Otis Adelbert Kline, Frank Belknap Long, unidentified, John W. Campbell, Jr., Otto Binder, L. Sprague de Camp, unidentified, and Manly Wade Wellman at First National Science Fiction Convention, Newark, 1938

Donald A. Wollheim in Philadelphia, 1937

Julius Schwartz, Otto Binder
and Raymond A. Palmer, 1938

Sam Moskowitz in Philadelphia, 1937

Right: Lester Del Rey,
who was a famous fan
under the name Raymond
Alvarez Del Rey

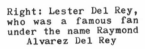

Below: Henry Kuttner, Clark
Ashton Smith and E. Hoffman
Price at Auburn, California

Below: Bob Tucker

Chapter XIII

THE SCIENCE FICTION ADVANCEMENT ASSOCIATION

PRIOR TO 1935 the West Coast had been involved in few activities of
national scope. The Los Angeles SFL chapter continued to hold
meetings on varying scales of interest, and there is no hint in all
available records of any serious discord in the group. Though fandom
at large envied their sometimes over-reported meetings, members
otherwise were well out of the public eye, enjoying the oblivion
that is the usual lot of an efficient well-functioning, localized
machine.

Claire P. Beck's *Science Fiction Critic* was the first attempt by a
West Coast fan to launch some project on a national scale, as has
already been noted. But Beck was in no way connected with the Los
Angeles group, nor was C. Hamilton Bloomer, the second fan from the
area to attempt something not merely local in scope. Bloomer resided
in San Francisco, and when Claire Beck moved there to live with his
brother Clyde (who was attending college) the two quickly became
friends. Bloomer's first appearance in the fan press was a
previously mentioned article in *The Science Fiction Critic*.

There is little available information on Bloomer the man, but he
was a chemist by occupation and would appear from the mature cast of
his writings to have been older than the average fan of the times.
Through association with Beck he was encouraged to strike out on his
own; the result was a national organization called the Science
Fiction Advancement Association. It was introduced to the fan world
through several advertisements in Beck's *Critic*.

No information as to the aims and ideals of the club are anywhere
to be found in its official publication. Apparently its title was
supposed to be self-explanatory. Joining the organization was not
even strongly urged. Bloomer merely asked its members to buy their
science fiction magazines from local newstands rather than purchasing
them second-hand, and decried also the practice of clubs buying
single copies that were subsequently passed among the memberships.
The SFAA offered virtually no advantages to members in exchange for
dues of fifteen cents, for even the association's official organ
cost them extra. Democratic processes were non-existent, for the
club had no constitution, merely being carried on under the
leadership of Bloomer, who headed a board of directors composed of
Lee Hertzberg, Claire Beck, Kathryn Kelly and Byron H. Geer.

The SFAA's official organ was called *Tesseract,* and was the first
fan publication to be reproduced by multigraph. Its first (March,
1936) number harbored little material of general interest, the bulk
of the issue being taken up with a short story of no outstanding
virtue, William Mitchell's "Stone Face On Venus," which significantly
contained many fragmentary bits of scientific information, such
as formulas pertaining to rockets and the like. Material of the
latter type, while it never predominated, nevertheless persisted in
being present during the magazine's entire life. Obviously a portion
of the SFAA's membership was composed of science-hobbyists, and

63

Bloomer thus made mild but continuous attempts to capture their support.

As issue after issue of *Tesseract* appeared, it became obvious that the Science Fiction Advancement Association was to be a success, and its membership list grew rapidly. Apparently there was a widespread desire at the time for a national fan organization, and fans were willing to support any attempt of such kind. Also it should be strongly emphasized that up until then lack of democracy in a club was never regarded as an unanswerable argument against it. From the very beginning fan organizations had been run by "strong men," and provided that their aim had been the common good of the multitude such procedure was never questioned. Some even went so far as to claim that because of the cameraderie among fans and their allegedly above-average intelligence and their willingness to work selflessly toward a common goal, no confining rules were needed. Thus we can see that fandom as a whole had an accepted code of behavior and ethical pattern which was generally acknowledged and conformed to, and which had the same authority as an unwritten law of society. It was felt that fans made up a fraternity rather than a congress, that those who were willing to do the work should receive the titles and the credit. In short, anyone who produced would be almost automatically recognized as the leader. Few if any men attained leadership on a promise to achieve—top positions were gained on the strength of past progress with little electioneering and campaigning present to confuse the issue. This code persisted until shortly before the first World Science Fiction Convention of 1939, when the maligning and invective of bitter feuds caused fans to look upon one another with suspicion that demanded stringent regulations in their official organizational affairs.

The membership of the Science Fiction Advancement Association climbed with surprising rapidity, virtually every prominent fan of the day being included. The real activity of the group, however, was promulgated by those members representing the third stratum of fandom—C. Hamilton Bloomer, Roy Test, Claire P. Beck, James Blish, Raymond Van Houten, William H. Miller, Jr., Nils H. Frome, Willis Conover, Jr., and Robert A. Madle. Indeed, many of these burst into activity for the first time in the SFAA. Some of them were comparitively recent followers of the genre, with little background of reading and collecting. Of the entire group, perhaps only Madle had a backlog of knowledge in the field equal to that of such leaders of the second fandom as Sykora, Wollheim, etc.

Third fandom was, at least so far as the SFAA was concerned, a neat, compact group. Lacking for the most part the large science fiction collections of the older fans, and coming into existence at a time when the genre itself was undergoing a recession in quality, it made fan publications its chief interest. And it was in this period that fan magazine collecting began in earnest, reaching its peak shortly thereafter. No young fan of those days would think twice about trading such a present-day rarity as a 1926 issue of *Weird Tales* for a copy of *Science Fiction Digest* that he did not possess. Your historian, who entered the field in the closing days of third fandom, recalls negotiating exchanges in which members of that stratum did not hesitate to give two copies of 1931-2 *Weird Tales* for every copy of a fan publication they did not own, regardless of intrinsic worth.) The average age of this new group of fans was between fifteen and sixteen, with an occasional eighteen-year-old gazing down from pontifical heights of maturity and youngsters of thirteen, such as Robert G. Thompson, not uncommon.

The SFAA's *Tesseract* appeared monthly for four consecutive issues, its constantly improving contents authored almost completely by neophyte fans who had seldom before been seen in print. The covers of the May and June, 1936, numbers were printed for Bloomer by Beck, and these, with the multigraphed interior, gave the magazine a very pleasing appearance.

The June number published the following notice: "We regret the necessity which compelled Claire P. Beck to give up science-fiction and return to his home in Northern California. He felt, and rightly so, that duty to his family came before hobbies. We shall miss him." But before Beck departed, Bloomer had made some very important arrangements with him. Plans had been concluded which, it was believed, would give to the Science Fiction Advancement Association a tone of national importance. These involved combining Beck's *Science Fiction Critic* with *Tesseract* under the latter title, thereby making the organization's organ a printed journal. By the time of its fifth number, *The Science Fiction Critic* had attained a fair amount of prestige. Its regular columns (expecially Clyde F. Beck's "Hammer and Tongs") were highly praised, and it even achieved the distinction of extracting an article from Hugo Gernsback explaining the sale of *Wonder Stories*. (Fan editors who have attempted to get material from Gernsback will recognize this as no mean feat.) *Tesseract*, on the other hand, offered the vigor and enthusiasm of a rising generation of fans represented in an already successful organization.

Beck announced the details of this planned consolidation in the July 15, 1936, number of the *Critic*. Apparently, however, he later thought better of his original decision—before that number of the *Critic* was completely type-set in fact—for further on he stated that the magazine would continue as usual with no changes. Whatever were Beck's reasons for a change of mind, reasons which he never bothered to clarify (and which later acts on his part seemed to stamp as little more than fickleness), he was inexcusably guilty of not informing Bloomer of the decision immediately. For Bloomer, feeling that everything was progressing as expected, sold his multigraph machine to Nils H. Frome, leading Canadian Fan of the day, who planned using it to publish a fan magazine to be titled *Supramundane Stories*. When Bloomer received the issue of the *Critic* announcing that its usual policies were to be continued he was thunderstruck. With Beck defaulting and his multigraph gone, it seemed he might as well give up continuing the SFAA altogether.

If the proposed arrangement had been realized, it would inevitably have had important effects. Third fandom would have emerged full-grown with a representative organization and club equal (if not superior) to the ISA's. It would have played a leading role rather than a subordinate one, manned as it was by a new, enthusiastic, capable bunch of youngsters. This was not to be, however, and now all that Bloomer could hope for was a way to fulfill obligations to members and subscribers. As if good fortune had opened her arms to him, he was suddenly presented with a way out of the dilemma—James Blish.

Blish had been one of *Tesseract's* most regular contributors, having even gone so far as to sign Frome's name to an article submitted. His own publication, *The Planeteer,* had improved continually, until with its sixth issue it had a large-sized format and included a story by the professional author Laurence Manning, the facts of whose purchase have already been outlined. Despite the fact that he boasted scarcely two dozen subscribers, Blish, together with the fan William Miller, Jr., speculated on something yet more elaborate—purchasing a press and printing *The Planeteer.* Upon learning of this idea Bloomer was immediately enthusiastic, and offered financial aid if *The Planeteer* would carry SFAA departments as a regular feature. Blish agreed, and the money was forwarded. Miller also contributed. The press was purchased, and with the naive innocence of which fifteen-year-old neophyte fans alone are capable, the two plunged eagerly into their dream world of grandiose plans, unencumbered by any irksome knowledge of the art of printing.

Months passed, months of toil and trouble. And the first printed number of *The Planeteer,* which was to have been dated May-June, 1936, was scheduled for September appearance instead. In early October funds ran out, and all work halted. Fourteen of the planned pages had been completed—two for the table of contents, one an editorial, one devoted to the SFAA, four of advertising, an equal number that began Blish's "Planeteer" yarn, "Death's Crystal Towers," and H. P. Lovecraft's poem, "The Wood," which for years made it a collector's item. Further material by J. Harvey Haggard, William Sykora and Forrest J. Ackerman was to have gone into the number, as well as a hektographed drawing by Morris Dollens.

When Bloomer learned that work on the magazine was being abandoned his state of mind may be well imagined. He had invested virtually all of the SFAA treasury in this project, and this he demanded refunded. Blish, being but a boy with no regular source of income, was naturally unable to comply. And Bloomer, seeing that heated words availed him nothing, and realizing that as a minor Blish could not be held responsible, "dishonorably expelled" him from the SFAA, referring to him as "a thief and a dispicable person unworthy of belonging to the legion of stf. fans." Miller, partner in the ill-fated enterprise, was exonerated of blame on the basis of his own financial loss therein.

On his part, Miller grew more and more restive concerning the fate of his invested money. His relations with his erstwhile partner were merely cool at first, but when Blish moved to a new location they became positively icy. The two eventually settled their differences in a good old-fashioned way: fisticuffs. And when the dust cleared, all love had flown. Miller went his own way with plans for publishing a literary fan magazine entitled *Phantastique.* Before this was completed, however, he was to be instrumental in inducing your historian, who lived in near-by Newark, to become active in fandom—but that is another story.

Blish never did mail out the unfinished number of *The Planeteer.* (This writer, on a visit to Blish's home in 1937, salvaged most of the remaining pages and assembled some two dozen copies, which he sold at ten cents apiece.) He did not abandon his publishing interests, however, producing *Grotesque* and *Phantascience League Digest,* both miniature humor magazines, the latter a caricature of Wollheim's

Phantagraph. In the former was virtually the only blow that Blish
struck back at Bloomer—a cartoon depicting him saluting a Nazi flag,
which was titled "Bloomer is elected to the Violet Star Order."
(The Violet Star Order was an honorary title given to those SFAA
members who had done the most in the best interests of the
organization.) Blish also announced plans for *Odd, Bewildering Tales*
and *Fantastic Tales,* with Wollheim in the associate editor's post;
but his enthusiasm had waned and none of these titles ever appeared.

In general, fandom frowned disapprovingly at James Blish, for it
could not be denied that he had not made good his promises, nor paid
his just debts. One fan, however, did not—Donald A. Wollheim. Blish
was a regular attendee of the New York ISA meetings, and there had
met and struck up a friendship with Wollheim. The latter was pleased
to make the acquaintence of the man who had been so enthusiastic
about his plans for *The Planeteer* in *Astounding Stories.* When he was
attacked by Bloomer, Wollheim remembered that the latter had written
the ISA and informed its members that while he liked their *International Observer,* he did not, as head of another fan organization,
feel free to join that group. Thenceforward Wollheim's "Sun Spots"
column made C. Hamilton Bloomer and the SFAA a preferred target.
Bloomer was denounced as a dictator, and his attitude on competing
fan organizations referred to as "childish." Blish was directly
defended by such statements as "...needless to say, Jim Blish is not
the childish person Bloomer would make him out to be." This campaign,
though not forced to a violent finish, was nonetheless maintained
throughout the entire life of the SFAA, with Wollheim characteristic-
ally taking a few licks at the organization after it had languished
altogether. His stand had some effect, however, for many of the
leading fans of the time refrained from showing activity in the SFAA
lest they incur Wollheim's disfavor.

Bloomer, meanwhile, was now forced to accept the inevitable. He
must maintain publication of *Tesseract* himself to make good his obligations. A mimeograph was procured, and in November, 1936, another
issue of the magazine produced. A short story by Robert A. Madle, a
Philadelphia fan, was featured, and J. Harvey Haggard's serial, "The
Planet of No Return," was begun. This presaged a new policy.

The December, 1936, issue was large-sized, and exhibited an amazing all around improvement. Louis C. Smith, one of the leading
collectors of the time, became literary editor and instigated his
column "Authorsophy." A copy of Merritt's book *Burn Witch Burn!* was
offered as a prize to the SFAA member who best answered the question
"What shall the SFAA do in 1937 to advance and better science fiction?" In all probability Bloomer himself had no plan, and was
marking time to learn what the members themselves thought.

The winner of the Merritt book was Roy A. Squires. He suggested
that plot outlines be furnished by those who had ideas, but not the
facility to utilize them, and that amateur writers who were members
of the SFAA should try their hands at turning them into finished
stories. (This idea, it might be noted parenthetically, was brought
to the fore again some years later by the fan magazine *Spaceways.*)
Squires also urged members to try converting more people to the
reading of science fiction.

Tesseract proved to be the biggest feather in the SFAA's cap. In
excellence and general interest the club organ surpassed almost

every similar publication then extant. It was far superior to *The Internattonal Observer* and *The Science Fiction Critic,* and virtually the only magazines that ranked above it were the fine printed journals. Worthwhile articles were obtained from Miles J. Breuer, E. E. Smith, J. Harvey Haggard, Arthur Leo Zagat, Clark Ashton Smith, Forrest J. Ackerman and others. The April, 1937, number was dedicated to Howard Phillips Lovecraft and carried the first printing of his story "The Crawling Chaos" that had been available to the fan world. Much fine poetry was published and, in addition to the magazine's regular science department conducted by A. R. Mink and a collectors' column run by Louis C. Smith, it encouraged the better amateur authors such as Raymond Van Houten, Russell Leadabrand, Walter Jamieson and others, featuring their fiction and articles. Willis Conover, Jr., contributed a humorous science fiction fan story. (For the edification of the uninitiated, a science fiction fan story is one wherein fantasy magazines, their editors, authors and the fans themselves play leading roles.) *Tesseract* stressed also aids for the prospective writer, and printed articles by well-established science fiction authors on that subject. In one of his editorials Bloomer urged his readers to join the National Amateur Press Association. This was an organization of amateur publishers who mailed out their productions jointly at intervals. Other fans of that period, such as Wollheim, Michel, Pohl and Shepard were already members of the group and their association with it was to foster the notion of the Fantasy Amateur Press Association late in 1937.

Taken all in all, selective collectors of fan magazines make a grave error when they overlook the large-sized later numbers of *Tesseract* for these are of a quality that unquestionably warrants preservation.

More and more Bloomer found his time being consumed by his occupational duties as 1937 progressed. As an initial expediant he discontinued all correspondence. Eventually, however, it became apparent to his that he could not hold his position and carry on with the SFAA too, and therefore gave up active interest in the organization. Squires, meanwhile, had been appointed assistant secretary by "unanimous vote" of the Board of Directors, in view of his interest in the club. With Bloomer retiring, Squires assumed leadership as managing secretary. But, for reasons which have never been adequately explained, he accomplished nothing. And for a long time it appeared that the Science Fiction Advancement Association had reached the end of its trail.

Chapter XIV

OTHER LOCAL GROUPS OF THE TIME

THERE HAD BEEN national fantasy organizations, international fantasy organizations and city chapters of various cliques, but until McPhail of Oklahoma City conceived the idea of the Oklahoma Scientifiction Association there had never been a state organization. McPhail had been an avid reader long before he became an active fan, and as early as 1929 had struck up with a kindred soul in the form of Louis W. Clark, whose interest in the field antedated even McPhail's. McPhail's history from that date must have corresponded with that of many other fans, with the important exception that he kept a record of his activities which he included in a little four-paged hand-printed sheet entitled *The Science Fiction News,* the first issue of which was dated June 1, 1931. After several numbers he procured a typewriter and typed the magazine in an assortment of shapes and sizes of paper, so that by 1934, with the aid of Clark he was pounding out twenty-four large-sized pages, making several carbons. With the many carbon copies on hand, McPhail proceeded to mail out numbers to every person with an Oklahoma address whose letter appeared in the readers' columns of the professional fantasy magazines. So successful was he in bringing these individuals together that in the early months of 1936 the Oklahoma Scientifiction Association was formed, with *The Science Fiction News* its official organ. Among its members were Louis Clark, Jack Speer, Austin Roquemore, James and Mary Rogers, Edgar Hirdler, Kenneth Jones, John Leonard and Francis Stewart, Jr. Of these, Jack Speer and James and Mary Rogers were to attain particular prominence in fandom.

After March, 1936, *The Science Fiction News* became available to fandom at large. "The newsmagazine for the science fiction fan" was a publication of unusual interest. The first six monthly numbers in 1936 had neatly printed covers on which were sometimes impressed hektographed drawings by James Rogers. The contents were neatly typewritten (or carbon copied), with illustrations and designs frequently being added in pencil or hektograph, and sometimes via printed linoleum cuts. The magazine boasted of belonging to "The Science Fiction News Service"—which, since it is nowhere else mentioned in fan publications, either was an affectation or an ostentatious method of referring to McPhail's correspondents' supplying him with news. The magazine featured many interesting regular columns, among them Ted Carnell's "England Calling," dealing in British news and views, and similar to his "London Newsreel" in *Arcturus;* "Radio and Comics," conducted by Jack Speer; a series of picturizations by James Rogers titled "Rambling 'Round the Universe"; and two pseudonymously authored columns, "Howls from the Ether" and "F-L-A-S-H-E-S!" both of which presented news items dealing more in fan personalities and activities than in the professional publications. The latter columns were leaders in a new trend which soon made itself obvious. Speer also proudly contributed the first science fiction crossword puzzle to the scrutiny of fandom. And by June of 1936 *The Science*

Fiction News was celebrating its fifth anniversary.

With its October number, the magazine underwent a radical change. McPhail, who was working at a printer's, successfully arranged to have the entire issue printed. This move elevated it into a class with *The Science Fiction Critic* and made it one of the leaders in a field overshadowed only by *Fantasy Magazine*. Many fans flocked to its banner of "the complete fan magazine" (as it called itself) because of its fine coverage of the field. The absence of fiction and the preponderance of news columns made it a live wire journal that mirrored completely the activities of the third fandom. More, McPhail himself gained the fast friendships of such up-and-coming fans as Miller, Blish, Kyle, Dollens and others. The OSA itself, meanwhile, continued to expand; in addition to Hirdler's Muskogee chapter. This latter group never thrived, however, and unfortunately lasted for but a short time.

When McPhail lost his printing-shop position it sounded the death-knell for the *News,* which was still accelerating in interest and quality, and thus indirectly dealt a severe blow to the OSA. It also abated McPhail's own enthusiasm, for he did not have the desire to continue the paper in less pretentious form, and its subsequent abandonment was hard to endure. Although he continued activity in sporadic bursts for several years, he never again attained a comparable position of eminence.

But from the bier of *The Science Fiction News* there was to rise a new Oklahoma champion whose fame and importance were far to outshine McPhail's. To fandom at large Jack Speer was simply a fifteen-year-old whose passion for fantastic cartoons seemed to augur a hope for no great future. So widespread was this impression that his pertinent article in the October, 1936, *Science Fiction News* "Science Fiction and History: An Unusual Parallel" was almost entirely disregarded Speer, whose only other activities aside from OSA membership had been a subscription to *Fantasy Magazine* and joining the Terrestrial Fantascience Guild, showed advanced powers of intelligent analysis that were to mature to a point of important consequence for the science fiction fan world. And James Rogers was to receive much attention at a later date as artist for Olon F. Wiggins' *Science Fiction Fan,* as was his similarly talented sister Mary.

Meanwhile, in Philadelphia, local chapter number eleven of the SFL was giving absolutely no inkling to the fan world of the importance it was later to assume. Within a few meetings after its formation (January, 1935) under leadership of director Milton A. Rothman members appeared to lose interest. Rothman had conducted several scientific experiments, but it was obvious that these did not arouse any great amount of enthusiasm, and shortly thereafter non-attendance at meetings caused a cessation of activity.

Unknown to Rothman, there existed an independant group of local fans which had formed itself at about the same time as the SFL chapter, but which likewise had no knowledge of the latter. This was The Boys' Science Fiction Club, and consisted of Harvey Greenblatt, John V. Baltadonis, Jack Agnew and Robert A. Madle. Rothman, who was still interested in forming an active local chapter eventually contacted these young fans through members' letters in readers' columns of the professional magazines, and thus local number eleven found itself on a firm footing once more.

Happily, this firm footing proved permanent. At the first meeting of the reorganized chapter (October, 1935) a substantial nucleus of both former clubs was present along with Oswald Train, a former correspondent of Rothman's who had recently moved to the City of Brotherly Love. Train was an old-time reader of the genre, and was the author of several science fiction stories published in small-town newspapers. Meetings as a rule emphasized science fiction rather than science-hobbying, and were devoted in the main to interesting informal discussions. Outstanding from the members' viewpoint was probably that of December, 1935, at which Hornig and Schwartz were guests of honor.

Early 1936 were several events of importance to take place. First, members voted to change the club's name to that by which it is known today: The Philadelphia Science-Fiction Society—more familiarly, simply PSFS. Second, there was a falling away of the older, veteran fans of the group—Raymond Peel Mariella, Paul Hunter, and their kind—and a sweeping to the fore of the young blood newly acquired, led by Agnew, Madle and Baltadonis. Finally, February, 1936, ushered into fandom the first publication of the group, *Imaginative Fiction.*

Imaginative Fiction was a carbon-copied journal bound on a sewing machine. Madle was editor in chief, Rothman his associate, and Baltadonis art editor. Unconsciously each man had settled into his proper niche. As most copies of the initial number were destroyed, readers had to wait until April for the second. In this, it is interesting to note, Charles Bert announced an intention of reviving Hornig's defunct *Fantasy Fan;* however, though many hopes were raised, nothing ever became of the project. After two issues it was all too obvious that the carbon-copied duplication was too restricting a medium, and so the producers cast about for something better. The answer was Morris Scott Dollens and his hektographed *Science Fiction Collector.*

Dollens was a sixteen-year-old fan residing in North Saint Paul, Minnesota. He had subscribed to *Fantasy Magazine,* and had been almost instantly bitten by the publishing bug. But for him no solution seemed forthcoming. He had no printing equipment, no typewriter, little money. What to do? He discovered that one reproduction method was within his means, and after some experimentation acquired the knack of coaxing purple impressions from the gelatinous surface of the capricious hektograph. What followed, for all its admitted juvenile crudity, was not without a peculiar beauty of its own. Entirely illustrated and printed by hand, Dollens turned out the first numbers of *The Science Fiction Collector.* The name he had chosen for his publication was excellent, and upon advertising in *Fantasy Magazine* he received a generous initial responce. To the fantasy reader such a title conjured up all manner of intriguing visions—items about rare science fiction books and magazines, well-written fantasy reviews, expositions by leading collectors, and any number of other mouth-watering possibilities. Consequently, the first issue of the *Collector* was a painful experience. An amateurishly-written serial story, an equally amateur cartoon, meager data concerning fantasy comic strips, a few jokes and some pitiful scraps of collector's material were what greeted their eyes. The only thing the editor had in his favor, besides sincerity, was a religious adherence to a tri-weekly schedule of publication and an undeveloped knack for illustrating.

Issue after issue appeared, but as subscriptions expired few were renewed as the magazine's improvement in quality was in the realm of the barely noticable, being even then confined to clearer reproduction and the use of several new colors in the print. So poor a comparison did the *Collector* make with other current publications that fans, always slow to contribute, finally contributed almost nothing, and the only subscribers who went along with Dollens were such "completists" in the field as Miller, Wollheim, McPhail and the like.

The poignant ups and downs of *The Science Fiction Collector* during the first three years of its existence are told in detail in your historian's article "Deep Purple," which appeared in the May, 1939, number of that magazine. Despite its many shortcomings, however, this journal was an inspiration to the fan who yearned to publish creatively, yet who did not possess the means. Dollens' example paved the way toward a publication that they could afford.

Fantascience Digest was the title that Madle and Baltadonis first planned to use, but somehow this was associated in their minds with something markedly superior; they felt it too good to waste on a run-of-the-mill fan magazine, and thus settled on *The Fantasy Fiction Telegram*. The first issue was brought out in October, 1936. This was poorer from a reproduction standpoint than was Dollens' *Collector,* but backed by an entire club as it was, it did not suffer from dearth of material; indeed, in addition to work by the Philadelphia group, they were able to obtain contributions from members of the first and second fandoms, such as G. R. Hahn, Donald Wollheim, Duane W. Rimel and others. Baltadonis produced some of his first art work, which, acceptable though it was, gave little hint of the latent talent that was to make him the most popular amateur illustrator in fandom. *The Fantasy Fiction Telegram* also marked the initial active entrance into fan circles of a live—wire group composed of Baltadonis, Rothman, Madle, Train and Agnew, with other PSFS members rising into prominence from time to time. And this auspicious beginning heralded what was to become one of fandom's most important groups. The *Telegram* lasted for only four numbers. A fifth was partially completed but never distributed, and later Baltadonis turned out another for the Fantasy Amateur Press Association.

But other fans, too, were entering a state of real activity, and among them was Olon F. Wiggins, the Colorado fan who had headed the Denver SFL chapter which had seceded, as we have read, to join the Independant League for Science Fiction during the ISA-SFL fracas. Wiggins made an error common with fans of the time: he attempted to compete with *Fantasy Magazine,* and so felt it incumbent on himself to have his publication professionally printed. The first neatly printed number was dated July, 1936, and apparently showed that the editor's funds had run out early, for it boasted a mere seven pages of material plus a wood-cut cover. Another Colorado fan, Mervyn Evans, was listed as associate editor. This issue was sent free to anyone who would ask for a copy, so that samples circulated far and wide.

Four numbers appeared in printed format, in all of which the standard of quality was quite good. Wollheim, the best of the columnists outside *Fantasy Magazine,* was represented by the popular regular feature "Fanfarade." Interviews, biographies and autobiographies of Jack Williamson, Clark Ashton Smith, John R. Fearn and Harold

Hershey appeared. Articles by Robert D. Swisher, Edward J. Carnell, Raymond Van Houten, Robert A. Madle, Willis Conover and others were likewise included.

Among the features in the first number was a short Esperanto column by Forrest J. Ackerman. In the second number it was not present, and Wiggins in his editorial remarked:

> Mr. Ackerman is no longer connected with *Fan* in any capacity due to he and myself not agreeing on the price he should receive for his column. I will not go into this any further, but anyone desiring to find out how unreasonable he was as to what he should receive for his column, can, if they wish, find out by getting in touch with Mr. Ackerman or myself.

This was the spark that flamed into the Ackerman-Wiggins enmity of several years duration. (It might be emphasized at this point that by far the majority of fan published magazines subsisted on material contributed free of charge, and even in instances where contributions were paid for, such payment was usually a mere pittance.) Wiggins was not the only one annoyed by Ackerman's demanding payment for material. Blish, who also used an Esperanto column by Ackerman in the penultimate issue of *The Planeteer,* likewise complained bitterly of being cheated, and as these and similar tales were noised about, Ackerman progressively became more unpopular with third fandomites, who felt that he was snubbing them in the same manner as the rest of the *Fantasy Magazine* clique, but with the irritating difference that they were being made to pay for this dubious privelege. Throughout almost all of 1937 Ackerman had comparitively little truck with the fan world at large as a result.

Wiggins was bewildered by the pitiful support his *Science Fiction Fan* received. He had envisioned subscriptions pouring in by the hundreds as soon as news of its release became generally known. Instead, he received only twelve subscriptions for his first number, most of them for but one, two or three issues. The second number fared little better. With the third, therefore, Wiggins mailed out three hundred sample copies to fans who had not seen the magazine before. Not even one postal acknowledgement—let alone a subscription!—came back. The bitter truth became apparent. There were simply not enough interested fans to support a printed journal like *The Science Fiction Fan*. An advertisement in *Fantasy Magazine* boosted Wiggins' circulation to thirty, however, and was continuing to give good results a yeat later. There seemed no question that the largest group of interested fans were concentrated under *Fantasy Magazine*'s leadership; but the example set by that sterling periodical was detrimental to the sale of anything of like (but inferior) nature.

Wiggins printed a fourth issue, larger than ever before, slanted distinctly away from the professional angle and toward news of the fans themselves. Typical of the material in this, the October, 1936, number, was a long article by Madle giving information on past fan magazines. But, outside of Wollheim, no one received a copy of the fourth for almost six months. Bitter over his failure, Wiggins had no intention of distributing the issue. And at that impasse the future of *The Science Fiction Fan* marked time.

Chapter XV

THE LAST DAYS OF *FANTASY MAGAZINE*

AFTER the September, 1935, third anniversary number of *Fantasy Magazine* had appeared, it found itself facing a serious situation. Ruppert, who had contributed such yeoman printing service at below paper cost, found that the increase in well-paying orders at his establishment made it impossible to carry on this charity any longer no matter how true the blood of the science fiction lover ran in his veins. It was a matter of sacrificing his livelihood or *Fantasy Magazine*.

This appeared for a while to be the death-knell of fandom's greatest journal. For months Julius Schwartz, who had held Ruppert's editorial post for some time, sought to find a way out of this dilemma. Finally an arrangement was made with William L. Crawford to do the printing. The terms of the agreement were never made public, but Crawford, himself an enthusiastic fan, was probably more than reasonable. But reasonable as these rates were, Schwartz still had difficulty in meeting costs with his small circulation. *Fantasy Magazine* did not reappear until January, 1936, and from then until its demise a year later maintained a roughly quarterly schedule of publication. This may have been partly due to Crawford's notorious undependability, but it is extremely doubtful that Schwartz was in any position to finance more regular publication even had Crawford been the essence of punctuality.

The January, 1936, number carried the announcement of Stanley G. Weinbaum's death on December 13, 1935, with appropriate eulogies and appreciations of his work. Weinbaum, who had been the best selling author of the Solar Sales Agency, would be sorely missed edonomically as well as spiritually.

The March, 1936, number announced the sale of *Wonder Stories,* and important as this fact was to the ISA in its clash with the SFL, it was equally important to *Fantasy Magazine* itself, for Weisinger, unofficial editor and writer on the staff, as well as partner with Schwartz in the agency, was soon elevated to editor of the new *Thrilling Wonder Stories* issued under the Standard Publications' banner. More than ever before Schwartz now felt himself alone. First Ruppert had left, and then Weisinger: the best friends he had were no longer able to share his fan activities. The full weight of responsibility for carrying on *Fantasy Magazine* now rested entirely upon his shoulders, and all around his was the ill-disguised envy and bitterness of the second and third fandoms, who, incapable of emulating his magazine successfully, would not be overly sorry to see it destroyed.

(Weisinger's dropping from the Solar Sales Agency was not without advantages, however, for Schwartz no longer had to divide his commissions, and now, with a close friend editor of a professional fantasy magazine, he had an "in" with *Thrilling Wonder Stories* of immense value. Authors were quick to realize the benefit of having Schwartz submit their manuscripts, and slowly but steadily the most prolific authors in the fantasy field began to sell substantial portions of their work through his agency.)

The June, 1936, issue of *Fantasy Magazine* was of unusually life-less appearance. Though the quality of the material featured had not suffered appreciably, the enthusiasm with which it had previously been presented was almost entirely lacking. It was obvious to Schwartz that something had to be done if his magazine were to maintain any semblance of its former size and prestige.

After some thought he decided to make one last all-out effort. Everything would be gambled on one superior number—the fourth anniversary issue due in September, 1936. A complete list of the 2,000 Science Fiction League members was obtained from Weisinger. Crawford, meanwhile, had acquired a linotype machine, and with the aid of this a fifty-paged issue of *Fantasy Magazine* was produced, in small-faced type to cram in as much material as was humanly possibly. From the front to the back cover it was packed with every item of interest that editor Schwartz could conceive, obtain or resuscitate. The feature of the number was a "round robin" story "The Great Illusion," written by Eando Binder, Jack Williamson, Edmond Hamilton, Raymond Z. Gallun and John Russell Fearn—the most prolific authors of the day. Binder's autobiography was present. There were articles by George Allan England, Festus Pragnell, H. G. Wells and others; columns by Julius Schwartz, Walter Gillings, Forrest J. Ackerman, Raymond A. Palmer and Robert Bloch. Appreciations of the recently-deceased author Robert E. Howard by H. P. Lovecraft, Otis A. Kline, E. Hoffman Price and Jack Byrne (editor of *Argosy* magazine at that time) were here also. A hitherto unpublished story by Stanley G. Weinbaum was included. A lithographed insert of fantasy authors' photographs was to be found. Book, film and magazine reviews, together with innumerable other odds and ends filled up the magazine.

Two thousand copies of this number of *Fantasy Magazine* were mailed out. The price, which had risen to fifteen cents a year previously, was reduced to ten cents once more. There is no question that this issue was a supreme fan publication. If any fan journal was worth a dime, this one was worth a dollar. Schwartz waited. Then subscriptions began to trickle in. But weeks went by, and the trickle never became a torrent. At last it ceased altogether. Then he knew that there was no use continuing. For four years he had given fans the finest effort in the field—and at the end of that time his subscription list stood at barely two hundred! One thing alone deterred Schwartz from abandoning the publication entirely: its outstanding debt of subscriptions. Most money had been spent almost as soon as received, and he was in no position to make extensive refunds. It seemed to be a vicious circle—he could no longer carry on the magazine, nor could he drop it.

Now in this fourth anniversary number of *Fantasy Magazine* was a full-page advertisement announcing a new printed fan publication to be titled *Science-Fantasy Correspondent*. The editors were Willis Conover, Jr., a former contributor to *Tesseract,* and Corwin F. Stickney, a virtual unknown in the field. Conover proved to be a nova in fandom, a go-getter who flared with unprecedented brilliance for a short time and then faded from sight, scarcely ever to be heard from again. Since interesting himself in fan activities, Conover had written dozens of leading fantasy authors, artists, editors and fans. His list of contacts was of extremely wide extent, and he was on good terms with both the second and third fandoms as well as the older *Fantasy Magazine* group. The fifteen-year-old Stickney was apparently markedly above average in intelligence. He had struck up an association with Frank S. Bogert, an elderly printer in Belleville, New Jersey, and in exchange for setting type for the latter was permitted to print his *Science-Fantasy Correspondent* for the cost of the paper. Bogert became interested in the sheet and offered to help subsidize it if he were allowed to handle its advertising, a field in which he had had previous experience. The editors consenting, he took over this branch of the work—with surprising results. In the very first number the *Correspondent* carried many well-paying advertisements of a general nature, and throughout its entire period of existence thus always managed to stay out of the red, despite the fact that several thousand free copies of every number were mailed out regularly to build up circulation for the benefit of advertisers.

The first issue of the *Correspondent* was a revelation to the fan world. Almost overnight there had arisen the most serious competition *Fantasy Magazine* had encountered since the advent of *The Fantasy Fan*. The ultra-neat format of the *Correspondent* impeccably printed on fine quality paper by Stickney (who throughout the entire life of the magazine made only one typographical error, and that one in the first issue), coupled with excellent material by David H. Keller, H. P. Lovecraft, Jack Williamson, Henry Kuttner and others, ranked it second only to *Fantasy Magazine,* whose background acquired after many long years in science fiction circles, was not easily equalled. This first issue sold out, and subscriptions continued to pour in. Subscribers then received an unexpected notice. The ten-cent, three-for-a-quarter price was to be halved. Bogert had ordered this in an attempt to build up circulation, for the more subscribers, the more advertising. He planned to operate the magazine on the same principle as the slicks and the newspapers, garnering operating costs from subscriptions, and letting advertising pay for the other expenses. Intrinsically this was extremely sound (as later events proved), though fans at that time loudly deplored the inclusion of non-fantasy advertising in a fan magazine.

At this juncture Julius Schwartz threw in the sponge. And on Conover's next visit to New York City arrangements were made to combine *Fantasy Magazine* with *Science-Fantasy Correspondent,* thus filling all of Schwartz's obligations. In exchange, Conover would have the prestige of leadership in the fan field and all of *Fantasy Magazine*'s stock of material. Conover regarded this achievement as a very bright feather in his cap (as indeed it was), and Schwartz considered it a great load off his mind (as it also was).

The very last—the thirty-ninth—number of *Fantasy Magazine* was dated January, 1937. Compared to the preceeding fourth anniversary issue it appeared slim indeed. The feature was "Thompson's Time-Travelling Theory," a short story by Mortimer Weisinger (later reprinted in *Amazing Stories*); a long autobiography of Neil R. Jones was included as well. The merging with *Science-Fantasy Correspondent* was announced, with the result dubbed "the Little Giant of the fan magazines."

To most readers the latter statement was little enough to go by.

Would *Fantasy Magazine* retain its identity? All that was definitely known was that a reduction in size to the *Correspondent's* six by four and one-half inch dimensions would take place. And which of the two titles was to have the dominating policy? The thought that this was really the end of *Fantasy Magazine* as they had known it did not enter the minds of most fans. They had no way of knowing how completely *Fantasy Magazine* was to fade from the picture—and of the damaging repercussions that were to follow.

The second issue of *Science-Fantasy Correspondent* which appeared shortly thereafter, provided little more in the way of enlightenment. After admiring its excellent Finlay cover and perusing excellent material by Raymond Z. Gallun, Robert Bloch, John Russell Fearn, Arthur J. Burks, Greye La Spina and Forrest J. Ackerman, the reader found this cryptic legend on page twenty:

> In our next issue will be published the most stupendous announcement ever made in the history of fan magazines! Do not miss this announcement, for it marks the renaissance of amateur fantasy magazines!

But again stark drama was preparing her lines for recitation, and what was to follow, coupled with the coincidence of simultaneous events, was to deal catastrophe to fandom as a whole. Ragnarok had caught the entire fan world napping!

Chapter XVI

FURTHER CLUBS AND PROJECTS OF 1936

IT MUST NOT BE IMAGINED that the Science Fiction Advancement Association was the only club of the period attempting to find its niche in fandom. Other groups and individuals were trying to found solid organizations, but with indifferent results.

One Hayward S. Kirby, a Massachusetts fan, attempted to form the Fantasy Fiction League on the strangest, most transparent basis ever presented by a club. To join, one merely wrote to Kirby, requesting a membership card and enclosing a three-cent stamp. Also requisite was the signing of a pledge of subservience to all rules and regulations that might be laid down by Kirby in his capacity of club director. No reason for forming the club was given, and the only prospective activity was the sponsorship of a short story contest, this being announced in the first issue of the club organ, *The Fantasy Fiction Digest*. The latter was bound in and distributed with the September 8, 1936, number of Dollens' *Science Fiction Collector*. The second issue, though continually announced as on the way, never did appear, and in the meantime Kirby's name became synonymous with procrastination in fan circles.

Discounting Dollens', the only written support Kirby ever obtained was from Wollheim, whose "Sun Spots" column carried the notice that the Fantasy Fiction League was being formed by some ISA members, and simultaneously decried the attitude of C. Hamilton Bloomer in singling out this new group as a competing organization. In again and again attacking the SFAA for "dictatorial control" and simultaneously supporting the Fantasy Fiction League he left the impression that the latter was the more democratic of the two. In actuality, however, it had not the most rudimentary vestige of a democratic limb emanating anywhere from its structure, while Bloomer's SFAA at least made a half-hearted stab at giving members voting privileges.

Had Kirby possessed some fair measure of initiative the Fantasy Fiction League, with Wollheim's support and the willing, hard-working hands of Dollens, might have caught on and made some sort of mark in fandom. But after many months of doing absolutely nothing, Kirby relinquished control of the organization to Dollens. The latter managed to produce a single number of the club organ which presented not a scrap of information on its aims, principles or hopes. Whether Dollens would ever have made anything out of the organization is debatable, for parental pressure at just that time forced him to curtail fan activities. This prompted his turning over all rights to both the league and its publication to Wollheim, who had long made a hobby of collecting such moribund items. The death of the Fantasy Fiction League, though postponed somewhat by these changes of hands, occurred unofficially but a short while later.

David A. Kyle, who had headed the Monticello, New York, chapter of the SFL, issued in February, 1936, a small mimeographed fantasy cartoon magazine that was titled *The Fantasy World*. The only other fan to have had a hand in its production (if we overlook the possibility of a nom de plume) was one Walter Schaible. The contents of this effort were, as might be anticipated, utterly worthless; however, its appearance is important, for it presaged Kyle's activity in the field.

This activity was forthcoming in late 1936, when he proposed the formation of the Phantasy Legion, an organization that was to be a "brethren of science fiction and weird fiction fans banded together for the common purpose and desire—to promote phantasy." (Wollheim, it might be noted, had for some reason campaigned for the spelling of the word *fantasy* with "ph" instead of "f" in the fan press. This practice caught on for a time, being prevalent from mid-1936 until early 1937.) Kyle claimed that this new group was derived from the Legion of Science Fiction Improvement that originated in November, 1934. If the latter organization ever existed, it was probably only in Kyle's mind, where it perished soon after conception. Reference to it was obviously an artificial attempt to give the Phantasy Legion a history, and is reminiscent of Wilson Shepard's similar hoax about an Impossible Story Club which has already been noted.

Membership in the Phantasy Legion was for life, a fifty-cent registration fee being all that was required. Existing side by side with this club was the Phantasy Legion Guild. Requirements for joining the latter were prior membership in the Phantasy Legion and a contribution of some creative work to any Guild magazine. Apparently it was planned to urge fan editors to place the legend "A Guild Publication" on their magazines, thereby loosely knitting together the entire fabric of fandom. *The Phantasy World* was the first Guild publication, and was erroneously regarded by many as the official club-organ of the Phantasy Legion itself—while in actuality the latter was *Legion Parade*.

Kyle gained almost immediate support. The newer fans, who had been unable to rally about the Science Fiction Advancement Association, who found nothing to back in the Fantasy Fiction League, who were no match for the politically minded ISA—these felt that they had in the Phantasy Legion an organization truly representative of their group. McPhail, Miller and Dollens, for example, hesitated scarcely an instant before throwing their lot in with Kyle's and campaigning actively for the new club. These fans—some of the most active in all of third fandom—easily were able to launch the Legion on an even keel.

McPhail campaigned vigorously in his *Science Fiction News*. Miller, by means of his extensive correspondence and strong influence with the Philadelphia circle, aided greatly in recruiting members. And Dollens was entirely willing to work like a Trojan to make *The Phantasy World* a truly exemplary magazine.

A flock of new names began to creep into the Legion's roster. There were Richard Wilson, Robert G. Thompson, John Baltadonis, James Blish, Daniel C. Burford—even Wollheim, who, on good terms with Kyle, lent his support. There was no question but that this was a do-or-die effort of the third fandom to gain for itself a representative organization. So far in their scant year in fandom its members had had no united voice in their own destiny—and they intended to have just that.

Exemplary was the mechanism for democratic election inherent in

the League's makeup. At the very first election, by an unusual quirk
Kyle, the originator, was not raised to president. This was
unprecedented. Instead, Miller was elected president; Kyle was vice-
president; Dollens, secretary, and McPhail publicity director.
Temporarily Kyle took over the treasurer's post as well.

One number of *Legion Parade* appeared, brimming over with
enthusiasm and unshakable in its confidence in the club's bright
future. But this first election had already sown the seeds of breakdown, for Kyle's feelings at not being chosen to head the group may
be well imagined. Also, fans reading this account will already have
noted some of the fatal weaknesses in its structure: the entire lack
of income from any source other than initiation fees; the general
air of juvenility; its most representative publication being at
first but an extremely poor cartoon magazine. Despite such drawbacks
the Phantasy Legion could probably still have prospered because of
most members' honest desire to keep it in existence. But most of the
publishing facilities were under the control of Kyle. Miller as
president was helpless against his lethargy, which again and again
delayed publication of *Legion Parade*. When the club after its brisk
start began to mark time, those who had resolved to join it desisted,
awaiting signs of further activity. The club's golden opportunity
came a few months later when every pillar in fandom collapsed,
leaving the field open to any newcomer with drive and ambition. But
so disorganized was the Phantasy Legion that it did not make the
slightest bid for leadership, and its failure to do so completely
discredited it as an active organization. Its death was then prompt
if unofficial, as were the hopes of third fandom, which the Legion
carried with it to its grave.

One great posthumous project was yet to rise out of the ashes of
Fantasy Magazine. This was the Stanley G. Weinbaum memorial volume,
Dawn of Flame. When Weinbaum died no group was more saddened than
the Milwaukee Fictioneers, his own intimate circle. Its members,
along with Schwartz and Weisinger, felt that some memorial should be
raised to the man's greatness. And finally they struck upon the plan
to publish privately a selection from his works. It was edited by
Raymond A. Palmer, who did the lion's share of the work involved,
managing finances and publicity. Ruppert, who had so long printed
Fantasy Magazine, was so much the fan that however busy he was he
nevertheless found time to print *Dawn of Flame* with no regard to
profit or loss. On his small press he ran the 313 page book two
pages at a time! This was first fandom's last project.

The volume appeared late in 1936. The title story was a hitherto
unpublished novelette, and along with it were included six other
short stories: "The Lotus Eaters," "The Mad Moon," "A Martian Odyssey,"
"The Red Peri," "The Adaptive Ultimate" and "The Worlds of If." These
were printed on fine quality book-paper, and the volume was bound in
embossed black leather stamped in gold. A full page photograph of
Weinbaum formed the frontispiece. The first edition that rolled off
the presses carried an introduction by Raymond A. Palmer, one of the
author's most intimate friends. When Weinbaum's wife Margaret read
this she branded it "too personal" and refused to allow the volume
to be distributed as it stood. Another introduction was therefore
written by Lawrence Keating, and with this substituted the book was
printed and distributed. But Weinbaum's closest circle of friends—

Schwartz, Palmer, Ruppert and a few others—retained copies carrying the original Palmer foreword, thus inadvertantly making it almost impossible for the average collector to obtain anything but a second edition.

Palmer's attempts to sell *Dawn of Flame* at $2.50 per copy were heart-breakingly disappointing. Fans in those days simply didn't have that much money to invest in their hobby at short notice. And he was more than willing to send the collection to anyone who would deposit fifty cents and agree to pay the balance due in small weekly installments. Final figures on sales placed the number of copies in circulation at approximately 250. Many copies were never bound at all, and may well have been disposed of as scrap by now. Today it stands as one of the rarest of all fantasy books—far harder to obtain than, for example, *The Outsider and Others*.

Chapter XVII

THE FIRST CONVENTION AND THE DEATH OF THE ISA

THROUGHOUT ALL THIS WELTER of fans, fan magazines and ephemeral organizations, the International Scientific Association continued to ride high in its tempestuous course, casting about as always for new fields to conquer.

Sykora, in an attempt to lead the science-hobbyists into some activity that would also engage the interest of the science fictionists, suggested that the ISA make a science fiction moving picture. He especially stressed the comparative cheapness of such a project. After initial skepticism, Herbert Goudket (who had long been interested in technical aspects of motion pictures) fell in with the idea, and plans were formulated for the production of such a film during 1937. Neither man was completely unfamiliar with the art, as films of fair quality had been taken previously of local meetings as well as of the several rocketry experiments which had been carried out by the ISA.

It was suggested by John B. Michel that the club join in a social outing of some sort; this agreed to, great controversy ensued as to the destination. Philadelphia was decided upon, chiefly because Wollheim had hit upon the novel idea of meeting with out-of-town fans and thereby calling the affair a science fiction convention. Intrigued with this plan, members made hurried arrangements. And on October 22, 1936, the ISA delegation, which included Wollheim, Pohl, Michel, Sykora, Hahn, Kyle and Goudket, was met at Philadelphia by a contingent headed by Rothman, Madle and Train. After viewing the town both groups convened at Rothman's home and engaged in a bit of officiality that gave them the uncontested title to the first convention in fan history. Rothman was elected convention chairman and Pohl secretary. It is interesting to note that but for this scrap of democratic procedure the honor would doubtless have gone to British fans, who held a well-planned gathering on January 3, 1937, in Leeds, England.

Aside from the expected banter and discussion among the fans present, the gathering resolved upon one very important fact. They laid plans to hold a second convention in New York the following February—plans which, as might be well imagined, aroused the greatest of enthusiasm from all present.

This forthcoming convention was to be sponsored by the ISA—and as if sponsoring a purely science fiction type were not leaning far enough away from the science-hobbyist angle, pressure was exerted upon Sykora to sanction the issuance of an all science fiction number of *The International Observer*. Never before in the magazine's history had science fictional material surpassed strictly scientific material in quantity, and the arguments that followed were tumultuous. Sykora bitterly opposed the proposal; later however (possibly realizing that the club's major activities were being accomplished by science fictionists, with the hobbyists playing, of late, a minority role) he acquiesced. His ostensible reason for a change of mind was that publication of such an issue for distribution at the convention would provide excellent incentive for new members to be recruited. But he had, actually, another thought in mind. Thus far the science-hobbyists were losing ground. If, now, a 100% science fiction issue of *The International Observer* appeared, perhaps they would then be startled out of their complacency, goaded into activity. And by such a move the entire ISA might be placed on the ground that had been contemplated at its creation. Thus, in his editorial in the January, 1937, number (which was labelled "special convention issue") he said:

> This issue is a challenge. It is a challenge to scienti-
> fictionists and experimenters alike. Will you each support us
> equally; or will one of you by your enthusiastic work and
> persevering support so overbalance the indifferent efforts of
> the other, that one group or the other must of necessity be
> eliminated almost entirely?

These were fighting words. They were the words of a president who through intimidation hoped to save the foundations of his organiza- tion. To Sykora everything depended upon the answer. And what was to occur should the reply be negative, few realized.

Wollheim and Pohl, meanwhile, worked like beavers to make this special issue a thing to remember. Wollheim, who had given the commendable fourth anniversary number of *Fantasy Magazine* a bitterly harsh review, may have wished that he had not been quite so caustic, for it was now incumbent upon him to turn out something not only equal, but better. To accomplish the latter was an almost impossible task, for *The International Observer* had no such far-reaching contacts or well-grounded columnists as did first fandom publishers, but Wollheim made a titanic effort. And when the issue appeared, the result was eye-opening.

The golden cover heralded the contents—H. P. Lovecraft, Dr. David H. Keller, Clark Ashton Smith, Laurence Manning, Dr. E. E. Smith, Jack Williamson, Edmond Hamilton, J. Harvey Haggard, Raymond A. Palmer, Robert Wait, A. Merritt—all in one number, and these in addition to the usual ISA features. This issue ran to forty large- sized pages, and at ten cents was unquestionably one of the biggest bargains ever offered in fandom. The response was almost immediate. No other fan organization had ever offered prospective members anything comparable to this, and at once the ISA commenced to absorb the leading elements of third fandom.

Work went on apace. Sykora proved to be no laggard when it came to publicising a convention properly. Hundreds of copies of a mimeo- graphed circular announcing the great event were mailed out, asking for a postal card from any fans desiring further information. Those who sent in such requests received a copy of the program and travelling directions for reaching Bohemian Hall in Astoria, New York City, where the convention was to be held.

Wollheim, Sykora, Michel, Goudket, Pohl, Kyle and Hahn, together with Robert W. Lowndes (whose name was familiar to readers of *Wonder Stories'* letter columns of 1935; as an early member of the SFL he had unsuccessfully attempted to form a Stanford, Connecticut, chapter, and had been an active participent in the Tucker-Wollheim staple war on Tucker's side of the fracas; he had arrived the

previous night) were on hand early, and the situation was tense
indeed as they waited for outsiders to put in their appearance.
Then, slowly, fans began to trickle in. James Blish and William H.
Miller, Jr., arrived from nearby East Orange, New Jersey. Rothman,
Baltadonis and Madle pulled in from Philadelphia. Richard Wilson
(not yet active in those days) and Raymond Van Houten, a Paterson,
New Jersey, fan came. But real sighs of relief were breathed when
the professionals reached the hall—Otis Adelbert Kline with his
brother Allen; Charles D. Hornig; Mort Weisinger, the new editor of
Thrilling Wonder Stories, and with him Julius Schwartz; the artist
Charles Schneeman; and the author Otto Binder. Also in attendance
were Dr. John D. Clark, Philip Jacques Bartel, Milton Kaletsky,
Robert G. Thompson, Arthur Leeds, John J. Weir, Jack Rubinson and
Harry Dockweiler, remembered more widely today as "Dirk Wylie." Even
Conover had journeyed from Maryland.

The most unfortunate aspect of the entire convention was the lack
of a complete and coherent account of the proceedings. A few
fragmentary sidelights found their way into the pages of *The Science
Fiction Collector* and *Helios,* but no authoritative account was ever
published at that time. The reason for this was the great prevalence
of fast correspondence among fans of that time. Everyone who was
interested got complete details from a correspondent in attendance,
and all that the fan press ever presented were a few trivial lowlights.

It is known, however, that Goudket served as chairman, and that
films of the New York ISA chapter meetings and their rocketry
experiments were here for the first time shown to the public. The
great interest fans showed in these could not help but make Sykora
wish that he had prodded members into action and thus been able to
present at the same time his projected science fiction movie.
Various fans and professionals were also called on to speak, though
it is doubtful if any except Weisinger (who supplied information on
his newly-revived magazine) supplied anything except such happy
trivialities as suited the occasion. However, the convention was
unquestionably a success.

In such a prevailing spirit of camaraderie it was inevitable that
some good would come out of the affair. For years the ISA and the
Fantasy Magazine group had been at bitter odds. Accounts of their
quarrels have already been outlined in this History. But now, amid
the atmosphere of good fellowship that existed, Julius Schwartz and
Donald A. Wollheim shook hands. This handshake was taken by
bystanders to symbolize the end of enmity, the start of a more
cooperative fandom. The ISA, however, secretly regarded it as a
victory, little suspecting with what cynicism Schwartz regarded the
act. The days when he and his clique would play leading roles in
fandom were over. Already Conover had the full rights to *Fantasy
Magazine;* Weisinger and Palmer had left the amateur field; nor was
Ruppert any longer active. And though he was later to play occasional
behind-the-scenes parts, this for Schwartz was to all practical
purposes a farewell appearance to the fandom which owed him so much.

Everyone knew that there was a world's fair scheduled for New York
in 1939. Why not hold another science fiction convention there the
same year? Not simply a localized gathering, but a worldwide show
that would draw fans from all over the country and perhaps from
England and Canada as well? Attendees received the idea with great

approbation. Machinery was put into motion immediately, a committee of four being chosen to do the groundwork. Wollheim was the chairman of this group, and his aides were Madle, Conover and Weir.

But a single, ominous, recurrent note marred the entire proceedings. Beforehand, throughout the convention itself, and afterwards, Sykora emphasized that the convention and the special science fiction number of *The Internattonal Observer* were to be the ISA's last strong efforts in that direction. Thenceforward the club would turn to science-hobbyist activities in earnest and push science fiction into the background. Some wondered if this was the price that must be conceded by recalcitrant members for their recent "spree." And because of it, too, the large membership that the ISA could have attracted on the basis of its recently powerful science fiction record never materialized. Fans were not sure that they wanted to pay for one night of pleasure by professing adherence to a hobbyist god that was distasteful to them. And therefore, although the ISA recruited many new members, it did not reap the harvest it deserved.

Behind the scenes discord now crept in. Sykora wanted to plunge pell-mell into his scientific plans. Pohl, Wollheim and many others, however, were reluctant to desert the sweet chestnut of science fiction that they had rolled from the fire of the ISA's scientific aplomb. And the next number of *The Internattonal Observer* showed them holding their own—for significantly the science fiction content had by no means fallen off to a bare minimum. The predominant science fiction departments were still taking up as much room as ever, and even the hobbyist articles had a noticable science fictional slant. Such a situation could not long endure—how could a pretense of being a scientific club be longer maintained? One side or the other would have to back down.

The break came in mid-April, 1937, and was the more startling for its lack of prelude, its unexpected abruptness. At that time all ISA members received a mimeographed circular letter signed by William Sykora. In it he spoke of his long cherished ideal of founding a democratic organization whose permanency would grow from the pursuit of an ideal; that ideal was to be the goal striven for by scientific and technical progress....

> Scientifiction had little to do with the attainment of this ideal, with only one important exception, namely to act as a stimulant. Scientifiction is only a means to an end, a bit of writing or a story that would make the reader want to get into the thick of the fight man is waging in his effort to better understand nature and life. But scientifiction, far from being the stimulus to scientific study it should be, had become an end in itself...a sort of pseudo-scientific refuge for persons either incapable of pursuing a technical career, or else too lazy to do so. ...Scientifiction therefore was a mistake in the makeup of my ideal club....

Sykora went on to decry readers who should have been interested in academic and technical work, but who were instead "more inclined to dilly-dally with pulp writing, editing and cartooning." In consideration of these facts, he had no desire to devote more of his limited spare time to what he felt had "proven to be a mistaken idea." He therefore resigned as president of the New York branch of the ISA.

The membership was too astonished to take any coordinated action. What had been in Sykora's mind? Had this been a drastic attempt to get them to beg him to return on the promise of their being good little scientists? No one knew, but the majority took his scathing denunciation of fans to heart, disliking him heartily for them.

Yet the resignation had been submitted in good order. In the normal course of events the vice president would have stepped into Sykora's place, and everything would have continued as before, with the final showdown of the science fictionists and the science-hobbyists yet to come. But fate played a hand. Michel, the vice president, had resigned some time prior. Judging from past experiences, Kubilius, the secretary, would have certainly continued things in good order—but Kubilius at that time was in the hospital, seriously ill, with little chance of emerging for some weeks time. The next officer in line was Wollheim, the treasurer. And Wollheim, in a decisive move as breathtaking as Sykora's, determined to disband the ISA entirely.

Before he took action, however, he was approached by Blish and Kubilius (then convalescent) with the request that they be allowed to take over the club and conduct it on a purely science-hobbyist basis. It may seem paradoxical that Kubilius, being the highest-ranking officer, did not insist that he be given charge, regardless of Wollheim's wishes. But Wollheim pressed his presidential claim on the basis of an election technicality and won. (In ISA elections the member receiving the highest number of votes became president; the second highest, treasurer; third highest, vice president; and fourth, secretary. This was Wollheim's argument against preserving the usual line of parliamentary succession, the point he achieved with Kubilius after—to quote his own words—"a bit of correspondence and some wrangling.")

Wollheim was well aware of the consequences that might arise from so swiftly dissolving the group if he did not back up his action with substantial reasoning. And the last (June, 1937) issue of *The International Observer,* indeed, contained in its twelve pages little else but explanations and defenses of his action. A list of the ISA membership was printed, and showed to Wollheim's satisfaction to be composed in the majority of science fictionists. He therefore contended that if the club were turned over to the science-hobbyists it would stagnate and die. As evidence, he pointed to the past failures of organizations of similar character. The very name "International Scientific Association" he claimed to be a farce. The club was not international, having few if any foreign members; it was scientific only in name, for its soul had become science fictional; and in the true sense of the word it was not even an association, since the bulk of the activity had been carried on by the New York chapter. To the argument of changing its name and retaining the cohesion of a purely science fictional group, he said: "...there are too many such clubs already and none amount to a row of ten-pins. ...In the span of eight years of stf clubs of all types not one has ever done anything in a national capacity."

Sykora's letter was reprinted in *The International Observer* in full, with appropriate and inappropriate interpolations by Wollheim. This damning document proved to be a fence shutting Sykora off from the rest of fandom, for his statement that he despised everything that fandom stood for could simply not be overlooked. Everywhere he turned in his later efforts to make a comeback in fandom this letter blocked the road.

But Wollheim did not stop here. Throughout the entire issue, in the fashion that marked the peak of his feuding ability, he again and again thrust the entire blame for the club's dissolution upon William Sykora's shoulders, reiterating that the ISA could have continued as a purely science fiction club, ignoring blithely its inner conflicts, but that "Sykora was not big enough to let it do so." In accounts of the latter's taking back his donation to the ISA library, and threatening to throw the remainder into the street if it were not promptly called for, he instilled in fans' minds doubts as to Sykora's sincerity in making any type of contribution to any individual or group. Further, he alleged that Sykora had through clever utilization of the constitution gathered all power into his own hands until he had become a virtual dictator, in one hundred per cent control of the club. Hence his resignation, contended Wollheim, meant the ISA's death.

Before Wollheim was through he had figuratively crucified his opponent. Nowhere could one see the slightest taint of sympathy for the man who had fought with him against *Wonder Stories* and the SFL, at whose side he had spent many memorable hours. Rarely has one fan ever so completely discredited another. Every road was blocked to Sykora now. He had no club, no publication in which to voice his opinions, few friends and little opportunity for gaining others. And worst of all, the respect of the fan field was lost to him.

Yet, the facts of the case show something that most fans, spellbound by the power of Wollheim's rhetoric, had not even stopped to consider. Sykora, as president of a democratic organization, had resigned in good order, leaving the club perfectly intact. Its treasury, indeed, was in the best condition of its entire existence. He had made no effort to injure the ISA, even suggesting Robert A. Madle and James Blish as possible good choices for his successor, wishing them luck in their task.

At a meeting of the New York branch of the ISA Wollheim had gained a majority vote in favor of the disbanding. He had contacted various other groups and claimed by proxy their sanction as well, and therefore a better than fifty per cent vote of the entire membership in favor of his action. Yet he seemed unable to present a list of names of those who had so voted, and admitted that a large portion of the membership had never been approached. He also admitted that there were at least two fans who wanted to carry on the club—one of them an officer of higher rank than himself. Despite this he had felt it incumbent upon him to disband the ISA, throwing the brunt of the blame upon a man who was granted no medium in which to defend himself. Such was Wollheim's prestige in fandom at that time that nowhere did a voice rise up in print against his action. Most fans regarded his summation of Sykora as "something growing horns" as fact. And Sykora became an outcast because he dared to resign the post of president in a democratic organization.

The Science Fiction Association, a prominent British group functioning at that time (concerning which we will hear more in later chapters) offered to take over all obligations of the ISA. But this offer was turned down because the ISA was completely solvent.

However, Wollheim devoted almost an entire page in *The International Observer* to extolling the virtues of this British group. He maintained that American fans had failed in their attempt to formulate and sustain a serious science fiction organization and that therefore Britain should be given an opportunity. His attitude hinted that fandom in America was through, and all that there remained to do was watch its limbs wither and die. In this insinuation he was closer to the real truth than most fans of the time realized. How close fandom came to extinction in less than a year's time will shortly be shown.

For all that, the day of the ISA was done at last. Its influence had been felt in every corner of science fiction fandom for two years. Rarely had any club boasted so proud, so eventful a history. In some ways, it was almost great. But except for a short time when Sykora faintly rolled the drums for its revival in 1938, this was virtually the final part that the International Scientific Association would play in the history of the field.

Standing, l to r: Donald A. Wollheim, Robert A. Madle, Richard
Wilson, Sam Moskowitz, David A. Kyle, Daniel C. Burford, Julius
Schwartz and Leon Burg
Kneeling: Robert G. Thompson, Edward Landberg, Jack Gillespie,
James V. Taurasi and Oswald Train in Philadelphia, 1937

Henry Kuttner, 1937

Virgil Finlay (right) and
Willis Conover, Jr., in
Rochester, 1937

Jack Agnew, John V. Baltadonis and Robert A. Madle, 1937

First row, left to right: Mark Reinsberg, Jack Agnew and Ross Rocklynne
Second row: V. Kidwell, Robert A. Madle, Erle Korshak and Ray Bradbury,
Coney Island, 1939

Jack Darrow (left) shakes hands with Forrest J. Ackerman
at the First World Science Fiction Convention, New York,
1939

Left to right: James V. Taurasi,
Sam Moskowitz, Louis Kuslan, John
Giunta
Kneeling: Alex Osheroff, Robert
G. Thompson, unknown fan, at
First National Science Fiction
Convention, Newark, 1938

Lew Martin (left) and Olon F.
Wiggins of Denver, Colorado,
1941

Standing: Marojo, Julius Schwartz, Otto Binder, Mort
Weisinger, Jack Darrow
Seated: Forrest J. Ackerman, Ross Rocklynne, Charles
D. Hornig, Ray Bradbury, 1939

Leo Margulies, foreground,
Will Sykora and Alvin R.
Brown

Below: Milton A. Rothman, Harry Warner, Jr. and Jack
Speer, Hagerstown, Maryland, 1940

Chapter XVIII

THE DARK AGES OF FANDOM

MEANWHILE, drama was being enacted in other quarters. Everywhere, interested fans were awaiting in a fever pitch of interest the appearance of the new *Fantasy Magazine*. What would it be like? Would it be an improvement upon the old? Many rumors ran rife, among them that the title of *Science-Fantasy Correspondent* would change to *Fantasy Magazine*. Stickney, however, had circulated a printed card announcing *Fantasy Correspondent*, "the little giant of the fan magazines." Lovecraft's essay "Supernatural Horror in Literature" was to be commenced again, and a biography of Virgil Finlay printed; in addition to this, material by Eando Binder, Robert Bloch, E. Hoffman Price and Donald Wandrei would appear. But all of *Fantasy Magazine*'s regular departments, like "Spilling the Atoms" and "The Science-Fiction Eye," would be discontinued.

Two months passed, and the *Correspondent* did not appear. Another, and still no sign of it. Finally, three and one-half months after the second number had been issued the third finally was distributed. And fans did not know what to make of it. Conover's name was nowhere in evidence. The magazine was still *Science-Fantasy Correspondent*, having seemingly "combined" with *Fantasy Magazine* only for the purpose of filling the latter's unexpired subscriptions. Not a scrap of the announced material was to be seen. Featured were two short stories by Philip Sutter and Robert A. Madle, both of good quality; acrostics by Lovecraft and R. H. Barlow; and a science article by Oliver E. Saari. But what horrified the fans was a section in the rear of the journal titled "Hobbyana"—and devoted to postage stamps and coins! This seemed a crowning touch of asininity.

In his editorial Stickney announced the beginning of a new policy. There would be no more line-ups of "big names," no more catering to fans' interests. Stickney was convinced that encouraging the amateur fantasy author was the important thing, and the *Correspondent* would welcome with open arms works of all such showing ability.

This was a startling turn of events. It was obvious that the old guard of *Fantasy Magazine* was through as far as Stickney was concerned. The last means of expression of this set was now denied it. For years its members had narrowed down their activities as their journals diminished one by one in number and their producers left the field one by one—until finally *Fantasy Magazine* was their sole stamping ground. It had been the center, the very base of fandom. It was the base of fandom because it was the strongest recruiting unit in fandom. Without it little new blood was infused into the broadening circles of the second and third fandoms. Its producers shuddered as they gazed out upon the welter of juvenile publications and organizations that surrounded them on every side. Some of these had acknowledged willingness to carry on the new *Fantasy Magazine*. But that avenue was now closed. And so, with spiteful swiftness, the door slammed shut on the old guard: on Schwartz, Weisinger, Ruppert, Palmer, Crawford, Bloch, Kaletsky,

Ferguson and Hornig, its leading members—and, to a lesser extent, on F. Lee Baldwin, Louis C. Smith, Duane W. Rimel, Emil Petaja, Forrest J. Ackerman and dozens upon dozens of the first fandom bystanders. The cream of fandom was no longer active in the field. Some did make rapprochements, but in most cases not until years later, when fandom had again "grown up."

This was catastrophe incarnate. Never had such a gold mine of talent departed simultaneously from the field. Survival of fandom in any mature sense of the word had devolved upon the ISA as the only remaining group possessing any number of advanced fans—but that too had departed for the limbo of forgotten things, and with it the science-hobbyists and semi-science fictionists Gee, Gervais, Sykora, Kubilius and many others.

By late 1936 Clare Beck's *Science Fiction Critic* had become a ranking fan journal. Its format and typography were consistantly excellent. The mildly vituperative attitude inherent in its "Hammer and Tongs" column throughout earlier numbers now accelerated to a raucous clamor of destructive volume. The policy of the magazine became to chastise the field of professional science fiction, suggesting little or nothing constructive. Its very first move was to announce that it did not recognize *Thrilling Wonder Stories* as a science fiction magazine, and to this policy it adhered, relenting only to the quoted degree:

> Henceforth, if and when stories of worthwhile scientific fiction appear in that magazine we shall gladly give praise and credit to the proprietors, but at present it is our belief that this is unlikely to occur, and until a definite change is evident in the material of the magazine, we feel there are now only two newstand publications worthy of the definition, "science fiction magazines."

To the *Critic's* mind there was no such thing as science fiction, but only scientific fiction. In this respect it was a leader in drawing fans away from whatever contact remained between them and the professional publications. But when Beck next turned to destructive criticism of fans and fan magazines themselves, it became immediately obvious that *The Science Fiction Critic* was not to be the rallying-point for reorganization of fandom's shattered ranks. Fans needed confidence in themselves, not condemnation.

As for the *Science-Fantasy Correspondent,* most of the remaining fans were too young to have much hope of soon becoming professional authors, and the non-science fictional advertising and "Hobbyana" repelled them. Then too, there was the scandal connected with the *Correspondent's* change of policy. What were the facts behind Stickney's break with Conover? Many tried to guess, and rumors were bruited about, but the only thing to see print was Wollheim's bitter condemnation of Stickney, whom he termed "contemptible and sneaky." All the facts that could be immediately ascertained were that Stickney, possibly grown jealous over Conover's success, had simply deposed his rival in an attempt to bask in the limelight alone. This was far from the truth, of course, but the entire story was not learned until much later.

Opinion rallied against Stickney, and he received many biting, sarcastic letters, cancellations of subscriptions, and condemnation by the field generally. This naturally embittered him in turn, and, having no medium through which to reply to his accusers save the *Correspondent,* and realizing the latter's circulation was too large to permit inclusion of a fan dispute, he merely rankled from within. So it became obvious that *Science-Fantasy Correspondent* would not be the rallying-point of fandom either.

What was left? Only an occasional stray fan publication (usually long overdue and started some time previously) and Morris Dollens' pathetic little *Science Fiction Collector,* which continued to appear at monthly intervals. And it seemed preposterous to expect this ever to be a center for a strong fandom.

To summarize, then— The ISA was dead, and therefore *The International Observer.* The Science Fiction Advancement Association was dormant, and with it *Tesseract.* The Phantasy Legion, moribund, was making no effort to assume leadership. The Fantasy Fiction League was hopeless. *Fantasy Magazine* was gone, and with it the great old fans of the past. William L. Crawford, having failed completely in his efforts to put *Marvel Tales* on the newstands, had followed in their footsteps. The SFL was an invertebrate thing, commanding no respect and obviously kept as an advertising point for *Thrilling Wonder Stories.* Stickney, more embittered than ever, was drifting still further from fandom by renaming his publication *The Amateur Correspondent,* with Wollheim still barking at his footsteps. Though for a short while stories persisted that he would revive *Fantasy Magazine* on his own, Conover, disillusioned, was making no effort whatsoever in that direction. *The Science Fiction Critic's* policy could not be harmonized with the needs of fandom at large. The Los Angeles SFL chapter, largest organized group in the country, continued to report large, successful meetings, with more and more celebrities present, but made no move to aid fandom in general— probably influenced by Ackerman, whose sentiments rested with the old *Fantasy Magazine* group, and whose experiences with the second and third fandoms had been unpleasant. Wollheim, the leading and most capable fan of the time, had frankly expressed his belief that American fandom had failed as a unified group, and could suggest no other course save union with Britain, whose youthful, virile, enthusiastic fandom was already sending skyscrapers of achievement upward.

The only thing to which the scattered remnants of fandom could turn was the Philadelphia Science Fiction Society, where Baltadonis, Madle, Rothman, Agnew and Train still showed some signs of activity. But even here things looked dark, for all meetings of the club had been suspended by mid-1937 because of non-attendance, and the society's *Fantasy Fiction Telegram* had collapsed after its fourth number. Without a published journal fandom could not nope to reorganize its broken and depleted ranks.

Here, then, were the dark ages of science fiction fandom. And if no champions arose to lead the way back to the light then fandom was through, and its existence would remain but a brief, amusing incident in the history of pulp publishing.

Chapter XIX

THE RISE OF BRITISH FANDOM

WE HAVE READ allusions to Britain's growing strength in the science fiction fan world. What then of England? How had she progressed since the early days of 1935 when her only organization was the British Science Fiction Association, merely a closed circle of correspondents which had glorified itself with a title?

Many of the country's writers whose work had appeared in American fantasy magazines were real fans of tremendous enthusiasm. Such names as John Russell Fearn, John Beynon Harris, Festus Pragnell and A. M. Low were in evidence.

Much science fiction and fantasy fiction had seen British publication in book form, but otherwise it was confined to juvenilities in "penny dreadfuls." For example, the British author Eric Frank Russell, addressing a fan gathering in the United States during his visit in 1939, cited an edition of *Mickey Mouse Magazine* as the chief exponent of the science fiction art in periodical form prior to the inception of Gillings' *Tales Of Wonder*.

Early in 1934 there appeared on the scene a letter-sized weekly publication known as *Scoops*. The only weekly professional science fiction periodical to appear, it staggered through some twenty consecutive issues before its collapse. In most of the early numbers the authors of the stories were not given, British writers apparently preferring anonymity to having their names—or even nom de plumes—associated with material of this nature. Toward the end of its existence *Scoops* improved the quality of its fiction and took on a less juvenile air. About this time, too, such recognized authors as A. Conan Doyle, A. M. Low, John Russell Fearn and P. E. Cleator commenced to appear in its pages. But the early taint of sensationalism and juvenility had turned many readers irrevocably against the magazine. The editor claimed to have been gradually building up an entirely new clientele, and felt that had he been allowed to continue a bit longer he would have been catering to a stable fan audience—but the shift of policy was too late. Too late, too, the editor had begun to organize a fan club through the magazine, similar in nature to America's Science Fiction League. By so narrow a margin did Britain lose an earlier fandom.

Thus, the only outlet for active British fans prior to 1936 was participation in American activities, and this was obviously difficult. However, John Russell Fearn ran numbrous columns in *Fantasy Magazine* on "scientifilms" and the state of science fiction in his country. And in the later issues of the same journal Walter H. Gillings had a regular column on British affairs having a fantasy slant. Edward J. Carnell was also active, contributing material to *The Science Fiction Critic, Arcturus* and *The Science Fiction News*.

But British fandom as we know it did not spring into life until *Wonder Stories* began its Science Fiction League. Many British fans, sometimes through devious means, obtained and read regularly the American fantasy magazines, and when the SFL was announced they did not lose their chance to organize. Douglas Mayer of Leeds was the first to apply for a charter for a British chapter. By early 1935 he had his chapter running with such prominent fans as J. Michael Rosenblum, Harold Gottcliffe and C. Bloom on its roster. The Leeds SFL soon became the largest and most active chapter in the British Isles as a result.

By mid-1935 the Nuneaton chapter, headed by Maurice K. Hanson, had been formed. About the same time the Liverpool chapter, which was of importance only insofar as it solidified British fandom as a whole, was also organized.

An additional large chapter was formed a little later. This was headed by Jack Beaumont of Yorkshire. Beaumont had been a member of the American ISA, and had for a time even planned to start a British chapter of that organization. By early 1937 he had obtained six members for his SFL chapter. This was unique among British groups inasmuch as it was predominantly composed of science-hobbyists. And, similar to like American groups attempting to subordinate science fiction to the active practice of science, this one soon collapsed under its own inertia. Indeed, the closest approach of science-hobbyists to being an important force in British fandom was the British Interplanetary Society, which was subscribed to by many of the country's prominent fans.

Once organization had been begun, it was but a matter of time before England's first fan magazine put in its appearance. One might have expected it to come from the chapter first formed—Leeds—but it did not. In March, 1936, Maurice K. Hanson and Dennis A. Jacques of the Nuneaton SFL founded *Novae Terrae* and captured the honors. While in no way comparable to *The Time Traveller* and *Fantasy Magazine, Novae Terrae* did compare extremely favorably with such American efforts as *The Science Fiction Critic, The Science Fiction News,* etc. It had the advantage of being edited by fans averaging four or more years older than typical American fans of the time. The magazine appeared on a religiously monthly schedule, its mimeographed pages and quarto size giving it a unique personality. To the younger members of chaotic American fandom in 1937 it appeared a bit too stiff, dry and formal; this, of course, was because fans in the United States were gradually turning away from science fiction in general and becoming interested in fans as personalities. The prominent British enthusiasts of the day were contributors to *Novae Terrae.* Walter H. Gillings, Edward J. Carnell, Leslie J. Johnson, D. R. Smith, Douglas W. F. Mayer, Eric Frank Russell, J. Michael Rosenblum, Festus Pragnell and John Russell Fearn were among them. The weight of the majority of the country's fans was behind the publication, and British fandom lacked neither writing nor analytical ability.

Proud of their progress, certain of their future, English fans did not hesitate to criticize their American cousins when the need arose. They found their opportunity when Forrest J. Ackerman contributed an article titled "Esperanto: Its Relation to Scientifiction" to the August, 1936, issue of *Novae Terrae.* In this, Ackerman exhorted British fans to turn to Esperanto, warning them that if the entire planet did not speak one common language by the time the Martians made their first landing the results would be disastrous; for the Martians, undoubtedly of an older civilization, would have anything

but respect for peoples having dozens of different languages with no
hard and fast rules of pronunciation and words meaning three or four
different things. It was essential for the world to Esperantoize
immediately, so that the Martians would be able to comprehend this
simple, new language when they arrived, etc., etc.

British fans were as one in indignation at Ackerman's article.
They felt that he was in some obscure fashion showing his contempt
for them by presenting an article no intelligent mind could stomach.
Spearheading this rapidly assembled opposition was no less a light
than Carnell. He maintained that

> ...if Forrest J. Ackerman can write scientifilm notes for a
> society calling itself the World Girdlers' International
> Science League Correspondence Club, surely all the fans in
> England are worthy of more than a mere Esperanto article.
> After all, the British Esperanto Association spreads its
> propaganda thoroughly over these isles. ...because we aren't
> a very progressive science fiction country as yet, American
> fans are apt to treat us too lightly, forgetting that any
> news of science fiction happenings in their country is
> eagerly sought after here, so that we may build this country
> into as enthusiastic a body as the U. S....

Carnell went on to say that he had heard Ackerman would not write
an article unless he were paid for it, and that fans were "already
asking" how much he had received for this one. (Needless, to say, the
World Girdlers' International Science League Correspondence Club,
originally announced in the last—January, 1937—issue of *Fantasy
Magazine*, was a classic of absurdity; nothing ever came of it.)

The December, 1936, issue of *Novae Terrae* printed "Whither
Ackermankind?" in which Ackerman turned on his opposition. In reply
to D. R. Smith, who had attacked his distortion and clipping of the
language in an article entitled "Hands Off English" (which was later
reprinted in the American *Science Fiction Critic)*, he offered the
weak defense that the tremendous amount of work he did necessitated
his using every short cut available, and that he felt *Time* magazine,
for example, did more coining and corrupting in a week than he could
hope to accomplish in a year. He stated his intention, moreover, of
"filosofically" carrying on, introducing inevitable "futuristic
forms." To the accusation of demanding payment for articles in fan
magazines he made the only defense in print that this historian has
ever seen:

> It seems, unfortunate, one receives considerable *erroneous*
> information, Person who told you I never write article unless
> paid was uninformed or misinformed *optimist!* I only wish it
> were true! Picture yourself in my position: approx thirty
> amateur imaginative mags already in existence; new pamfs
> popping up at frequent intervals. And publishers of about
> every one of these periodicals writing me—friendly, but
> fundless—requesting articles on Esperanto or fantascience
> films or allied subjects.
> What am I expected to do dear friend? Ten years now, I've
> been effervescently enthusiastic about stf. and, after
> college, commenced putting into practice idea I'd conceived
> some time long before—briefly that of "hanging out my
> shingle" as world's first professional "scientifictionist"!
> Meaning to make living as authority on scientifiction field.

I've enlarged that since to scientifantasy field as outlined.
But it's "floppo"! For this pioneer in newest and most noble
profession is expected to give away gratis products of time
and "training."

The staff of *Novae Terrae* called a halt to the debate, stating
that both sides of the question had been presented. But the damage
had been done, and in England as well as in the United States
Ackerman had become unpopular with the new group of fans.

In Leeds, meanwhile, Douglas Mayer was supporting the idea of
holding the first science fiction conference. At first more
centralized sites than Leeds were considered, but these were finally
abandoned since this chapter, having the largest membership of any
in England and being composed, perhaps, of the country's most active
fans could more easily make arrangements in its own city. There was
to be no fee for entry to this convention. However, fans were
required to write in advance for tickets. Publicity and speakers
were arranged for, many of the nation's most prominent fantasy
authors promising to attend. There were many pressing problems
before British fandom, and there seemed little doubt but that this
conference would unify all its elements, leaving the group free to
work cooperatively toward a common goal.

On Sunday, January 3, 1937, then, the first British science
fiction conference was held. Hopes for a banner turn-out were
blasted, however, by an epidemic of influenza then prevalent. Many
prominent authors and fans decided at the last moment not to attend
because of this. But to the young, growing British fandom an
attendance of twenty was virtually equal to a thousand. At 10:30
that morning Herbert Warnes, the chairman, called the proceedings to
order and then asked Douglas W. F. Mayer to read messages to the
delegates which had been received from Professor A. M. Low, Dr. Olaf
Stapledon, the Oklahoma Scientifiction Association, John Russell
Fearn, Festus Pragnell and H. G. Wells.

Walter H. Gillings gave the first talk of the day, recounting how
very close he had come to convincing Newnes, Limited, of the
feasibility of issuing a professional science fiction magazine.
Plans had been abandoned at the eleventh hour because of Newnes'
fear of competition in the form of American "pulps" remaindered in
Britain. Later on Gillings outlined his plans for a projected
printed fan magazine to be titled *Scientifiction*. This was to be the
most elaborate fan effort Britain had yet produced—and, it might be
added, the magazine actually did eventually appear.

Edward J. Carnell spent most of his talk belittling American fans
and their activities and warning Britons against repeating the
blunders of their overseas brethren.

Maurice K. Hanson, editor of *Novae Terrae,* briefly outlined the
history of the Nuneaton SFL chapter and of its publication.

After recessing for dinner the main business of the day was
reached. Mayer proposed that "a British non-commercial organization
should be formed to further science fiction"; this motion was
promptly seconded by Carnell and passed unanimously. After some
discussion it was decided to name the organization "The Science
Fiction Association," and Hanson agreed that *Novae Terrae* should
become the new club's official organ. The choice of president was
left open (even H. G. Wells being suggested for the post), but Mayer

was appointed secretary with Warnes his assistant. The customary high-sounding idealism voiced with the launching of such organizations was forthcoming, and everything proceeded with apparent unanimity, even to the passing of a resolution that fans dissolve all connections with American clubs and throw in their lot with the SFA.

Despite its meager attendance the conference was eminently successful and the plans it decided upon were within a short time to mature. But into the scene now sprang discord. At the January 24, 1937, meeting of the Leeds chapter Mayer moved that the club secede from the Science Fiction League and thenceforth call itself the Leeds Science Fiction Association. He mentioned that cutting all ties with American groups had been stipulated in the SFA prospectus. Then—perhaps for the first time—many of the members began to realize the significance of this resolution. Association with America in the past had been pleasant and often to mutual advantage. Was it necessary to drop these ties in order to show loyalty to the British Club? There was opposition, then, to Mayer's motion, but it was passed nevertheless. Opponents promptly rallied under the leadership of J. Michael Rosenblum and Harold Gottcliffe, and when Gottcliffe announced that his group was still behind most of the principles of the SFA and was continuing to solicit memberships for it as usual the initial fires subsided. Nevertheless, members of the new Leeds SFL were in a fashion outcasts from British fandom for a time.

Mayer, on his part, issued a *Science Fiction Bibliography,* which listed a selection of fantasy books. It was the first of its type to be issued in Britain and the second in fandom as a whole (the first ran serially in the American *Science Fiction Digest*), and though pitifully incomplete compared to those which were to follow was a strong effort for its period. Mayer's group also paid a visit to the London branch of the SFA (which had been organized since the conference under the leadership of Eric Williams), one of its strongest chapters, which was progressing healthily with such names as Arthur C. Clarke, William F. Temple and Kenneth Chapman on its roster. For a time, several of these London fans rented an apartment together, the first instance recorded of fans banding together in "Futurian House" fashion.

The SFA continued to prosper. The Los Angeles SFL, which entirely ignored the American scene during the chaos of early 1937, sent enough memberships to the SFA to qualify Los Angeles as the first overseas chapter. Thus the only group in the United States powerful enough to grasp leadership during troubled times turned far-sighted eyes away from the local scenes to form a link with the virile new blood of England.

Amateur Science Stories, a legal-sized fan magazine composed of fan-written fiction chosen by a board of review, was another project the SFA consummated. Three issues appeared and several stories it carried were later reprinted by professional publications in Britain and America. The club library was growing steadily and a librarian was busy shuttling books out to members at an ever-increasing rate. British fans had no objection to obtaining their reading-matter gratis and the club library was constantly being utilized—in contrast to American groups, where a club library is a formality, few American fans being satisfied with less than complete ownership of their books and magazines.

With its February, 1937, number *Novae Terrae* began complete coverage of SFA activities. Plans for printing the magazine professionally had to be abandoned for lack of funds, but despite this England did not lack a fine printed fan journal. John Russell Fearn, British author, let it be known that a proposed English science fiction magazine to be titled *Little Science Stories* died before appearing when its financial backer perished in an automobile accident. (Walter Gillings later branded this story a complete fabrication from beginning to end.) Gillings' announcement at the Leeds conference of a printed fan magazine was not premature, however, for shortly thereafter his *Scientifiction: The British Fantasy Review* appeared. This was a superb effort, surpassing in clearness of impression and absence of typographical errors all fan productions save America's *Amateur Correspondent*. The material featured was mostly staff-written. To the American fan of average experience much of the information was a little dated, but for his English cousin it was ideal. *Scientifiction* indulged in no hazy references or vague generalities, but proceeded on the assumption that the reader knew nothing and must have everything explained. This was done in its news columns, book reviews and other features. Julius Schwartz, who had turned down offers of several American fan magazines to carry on his popular *Fantasy Magazine* column, "The Science Fiction Eye," virtually offered it to Gillings, who carried it in the magazine's final issues. So again was manifest the tendency for leaders or former leaders in American fandom to let the home boys muddle through as best they could while they jumped on the British band-wagon. *Scientifiction* also gained distinction by publishing the first biography and photograph of Olaf Stapledon, famous author of *Last and First Men,* ever to appear in a fan magazine.

It is entirely possible that Gillings, in publishing *Scientifiction,* intended to use it in approaching publishers as showing his familiarity with fantasy fiction and its background, his ready contacts with its authors, his knowledge of the reading public's tastes. Credence is lent to this view by the announcement a few months later that Gillings had contacted the World's Work Firm, which was to publish a quarterly science fiction magazine to be titled *Tales Of Wonder*

And so it was that British fandom itself created its own professional science fiction magazine. This was the clenching argument that the fans themselves, though regularly sneered at by professional editors, were in no way dependent on existing professional periodicals. Few individuals—in fandom or out of it—absorbed this lesson of applied enthusiasm.

In *Tales Of Wonder* Gillings again advanced on the assumption that the reader knew nothing and that all elementary scientific facts must be included in the stories. Advanced "thought-variants" (such as editor Tremaine so successfully used in *Astounding Stories* in 1934-6) were definitely out. But Gillings was sympathetic to the efforts of the more talented members of British fandom, giving many of them a real boost into professionalism.

In the spring of 1937 the organ of the SFA intended as its "front" appeared. It was entitled *Tomorrow,* and had as its forerunner several issues of *The Science Fiction Gazette.* *Tomorrow* boasted a printed cover, and was mimeographed extremely neatly in purple ink. It carried articles on science and science fiction and devoted a little space to regular columns. Mayer was editor.

The membership of the Science Fiction Association continued to increase so that by the end of 1937 over eighty fans had enrolled. About two hundred copies of *Novae Terrae* were being mailed out. The SFA is believed to have gained eventually an international membership of 120—one of the highest ever claimed by a fan club. As 1937 drew to a close British fandom was laying plans for their second conference, to be held in London.

For its size and late start, the British fandom was by all comparisons far ahead of American fandom in unity, quality and general maturity.

Chapter XX

RENAISSANCE

IN AMERICA little rustlings became apparent in the debris of the old order; green plants began to sprout from the rot of dead wood. These were insignificant at first and lacked unified pattern—but they were to be of great importance to science fiction fandom.

Of the old groups, few had survived. There was, of course, Wollheim, with his comparatively inactive circle of adherents— Michel, Pohl, Dockweiler, Kyle and others—who could be pricked into life long enough to help him in some feud, but who were of little or no general help to fandom at large. There was also the Philadelphia Science Fiction Society, fronted by Baltadonis and Madle, who were carrying on a vigorous correspondence with other fans scattered throughout the country. Morris Dollens, after a delay of some months, began reissuing *The Science Fiction Collector* in slightly improved form. However, it still seemed to deal more with the fans themselves than with science fiction.

In April, 1937, Olon F. Wiggins, embittered by previous failures, but equally determined to distribute his *Science Fiction Fan,* revived the magazine in hektographed form—skimpy, uninspired, its Dollens covers its main attraction. With the May, 1937, number Wiggins announced that no subscriptions smaller than one dollar would be accepted. Today, such a note would not seem so unusual, but in those times, with the country scarcely pulling out of a depression long enough to slump into a recession, when a fifteen-dollars-a-week job was considered good pay, and with the average fan having very little spending money—this was an outrageous demand. It was the more so because the fan of 1937 religeously collected every fan journal issued. Nothing was more horrible in the mind of the fan of that day than missing an issue. Not even feuds reached the extreme where one fan would cancel another's subscription and refund him his money. Wiggins, in caustically turning away subscriptions of less than a dollar, made it virtually impossible for many to subscribe. Many fans hated him bitterly on this account, though it was not generally realized that Wiggins sent free copies to many simply because he believed they were sincerely interested in getting the magazine, never remitting a bill. Nevertheless during 1937 Wiggins was not highly thought of, and though he managed to get his *Science Fiction Fan* out with monthly regularity only Wollheim ever contributed any material to its pages; the rest was scraps culled from chance sources.

Slowly now names began to make themselves apparent—or as apparent as anything could be amid the publishing dearth of the time. The February 14, 1937, issue of the *Science Fiction Collector* announced that Sam Moskowitz had contributed a story and three articles, and simultaneously Miller's *Phantastique* carried the notice that Alex Osheroff and Sam Moskowitz, two Newark fans, were to issue a fan magazine entitled *Helios*. Moskowitz had helped organize the Newark SFL chapter in July, 1935, and had attempted to get into the active stream of fandom in early 1936 without success. The fourth anniversary issue of *Fantasy Magazine* (which, it will be recalled, was sent to all SFL members gratis) proved to be an open sesame to the entire fan field, however, and he proceeded to subscribe to every fan journal mentioned. This led to acquaintanceship with Miller and Blish, who lived in neighboring towns, and with Osheroff, who lived around the corner. Though but sixteen years old, Moskowitz possessed a broad background in science fiction, having—like Madle —collected most of the professionally published magazines and read them all.

At the first convention in New York there had been present a fan known as Richard Wilson. Wilson was a tall, slim, taciturn individual, intelligent in appearance, whom no one of note had seen or heard of in fandom previously. His eighteen years was in contrast to the less mature fans of fifteen or sixteen, and he was one of no mean capabilities.

Wilson helped bring into active fandom another science fiction reader whose name he had seen in magazines' readers' columns. This was stocky, black haired, blunt James V. Taurasi, whose chief assets seemed to be energy, ambition and ideas, though he was sadly unqualified for artistic or literary pursuits. Taurasi helped Wilson set type for the latter's *Atom,* a slim, envelope-sized magazine he was issuing. But friendship of enduring quality between the meticulously correst Wilson and the often uncouth Taurasi seemed out of the question. And it was not long before Wilson's acid comments on Taurasi's failings severed their initial friendship. Like many others after him, Wilson failed to discern that Taurasi, for all his crudities, was an extremely capable and intelligent person, and possessed like himself a very good background in science fiction.

These three names—Taurasi, Wilson and Moskowitz—were to be the most important in the reconstruction of fandom outside of the Philadelphia group, which worked with them almost as a unit.

Fandom at first attempted to revive the printed journal, patterning its efforts after Wollheim's midget-sized *Phantagraph.* Wilson issued *The Atom* on his own press, this being a good effort for a first attempt. Moskowitz and Osheroff paid Wilson three dollars to print their first eight-paged *Helios,* which boasted a linoleum cut on the cover; this cut was the work of Dollens, with whom Moskowitz had struck up a strong friendship. It, too, was reasonably good for a first number, though following a trend of the times in being more of a magazine about fans than about science fiction. Kirby, who had failed so conclusively to make a success of his Fantasy Fiction League, now presented a one-paged, printed, monthly news-sheet titled *The Science Fiction World;* the second issue was promptly reduced to the six by four-and-a-half inch size then prevalent. All three of these titles had one thing in common: they lasted for but two numbers in printed format. *The Science Fiction World* gave up the ghost without bothering to refund outstanding subscriptions. *The Atom* folded with a third number partly completed. *Helios,* after a second issue printed by Stickney, announced that it would henceforth continue as a hektographed journal.

It was obvious that printing was an impossible medium. There simply was not enough support to be had to pay for printing even the most modest fan magazine. The initial cost of mimeographing equipment also was steep in those troubled days. So fans arrived at the conclusion that hektographing was the only solution to their problems. Morris Dollens then became the center of attraction. For the first time he received sizeable literary and artistic contributions from fans who had few other outlets for their work save his *Science Fiction Collector*. Because of this sudden prosperity he increased the size and number of pages in the magazine, producing a first anniversary issue that was such an improvement over past numbers as to cause fans to look up and take notice. The next—the thirteenth—number saw the *Collector* as it should have been—a mature, entertaining, intelligent publication, more than holding its own with others in the field. The contents-page read like a *Who's Who* of fandom at the time, with material by Stiles, Dollens, Wollheim, Kyle, Beck, Baltadonis, Chapman and Moskowitz. But cooperation had come too late, for the issue also contained an editorial announcing the magazine's discontinuance.

Then did the end of American fandom seem very near indeed. Here, and on all other sides, every attempt ended in collapse. But the darkest hour is always just before the dawn.

Dollens announced that he had given full rights to the title *Science Fiction Collector* to a prominent fan who wished for a time to keep his identity secret. Finally, however, the facts leaked out. Baltadonis, aspiring Philadelphia artist and former associate editor of *The Fantasy Fiction Telegram,* was the one who had received all rights to Dollens' *Collector*. Soon afterward there came word that the first revived issue under new editorship "would be the best hektographed fan magazine ever." This boast was met with much cynicism, and the summer of 1937 dragged on, the slim hope of fandom resting on Baltadonis' energy, ambition and ability, with no rallying-point appearing elsewhere.

Meanwhile, Moskowitz had contacted Corwin Stickney, who lived in Belleville, New Jersey, about five miles from his home. This acquaintanceship was cemented into friendship by the hard cash Moskowitz paid him to print the second number of *Helios*. Moskowitz's aim was to win Stickney back to fandom's cause, and in this he was moderately successful, becoming an unofficial editor of *The Amateur Correspondent* in the sense that he had a good deal to say about its policy thenceforward. Science fiction articles and features began to reappear; a fan magazine review popped back in; art work by fans was accepted; and, in the journal's final issue, the infamous "Hobbyana" column was ousted.

In correspondence Moskowitz carried on a vigorous defense of Stickney's attitude toward Conover, particularly vehement exchanges being made with Wollheim, who was heading the Stickney attackers. In this attitude Moskowitz was guided by the fact that regardless of past events shattered fandom could not afford to lose a magazine like *The Amateur Correspondent*. In reply to Wollheim's assertion like what Stickney had done was "contemptible and sneaky" he revealed what he had learned of the break with Conover. The deadline for receipt of material for the third number had been reached and passed with nothing for it having been received from Conover, who had ignored repeated pleas. Ordinarily, deadlines for fan journals are flexible in the extreme (if not an editorial affectation), but the *Correspondent* happened to be one of the very few financed by its advertising, and hence its publication could not be delayed.

Stickney therefore scraped together what material he could, writing a story himself under the pen name of Philip Sutter, and proceeded to print the issue. While thus occupied a part of the promised contents belatedly arrived from Conover. Feeling him to be unreliable, however, Stickney severed all ties with him. The hue and cry that arose from Conover filled the fan world with indignation, and since Stickney had at no time made clear his side of the story his silence was accepted as a full confession of guilt. Through publicizing the truth of the matter Moskowitz succeeded in winning over such fans as Madle, Baltadonis, Weir and Miller to his side of the controversy.

Moskowitz was also courting Claire Beck in an attempt to induce him to let his *Science Fiction Critic* serve as a rallying-point for American fandom, but Beck's opinion of fans of the time was still low, so that he felt he would be stooping to their level regardless of the cause. Moskowitz did help seal a cooperation pact between Beck and Stickney, however, though he failed in inducing them to go much further. He managed to place his articles in both of their magazines, which, along with appearances in other journals of the time, helped build his reputation as a writer in the fan world. The article in the *Critic*, titled "Was Weinbaum Great?" (in which Moskowitz decided in the negative), was replied to by Robert W. Lowndes with an article "Weinbaum Was Great." Although Lowndes' reply was politely formal the incident may have instilled in his mind a subconscious dislike for Moskowitz which was to result in an overt attack at a later date.

In late August, 1937, the first issue of the new *Science Fiction Collector* appeared under the editorship of Baltadonis and staffed by Train, Madle and Moskowitz. The result set the fan world agog and unified its struggling remnants. For Baltadonis had done the near-impossible: not only was the *Collector* ahead of the old insofar as quality of material was concerned, but Dollens' hektography had actually been surpassed. Some of the most important names of fandom were contributors, and in the space of one issue the *Science Fiction Collector* became the leading representative fan journal.

At about the same time the first issue of *Cosmic Tales Quarterly*, edited and published by James V. Taurasi, made its appearance. Taurasi had attempted to produce *Junior Science Fiction* earlier in the year, but had never completed the number; however, he mailed out fragments of this abortive journal with the bulky *Cosmic Tales Quarterly*. This latter contained fiction written by Taurasi, Wilson Kyle and Edward E. Schmitt (the actual name of a real individual). Wilson's effort in particular showed narrative ability, and the mere thought of the amount of work involved in producing the number was enough to give the magazine a leading position among the scant ranks of fan publications.

Baltadonis, in an attempt to integrate the numerous titles produced by the PSFS, announced the Comet Publications banner. In addition to the *Collector* this embraced *Imaginative Fiction* originally carbon-copied but now reappearing in small hektographed format; *Science Adventure Stories,* a brainchild of Dollens which he never issued, but now brought out by Baltadonis; and *The Brain,* pamphlet of three stories by Oswald Train, copiously and colorfully illustrated but typographically all but unreadable.

Taurasi followed Baltadonis' lead with Cosmic Publications, whose longevity through many vicissitudes proved phenomenal. He listed under this banner *Cosmic Tales, Phantasy World, Future Science Stories, Solar* and *Tempopossibilities*. Aside from the first title, the only one actually to appear was *Solar,* which won a Fantasy Amateur Press Association award some time later. Taurasi also contemplated further issues of *Legion Parade* and *Phantasy World,* as he had taken over the Phantasy Legion from Kyle; however, he soon lost interest in this organization, and nothing ever came of his plans.

Moskowitz now metamorphosed his printed *Helios* to a hektographed journal of a greater number of pages. This third number had a definite literary tone, and featured contributions from David H. Keller, John Russell Fearn, Clark Ashton Smith and other notables. A collectors' column by Louis C. Smith was begun. The news sections listed over two dozen tales and poems of H. P. Lovecraft to be printed posthumously by *Weird Tales,* along with the list of stories returned by *Amazing Stories* to reduce its overstocked condition. There were also critical articles and literery definitions of science fiction. This number met with some praise, but Moskowitz, realizing that he was publishing material which could not hope to reach the audience preferring it, returned with the next *Helios* to its former policy of catering to the fans. This reached its culmination in the fifth issue, and caused an immediate rise in the magazine's circulation. If Moskowitz had convinced no one else, he had convinced himself that the fans of 1937 were interested not in the literary side of fantasy fiction or its publishers, but solely in themselves—their personalities, the uniqueness of their type. Many, for example, collected fan magazines exclusively, caring not a bit for the professional fantasy publications. And no doubt a large part of this attitude can be traced to the poor quality of the latter, which were sinking gradually at the time toward a new literary nadir.

Chapter XXI

THE NEW ORDER PROGRESSES

DOZENS OF NEW FAN MAGAZINE titles were being announced everywhere. *The Scientifictionist, Luna, Future Science Stories, Fantasia, Tales of Time and Other Dimensions, The Anti-Time Traveller, Cosmic Call,* and *Hackneyed Tales* were among these. Some titles thus forecasted—like *Science Adventure Stories* and *Fantascience Digest*—did not appear for a year or more; others never appeared at all. The general impression received from reading such advertisements was that of a fan field weighed down by its own publications. In actuality, however, fan magazines were pitifully few and far between, and most of those which did appear seldom survived more than one or two issues. Everywhere the lament was the same: lack of material. Fans had the time and energy (though not always the ability) to publish, but they had nothing to print. Most professional authors refused to contribute to hektographed or mimeographed periodicals. The older fans contacted, probably unwilling to associate with a more juvenile element, evinced no interest. Of the newcomers and publishers themselves, very few had the ability or background to help—and some who tried were roundly criticized for their amateurishness, when they should have been praised for their willingness to try in the face of their acknowledged handicaps.

Of the comparative newcomers, Moskowitz was one of the few to produce any number of articles and short stories for the fan press, and he too possessed noticeable deficiencies in spelling and grammar —though still managing to string words together well enough to sound natural when read aloud. (And it should be understood that most of the fan editors of that time not only printed material with all grammatical errors intact, but were unconscious of the fact that any of these were present. More, a large enough percentage of the readers were incapable of recognizing them to make a generally harmonious fan world.)

In the October, 1937, issue of *Helios* there appeared an announcement of an organization titled Unofficial Society for the Aid of Fan Magazines in Need of Material—later known as Moskowitz's Manuscript Bureau. Moskowitz made a plea for all readers to send him their articles and stories; he would act as central distributor and guarantee that all contributions would be placed with some fan editor. Those who needed material were invited to apply for help. In this way he hoped that not only would existent writings be placed for rapid publication, but that more material could be coaxed from indifferent potential producers.

Editors needed no second invitation. With a swoop they descended upon the Manuscript Bureau. Moskowitz's hopes for incoming material were not realized, however, and situations of supply and demand frequently reached the point where Moskowitz was forced to sit down and grind out literally dozens of articles, using numerous pen names, in order to keep up with requests. As a result, he was jeered at by some as a "fan hack," but his efforts in behalf of others was selfless enough to gain for him from the fan editors, the keystones of the field, a reservoir of good will that later was to serve him well. Moreover, he was beginning to build for himself a following of readers that, partly or wholly, saw eye to eye with the philosophy of fandom and science fiction that his articles outlined.

Olon F. Wiggins, meanwhile, had been plodding along methodically with his *Science Fiction Fan*. Though recieving scarcely a word of encouragement and the barest modicum of contributions, he still adhered to a monthly schedule of appearance with determined stubbornness. When Morris Dollens had to give up illustrating the magazine Wiggins was in sore straits indeed. James Taurasi, who had been contributing crude back-cover illustrations was rushed in to fill the gap. Taurasi's art work was atrocious. The only saving graces it possessed were good underlying ideas and a superior layout —the latter quality traceable to ability acquired through his position as an architectural draftsman. Taurasi also was responsible for some science fiction scarcely superior to his art.

The Manuscript Bureau beckoned enticingly to Wiggins. There was only one hitch: Wiggins had refused to carry Moskowitz as a *Science Fiction Fan* subscriber because of the latter's inability to send in dollar subscriptions. But now he swallowed his pride and virtually begged for material, either from the bureau or from Moskowitz himself. To Moskowitz it would have been inexcusable to supply material to a fan magazine as yet unborn and at the same time refuse it to *The Science Fiction Fan,* which had proved its sincere desire to continue publication and had maintained a regular schedule despite almost insurmountable difficulties. And so, personalities having been put aside, Moskowitz sent Wiggins a contribution from the Manuscript Bureau.

This action amounted to a mutual rapprochement. To Wiggins it meant more than a regular supply of material: for other fans who had been antagonized by the dollar-or-nothing subscription policy he had instituted likewise began to forget their enmity and lend their aid. And finally Wiggins announced that he would issue his magazine weekly for a month in order to close the four-month gap between printed and hektographed issues that had occurred some time back. James and Mary Rogers were engaged as illustrators for the *Fan,* and all this improvement presaged the leading role that the magazine was to play in early 1938.

It should not be thought that all fandom was in the throes of turbulent mutation. The editors of the two leading printed periodicals in the field—*The Amateur Correspondent* and *The Science Fiction Critic*—were launching worthwhile publishing projects.

Corwin Stickney decided upon receipt of the news of lovecraft's death in 1937 that he would like to publish a lasting memorial to the man's greatness. This was a not unexpected gesture, for he was a great admirer of Lovecraft; and he had dedicated an issue of his *Correspondent* to the man, including his portrait by Finlay (a remarkable likeness despite the fact that Finlay had never seen his subject), Lovecraft's own "Notes on the Writing of Weird Fiction," and "The Sage of College Street," a personal appraisal by E. Hoffman Price. Now Stickney decided to issue a small brochure of Lovecraft's select poetry in a limited edition, distributing it free to new subscribers of *The Amateur Correspondent* and to regular ones sending in renewals. This brochure, printed on high quality paper and enclosed in a leatherette cover, was titled simply *H. P. L.* The Finlay portrait previously mentioned was used as a frontispiece. There was an introduction by Stickney himself and eight of Lovecraft's poems were included: "In a Sequestered Graveyard Where Once Poe Walked," "The Wood," "Homecoming," "Nostalgia," "Night Gaunts," "The Dweller," "Harbour Whistles" and "Astrophobos."

But there was a totally unexpected aftermath to this brochure. August W. Derleth had, shortly after Lovecraft's death, acquired rights to most of the latter's works. Stickney had no knowledge of this; and, since Lovecraft's kindness to fan editors had been strikingly evident by his numerous contributions to fan magazines, and since all of the above poems had been reprinted from these sources, Stickney had felt that he needed no more than the fan editors' permission to reprint them. (In point of fact he did not require even that: most fan magazines appearing in those days were not copyrighted, and consequently anything appearing in them automatically reverted to the domain of the free press. Since all of Lovecraft's poems in fan journals were printed with his permission, they too were in this category—as, indeed, they are today.) Derleth, in all probability, was not aware of these poems' prior publication. In any event, he promptly threatened to due Stickney for publishing Lovecraft's material without his permission. Nonplussed, Stickney explained that he could scarcely have had any ulterior motives for producing the brochure: only twenty-five copies had been prepared, and these had been distributed gratis; the whole action had been merely out of respect for a great author's memory. Derleth took no further action, but this incident left many fans who possessed material of Lovecraft, along with permission from him to publish it, wondering what their position was.

Such a one was John J. Weir, editor of *Fantasmagorta,* a little magazine emanating from Perth Amboy, New Jersey. Weir had given Stickney permission to reprint "Astrophobos" from his magazine, and had on hand for future appearance Lovecraft's poem, "The Tree." So infrequent was *Fantasmagorta's* schedule of publication, however, that *Weird Tales* beat him to printing of the work. (This writer will quietly sidestep the question of who—if anybody—is the legal owner of the copyright of this poem, leaving it for someone more versed in law than he to decide.) *Fantasmagorta,* it might be remarked, though at times poorly hektographed, contained in the space of its five issues much excellent material by H. P. Lovecraft, Robert Bloch, Henry Kuttner, Hazel Heald, William Lumley, Manly Wade Wellman, Emil Petaja, Robert W. Lowndes, Duane W. Rimel, Clark Ashton Smith, Bernard A. Dwyer, J. Harvey Haggard and others. Its illustrations by Baltadonis were exceptionally fine. But, like other literary publications in the field at this time, it enjoyed small success.

In addition to producing his *Science Fiction Critic,* Claire P. Beck had founded "The Futile Press" for publishing small books and pamphlets. The first of these was *Hammer and Tongs,* which reprinted a series of articles of the same title from the pages of earlier *Critics.* It was neatly printed, bound in boards and sold for twenty-five cents. Though very few copies were sold, its distribution, considering the emaciated aspect of the field, was fairly good. Beck followed this effort with *Nero and Other Poems* by Clark Ashton

Smith; this was identical in typography, binding and price with the first volume. In addition to ten poems it contained a long apprecia- tion of Smith and on separate sheets "The Outlanders," which Smith later sold to *Weird Tales*. The volume was, moreover, autographed by Smith. Later in 1938 the Futile Press issued Lovecraft's *Common Place Book,* which later appeared in the Arkham House volume *Beyond the Wall of Sleep*. It was a neat little volume produced in an edition limited to seventy-five copies; it sold for a dollar. Like Beck's other productions, it sold poorly.

Another high quality periodical of the time was *Supramundane Stories,* published by Canadian fan Nils H. Frome. Frome illustrated it by hand, and although he possessed no little artistic ability he showed a disquieting dislike for uniformity by illustrating every copy of the magazine differently. For the particular fan collector it would have been necessary to obtain every copy of the periodical in existence in order to own all variations. In his second number, however, Frome hektographed the illustrations. He also presented a selection of superior material, including Lovecraft's "Notes on the Writing of Weird Fiction," poems by Clark Ashton Smith, and other prose by J. Harvey Haggard, Duane W. Rimel, Lionel Dilbeck and others. The Lovecraft contribution was not challenged by Derleth; apparently, then, he had no intention of questioning prior per- mission of Lovecraft himself. (That he saw this particular number is probable, as it contained a news item he had submitted.) When *Supra- mundane Stories* collapsed "What the Moon Brings" by Lovecraft was sent by Frome to Taurasi, who published it in the widely-advertised third anniversary issue of his *Cosmic Tales,* again without provoking challenge from Derleth.

Thus we see that while fandom in late 1937 possessed little interest in the more literary amateur publications, a sufficient number of tough-minded editors were attempting—not with marked success—to buck the trend. Such titles as *The Science Fiction Critic, The Amateur Correspondent, Fantasmagoria* and *Supramundane Stories* showed this tendency, as did occasional experimental issues of others, such as *Helios*.

We have seen that both the Los Angeles SFL chapter and the Phila- delphia Science Fiction Society had survived the changes undergone by *Wonder Stories*. It has also been shown that in England this change actually resulted at first in additional SFL chapters. How had the fans of New York fared during this reorganization? The first attempt to produce a new group there was made by Frederik Pohl, who announced the new Brooklyn chapter. The doings of this group (com- posed of Pohl, Kubilius, Dockweiler and a host of Pohl's pen names) was erroneously reported at length in the SFL column of *Wonder Stories* (October, 1937): all these activities were figments of Pohl's imagination, as was *The Cosmic Call,* announced as a forth- coming publication. Apparently Pohl derived much amusement from this hoax. It was left to Taurasi to form the first serious SFL chapter. Prominent also in building up the group was Richard Wilson, who later succeeded in drawing new fan Jack Gillespie into the circle. Robert G. Thompson and Abraham Oshinsky were among those present at the first meeting in July, 1937. Though small in numbers, the Flushing SFL made up in enthusiasm what it lacked in experience. Older fans in the New York area, however, paid little attention to its meetings. A short time later the Washington Heights SFL was formed. This group is of interest only in that it contributed to active fandom two members: Chester Fein and Cyril Kornbluth.

Forming itself slightly previous to these last two groups was a Minneapolis SFL chapter under the leadership of Oliver E. Saari and Douglas Blakely. Prominent authors such as Donald Wandrei and Carl Jacobi attended meetings, but the geographical isolation of the group from other fans conspired to keep it from forming any strong link with others.

Chapter XXII

THE FANTASY AMATEUR PRESS ASSOCIATION

AS HAS BEEN NOTED, Donald A. Wollheim was the leading fan during the first six months of 1937. And when fandom felt its foundations swept away, naturally all looked to Wollheim for leadership. His first answer was that American fandom had failed, and that all should look to Britain. To those who still wished to publish Wollheim set the example by issuing a series of envelope-sized mimeographed leaflets which he nicknamed "mijimags." These carried such titles as *The Science Fiction Bard, The Mentator, Voice of the Gostak* and others. Some of these were the work of Pohl. Here, said Wollheim, was a cheap form of publishing—"magazines" which could be contributed free to correspondents.

But fans did not take to this idea. Some of them, viewing the large numbers of titles, imagined the field to be as flourishing as ever; they recognized no general collapse, but nevertheless could not help feeling the lack of integration in the field. Wishing to do something about it, they attempted to publish as before, but were met by the obstacles we have already noted and could not understand why conditions were not alleviated.

Then Wollheim, bowing to the desire of fandom to continue on its own, came forward with a second idea, not only much better than his first but of such surprising foresight as almost to fail because the youthful fans were not ready for it. For some time such fans as Wollheim, Shepard and Bloomer had been active in amateur press associations. Indeed, in the fall of 1936 Wollheim had actually discussed with Miller and Blish the possibilities of organizing such a group in the fan field; nothing came of it at that time, however. In mid-1937 he not only proposed the idea as a solution to fandom's problems, but began immediately to work on the material factors needed for its success. Through correspondence and personal contact he convinced such rising leaders of fandom as Baltadonis and Taurasi of the efficacy of his new idea. Then the leading fans of the time received a sample mailing from "The Fantasy Amateur Press Association." This mailing consisted of a number of fan magazines; outside of *Solar,* the work of Taurasi, all of them had been published by Wollheim and his friends.

Wollheim's article "Why the Fantasy Amateur Press Association?" in the first issue of *The FAPA Fan* was a masterpiece of simple, concise, patient explanation. He explained that there were about two dozen titles in the field at the time, appearing with great irregularity. The average circulation of a fan magazine was between twenty and thirty-five. Those surpassing that range were rare exceptions. Was a circulation this low worth the effort expended? The answer, contended Wollheim, was No. Obviously, then, the only gain was the publisher's personal satisfaction.

He told of the amateur press groups, whose members could publish at any intervals they wished magazines of any shape, size, form or description. The distribution of these publications was emphasized:

all members produced enough copies of their magazines to cover the entire membership. These were sent to a mailing manager, who mailed to members at stated intervals a copy of each magazine so contributed. In this way every editor and author could be certain that his work received the widest possible distribution. Wollheim emphasized the money, time and energy saved by eliminating separate postings of magazines by individual editors to subscribers. There were no deadlines to meet, no subscription lists to keep up by advertising, and so on; no fan need be obliged to continue printing a magazine he was no longer interested in because of outstanding subscriptions or any other reason. Concluded Wollheim:

> We limited FAPA to fifty members because hekto magazines cannot exceed that. We limit officers to one term because we do not want this organization to remain in the hands of any single person or group. We limit membership to active fans because we do not want any dead wood. All members must be willing and able to do their share to hold up the fan magazine standard. The number of eligibles exceeds fifty. We believe that we will reach our limit in short order.

Had the fans been a bit older, a bit more mature, they might have realized that here was at least a temporary salvation for them. Active fans then numbered less than fifty—the Fantasy Amateur Press Association could have included *every* fan of importance. Wollheim's statements anent the circulations of fan magazines were unquestionably true. Thus it might have been expected that fans would flock to the organization immediately, and enter into its activities with enthusiasm. But they did not.

Despite Wollheim's crystal-clear explanation the fans did not understand the FAPA. They did not understand it because nothing of comparable nature had ever entered the sphere of their interests before. The idea of giving fan magazines away was regarded as almost fantastic; "We lose money as it is!" they protested. Some, because of past fracases, distrusted Wollheim himself, mistakenly feeling that the organization belonged to him along just as a fan magazine belonged to its publisher. In vain Wollheim pointed to the democratic constitution, providing for annual elections, which had been sent out with the mailing. Fans didn't understand that either. There had been plenty of fraternity but little democracy in previous organizations. They remembered the ISA where one group was always ahead of another in its interpretations of the constitution.

Then why didn't the association fail? The answer to that is twofold: Firstly, as we have previously noted, fans of that day were fanatic collectors of their own publications; FAPA magazines could be obtained in only one way—by joining FAPA. And so many joined, probably feeling that for fifty cents they were striking a bargain. Secondly, Wollheim virtually begged fans to join. He campaigned continually with all of his plentiful energy. As a result, many fans "did him a favor" and joined. But most of the joiners soon became intrigued after a while, and wondered how they ever could have considered staying out. And still later many fans confined most or all of their activity to FAPA, thus contributing much to the progress and welfare of the group. But that is another story.

By December of 1937 the roster of the association included

Rosenblum, Wollheim, Michel, Carnell, Pohl, Kyle, Schwartz, Lowndes, McPhail, Speer, Osheroff, Thompson, Taurasi, Wilson, Wiggins, Baltadonis, Madle, Moskowitz, "Vodoso" (the name under which a Los Angeles group received mailings), Thomas Whiteside and H. C. Koenig. As yet probably no one dreamed that FAPA would amount to much more than a passing fad. For FAPA did not become science fiction fandom; it simply became another facet of the whole field. Fans continued to publish their own subscription magazines, and contributed worthless little sheets to FAPA. Fandom did not recognize a solution to its problems when it was offered; it continued to work out a salvation in the traditional, if fumbling, fashion.

Perhaps it is fortunate, in the long run, that the Fantasy Amateur Press Association did not achieve its aim of becoming fandom itself. For this would have doomed fans to a cramped and isolated sphere, an obscure unit which might well have stagnated and died for lack of new blood. As an integral part of fandom, however, it continued to remain virile throughout its life.

Chapter XXIII

THE THIRD CONVENTION AND MICHELISM

THE MEDIUM of fast news dispensation in 1937 was first class mail. And some of the most exciting news carried that year emanated from Philadelphia when with thrilling suddenness PSFS members began to tell their correspondents of the convention that the society was planning for that October. Rumors of possible cancellations ran rife, and it was not until a few days before the scheduled date that circulars announcing that it was to take place on October 31 were mailed out. These told interested fans to write Baltadonis for information (which there was simply insufficient time to do) and neglected even to name the meeting-hall. Optimistic out-of-towners simply headed Pennsylvaniaward, trusting to luck. Unquestionably poor handling such as this cut down attendance.

In the background, meanwhile, an event of great future significance had taken place. William Sykora, thought out of fandom forever, the man who had decried the science fiction fan as hopeless, had unexpectedly attended a meeting of Taurasi's Flushing SFL chapter and been voted into membership. At this same meeting it had been decided to change the name of the group to the Queens Science Fiction League.

Sykora left for Philadelphia on the evening of October 29. There was much speculation in the Wollheim camp when this, as well as Sykora's return to fandom, was learned. What were the significances of these moves? Did the man hope to swing the Philadelphia group into line with some scheme he had by utilizing his day's advantage in speaking to them? It was all quite mysterious.

All other fans in the New York area (save Mario Racic, Jr., who had taken an earlier train) departed for the convention on the morning of the 31st. They comprised Schwartz, Wollheim, Burg, Burford, Taurasi, Wilson, Pohl, Michel, Gillespie, Thompson, Dockweiler, Landberg, Kyle, Van Houten, Duncan and Moskowitz. On the train Moskowitz and Taurasi met for the first time, and a strong friendship developed between the two immediately, for both saw eye to eye on many points of fan interest. At Philadelphia the group was met by Sykora, Madle and Train, who were to act as their guides.

To add to the conventioneers' troubles, it became necessary at the last moment to find a suitable meeting-place. (It had originally been planned to hold the meeting in a spacious room in the rear of Baltadonis' father's tavern—but suddenly-remembered city ordinance forbidding this, new quarters had to be located.) While frantic efforts in this direction were under way, fans congregated at Baltadonis' home and began to fraternize with earlier arrivals. It should perhaps be emphasized at this point that fans in 1937 were not meeting in order to solve any problems that might be vexing the field. If these happened to be cleared up, well and good; but the prime reason for attending a convention was to meet and talk with other kindred personalities. Indeed, the very concept of a convention was at that time so unusual as to make the gathering together

of any group for the purpose of talking about science fiction an
eminently satisfactory end in itself.

Baltadonis had hektographed a special convention booklet for the
occasion, and the fashion in which fans began to solicit one
another's autographs like high school seniors was incredible. Madle
had managed to complete the first issue of the long-awaited *Fantascience Digest* for the occasion. His grandiose plans for having the
magazine professionally printed had at the last minute been dropped,
but the resulting hektographed publication was definitely above
average. Almost every fan had brought along some fan magazines of his
own to sell, and the bargainers were setting up shop everywhere.

But amid all the hilarity of talking, shouting, buying and selling
one sombre fact persisted. One fan drifted aimlessly through the
scattered groups, finding common ground nowhere. That fan was
William Sykora. If he had hoped to win the Philadelphia group over
to some plan of action (possibly the resurrection of the ISA) it was
obvious that he had failed. He searched the faces of those present
penetratingly, as if seeking allies, and seemed to find little
solace in what he read in them.

In one corner of the room Moskowitz had set up business with an
entire shoe-box full of fan magazines. Sykora edged forward,
examined a few, and proceeded to question the big, seventeen-year-
old Newark fan. In Moskowitz's replies there was none of the cold-
ness he had found elsewhere. Between sales Sykora engrossed
Moskowitz deeper and deeper into conversation. When the selling was
over, the conversation still continued. Moskowitz suggested that
Newark would be a better site for a convention than Philadelphia,
and Sykora was urging him to sponsor one, even offering to back the
event financially. By the time the conversation had been concluded
Moskowitz was considering this proposal half-seriously, and the
first link had been forged in a friendship that was to be of
paramount interest to fandom.

Milton A. Rothman, the chairman, finally opened the convention at
2:37 p.m. with a welcome to the attendees and the introduction of
secretary Baltadonis. (Conover, who was to have held this post, was
not present.) The minutes of the preceding convention were read, and
then Rothman plunged into his talk "Literature in Science Fiction."
He held that the future of science fiction rested upon fans'
recognizing that certain stories—such as McClary's *Rebirth*—contained all the essentials of good literature. He concluded with an
invitation to others to air their views on the subject.

The guest of honor was R. V. Happel, associate editor of
Astounding Stories magazine; he was the most important professional
present, and most fans were doing their utmost to give as good an
impression of themselves (and therefore of fandom as a whole) as
possible. Happel spiked rumors to the effect that *Astounding* was
losing circulation. Indeed, he revealed that it had been the only
one in the Street and Smith chain to show a gain in 1937. He spoke
of the new editor John W. Campbell, Jr., and of his intention to
maintain and better standards set by the previous editor, F. Orlin
Tremaine. Campbell had written a talk for the occasion, and this was
read by proxy.

Julius Schwartz of *Fantasy Magazine* fame was next introduced. He
electrified the gathering by announcing that *Thrilling Wonder*

Stories would soon be joined by a companion science fiction magazine, possibly a quarterly.

Then drama was enacted. The next scheduled speaker was John B. Michel. When Michel was called upon, Wollheim arose in his place and asked that he be allowed to present the speech, since Michel suffered from an impediment of speech which made public speaking difficult. No objection was raised. It was obvious from Wollheim's manner that something unusual was afoot. There was an almost defiant tone to his voice as he began to read. Before he had gone very far fans were startled to hear:

> The Science Fiction Age, as we have known it during the past few years is over. Definitely over and done with. Dead, gentlemen, of intellectual bankruptcy.

How often was that phrase to ring out, again and again!

> In a few words let me put forth my opinion on what we are doing. My opinion is that we are baloney bending, throwing the bull, indulging in dull flights of fancy, tossing barrels of rhodomontade all over the place.

That, too, was to be heard many times more. How is your rhodomontade today? The older opinion of Wollheim that science fiction had got nowhere, that it was in a hopeless rut, that it had neither aim nor purpose was repeated. Those present were told that although they possessed imagination and ability superior to that of the average man they were satisfied to do little with it. Simply discussing science fiction was a senseless routine. Science fiction must have a purpose. Science fiction must help lift humanity from the morass of stupidity in which it had become imbedded.

As the speech progressed many of the younger fans lapsed into a mental coma because of their inability to make head or tail out of it. To some it seemed that an unwarranted amount of abuse was being flung at their hobby and indirectly at themselves—but this they felt must be endured because Wollheim was an important fan and crossing him might mean personal extinction as far as science fiction fandom was concerned. But the older fans present strained for the meaning and implication of every word. They knew the talk was leading up to something. But what? Finally the revelation came—

> And how sick we are at the base of this dull, unsatisfying world, this stupid, asininely organized system of ours which demands that a man brutalize and cynicize himself for the possession of a few dollars in a savage, barbarous, and utterly boring struggle to exist.

Communism!

In 1937 the press of America had made "communist" and "red" things to be feared even above Fascism. These were the labels all too frequently applied to liberals who wished to better their status, who asked for the right to live like respectable human beings without having their spirits broken on the yoke of WPA, CCC and "relief." Despite this, there were those present intelligent enough to realize that because a man had ideas of a leftist nature he was not automatically a fiend. But that was not the issue. To most attendees reading and discussing science fiction was merely a hobby, a

diversion. They felt that if organizations for world-betterment were
to be formed, they should be formed separately, outside of science
fiction. And they probably had less respect for Michel and Wollheim
for attempting to disguise cleverly their injection of communistic
ideas into fandom than they would have had for open admission,
advocation and recruiting for the party. And thus the true issue was
not what ideology the majority favored, but rather simply "should
there be politics in science fiction?"

Michel's speech ended in this fashion:

> Therefore: Be it moved that this, the Third Eastern Science
> Fiction Convention, shall place itself on record as opposing
> all forces leading to barbarism, the advancement of pseudo-
> sciences and militaristic ideologies, and shall further
> resolve that science fiction should by nature stand for all
> forces working for a more unified world, a more Utopian
> existence, the application of science to human happiness, and
> a saner outlook on life.

Such a Utopian resolution seemed harmless enough, being worded in
such a way as to make it difficult to reject. But when discussion
was called for plenty of it was to be had. The author Lloyd A.
Eshbach was vehemently against what he plainly called "The
introduction of politics into science fiction." William Perlman, a
Baltimore fan considerably older than most of those present,
attempted to moderate extreme views by saying that although the
ideas expressed in the talk (which was later printed under the title
Mutation or Death) were "wonderfully and idealistically expressed,
the world was not yet ready for such action." Wollheim and some of
his friends of course supported the speech on all points. Finally,
Sykora entered into the discussion and managed to sidetrack the
issue, so that controversy was soon centered on "the advisability of
a world state." And there it remained permanently mired.

It has been stated by other writers that elaborate plans had been
laid by Wollheim and Michel to insure acceptance of this resolution.
This has been stated because Wollheim's inner circle of friends—
which included Pohl, Kyle, Dockweiler and others—was supposed to
have voted *en masse* for the resolution on previous instruction.
Opinion has also been expressed that the speech actually was written
by Wollheim and accredited to Michel as a matter of strategy. Your
historian does not agree with either of these views. The style of
Mutation or Death is definitely Michel's. It is the fiery, awake-
the-future-is-upon-us type of style that he has utilized on so many
other occasions. The idea of "Michelism" (as the movement embodying
these ideas later came to be known) is also Michel's for he was the
first to express such ideas (cf. his article "Look to the Stars!" in
a late 1936 *International Observer*). Wollheim has admitted being
indoctrinated by Michel's ideas, besides. And Michel is known to
have been the first of the clique to join the Young Communist
League. Generally, Michel's influence has been sadly underrated,
mainly because he let his friends do the bulk of the talking and the
writing.

Scarcely noted was the fact that Kyle, one of the Wollheim inner
circle, harangued at great length *against* the Michel speech.
Dockweiler and Pohl may, peculiarly enough, never have voted on the

resolution at all, since both were inebriated during the proceedings and out of the room much of the time. Ignored by fan writers also was the fact that although the Michelistic resolution was defeated by a vote of twelve to eight (with many taking neither side), both Moskowitz and Taurasi voted for it! This was not an acceptance or an understanding of its ideas on their part. They were among the younger fans bored by the talk and scarcely understanding or caring what motion was on the floor. Probably others present voted with a similar lack of knowledge.

In later written reviews of the convention Wollheim asserted that for the only concrete proposal for the betterment of science fiction advanced there to be voted down to thoughtlessly was a stinging slap in the face for all fans. But if it was thought that this defeat disposed of Michelism, that belief was wrong indeed.

Chapter XXIV

THE AFTERMATH

IT WAS A STRANGE paradox that a convention that took place for sheer exhiliration should have been followed by a singular resurgence of life in the turgid mass of the field. It was all the more unusual when one recalls that all conferences and conventions have been notorious for the sorry slump in activity that followed in their wakes. Perhaps all that fandom needed in late 1937 was an assurance that genuine interest still endured, that all had not been swept away with the old order.

Cosmic Tales, The Science Fiction Collector, Fantasmagoria, The Science Fiction Fan, Heltos, The Science Fiction Critic, The Amateur Correspondent —all of these continued to appear, consistently enlarging, consistently improving in content and interest. These publications comprised the very backbone of the field. If they were not printed they were hektographed—for the hektographing era was now in full flower. The consequent flavor and atmosphere of the field was intriguing. The personality of this new fandom was well defined.

Fantascience Digest and the *PSFS News* continued to appear from Philadelphia. The Fantasy Amateur Press Association was growing steadily to a point where president Wollheim asked for a discontinuance of sample mailings. From the Queens SFL chapter now came its official organ, *Jeddara.*

To the latter club Moskowitz paid a visit when such intercity travelling was still infrequent. At this meeting he renewed acquaintanceship with Sykora, who again broached the matter of a Newark convention. Moskowitz asked him point-blank precisely how much capital he was willing to risk on such an affair. "One hundred dollars," replied Sykora, and offered to put the pledge in writing. "It's a deal," said Moskowitz; and there remained little question now that a major science fiction event was now in the offing for 1938. That the convention, when finally held, didn't cost anything near that figure is irrelevant. If Sykora had not agreed to advance a sizeable sum for its presentation, if he had not virtually called Moskowitz's bluff and pushed him to the brink, the convention might never have materialized. For it was an undeniable fact that Moskowitz was endowed with a degree of conservatism all out of proportion with his youth. In order to move him to long-term action it was necessary to convince him of the soundness of every part of the proposed plan. Once convinced that he was setting out on the right road, the zeal with which he pursued his object gave the erroneous impression of impulsive, inspired action. Actually the stubbornness with which he sometimes resisted progressive plans was enough to drive his friends to tears.

At this time two events of great importance occurred. The first of these was the appearance of what this writer recognized as the first true weekly fan journal devoted to the dissemination of news. It was titled *The Science Fiction News-Letter,* and was the work of Richard

Wilson, former editor of *The Atom* and *Jeddara,* and one of the brighter lights among the younger fans. This publication proved to be a banner achievement in his career. Its first issue was dated December 4, 1937, and though fans at first grumbled over paying five cents a copy for a single-sheeted journal, the value of a regularly-appearing weekly devoted exclusively to news soon became self-apparent. No one realized it them, but this news weekly began a slow but sure reduction in the volume of correspondence among fans. Of what use was it to write voluminous letters to a dozen fan editors when the *News-Letter* provided all the up-to-the-minute information about these notables in cheaper, less time-consuming and better integrated form? The day of bragging about one's two dozen correspondents was gone forever.

The second important event was the distribution of *Imagination!,* which was a poorly hektographed, twenty-paged journal replete with "streamlined" English, Esperanto, atrocious puns and no end of enthusiasm. This magazine is not important because it was the forerunner of the long-lived *Voice of the Imagi-Nation.* The true significance of *Imagination!* lay in the fact that it marked the entrance of the Los Angeles SFL chapter into the main stream of fandom. Through this publication, edited by T. Bruce Yerke and Forrest Ackerman, the world's largest fan club gave notice that it was now a factor to be reckoned with. No longer would it remain aloof, disdaining to do more than subscribe to a few fan journals. It was signalling its desire to mix with the Taurasis, Wollheims, Baltadonises, Wilsons and Moskowitzes that made up the vigorously growing fan world of early 1938. It meant that the field was again on a solid basis of near-unity, and that its appearance would henceforth attract new fans rather than repel them.

As 1937 drew to a close, a formerly quiescent fan of unusual ideas and abilities began to project himself more and more into public attention. This fan was Jack Speer, former member of the Oklahoma Scientifiction Association and collector extraordinary of fantasy comic strips. Speer at first contented himself with producing articles about the collecting trend and about the appearance of a new school of fan writers headed by Lowndes and Moskowitz, which was presenting in its essays a pattern of fan philosophy. He modestly neglected to state that he himself was a leader in this field of fan analysis.

Inspired by the Gallup Poll, Speer founded what he termed The Oklahoma Institute of Private Opinion (usually referred to as the IPO), which was to find out general fan opinion on a number of subjects. Speer was initially interested in the average fan age (which turned out to be in the neighborhood of eighteen), but added other topics as the polls progressed. Ballots for these were mailed out with Wiggins' *Science Fiction Fan,* and were usually forty in number. Results of these polls were published in that magazine, and showed, among other things, that fans were against a national federation (by almost two to one); that Wollheim was by far the "top" fan; and that *The Science Fiction Fan* was the most popular fan journal.

This last was due not only to Wiggins' magazine being the one in which the polls were conducted, but also to its generally high quality. Such features as the IPO, Wollheim's "Fanfarade" column, the improved art work and the regular supply of articles both from the Moskowitz Manuscript Bureau and from unsolicited sources placed it high in fan esteem.

Initial returns in the poll for the "top" fan showed Moskowitz in second place, well behind Wollheim, and Baltadonis in third. Later votes completely altered this picture, sliding Moskowitz to fifth place, elevating Ackerman to the runner-up spot and giving Wiggins the fourth position, Baltadonis remaining in third. But between the publication of early and complete returns a month intervened. This is mentioned because it was a period in which Moskowitz was psychologically regarded as the country's number two fan, and this was important in shaping his mental attitude during his feud with Wollheim.

For those who may be interested, complete files of the IPO polls may be found in 1938 issues of *The Science Fiction Fan;* in a special FAPA publication later issued by Wiggins; and in the May, 1944, number of *Fantasy Times*.

Wollheim was responsible for initiating yet another topic of fan interest in 1937. In the November-December issue of *Cosmic Tales,* in his column "Phantaflexion," he brought out a sharp attack against religion and fans who accepted it. (This was later reprinted in the first number of *The Science Fiction Advance* as "Science Fiction and Religion.") The next issue of *Cosmic Tales* contained an indignant reply from Chester Fein of the Washington Heights SFL chapter. Subsequently Wollheim answered this reply, quoting among other things figures compiled by H. P. Lovecraft on the subject which gave overwhelming support to the materialists. Somewhat surprisingly, the topic never became a bitter issue, and with the exception of one item that will shortly be mentioned was confined almost completely to *Cosmic Tales*. This was probably due to the fact that little opposition to the materialists was brought up, most fans either possessing already such an outlook themselves, or, lacking it, believing that religion was scarcely a subject that could be resolved satisfactorily by objective debate. McPhail as well as Fein broke with Wollheim on the matter, however, and it seems likely that later anti-Wollheim blocs were contributed to by others who still adhered to the religious principles taught them in their youth.

The one item mentioned in the paragraph above was "Anent Atheism and Stf.," an article published in the March, 1938, number of *Imagination!*. This bore the byline of "Erick Freyer" (a pseudonym of the California fan Frederick Shroyer), and in expressive style suggested that fans read science fiction because they already were either agnostics or atheists. Shroyer felt that they were not true escapists, however, because they "realized" what they were doing when they lost themselves in fantastic literature. Religious adherents were labelled the worst type of escapists, since they believed what Shroyer termed the "mumbo-jumbo of the latter day witch-doctors."

One other event of importance should be mentioned here, an event whose genesis takes us back to a few weeks before the Philadelphia convention. At that time Roy A. Squires, who, it will be remembered, had assumed directorship of the Science Fiction Advancement Association upon the retirement of its former head, C. Hamilton Bloomer, turned the SFAA over to Raymond Van Houten, as he himself had been unable to accomplish anything after some months of trial. Van Houten had been a staunch supporter of the organization since its inception, had contributed liberally to the pages of its official organ *Tesseract,* and appeared from his published work to be a fan of better than average abilities. His cross was lack of funds and a previous aloofness from most of the fan field outside of the SFAA which left him with no circle of active friends on whom he could rely for aid. His sole helper was a fellow Paterson, New Jerseyite named Peter Duncan, whose vituperative articles in *The Science Fiction Critic* had earned for him the not necessarily complimentary appelation of "the Poison Pen of Paterson."

When Van Houten took over the SFAA it still had 78 members, but not all of them were subscribers to *Tesseract.* (This contradictory state of affairs was due to the fact that membership in the organization did not include distribution of its official organ, which was obtained separately.) Under Bloomer's ministrations *Tesseract* had evolved into a neatly mimeographed magazine of high quality. But Van Houten, with disadvantages already mentioned and a hektograph run by inexperienced hands, produced issues of the magazine that compared sadly with the older ones. Its contents were still interesting and readable, but the typography could scarcely be expected to elicit enthusiasm. The lack of responce that resulted was not surprising, and was reflected at first in Van Houten's ever more caustic editorial remarks. In a more positive effort to revive lagging interest, he then began printing a series of Duncan's articles, some under the latter's own name and some under the pseudonym of "Loki." He also carried on a one-man campaign to induce John W. Campbell, Jr., to publish a companion quarterly with *Astounding Stories*—which, incidentally, was unsuccessful. But by March, 1938, when four numbers had not awakened fan interest in *Tesseract,* Van Houten realized he could no longer carry on.

He then approached Moskowitz and urged him at least to aid the SFAA on a cooperative basis, if not take it over entirely. "You," he said, "have a large following in the field, many friends who would help you; large numbers of fans like what you write. With you behind it, the club could 'go places'." Moskowitz ridiculed the notion of having a fan following and declined.

But Van Houten had obtained a more accurate perspective of Moskowitz's position in the field at that time than Moskowitz himself realized. Van Houten was well aware that in his manuscript bureau Moskowitz possessed a weapon for political maneuvering unequalled elsewhere in the field. Desperate fan editors would certainly think twice before antagonizing their bread and butter. And so, while the resurrection of the SFAA scarcely affected the course of fandom at all, its availability to Moskowitz on request was to become a vital factor, as will later be shown.

Chapter XXV

THE WOLLHEIM-MOSKOWITZ FEUD

DESPITE ALL DISRUPTING forces, fandom was slowly progressing,
holding fast to its gains as it achieved them. Let us examine the
panorama of the 1938 fan field spread before us. There is a weekly
newspaper, an amateur press group, a manuscript bureau. There are
several regular monthly fan magazines and a half dozen regular
bimonthly periodicals. A national convention is being planned. Two
large SFL chapters hold meetings at opposite ends of the country.
Hitherto lethargic groups have been stirred into activity. The field
is vital, alive, progressing; and then—conflict. Not merely a petty
argument or heated debate, but a destructive feud that ran rampant
and left shattered plans, broken friendships and dead inertia in its
wake.

We have read of the Philadelphia convention and its introduction
of Michelism. Accounts of this convention were written by various
fans, among them Sykora, Wollheim and Moskowitz. Sykora's account,
while it gave excellent coverage to the affair, naturally did not go
out of its way to shower bouquets on the Michel-Wollheim speech.
Wollheim's account covered the convention poorly, three-quarters of
its bulk being quotations from or comments on the "Mutation or
Death" talk. Moskowitz's account, titled "Convention Happenings,"
was published in the January 14, 1938, issue of *The Science Fiction
Fan* under the pseudonym of William M. Weiner. (Moskowitz had
employed a nom de plume in order to facilitate writing of his own
actions as well as others'.) "Convention Happenings" had this to say
of the "Mutation or Death" speech:

> Then the bombshell of the evening was perpetrated by Donald
> A. Wollheim who expressed some very good arguments as written
> by John B. Michel but degenerated these arguments into a
> political issue. For over an hour pros and cons were rung on
> the subject by D. A. Kyle, J. Perlman, J. B. Michel, D. A.
> Wollheim and L. Burg who were apparently talking about the
> possibilities of a world state. Mr. Eshbach squelched the
> discussion very effectively by proposing that a motion be
> made that the convention be adjourned. He came, he said, to
> listen to a science-fiction discussion and not a pseudo-
> political argument. The motion was carried and the meeting
> was called to an end.

This account was referred to by *News-Letter* editor, Richard Wilson
as "the first unbiased views of the Third Eastern Science Fiction
Convention."

But Wollheim, in the next (January 21, 1938) issue of *The Science
Fiction Fan,* dubbed it "the most inaccurate piece of reporting" he
had ever seen:

> There was not a single paragraph without at least one error,
> and I may add few sentences likewise. The most outrageous
> misreporting was the remarks about the final part of the con-
> vention which is almost 100% wrong. But without essaying the

arduous task of pointing out all the errors, I will merely
sum up by saying that the Weiner-Moskowitz account is final
and conclusive proof of the utter stupidity of a large
portion of the so-called fans. The speech made by Michel hit
deep into those shallow fans, which is probably why they
refrain from giving any account of the actual issues of
Michel's speech. ...The account given by Moskowitz which
ignores all the intellectual aspects of the convention for
the purely inane and frivolous, gives perfect proof.

Back in Newark Moskowitz was in a quandary on reading these words.
His "Convention Happenings" had been written in naive sincerity. He
had had no axe to grind. Michel's statements had not "hit deep" into
him—rather, he had been interminably bored. He had told the truth
as he saw it, with no intention of antagonizing Wollheim or anyone
else. He was aware of Wollheim's tendency to go to extremes even in
supposedly mild critical articles. And, knowing his critic's past
record of successful feuds, he had no particular desire to become
embroiled with Wollheim. But—what did others think? In Moskowitz's
mind the situation boiled down to this factor: Had fans reached the
point where they too regarded Wollheim's attacks as meaningless out-
bursts of temper, or would lack of reply to this new assault cause
him to lose face in their eyes?

Louis Kuslan of Connecticut answered the question when in a letter
to Moskowitz he asked, "What are you going to do about Wollheim's
attack in the last *Fan?*" This was the convincer. If Kuslan, at that
time a very neutrally inclined fan, felt that action should be
taken, then the entire fan field probably felt the same way.

In supplying additional motive for Moskowitz's decision to feud
with this opponent, one must take into consideration his admitted
initial dislike for the man, the earlier argument over the Conover-
Stickney dispute, and, even more important, a visit by Wollheim,
Pohl and Michel to the Moskowitz home shortly before the convention.
At this meeting Wollheim stated that he was able, by the proper
application of psychology, to "drive any fan from the field." He
alluded with satisfaction to the George Gordon Clark incident. When
Moskowitz attempted to change the subject it was reiterated with an
emphasis that he took to mean "You'd better be a good little fan—or
else!" And Moskowitz then and there determined that he would never
be thus driven from the field. Lastly, in one of his "Fanfarade"
columns, Wollheim had written that Moskowitz had ambitions of
becoming a "fan hack," and that "four out of five" of the articles
he wrote were rejected. Here he touched a point of extreme
sensitivity, for Moskowitz was extremely proud of his writings,
written as they were sheerly as a labor of love, and given to fan
editors in urgent need of material. The falseness of this attack was
unforgiveable.

Wollheim probably did not expect much of a reply from Moskowitz.
And if he did not, he was doubtless unprepared for the "Reply to
Donald A. Wollheim," which appeared in the February, 1938, *Science
Fiction Fan:*

"Convention Happenings" was elaborately checked after
Wollheim saw fit to devote an entire page to slamming it.
Errors were found—two or three. The major one consisted of
stating that Pohl and Dockweiler accompanied Wollheim to a
nearby automat: Correction—Wollheim proceeded to the automat

...and Pohl and Dockweiler went to the home of Baltadonis.
...The other errors consisted of the heinous crime of
exaggerating a point or two for the sake of humor.

Wollheim's "Fanfarade" has since its inception been
notorious for inaccurate statements and general falsity. To
name all such would be an exhausting task, but the writer is
concerned with one involving himself. In the October, 1937,
issue of the *Fan,* Wollheim stated as an unalterable fact that
Sam Moskowitz gets four out of five articles rejected. I
challenge him to produce even one proof of this statement
with the signature of the editor. It goes without saying that
he cannot.

Fandom was rocked by this unexpected resistance, and the unexpected occurred: opinion rallied to Moskowitz's side. Not unexpectedly,
Wollheim's cutting comments and sharp criticisms in the past had
stored up for him much resentment. Speer spurred Moskowitz on with
the comment that his reply to Wollheim had been "well taken." And
typical of the attitude among the younger clique of fans in which
Moskowitz had become prominent was that of Robert A. Madle, who
remarked in a letter: "Three cheers for Sam Moskowitz! He has really
started the ball rolling—and I'm quite sure some fans are going to
side with him. He has the sympathy of the Philadelphia fans I know.
DAW says what he pleases in his columns, and many of the readers
think he is telling the truth."

Still, it was some time before the moral support of his friends
was transposed into action. And in the meantime Moskowitz desperately
matched blows with a more experienced opponent. To the casual
onlooker the odds seemed greatly in Wollheim's favor. He was six
years older than Moskowitz. He had a better education and financial
background. He was the victorious veteran of a number of fan feuds.
He had a loyal circle of friends willing to follow his lead. And he
was the top fan of the field.

Some time previously Moskowitz had initiated in *The Science
Fiction Fan* a regular feature titled "As Others See Us." In this
column, under the pseudonym of Fred Wollonover, he gave humorous
resumes of other fans' characteristics. The subject of one of these
write-ups was Frederik Pohl. Moskowitz alluded to Pohl's use of many
pen-names; his habit of signing other fans' names in autograph
books; his alleged inebriety; and so on. Wollheim, upon seeing these
things, promptly mailed a protest to Wiggins, demanding that the
real name of the "culprit" writing "As Others See Us" be revealed,
and saying further that

> There are a number of very juvenile irresponsibilities
> infesting science-fiction these months, who know nothing of
> the tradition of stf. nor of the ethics of writing and
> publishing. Their childish and wild antics are becoming a
> constant nuisance, and you as an editor will do well to keep
> an eye on them.

The dual nature of Wollheim's attack now led Moskowitz to believe
that plans had been laid to drive him out of fandom. He felt,
perhaps erroneously, that Wollheim was worried about his rising
popularity. So when Wiggins forwarded to him a letter from Pohl
expressing Pohl's suspicions that Moskowitz was Wollonover and
threatening to sue Wiggins for libel, he felt that it would

strengthen his position to have some one else revealed as the author
of "As Others See Us." Alex Osheroff agreed to accept the "blame."
And in a coached reply to critics he expressed amazement that
Wollheim and Pohl should object to a column that was intended merely
to provide a little "light entertainment for fans." He pointed out
that Pohl was the only subject to take offense. He reminded his
critics that Wollheim's past statements in *Arcturus,* under the
Willy-the-Wisp byline, had been far more malicious than anything in
"As Others See Us," and that Wollheim had not revealed his identity
until more than a year after he had dropped the column. In answer to
Pohl's threatened suit he said, "I will not retract one statement
that I have made!" (And Pohl, as might be guessed, never made good
his threatened legal action.)

The fans in general, it might be noted, were enthusiastic over the
"As Others See Us" column, and Pohl was generally regarded as a
"sore-head." Speer, Gillespie, Kuslan, Taurasi and Madle were among
those who went on record as favoring it and denouncing its critics.

At this point Wiggins informed Moskowitz that both Wollheim and
Lowndes had sent him long rebuttals of the "Reply to Wollheim."
Moskowitz was startled to learn that Lowndes also had taken up the
cudgel against him since he had had virtually no association with
the man save the *Science Fiction Critic* episode already mentioned
(Chapter XX). He realized that his opposition was rallying and that,
given a little time, he might well be smothered by its very volume.
So he induced Wiggins to drop the feud in the *Fan* (although it was
tremendously interesting to readers), hoping that Wollheim would
find difficulty carrying on outside its pages. And when the
editorial of the March, 1938, issue carried the statement "Inasmuch
as it seems to be the combined opinions of all fan readers that this
magazine should not become the arena for fan squabblings, no more of
the Moskowitz-DAW-Pohl affair will be run" it meant that in his
series of exchanges with Wollheim Moskowitz had taken the first
round.

But this small victory was short-lived, for Wollheim, veteran
campaigner that he was, mimeographed a four-paged rebuttal himself,
and mailed copies of it to Wiggins to be distributed with the *Fan.*
Technically the material was not "in" the magazine, and Wiggins
could supply eager readers with sidelights on the latest "feudings"
without breaking his promise to Moskowitz. It was stretching
principles a bit, but it worked.

In this "In Answer to Sam Moskowitz" Wollheim swung into the style
that had crushed opponent after opponent in the past. He termed
Moskowitz's reply "a thoroughly vicious article," and denied
provoking cause for another "hymn of hate" campaign, saying:

> It is true that, along with many of the most progressive
> and intelligent fans, I have joined in an effort to raise
> science-fiction from being merely a childish puerile hobby to
> being an active force towards the realization of those things
> that science-fiction has always believed. In the course of
> this work it becomes necessary to expose such juvenility and
> puerility as raises its head. Since Mr. Moskowitz is one of
> the foremost advocates of childishness in the field today, he
> was one of the first to get his little tootsies tread on....

Wollheim then went on to list those portions of "Convention

Happenings" which he considered false and misleading. This took up the bulk of the leaflet. He revealed that the erroneous information concerning fan magazine rejections had been given him by William H. Miller. The original attack on "the utter stupidity of a large portion of the so-called fans" was repeated. Moskowitz was accused of mud-slinging to evade the issue, and of being a "contemptible scoundrel" for writing the "As Others See Us" column under a pseudonym. Wollheim then went out of his way to drag poor, oft-maligned Will Sykora into the argument (on the excuse that Moskowitz had praised him in one of his columns), and spent a long paragraph rehashing the ISA fiasco. (This, of course, was in line with his tendency to harry a defeated foeman.) He concluded with this flattering play for popular support:

> I wish to again warn all intelligent and understanding fans, those who really think that science-fiction can be a force which will help the world, even a little bit, toward a brighter future, against those shallow minded adolescents who dabble in "fan activities" and find it a source of self-glorification. If science-fiction is ever to become such a force, these pseudo-fans must be kept down.

Probably Wollheim and his followers now felt that Moskowitz was completely squelched. The opinion of fans at large, however, was somewhat different. For when Wollheim attacked "shallow minded adolescents" and "pseudo-fans who must be kept down" he was attacking every one of them as surely as he was attacking Moskowitz, for the rank and file was little better or worse than he with respect to methods, motives or activities in the field. And Moskowitz's philosophy of fandom seemed to appeal to them more strongly than did politically-based Michelism. The average fan preferred to remain "intellectually bankrupt" and enjoy fandom about him rather than set off on a quixotic crusade, however inspiring the visions of its goal might be. Thus when Moskowitz prepared a second reply (entitled "Ho-Hum, or the Further Enlightenment of Wollheim") it was evident that he would not wilt under a barrage of words, and material support for his stand was not long in appearing.

In this second reply he inquired why Wollheim bothered to associate with "us chillun." "Why not desert this field 'dead of intellectual bankruptcy' for fields of greater and finer intellect?" He contended that Wollheim had never benefited the field up to that time (which was somewhat exaggerated), but had been a destructive influence in driving many members from it (which was not). One by one he dealt with the "errors" Wollheim had pointed out in "Convention Happenings," and refused to concede a single one, referring interested parties to eye-witnesses for support. Most of the points involved were indeed trivial, and it became clear that Moskowitz's regarding them as excuses for an attack against him was by no means illogical.

> My account of the speech was given as I saw it. That is most certainly my right and obviously the reason for Wollheim's attack. What does DAW expect me to do, make a good lively account of a convention dead and uninteresting by reprinting a communistic speech that some way found itself away from its Astor Park soap box? Michel makes no bones over the fact that he is a communist, and his speech was without a trace of a doubt an attempt to get new converts.

The end of the second round saw neither opponent decisively beaten, but what started as a feud was beginning to shape into a veritable fan war, with fans rapidly choosing sides and priming for the encounters that it could be seen were soon to take place. More, the tide of battle was shifting gradually from an attack on Wollheim to one on Michelism, from the time of the convention the basic cause of all the squabbling. And in his attampt to chastise Moskowitz for his disregard for Michelism, Wollheim was creating the nucleus of an active resistance against the movement, where little had originally existed.

Wollheim's next move was in a totally different quarter. In his FAPA publication *The FAPA Fan* he printed an article titled "Manuscript Bureau." Here he urged members to recognize the necessity of a centralized manuscript bureau in the association, citing other amateur journalistic groups where such bureaus had proved of genuine worth. Now, the nearest thing to this that had so far appeared in fandom was the Moskowitz Manuscript Bureau. This, however, functioned only with respect to subscription (non-FAPA) journals, and its stock — in a time when such submissions were at a premium — could scarcely be stretched to cover fan periodicals in FAPA as well as out. And if it were diverted to FAPA exclusively Moskowitz would lose the "pull" he had gained from the editors that he was already supplying. Wollheim, of course, knew these facts. He then announced in his article that Moskowitz, the only one in fandom with experience along such lines, was the logical choice to head such a FAPA bureau. He further inferred that Moskowitz would be double-crossing his friends should he refuse the post. Moskowitz realized immediately that he had been put in a position where, regardless of his decision, he would surely displease some group of fans.

His reply was to circulate in FAPA an open letter, in which he agreed to accept the post if offered him, but only upon acceptance of three conditions:

> 1.) That I am not made the object of further slander in FAPA mailings.
> 2.) That the FAPA members are willing to cooperate by sending in material.
> 3.) That I may keep my independant organization functioning.

(The first condition was engendered by Wollheim's having circulated "In Answer to Sam Moskowitz" in the previous mailing.) It seemed a reasonable set of conditions, asking as it did that FAPA members cooperate for their own best interests and that he be allowed to continue aiding independant publications as usual. In addition, Moskowitz promised to help the bureau by writing material himself. He also wrote a letter to Wollheim, stating his suspicions openly of the latter's actions in the matter.

Wollheim sent abbreviated quotations from this letter, a defense of the accusations, and a copy of the open letter to Daniel McPhail, the vice — president of FAPA, requesting that he exercise his constitutional powers and rule thereon. McPhail, without contacting Moskowitz for further information, rendered a verdict against him on every point brought up by Wollheim. He even decided that "the existence of two bureaus run by the same person would be mutually destructive and otherwise irrational," and that his "careful search

...of the three mailings to date fail to reveal any slander against Mr. Moskowitz's name." By this short-sighted procedure McPhail settled none of FAPA's problems and effectively cancelled its last hope of possessing a manuscript bureau. This round was quite definitely Wollheim's.

When Lowndes learned of Wiggins' intention to soft-pedal the feud in *The Science Fiction Fan* he too published a rebuttal he had sent himself. Moskowitz's original reply to Wollheim had been four paragraphs in length, taking up less than half a typewritten page. Wollheim had found it necessary to use four pages to reply to it. Lowndes needed eight. In fact, he devoted the entire issue of his magazine *The Vagrant* to the fight. Indeed, so much material in two FAPA mailings was devoted to the feud that the fan Walter E. Marconette brought out *The Protestant,* a small sheet that begged for a sane ending to the squabble. Lowndes attempted an extremely pseudo-impartial-intellectual approach. How impartial it was may be judged from such statements as this: "...despite the fact that Moskowitz's accusations are *all* beside the point we must examine them...." In summation, Lowndes offered two alternatives. Either Moskowitz suffered from "mental poverty," or he was "a mental pervert, a literary whore, or, what is worse, a would-be literary prostitute." He hoped for Moskowitz's own sake, he said, that it was the former. It is amusing to recall now how, with lines such as these to their credit, Michelists in later quitting the argument deplored the fans' "inability" to meet them "on intellectual grounds."

Jack Gillespie, who had fallen in with the Michelist crowd, contributed to the feud *Just Things;* the only original remark in this leaflet, which was printed upon different-sized pieces of yellow second-sheets, was a query as to how Moskowitz "ever got the idea that Michel's was a Communistic speech."

The variety of anti-Moskowitz material emanating from Wollheim's circle of friends prompted Moskowitz to coin the nickname "Wollheim's stooges" for them. This nickname stuck—probably because fans began to believe that there was no other explanation for entrance into the fray on Wollheim's side of people who had previously held no enmity against Moskowitz.

The abrupt entrance into the feud on Moskowitz's side of Jack Speer came as a surprise to both contestants. And Speer was a potent ally indeed, for he was strong on every point where Moskowitz was weak. This was especially noticeable in the matter of written statements; Moskowitz was often careless in their preparation, leaving himself open to various interpretations, while Speer's wording was meticulously correct and unambiguous. Speer called for fans to consider charges and counter-charges carefully, pointing out that contentions lacking concrete proof were worthless. He cited several errors in "Fanfarade," and reminded readers that Wilson, an admitted "friend and admirer" of Wollheim, had called Moskowitz's report of the convention the only unbiased one. He then reprimanded Lowndes for the use of improper language, and challenged him to find a grammatical error in his own writings (Lowndes having previously stated that the demand was for writers rather than publishers in FAPA, thus inferring that the organization had blundered in so quickly casting away prospects for a manuscript bureau.

Shortly after this the oft-provoked Philadelphia fans directed their fire against Wollheim, and the latter's days of easy victory were soon over. But there are other threads to trace before that story is continued.

Chapter XXVI

THE BACKGROUND IN EARLY 1938

IN ORDER BETTER to understand the explosive-packed events which transpired during the late spring and early summer of 1938, further description of the field during the early months of that year is essential.

Corwin Stickney's *Amateur Correspondent* collapsed with its November-December, 1937, issue. Due to the many advertisements it carried the magazine had never lost money, but just as surely it had never made any. Little praise for the effort had been forthcoming from fandom, and even omission from the last number of the hated "Hobbyana" column, the inclusion of a new amateur story contest, and a generally stronger slanting toward fan-interests had elicited only faint approval. With the effects of a national economic recession deepening, Stickney was obliged to drop *The Amateur Correspondent* in favor of his home town weekly, *Topic News,* which at least showed a profit, though its fantasy content was nil.

In California, Claire Beck was faring as badly with his *Science Fiction Critic,* which had just merged with Miller's *Phantastique.* With this combination he was enabled to publish several letters from H. P. Lovecraft, which gave the magazine a literary as well as critical tone. But, as has been stated before, Beck specialized less in carefully thought-out analyses than in destructive criticism, and did not hesitate to edit submissions to fit the latter description. When Moskowitz sent him an article analyzing the state of cooperation between American and British fans of the time, for example, Beck deleted almost all of its interpretive, explanatory and mitigating phrases, reducing it in print to a string of insults offering neither hope nor suggestion for improvement in international fan relations. Typical of the more rabid tirades appearing in the magazine were the effusions of Peter Duncan. In his many, interminable good-byes to fandom Duncan expressed himself so succinctly on the failings of science fiction authors, editors and fans as to make himself cordially disliked throughout the field:

> But, nevertheless and despite the fact that I am fully aware of the horrendous penalties awaiting the errant heretic, I hereby propose to do that very thing; to boot the sacrosanct fan in his doubly sacrosanct rump; to do a little stamping on his consecrated toes. For the scientific-fiction fan is no god, no intellectual colossus, and no paragon. He is, as a matter of fact, no kind of superior being at all, but merely a stupid imbecile and buffoon, unworthy of anything but scorn and contumely. The very fact that he believes all the buncombe that is editorialized about him is sufficient to reveal him as a gullible simpleton ready to lap up any flatulent metaphor just so long as it intumesces his already overgrown cranium.

Beck's last worthwhile contribution to fandom was the completing of R. H. Barlow's literary publication *Leaves.* In May, 1937, Barlow

had published the first number of *Leaves,* a superb amateur fantasy
publication that ran to fifty large-sized mimeographed pages. It
featured such things as a reprint of A. Merritt's "People of the
Pit," Letters written by Lovecraft under his pseudonym of Lewis
Theobold, Jr., fiction and poetry by Clark Ashton Smith and a
reprinting of Wandrei's "Red Brain" with its theretofore unpublished
ending and sequel. Stencils for the second number had been prepared
by Barlow, and Beck's contribution was the actual mimeographing.
This second (and last) issue is noted for a Northwest Smith story by
C. L. Moore that has never appeared elsewhere, a Henry Whitehead tale
reprinted from *Weird Tales,* original contributions by Lovecraft and
literary work in a similar vein. Virtually ignored when it appeared,
Leaves today is a collectors' item of extreme rarity, and easily
holds a prominent place among the finest journals ever to be turned
out by the fan field.

The collapse of *The Amateur Correspondent* and *The Science Fiction
Critic* left but one printed journal in the field. This was *Unique
Tales,* which was published by Russell A. Leadabrand of Dinuba,
California. The first number was dated June, 1937, but the magazine
was circulated so poorly that few fans heard about it until early
1938. In all, three issues appeared, the last being dated April,
1938. *Unique Tales* published mostly fiction (the majority of it
editorially written), and was of no great worth, its neat format
being its chief asset.

The disappearance of *Unique Tales* left what had been called the
hektographing era of fandom in full swing. The two leading journals
of the time were *The Science Fiction Fan* and *The Science Fiction
Collector.* Other ranking titles were *Helios, The Science Fiction
News-Letter, Cosmic Tales, Fantascience Digest* and *Imagination!.* Of
these only the last was mimeographed, at that time no mean
distinction.

The comparatively large number of regularly appearing fan magazines, coupled with the quarterly FAPA mailings and numerous "one-
shot" pamphlets, gave the impression that a tremendous number of
fans were engaging in a welter of activity. In a sense this was
true, for the early months of 1938 probably saw more per capita
activity than at any other time, before or since. Yet the field had
gained few new fans since its emergence from the chaos of 1937.
There was virtually no medium other than personal contact for
recruiting new members to its ranks. And there was little or no
cooperation between fans and professionals except occasional notices
in six-point type that appeared in the SFL column of *Thrilling
Wonder Stories.*

Thus when in January, 1938, a new fan named Walter Earl Marconette
made his appearance with a new magazine, *Scienti-Snaps,* it was an
event indeed. Possibly Marconette thought that financial and
material support would be speedily forthcoming—but if so, he was
greatly in error. Were it not for his own abilities along literary
and artistic lines, plus a prompt transfusion from the Moskowitz
Manuscript Bureau, his demise might have been rapid. But the
combination proved fruitful. *Scienti-Snaps* boasted meticulously neat
hektographing, and was as carefully illustrated. One would sooner
have suspected its editor of being a timid aesthete than one of
the physically biggest fans on record. Along with *Scienti-Snaps*

Marconette issued five numbers of *Science-Fantasy Movie Review,* a tiny journal that contained illustrated reviews and synopses of "scientifilms."

Late in 1937, Taurasi, Wiggins and Kuslan had attempted to establish an American counterpart of the British Science Fiction Association. This they called the American Fantasy Association. Tentatively Wiggins took the director's post, Taurasi that of vice-director, and Kuslan became secretary-treasurer. Immediately Taurasi began work on *The American Fantasy Magazine,* a small hektographed publication that was planned as the club's official organ. Only four pages of it were ever completed. Kuslan advertised the organization in almost every leading fan magazine, but cooperation was weak and sporadic and its leaders were inexperienced, so that within less than a year it died in embryo.

Taurasi, however, was the earliest popularizer of another type of organization which was successful. This was a series of publishing-groups, which within a short time virtually divided fandom into something like an interconnected series of feudal castles. Taurasi marked his early numbers of *Cosmic Tales, Junior Science Fiction, Weird and Fantasy Fiction,* etc., as Taurasi Publications. This metamorphosed into the more general house-title Cosmic Publications, which allowed leeway for newcomers to join the circle. Most of the publications listed under this banner never actually appeared at all, and there are so many of these that it would take up too much space to list all of their titles. But in November, 1937, Taurasi made a commendable effort to concentrate his energies and those of his friends upon a single project. This was in the form of a proclamation to all at large that he, Gillespie and Thompson would pool all of their projects (the latter two had never thus far completed any of their planned journals) and issue a single publication to be titled *Cosmic Tales.*

The extravagance of the plans for this new *Cosmic Tales* knew no bounds. Illustrations were hektographed, and Taurasi borrowed Kyle's mimeograph for reproducing the rest of the magazine. It ran to forty large-sized pages, truly an unheard-of thickness for a 1938 fan effort. But the tremendous task of assembling material and allocating work efficiently; the extreme youth and mechanical ineptitude of Thompson; the constant prodding necessary before creative effort could be derived from Gillespie; and Taurasi's own lack of grammar and spelling—these things added up to a general mess. By the time the fourth number of *Cosmic Tales* appeared the magazine had been so roundly criticised by fans in general (and by Richard Wilson in particular) that Gillespie quit in disgust. Completely overlooked by readers were the time, effort and money involved, and the better than average quality of articles and fiction published. These latter included reviews of the professional fantasy publications, "scientifilm" reviews by Mario Racic, Jr. (his first printed work), a debate on religion between Fein and Wollneim, an article on rocketry, and a summary of fan activity during the past year by Moskowitz. *Cosmic Tales,* moreover, was the magazine which introduced artists John Giunta and Jack Agnew to the field. It had all the ingredients needed for success except experience, which could have been gained with perseverance.

Shortly after this Taurasi suffered a nervous breakdown because of

overwork at his place of employment, and was forced on medical
orders to drop *Cosmic Tales*. (The rights to the title went to
Thompson.) Upon being asked, the doctor said he could see no harm,
however, in his patient's publishing occasional minor efforts for
relaxation. So Taurasi, instead of issuing one large magazine,
promptly brought out fifteen or twenty small ones.

Once he had regained his health Taurasi lost no time in
reestablishing Cosmic Publications. With this second series, what
had started as mere affectation grew until it was by far the most
powerful interconnected group of fan magazines in the history of the
field. When he founded *Fantasy News* it became the nucleus of the
Cosmic group, which at one time or another included *Cosmic Tales,
Helios, The Science Fiction Fan, Scienti-Tales, D'Journal, Le Zombie*
and many, many others. The weight of its opinions in fan circles was
pronounced, and by late 1938 it became the virtual center of
activities.

Were it not for its local character, Comet Publications, whose
nucleus was Baltadonis' *Science Fiction Collector,* might well have
overshadowed Cosmic Publications. Composed almost entirely of
Philadelphia publishers, it encompassed Madle's *Fantascience Digest,*
which later became a leading journal in the field, and Train's
Science Adventure Stories among others. The latter was a mammoth
publication for its day, running to sixty-two pages, and being
illustrated in color by Baltadonis and Rothman; it featured material
from the pens of such well known fans and professionals as Eshbach,
Saari, Chapman, Farley, Wilson and Rothman. Both of its two issues
are well worth owning. *PSFS News,* which started as the official
organ of the Philadelphia Science Fiction Society, gradually became
of more general tone. From the date of its establishment in the fall
of 1937 it has never ceased to appear, and remains a valuable source
of the society's history. Publications of lesser importance, such as
Fantasy Herald, Imaginative Fiction, Fantasy Fiction Telegram and
Fantasy Pictorial were likewise members of the Comet chain. The
result of this powerful concentration of published matter in one
city has been one of the most harmoniously run and continuously
active of all science fiction clubs. Easy-going generally, the PSFS
has presented a united front to all opposition, and never has
suffered disruption from internal or external pressure.

Though Cosmic and Comet were by far the most powerful, there were
other groups not without similar importance that followed the trend.
One of these was Empress Publications, which represented the efforts
of Richard Wilson and of Walter Marconette. These two had many
things in common. They attempted to be punctiliously correct in
their grammar and spelling, extending extra efforts to produce
neat publications—and usually succeeding. Their organization was
announced in the August 6, 1938, issue of *The Science Fiction News-
Letter,* one periodical of the group. Marconette's *Scienti-Snaps,*
which was steadily building a reputation for itself, was the other
strong partner. Included under the banner were also such minor
titles as *Science-Fantasy Movie Review, Queer Tales,.Incredible, et
al.*

Perhaps the most individualistic of all was Wiggins' Galactic
Publications, under which masthead were published *The Science
Fiction Fan, Galaxy, The Technocrat.* It was untypical in that it did

not represent a pooling of resources by more than one person, as did the others.

In April, 1938, the Los Angeles-New York Cooperative Publications (LANY) was formed. This is how it came to be established: Some time before, in his *Phantagraph,* Wollheim had begun (but never completed) serialization of Robert E. Howard's story "The Hyborian Age." Howard's death revived interest both in this story and in the author's background, and the time was ripe for issuance of a memorial pamphlet on the subject. Wollheim contributed some of the material and several Los Angeles fans (Ackerman, Douglas and Hodgkins, who, because of their socialistic, Esperantic or techno-cratic interests, felt some kinship with Wollheim's and Michel's ideals, as expressed by Michelism) contributed more as well as the actual publishing of such a pamphlet. It appeared in an edition limited to one hundred copies, and was LANY's most notable achievement.

If we attempt to trace the concept of fan publishing groups back into the past, we come first upon Kyle's Phantasy Legion, which had a similar idea in mind, but which never brought it to fruition. Earlier still we encounter Pohl's EGO-Cooperative Publishers Association, formed in late 1936 and publicized in *The International Observer.* This group announced titles by many publishers, of which *The Mind of Man, The Mutant* and *Legion Parade* actually appeared. They were of no more than passing interest.

The large number of fan publishing houses that existed in 1938 were an attempt by fans to form cliques with others of similar temperament and group their energies for greater achievements. They were far from being failures and the influence of their psychology in the framework of national fan organizations will later become apparent.

Led by Dale Hart, meanwhile, a Texas group that was shortly to be-come very active in the fan world was organizing. This group formed a "Tri-Cities Chapter" under the SFL banner, and embracing interested fans in the communities of Baytown, Goose Creek and Pelley. A. S. Johnston, author of several tales in the old *Amazing Stories,* was a member, as were Percy T. Wilkinson and Arthur Nelson. By dint of diligent effort Hart eventually assembled in the Houston area, from this nucleus, one of the largest fan groups Texas had ever known. This Tri-Cities chapter later proved quite active, and was noted for the delegations it sent to the World Science Fiction Convention in New York and later events. Associated directly or indirectly with it by 1939 were Alfred Moskowitz, John Ellis, Julius Pohl, Jr., Louis Bains, Chester Jordon, Allen R. Charpentier, Robert Young and many others.

In upper Manhatten the Washington Heights SFL chapter had begun a series of mutations of name and policy that carried it through the titles of the Washington Heights Scientifiction Club, the Inter-Fantasy Circle, and finally the Fantasy Circle. The eventual inclin-ation of the club was toward fantasy and the supernatural rather than science fiction, and for this purpose its director (then Chester Fein) obtained from James Taurasi the rights to the title *Weird and Fantasy Fiction* for use as the official club organ. As far as your historian can determine, however, no magazine bearing this title was ever published by this group. From reports of Richard

Wilson and Jack Gillespie, the meetings of the Fantasy Circle were
largely rounds of tomfoolery. Not surprisingly, the club was soon
heard from no more, though it is not known whether it dissolved
officially or simply petered out through lack of interest. However,
such members as Cyril Kornbluth, Chester Fein and David Charney
played later parts in this History.

Neither this account nor another of similar length can be expected
to do justice to the long history of activity of Science Fiction
League chapter #4: Los Angeles. The LASFL had been back into the
swing of fandom since the fall of 1937, but despite its crescendo of
activity it gave the impression of being apart and different from
the field at large. This view was heightened by the innumerable
affectations adopted by club members on their stationary, publications, etc.—such as support of "simplified" spelling, technocracy,
Esperanto. Much of this was but a superficial veneer applied by
Forrest J. Ackerman, leading light of the organization for many
years, and was often an issue hotly debated at meetings, though
little mention of such opposition ever leaked out.

A very fine personalized history of the club's activity during
1937-38 may be found in T. Bruce Yerke's booklet *Memoirs of a Super-
fluous Fan*, which was distributed through a FAPA mailing in 1944. It
was the first of a projected series of four such booklets—but was
the only one to appear. And truly, a club of the size, duration and
all-around importance of the LASFL needs a novel-length resume to do
it credit.

The framework of the organization was the interests of the numer-
ous fans who composed it. Included on its roster were such names as
Forrest Ackerman, Ray Bradbury, Frederick Shroyer, T. Bruce Yerke,
Morojo, James Mooney, Paul Freehafer, Russell J. Hodgkins, Pogo, Roy
Squires, Franklyn Brady, and A. K. Barnes.

So often did members convene that gatherings were little more than
gab fests. Almost every time a new member joined, as in the case of
Shroyer, a plea for planned programs would arise. The club might
take this seriously for several meetings, but as soon as the new
member became acclimated to the group a slump back to the old informal order of things proved inevitable.

This attitude did not preclude worthwhile activity, however, for
in 1938, in addition to publishing *Imagination!, The Hyborian Age*
and *The Television Detective,* the club distinguished itself by sponsoring such lively discussions as a debate on the relative qualities
of weird and science fiction, with Henry Kuttner championing the
former. Besides, numerous excursions to places of fan interest were
made by members, such as those to a mathematical lecture by Eric
Temple Bell ("John Taine") and to the home offices of Edgar Rice
Burroughs, Inc., in Tarzana, California.

The LASFL itself received many visitors. Dr. David H. Keller,
Joseph Skidmore (since deceased) and Arthur J. Burks were among
these. Hannes Bok, then an unknown, aspiring artist, stopped in once
in early 1938. The resultant friendship between him and Ray Bradbury
proved of much ultimate benefit to Bok. The only evidence of his
visit to the club, however, is a rather poorly mimeographed drawing
which appeared on the cover of the May, 1938, *Imagination!*

Charles D. Hornig, the former science fiction magazine editor,
dropped in on the LASFL also, and caused a furore by guest-editing
the June, 1938, number of the club magazine in normal style—i.e.,

with all of Ackerman's innovations omitted. Though many preferred *"Madge"* (as *Imagination* had come to be nicknamed) in this format, it was evident that much of its charm and atmosphere had been sacrificed in the process. A chapter vote was taken, and by the slim margin of two ballots it was decided to retain the old form.

Prior to Hornig's experiment, it should be remarked, there had been considerable discussion in the club as to the advisability of discarding "simplified" and "phonetic" spelling in the magazine, as well as many other of its ruffles. When the issue was forced, editors Morojo and Ackerman offered to withdraw in favor of anyone else who cared to edit *Imagination!*. It was a safe offer, for none of the critics were willing or able—and so the material was printed in more or less standard format, with more emphasis laid on cleverness of handling than on uniqueness of language.

Thirteen was a very unlucky number for *"Madge,"* for with the issue of that number she stumbled, sighed and gave up the ghost. What was to have been a magnificent anniversary issue dwindled down to a dozen pages of readers' letters and editorial excuses. To few people had been bearing the brunt of work on the magazine; and now that Ackerman was working at irregular hours the coordination of editorial effort became impossible.

But from the corpse of *Imagination!* there arose a small, quarterly periodical composed entirely of readers letters—in short, a sort of expanded version of the *Madge* letter column, which had long been one of the most popular of its features. This new periodical was titled *Voice of the Imagi-Nation* (for short, *Vom*).

The material on hand for publication in the now-defunct club organ was published in several new individual titles that appeared irregularly from time to time. Some appeared in two untitled issues of a magazine later named *Mikros,* and used to propagandize the gospel of technocracy throughout fandom. However, most of the articles saw print in a pamphlet entitled *Madge's Prize Manuscripts* (thus named because most entries were submissions to a fan contest intended for the ill-fated anniversary issue). Among them was Jack Speer's "After 1939—What?" Whatever interest Speer had lost in professional fantasy itself had been more than compensated for by his increased interest in fandom and the psychology of the fans themselves. In this prize-winning article he predicted that the first world science fiction convention would mean greater cooperation and publicity from the professional magazines and hence an influx of new fans into the field—which would in turn raise the circulation of fan journals into the hundreds and necessitate their using a more general type of material. He further considered the possibility of a war and its probable results on the field.

During its early numbers *Imagination!* had been disliked by many, but as the magazine maintained its mimeographed format and twenty large-sized pages month after month it slowly attained not only popularity but a certain amount of respect. This was partly due, no doubt, to the fact that a mimeographed journal in those times of hektography was roughly equivalent to a professionally printed one today. And its demise was marked by sincere regrets, even from some of its severest critics. Yet although *Imagination!* was in point of reproduction ahead of its time (mimeography did not come into general usage until almost a year later) this made it in a sense a magazine apart, one which augmented other activity in the field rather than worked hand in hand with it.

Chapter XXVII

THE FACTIONS ALIGN THEMSELVES

MEANWHILE the Wollheim-Moskowitz feud was continuing to run full-tilt. Here and there were still some who teetered on the tight-rope of diplomacy, but who realized that sooner or later they would probably have to choose sides. Among these were Richard Wilson and Jack Gillespie. Wilson was of course well known as publisher of the weekly *Science Fiction News-Letter,* and was among the ten most popular fans of the day. He had previously printed an issue of Moskowitz's journal *Helios.* Gillespie had time and again, in uncertain fashion, attempted activity in the field, but had somehow never quite entered the main current of the stream. He was well known to Moskowitz, who had in fact personally initiated him into the whys and wherefores of the fan world much in the fashion of a Dutch uncle.

The curious set of circumstances which led to the open break between these two and Moskowitz has many extremely humorous aspects. Much of the account was told by Wilson in "Newark Pilgrimage," an article that appeared in the second issue of his news-sheet supplement, *The Science Fiction Dividend.* "It all began sanely enough," he stated. "Donald A. Wollheim, John B. Michel, James V. Taurasi, Jack Gillespie, Robert G. Thompson, Fred Pohl and I gathered at the home of Herbert E. Goudket on the night of Saturday, March 12, 1938, in order to see our unlovely faces in the movies he had taken of us the previous Sunday." On conclusion of this visit all but Taurasi and Thompson treated themselves to a showing of a surrealist film *Blood of a Poet* and the fantasy *The Crazy Ray* at a Greenwich Village theater. This was more than adequate fare for putting a science fiction fan in a peculiar state of mind, so after a very late cafeteria repast Wilson and Gillespie took leave of their friends and strolled uptown to the ferry, which they took to Weehawken, New Jersey. On impulse they decided to pay a visit to Moskowitz who lived in nearby Newark, and after a somewhat roundabout trip reached the door of the Moskowitz abode at exactly 5:45 a.m.

Neither Sam Moskowitz nor the other members of his family had any acquaintance with the spectre of insomnia, and when the bell interrupted their repose with its insistant clamor at that hour of the morning, speculations soared from such trivialities as the house being afire on up the scale of imagination. On being confronted by Wilson and Gillespie, Moskowitz demanded to know what urgency prompted visiting him at such an hour of the morning. With eyes almost brimming with tears, Gillespie broke the "news" that William Sykora had "passed on." Moskowitz was assured that this was an irrevocable fact, having been ascertained by Jack Rubinson, who, when he happened to pass the Sykora residence, had seen a wreath of flowers on the door. Upon inquiring, he had been informed of the event, but had not, he said, queried the bereaved further as to the cause.

The strangeness of the early visit, the vividness of the detail and the note of sorrow in their voices added up to the real McCoy to Moskowitz, who told the news to his family (who knew Sykora well), all of whom swallowed the story with incredible naiveté and much sympathy. Gillespie and Wilson were given refreshments, and offered the use of a bed if they wished to sleep. Moskowitz now had every intention of calling off the Newark convention, since it had been Sykora's idea. At this point his visitors apparently realized that their prank was getting out of hand, for they tried to dissuade their host from such an action. However, during the dawn hours while they sat waiting for the world to wake up, their remarks concerning Moskowitz, his family and place of residence were insultingly caustic. Quite naturally Moskowitz took offense, though he remained silent.

An early morning visit was made to Alex Osheroff, and quite deliberately (since he was still somewhat annoyed by their behavior) Moskowitz conducted Gillespie and Wilson several miles to the residence of William Miller, who was not at home, and then to an address of James Blish which proved to be incorrect. Extremely worried, the two departed for New York—without disclosing their hoax.

Fortunately Moskowitz dispatched a letter of condolence to the Sykora family on the same day of the visit; upon receiving it Sykora himself made a quick trip to Newark in time to forestall Moskowitz's intentions to dismantle convention preparations. Just before his arrival he received several sarcastic postal cards from Wilson and Gillespie, informing him of the truth.

The relief felt on learning that Sykora was still alive almost cancelled an explosion Wilsonward that would have been Moskowitz's normal reaction. However, he was definitely affected by the whole affair, since he had always played the fan game naively "straight," and since this experience was a sort of climax to many shoddy stories he had heard. Previously he had written for Wiggins' *Science Fiction Fan* an article titled "They're Grand," in which the virtues of fans in general were extolled to the skies. Now his views swung to the other extreme and he found psychological relief in penning for *The Science Fiction Collector* an essay "They're Grand—But They Have Their Faults." The appearance of such lines as the following was a shock to the fan world of 1938:

> Imagine for yourself the terrific shock I received when upon acquaintance with these "top" fans I found a number of them reeling unsteadily about, definitely under the influence of alcohol. I took all that in, being careful not to let one example influence my opinion of all others. I made reservation for the fact that black sheep were present in all circles. The crowning blow came when I met one time a few fans whom I had always respected, whom I thought tremendously of, prancing crazily about at all hours of the night, obviously intoxicated or the next thing to it. One was fifteen years old!

In this day, when the average fan age is higher, drunkenness is more common and regarded more liberally, but in 1938, when most fans were from fourteen to nineteen years of age, imbibing alcoholic beverages by fans was looked upon as outright perversion—as, indeed, the law has always recognized it for minors.

The response to this article was rapid. Both Oliver Saari and Milton Rothman wrote lengthy replies of analysis and comment, concluding that New York fans were not typical of those throughout the rest of the country, and chastizing Moskowitz for his "hero-worship and idealism." Richard Wilson had also read the article, and, despite the fact that no names had been mentioned, he took it personally and stoutly denied being a drunkard. "Moskowitz," said he, "is a liar."

And henceforth all Moskowitz publications, articles and projects began to receive decidedly sour notices in Wilson's own publications and in those where his influence was considerable. For some months Moskowitz made no reply, but when silence and attempts to smooth out differences alike did not alter Wilson's attitude, Moskowitz took steps which were directly responsible for cutting down *The Science Fiction News-Letter's* influence in the field, and in some measure prompting its eventual discontinuance.

Meanwhile, Will Sykora, still attempting to reaffirm his newly-won foothold on the fan field, did not content himself merely with the belief that Moskowitz would carry out with him plans for a science fiction convention. He continued to probe incessantly for other possibilities. When it seemed that Stickney would suspend publication of *The Amateur Correspondent,* Sykora wrote to Willis Conover, and inquired if he still had the rights to the title *Fantasy Magazine,* and proposing, if so, that it be continued with Conover as editor and he business manager. For a short time it appeared that some progress in this direction was going to be made; but as soon as Stickney caught wind of these plans he promptly announced that he himself intended to continue *The Amateur Correspondent* (though he never actually did), and since the latter title was the successor filling *Fantasy Magazine's* obligations, Stickney probably had legal grounds for spiking Sykora's revival plans had he chosen to do so. In any event, nothing further ever came of the matter.

Nothing daunted, Sykora next tackled a matter vibrant with potentialities for disaster. He set about to prove that the dissolution of the ISA had been accomplished illegally. He organized what he termed "the ISA Committee for Reorganization." Robert Madle was contacted and offered the presidency of the resurrected club. Madle was amenable to the suggestion, and supported the idea in an editorial of the March-April, 1938, issue of *Fantascience Digest.* But the surprise came when Sykora announced that he had contacted members of the old ISA and alleged to have in his possession signed statements from a majority affirming that they had had no voice in the dissolution of the group.

Sykora's claims were naturally thoroughly alarming to the Wollheim faction which he held responsible. The result was concerted action against him by the Committee for the Political Advancement of Science Fiction (CPASF), the group into which such leftist-inclined fans as Wollheim, Michel, Lowndes, Pohl, Rubinson, Dockweiler, Cohen and others had united shortly after the 1937 Philadelphia Convention for the purposes of propagandizing Michelism and similar purposes. Sykora was ill-prepared for countering their actions.

Next, Sykora announced the formation of the Scientific Cinema Club of New York (whose function in all probability was that of a "front" for ISA-revival activities), and named January 30, 1938, as the date for a get-together meeting. At this time, related announcement circulars, there would be shown a revival of the science fiction film *The Lost World* (from the Doyle novel of the same title) as well as a short fantasy cartoon and a film showing former ISA activities (the rocketry experiments).

On the scheduled Sunday this meeting took place at Bohemian Hall, the site of the New York convention of the previous year. Not only were several fans from the metropolitan district present, but a Philadelphia delegation composed of Agnew, Madle and Baltadonis as well. Upon conclusion of the showing of the films, Sykora, Goudket and Fein presided over a discussion as to plans for a local club whose chief interest would be the production of an amateur "scientifilm."

Only a short bit of *The Lost World* had been shown, however, when Harry Dockweiler (a CPASF member), influenced by liberal imbibation of alcoholic beverages, began to misbehave. His actions became so annoying that a police officer had to be summoned to remove him from the hall. Frederik Pohl decided to leave with him. If Dockweiler's action had been prompted by a desire to disrupt the meeting (which your historian doubts), certainly the attempt had been fouled by the expedient of summoning the law to the scene. But the CPASF did not have to rely on such crude devices; it had far subtler methods at its command.

When Sykora walked into the next meeting of the club at the home of Goudket he found himself confronted by a major delegation of his opposition in the persons of Wollheim, Michel, Pohl, Gillespie and Lowndes. The only one present (with the exception of Goudket) that he could count on as favoring him was Mario Racic, Jr. Shocked by this turn of events, Sykora refused to meet the members of the CPASF, and retired to another room. No amount of argument could persuade him that these fans were sincere in their desire to aid in the production of a fantasy film. And in desperation he threatened to resign from the organization should they be elected. They were elected however. Sykora promptly resigned, predicting that the club would be destroyed by the actions of the newcomers, and promising to return to Goudket after the inevitable disruption and start anew.

This prophesy materialized with clock-like precision at the following meeting of the Scientific Cinema Club in June, when it was unanimously resolved to disband the club. Unable to resist the opportunity for placing this, too, on the shoulders of Sykora, members "bemoaned the manipulations" by which he had "crassly" arranged to reimburse himself for the bare expenses of showing *The Lost World* at the expense of the club treasury.

But Sykora had not waited for the disbandment before striking out anew on his own. In early May, 1938, he launched a club known as The Scientifilmakers and even distributed one issue of its official organ (*The Scientifilmaker*) at the convention held in the same month. The back cover of the magazine carried an advertisement for the ISA, which was characterized as "never legally dissolved!" In the same number was an article, with diagrams, "Make Your Own Cartoon Movies," by James Taurasi. Even more pertinent, however, was Sykora's editorial "What I Have Done to Get *Metropolis*." In this he claimed to have failed in his attempt to procure a print of that famous fantasy film originally produced in Germany eleven years before, but stated that he had begun negotiations with UFA, the original makers. This last remark was to have later repercussions, as we shall see.

Chapter XXVIII

THE FIRST NATIONAL SCIENCE FICTION CONVENTION

ALTHOUGH MOSKOWITZ and Sykora had in common the desire to sponsor a successful convention, and the fact that both had been attacked by Wollheim, they had theretofore cooperated little along other lines. Moskowitz had done nothing to aid the proposed revival of the ISA, for example, other than announcing in his magazine *Helios* that Sykora intended to resurrect it. He was not, at that time, actually aware of many of the currents of fan politics that eddied about him, and maintained a patently naive and idealistic attitude toward both the convention and fans' actions in general. On his part, Sykora offered little or no enlightenment to Moskowitz prior to the convention, not even advising him regarding the trouble he was having with Wollheim. These facts should be kept in mind by the reader as we lift the curtain on events transpiring at the Newark convention.

As this gathering proved to be the most successful up to that time on the bases of both attendance and program, it behooves us to consider in some detail the preparations preceding it.

Newark had been favored as the convention site for several reasons. First of all, it was a city close enough to New York to assure maximum attendance from that source, as well as being near Philadelphia, home of the PSFS. Secondly, since many New Jersey names had been noted in fantasy magazine readers' columns, it was hoped that many of these could be lured to a local site. Thirdly, Moskowitz's work on the convention would be facilitated, since he lived in Newark. Finally, prices were generally lower there than, for example, in New York; as a criterion, the well-kept Slovak Sokol Hall (which was finally chosen as the meeting place) which boasted two podiums and seats for a hundred people was obtained for the modest sum of three dollars.

Originally it had been intended to hold a three-day convention. Ultimately, however, this idea was discarded. Instead, a one-day affair that would not try (as previously announced) to be as much an end in itself as a trial for judging the feasibility of a longer, world convention in 1939 was decided upon. Originally, too, the provision of a complete dinner for attendees was contemplated; but in view of the hoped-for large attendance a buffet was scheduled in its place. Even the titling of the affair had provided food for thought. In early stages of planning "The First National Fantasy Convention" was considered suitable; but eventually this was altered to "The First National Science Fiction Convention," it being felt that the word "fantasy" might lead people to misconstrue the scope of the gathering. An elaborate printed program (such as later conventions featured) was vetoed on the grounds of the difficulty that would be encountered in obtaining advertisements to support it considering the economic state of the country at that time.

Publicity for the convention was disseminated in the form of posters, mimeographed circulars and notices in fan magazines. In the fan press this was poorly organized, but what did appear contained the proper appeal. *Heltos* ran sizeable notices in its fifth and sixth issues; Taurasi's *Cosmtc Tales* published another; and a convention flyer, *The First Nattonal Fantasy Bulletin,* was circulated among FAPA members. For the first time a convention was advertised by professionally printed posters, which were displayed in Newark and New York museums, libraries and schools. These furnished essential information about the affair in compact, eye-catching manner, and are known to have been responsible for luring at least two visitors to the hall. But the most important device utilized to attract attendees were the circulars, which were mailed to a large list of near-by fans. These drew the crowd. They included a brief description of the affair (with a program), an explanation of the stake every reader, author, artist, editor and fan had in the convention, and complete travelling instructions. The writing, mimeographing and mailing of these circulars was entirely the work of Sykora. It will be noticed that there was no publicity whatever in the professional fantasy publications. This should not be surprising, inasmuch as rapprochement between the fans and professionals had not as yet been consummated. In fact, the convention proposed to do that very thing.

It was announced that sponsorship of the convention was the joint project of *Heltos,* the Scientifilmakers and the ISA Committee for Reorganization—but this was the veriest of camouflage, for the task was pure and simple the personal burden of Sykora and Moskowitz.

At first Sykora had intended to pay the entire bill for the convention and not try in any fashion to retrieve his money; but, prompted by the urgings of Moskowitz, he decided to make some attempt to cover the expenses. In those days, when fans were avid collectors of their little amateur journals and steep prices were paid even for announcement circulars, selling fan magazines was a possibility to be considered. But where could these be obtained? Moskowitz conceived the answer: have fans publish them—magazines of not less than twelve pages, in fifty-copy editions. These would be sent to the convention sponsors, and in exchange each publisher receive a free copy of every other magazine similarly contributed, plus a premium—this being a bound set of eight issues of Alex Osheroff's *Science Ftction Scout.* Excess copies would be sold.

The plan had tremendous appeal to distant fans who had no hope of being present, yet who all but wept at the thought of having a dozen or more magazines missing from their collections. The response was immediate. Ackerman contributed *Baroque, Bagatales, Brobdtngnagtan,* a pamphlet for attendees' autographs. Marconette turned out a special issue of *Sctentt-Snaps.* Wiggins published *The Science Fiction Conventioneer.* Madle brought out *Cosmos.* Wilson published *The Convention Crier.* The Canadian fan Nils H. Frome hektographed a *Fantasy Ptctortal.* McPhail mailed in *Stf. and Nonesense.* Thompson contributed a short story titled *The Magtc Drug of Witch-Dr. Boog.* Taurasi submitted *Wonder Ftction Annual.* Larry B. Farsaci mimeographed a collectors' magazine, *Fantasttc.* Both Sykora and Moskowitz had their convention journals, titled respectively *The Sctenttftlmaker* and *Different.* Even the CPASF members came through with *The Science Fiction Advance* and *Rejected—Convention Committee,* neither of which was calculated to do the gathering any good.

The auction idea was used for the first time at a fan convention when a contribution of professional fantasy publications and fan

journals was received from Forrest Ackerman. In deciphering Ackerman's ambiguous wording and spelling eccentricities it was understood that half of the money received from auctioning these items
was to be applied to defraying convention expenses and that the
other half Ackerman would accept in the form of convention publications. In view of the fact that he was a dealer who bought and sold
such items, this agreement appeared perfectly understandable. But
when it had been fulfilled in this way Ackerman wrote Moskowitz
indignantly:

> My meaning was; 50% of the sales I was to receive in cash to
> offset my expenditures, U to keep the other ½ & send me fan-
> mags. I'll concede it's conceivable U coudve interpreted
> "fanmags" as Convention mags; what I really had in mind,
> however, was issues of *Heltos* & other duplicates in Ur pos-
> session. In other words, if U disposed of my stuff at $3 I
> got $1.50 & U the opportunity to sell me $1.50 worth of Ur
> stuff for Ur "trouble" (fun). I wonder how U woudve disposed
> of all those Con-mags if U hadnt unloaded m on me???...Seri-
> ously—I shall really scandalize U in scientifictional cir-
> cles, Samuel, letting all the lads *know*.

The above quotation will give the reader a rough idea of the difficulties under which correspondence with Ackerman operated at that
time. Moskowitz refused to remit him further consideration, maintaining that Ackerman's original letter suggesting the agreement
would remain in his files as evidence that his interpretation had
been reasonable; that the contribution had been unsolicited; and
that, even without Ackerman's contributions, the extra convention
journals would have found ready buyers. He returned to Ackerman,
after some delay, a copy of the first issue of *Imagination*, which
had not been sold at the auction. (Ackerman had intimated that
Moskowitz intended to keep and eventually sell this item for a small
fortune.) This exchange was the foundation of the anti-Moskowitz
attitude held by Ackerman thenceforth.

As luck would have it, the weather was exquisite on Sunday, May
29th. But this was small consolation to the fingernail-biting convention committee, as by three hours before convention time, no one
had yet arrived in the hall. This lack of early-birds was a matter
of grave concern, for at past gatherings fans usually arrived many
hours in advance. At two o'clock, one hour before starting time, a
scant fifteen people had put in their appearance. Thus arrival on
the scene of *Astounding Science Fiction*'s new editor, John W.
Campbell, Jr., was the cause of more trepidation than rejoicing, if
this skimpy showing was the best that could be made. Campbell's mur-
mur of "Better than I expected," (which might have referred either
to the attendance or the hall) was noted with uneasiness. Twenty-
five attendees now appeared the maximum to be hoped for. Then abruptly, just twenty minutes before commencement time, a veritable cloud-
burst of people converged on the hall. The scene grew with amazing
speed to the aspects of a mob. There was a wild melee of talking,
drinking, gesticulating, photograph-snapping fans. The hundred available seats filled up almost immediately, and a mass of standees
began to assemble in the rear of the hall. It was fantastic, it was
unbelievable—but in the vicinity of 125 people were jammed into the
room—more than had attended all past conventions put together!

They had turned out from every nearby state—New York, Massachusetts, Pennsylvania, Delaware, Maryland, Rhode Island, Vermont,
Maine, New Hampshire. It was virtually a *"Who's Who"* showing of past,
present and future fandom. Professionals were represented, among
them being authors Otis Adelbert Kline, Eando Binder, L. Sprague de
Camp, Frank Belknap Long, Manly Wade Wellman, Lloyd A. Eshback and
John D. Clark; in addition to Campbell, Mortimer Weisinger (editor,
Thrilling Wonder Stories) was present, and with him Leo Margulies,
the editorial director of Standard Publications itself.

This last-minute onrush of fans resulted in the convention being
called to order one-half hour late. At 3:30 p.m. chairman Moskowitz
rapped the gavel on the speaker's stand for order. Robert Madle,
taking the place of Baltadonis (who was too ill to attend) read the
minutes of the Third Eastern Science Fiction Convention held in
Philadelphia the previous year. Then the chairman launched into the
welcoming address. He emphasized the fact that present were representatives of every category in the field—the publisher, the editor,
the author, the artist, the reader, the active fan, the science-
hobbyist. This, he maintained, was the ideal opportunity for ironing
out misunderstandings.

Sykora, the first speaker on the program, swerved from the sweeping generalities of the chairman's address. He emphasized that the
large gathering before him assured the success of a world science
fiction convention. He proposed that such a major event be held in
conjunction with the World's Fair in New York City in 1939. With the
active cooperation of all parties concerned, he maintained, there
were virtually no limits to the possibilities offered.

Rothman, the chairman of the two previous Philadelphia conventions,
expanded still further these possibilities, and then veered into a
talk drawing an analogy between the past histories of music and
science fiction. He concluded by asserting that he felt a golden age
was in prospect for both.

Inspired by this support, Sykora moved that the chairman be given
power to appoint a temporary or a permanent committee to lay the
groundwork for such an event. This motion aroused general comment.
Herbert Goudket asked if editors would pledge their aid to a 1939
world convention. The chair remarked that it would be unfair to coerce the editors into a hasty decision. Goudket then moved that the
motion be tabled for later discussion. Here occurred a peculiar event
that has often been misinterpreted. Moskowitz had never heard the
expression "tabled" before. Befuddled, he requested Goudket to
repeat his words, which Goudket did to no better effect. Moskowitz
then conceded his position to Sykora, under whose chairmanship the
motion was passed. Moskowitz after this resumed the chair.

Campbell, the feature speaker, was then introduced. His topic
aroused much surprise: he was going to speak about science fiction
fandom. For the first time an editor was publicly acknowledging the
existence of such an entity. Campbell outlined his views of an inner
circle of fans (the letter-writers, amateur publishers and participants in associated activities), and the outer circle of fans (those
who were merely readers). He announced his intention of aiding this
inner circle by offering to print in "Brass Tacks" (*Astounding's*
readers' column) a letter of what amounted to free advertising to
any fan publication that could support an expanding audience. (This

would of course exclude hektographed journals.) Also he was honestly interested in obtaining more of these amateur periodicals. As this and later events proved, Campbell was undeniably a very real fan himself. He answered Goudket's question anent editorial support for a 1939 world convention by implying that he was ready to support the efforts of any generally recognized group to sponsor such an event.

In the address of Mort Weisinger which followed, however, there were no such qualifications. He pledged that *Thrilling Wonder Stories* would give such a convention a prominent advertisement at no cost. Then he revealed that plans were afoot to publish a companion magazine to *Thrilling Wonder*. This proposed magazine would specialize in printing full-length novels, and Stanley Weinbaum's "Black Flame" was then under consideration for use in it.

Goudket expressed a few definitely uncomplimentary opinions of the Science Fiction League, and asked Weisinger what would be done to remedy the stagnant status into which it had deteriorated. Weisinger replied somewhat evasively that a remedy would be apparent in the next published column.

A fifteen-minute recess was called, and motion picture projectors were set up. Then the showing of the scheduled films began. First There was a "Stanley Ink" cartoon portraying a trip to Mars. Next on the program was a short picture illustrating Einstein's theory of relativity, and close upon the heels of this a comedy titled "Aladdin and the Wonderful Lamp." Presentation of the main feature, "The Lost World," had to be terminated after fifteen minutes because of the dullness of the silent film technique and the poor print that had been obtained.

An intermission was called and buffet refreshments brought in. These might have served a maximum of fifty people but under the onslaught of 125 the result was so farcical as to inspire Richard Wilson's article "Way Down East" (published in *Imagination!* for July, 1938). Under the heading of "The Battle of the Buffet" he related a very funny and painfully authentic account of his attempts to assuage the urgings of the inner man.

During this intermission a telegram was received from the newly-published *Marvel Science Stories* in which its editors asked for an account of the convention for publication and wished attendees an "effective and enjoyable" time. The New York *Times* also telephoned for information, but neither periodical ever actually published news of the affair. A short squib in a Long Island paper was the closest thing to a professional write-up the convention obtained.

After the eulogies were over the next item on the agenda was fan business. And anticipating trouble, the professionals began their hasty departure. They had ample justification for concern, since CPASF members present had come well loaded with ammunition. Moskowitz had been handed (as convention booklets) by Wollheim and Michel *The Science Fiction Advance* and *Rejected—Convention Committee,* the latter bearing the subtitle "Speeches by Donald A. Wollheim and John B. Michel Suppressed by the Committee of the Newark Convention." Both of these were placed on sale at the official table with all other convention publications. (*Advance* sold out completely, and Wollheim of course received a set of booklets in exchange for its submission. *Rejected* failing to sell, Michel agreed for it to be given away; he was denied a set of booklets, however, when he later claimed undistributed copies.)

Prior to the convention a rule had been stipulated to the effect that all speeches should be submitted in advance to the convention committee. Both of these speeches had been rejected for specific and fair reasons. Wollheim's talk "Science Fiction and Science" had been excluded because it contained passages which might offend Campbell, the feature speaker, who had a technical education. For example:

> Does a man study science in high school and college, master a B.D., an M.S., or finally perhaps a Ph.D. only to b·:ome the editor of a pulp magazine? Why did he not utilize this hard won technical knowledge to pursue a research career? ...The answer is easy but sad. Society had no place for this trained mind....

Michel's proposed speech, "The Position of Science Correlative to Science Fiction and the Present and Developing International Economic, Political, Social and Cultural Crisis," was rejected because it was considered too dull and too far removed from probable interests of attendees. The following are typical passages from it:

> The dialectic is a process resulting from the conflicts of the varied interests of humanity which coalesces the nebulous forces released by these conflicts into a rigid thread running through history which determines irrevocably the course of human affairs and which lasts as long as opposing interests exist in human intercourse.

And:

> This [the perversion of science to war] is due entirely to the economic contradictions of the present economic system, namely capitalism. On every hand these contradictions appear, throttling the very life out of scientific research.

Also in the booklet with these two speeches was an exceedingly uncomplimentary editorial regarding the convention and its sponsors.

The Science Fiction Advance, official organ of the Michelistic CPASF, was simply an easy-stage education in communism. As such, it was by 1938 standards blatantly obvious, though today, when many scientific tenets have been more thoughtfully evaluated by sober liberals, it would seem quite mild. This issue contained a cartoon-illustrated poem by Pohl poking fun at Moskowitz, Sykora and Speer in decidedly unpleasant fashion.

But this was not all. In addition, CPASF members distributed by hand four different leaflets. One protested the discharge of a *Thrilling Wonder Stories* printer who was a member of the CIO. Another, aimed to counteract the possibility of Sykora's debating the legality of the ISA dissolution, announced that formation of an organization titled "Friends of the ISA"; this group was opposed to "the efforts of those who would willingly distort to selfish and inimical ends the history of the ISA and the facts concerning it," etc. A third circular asked fans to vote for Michel as president of the FAPA on a free speech, free copies and no censorship platform. And the last of the quartet contained lyrics by Michel titled "Science Fiction Internationale" which were to be sung to the tune of "The Internationale."

At no time was an attempt of any nature made to curtail the distribution of all this CPASF literature, which quite obviously was not calculated to promote a harmonious gathering. This pertinent fact should be kept in mind when one remembers the later charges of "dictatorship" and "suppression" that were launched at the convention and its sponsors.

Sykora conducted the business portion of the convention, since obviously his knowledge of parliamentary procedure was superior to that of Moskowitz. Sykora first spoke of the necessity of having a special group formed to sponsor the proposed 1939 convention. David Kyle, agreeing, moved that an organization be formed for this purpose; the motion was carried unanimously, a few not voting.

Immediately following this, another motion was made to the effect that a temporary committee be appointed by the acting chairman to work on the project, and that this temporary committee be invested with the power to choose a permanent committee of at least twenty members. At this point it was recalled that a similar committee had already been appointed at the second convention in New York in February, 1937. This committee had done virtually nothing in the interim. Sykora stated that if a majority of those present voted for the motion on the floor the old committee would automatically be disbanded, since such a majority would exceed in number those who voted to create the original committee. Upon being put to a vote, the motion was then passed with only a few dissenters.

Sykora appointed Goudket, Fein, Kubilius, Moskowitz and himself to this committee. It might be mentioned that of these the first three named had proved themselves generally more friendly to the CPASF than to Sykora. Kyle protested the choice on the grounds that there was a group present (the CPASF) not represented. Sykora replied that in boosting science fiction he recognized no group distinctions, and that in any event several other factions present, such as the Philadelphia fans, were likewise unrepresented. But since this committee was temporary in nature, he said, such faults—if faults they were—could be remedied when the permanent membership was appointed. This discussion might have proceeded further had not Alex Osheroff moved for adjournment; this motion was carried, and the group began to disband.

This official closing was followed by the first auction ever held at a science fiction convention. Moskowitz, who was to be seen in this role in later years, officiated. By the standards of today, when many beautiful and valuable original drawings, great piles of rare fantasy magazines and books, and unusual collectors' items of every sort are commonplace sights at such affairs, this initial auction, at which a small box filled with fan magazines was the main attraction, may appear extremely modest. Yet in those depression years fans whistled in amazement to hear two dollars bid for a set of twenty stills from films, or the bidding on issues of *The Time Traveller* and *Science Fiction Digest* rise to a dollar a copy. An advertisement for a West Coast fan journal on a single sheet of paper was knocked down at fifty cents, on bids raised a penny at a time. Similar selling prices prevailed on other rare items. Yet despite this the convention was a financial failure—approximately twenty-five dollars having been expended, and only fifteen regained. The deficit was footed by Sykora.

Before and during the auction many events of political significance had been transpiring. The group headed by Wollheim had been giving its circulars the widest possible circulation. David Kyle had written a petition protesting against methods used for choosing the committee (spoken of above) in the blank pages of the convention autograph book *Baroque, Bagatales, Brobdingnagian*. With this he solicited signatures, obtaining many from the closest friends of Sykora and Moskowitz, who in most instances had no idea that they were signing a petition, since Kyle never bothered to explain that he was doing more than soliciting autographs. The petition thus obtained was duly notarized, and Frederik Pohl at a later date delegated to show it to various New York science fiction magazine editors.

The far-reaching consequences of the First National Science Fiction Convention have never been clearly delineated. Today fans read of a gathering with 125 attendees and tend to regard it as a freakish development in an otherwise orderly history. The sole reason for this is the fantastically poor news coverage the affair received.

The one weekly journal in the field at the time was Richard Wilson's *Science Fiction News-Letter*. Wilson had attended the convention, published *The Science Fiction Crier* for distribution there, and had shown himself sufficiently interested in the event to print, beforehand, such derogatory remarks as "It probably won't be worth while." His weekly was in its twenty-sixth issue at convention time, and subscribers looked forward to the twenty-seventh—June 4th—number, which might reasonably be expected to carry an account of the affair. But when that number appeared its entire space was found to be devoted to reviewing in detail the convention booklets. Neither did the twenty-eighth number have a single line apropos the convention, being devoted instead mainly to a review of the latest FAPA mailing. Paradoxically, Wilson's article "Way Down East," which has been mentioned earlier in this chapter, contained more information about the convention than did his own journal.

Thus it happened that a magazine which did not appear until fully a month after the event had a news scoop of the convention. This was McPhail's mimeographed *Rocket,* a quarterly FAPA periodical. Yet even here the bulk of the account was devoted to a description of the wrangling of various factions over the choice of fans for the temporary convention committee. Still later the June-July, 1938, issue of *The Science Fiction Collector* published an unsigned commentary—titled "Comments on the Convention"—which mentioned merely the "lowlights" of the gathering. Not until the long-delayed last issue of *Helios* appeared almost three months later with seven pages of pertinent information did fandom have a well-rounded picture of what had transpired. Since none of the journals named above had a circulation of more than fifty, the passing years have screened the important influence of a convention that boasted an attendance of twice as many fans as there were believed to be in active fandom at that period.

The subsequent account in the SFL column of *Thrilling Wonder Stories* for October, 1938, contained the only widely-circulated account the convention received. And, oddly enough, this account was contributed, without the knowledge of the convention committee, by one of its opponents, who labelled the gathering the Fourth Eastern Science Fiction Convention in an effort to minimize its importance.

Although the designation "First National Science Fiction Convention" did eventually triumph, there was for a time a field-day for advocates of the what's-in-a-name? philosophy.

By the statements of cooperation drawn from editors of professional fantasy magazines this convention was vitally important in redirecting the interest of fandom from the fans themselves back to the professionals. Just as surely its very size and general air of success convinced the editors that fandom was not without its potent influence, and that it would be wise not to disregard it. Finally, it was a new type of activity that differentiated the newer fandom from the old. The *Fantasy Magazine* group had produced publications which its followers were unable to match; the newer fans produced conventions, which their forebears had never dared to attempt, and which as a factor for boosting science fiction were infinitely superior in range of influence.

Chapter XXIX

THE FAPA ELECTIONS OF 1938

THE FANTASY Amateur Press Association had worked under a temporary slate of officers until such time as the membership became large enough to warrant a general election. Donald A. Wollheim was president, and he also assumed the duties of secretary when William H. Miller, Jr., resigned that office. Daniel McPhail was vice-president and John B. Michel official editor.

By the time the third mailing was dispatched (December, 1937) the membership totalled twenty-one. Though this was less than half the organization's intended roster of fifty, the fans included were of such prominence in the field at the time that it was decided an election could reasonably be held. The electioneering was of the mildest sort, few beyond the candidates themselves feeling much excitement—or even interest—in the outcome. Wollheim, virtually unopposed, easily retained the presidential post with fifteen votes in contrast to seven votes distributed among five other "write-in" candidates. McPhail eked out a close victory over Robert A. Madle, polling eleven ballots to the latter's ten. John V. Baltadonis easily defeated a quartet of would-be secretary-treasurers by a sixteen-to-six count. Finally, Frederik Pohl took the official editorship from Michel, twelve votes to nine.

Superficially there was little wrong with this election—save the fact that alghough there were only twenty-one registered members, a total of twenty-two votes had been cast for two of the offices. This together with the fact that Wollheim had appointed three of his close friends as ballot-counters—Pohl, Wilson and Michel—caused a mild rumble from the Philadelphia faction. Temporarily it remained subdued, however, for not only was there but one tally where a single vote would have changed the result, but all evidence was in New York.

As has been previously pointed out, the FAPA was, in the early part of 1938, an open avenue which was frequently traversed by political maneuverings of the field. The organization was still a long way from being a fandom within a fandom. Thus many of the broadsides occasioned by the Wollheim-Moskowitz feud had been circulated in the mailings, which had almost become a major battleground for the two contestants and their supporters. Jack Speer, it will be remembered, had just sprung actively into the fray. And it was under these fire-brand influences that the FAPA moved towards elections in June, 1938.

Not surprisingly, then, this second election was far different from the first. There was no lackadaisical attitude on the part of the members; rather, bitterness and strife predominated. Each group and faction seemed to feel that it had desperate reason to see the other defeated.

The anti-Wollheim faction was growing, and it filed as candidate for president John Baltadonis, immensely popular and one of the most prominent fans of the day. Wollheim, confronted by a constitutional

153

provision of his own devising which did not permit a FAPA member to be elected to the same office twice in a period of five years, backed his friend Michel for the post. Olon F. Wiggins also filed.

Baltadonis issued a four-paged hektographed pamphlet entitled *The FAPA Election* in which he charged the administration with the following: (1) "Gross incompetency in the matter of mailings...every one of the first three mailings has been late and the last terribly so." (2) "...abrogating of the constitution they themselves wrote" by charging compulsory postage to FAPA publishers without putting the matter to a vote. (3) "...juggling the membership list and sending out ballots calculated to secure votes for the Wollheim group; 21 were on the list December 15, and...22 voted...two who joined right after the mailing were not sent ballots." (4) "...putting publications in the third mailing that had no right there." This was a reference to the constitutional requirement that all publications submitted for use in the mailings must total fifty copies; Lowndes had sent in but thirty of his magazine *Strange*.

This little leaflet had dynamic results. The mailing that was to have carried the election ballots was again late, but the ballots themselves went out, mailed separately by Wollheim with a history-making *Open Letter*. The ballot itself raised consternation in one segment of the anti-Wollheim ranks—for neatly inscribed as a candidate for president was the name of Sam Moskowitz! Moskowitz had never filed candidacy, since he had pledged all his support to Baltadonis. At a meeting of the Greater New York SFL chapter shortly thereafter Moskowitz accosted Wollheim and openly accused him of trying to split the vote by listing him as a candidate without permission. Wollheim blandly short-circuited Moskowitz's indignation by informing him that Taurasi had filed for him. Taurasi had done so merely out of friendship. And Wollheim shrugged off Moskowitz's accusations of negligence for not informing him of the matter beforehand. There was little that Moskowitz could do except write explanatory letters to Baltadonis and those who might conceivably vote for him. However, when Sykora saw his friend's name on the ballot he immediately published and sent to most of the members a campaign flyer in Moskowitz's support. These communications crossed in the mails—and confusion was the order of the day.

In Wollheim's *Open Letter* no small part of the blame for the mailings being tardy was put on the shoulders of Baltadonis, who was accused of being so slow in sending reimbursements for official expenditures that the mailing office was constantly "bankrupt." It was alleged that such tactics had been purposely resorted to in order to "sabotage" the organization. As further evidence of "sabotage" Madle was accused of writing for publication unfavorable remarks concerning the FAPA. The reference was to a pseudonymous "Panparade" (a burlesque of Wollheim's "Fanfarade" column) that appeared in the March-April, 1938, issue of *Heltos*. Wollheim took especial objection to the following paragraph:

> Knowing with what great respect fans hold my opinion and sense of decency, honesty and fairness, in the forthcoming FAPA election I will take it upon myself to count the votes. You will be assured still further of my unquestionable honesty by the fact that I am one of the candidates.

Actually Moskowitz had authored the piece as part of his campaign against Wollheim, and Madle was angelically innocent of blame. With regard to the mailing office being "bankrupt," it was true that Baltadonis was frequently slow in answering his mail—but it was also true that just before this time Baltadonis had been ill and therefore unable to attend to his secretary-treasurer's correspondence. Moreover, according to postmarks and dates on letters, missives from New York would not be mailed to Baltadonis until several days after they had been written. Thus connections deteriorated. Most important of all statements found in the *Open Letter,* however, was the request that ballots be returned as promptly as possible (since they had been posted somewhat later than the constitution provided); thus there was little chance for those accused to reply to the charges made against them. Members were consequently left in a pro-Wollheim state of mind when they voted.

Running on an anti-Wollheim ticket for the FAPA vice-presidency was Jack Speer. Opposing him were Lowndes and Wilson. Speer's recent defense of Moskowitz plus his present alignment with the Philadelphia faction gained for him the immediate attention of Wollheim. Although Speer often pointedly denied any blanket support of fascism, he had on occasions orally remarked (and once stated in print) that he could see good points in even such a dictatorial system of government. Wollheim and his cohorts promptly seized upon this last statement as a sufficiently good excuse to refer to him as "an avowed fascist." Quite possibly Speer's known anti-communistic attitude played a part in this as well.

Wollheim himself was opposing Madle for the office of official editor and mailing manager, and there seemed little doubt that he would win out over his younger opponent. Taurasi had filed for secretary-treasurer, and was virtually unopposed.

The late fourth mailing which followed the ballots was devoted predominantly to Wollheimist campaign arguments. The charges in Baltalonis' pre-election pamphlet were answered by Wollheim in detail. He maintained that the idea of a mailing deadline was one which in practice never worked out in any amateur press group. The constitutional breach of allowing members to distribute material without paying postal charges was admitted and defended on the grounds that to do otherwise would have found the FAPA "strangled from lack of blood." As to the extra ballots cast in the earlier election Wollheim admitted that several fans had joined before the end of December and given ballots. Jack Speer was then accused of being s fascist—a charge that others of the clique repeated with Minor variations to great length, even going so far as to label *Loke,* his FAPA publication, "an apology for Fascism and general upholding of anti-progressive tactics and barbarism." As Speer's denials were simply used as bludgeons to reaccuse him of the same unfounded charges, he good-naturedly commenced to sign his name Jack F. (for "Fascist") Speer soon after, tactics which in some measure were effective in countering his opponents' accusations.

The election results were first announced in the July 17th number of Taurasi's weekly *Fantasy News* (a periodical about which much will shortly be related). Michel had gained the presidency, rolling up twenty votes to eleven for his nearest competitor, Baltadonis. Lowndes became vice-president with fifteen votes, while Speer and

Wilson recieved twelve apiece. Thirty-one gave Taurasi the secretary-treasurership decisively, with but ten votes scattered among three "write-in" candidates. And Wollheim overwhelmed Madle for official editor, twenty-eight to thirteen. The Wollheim faction had been elected to all offices but one—and Taurasi, then a neutral, held that. The Speer-Philadelphia group had been conclusively out-maneuvered by more experienced political workers and had suffered a drumming defeat. But they had no intention of taking it lying down. Outraged by the methods that led to their downfall they quickly began a counter-attack that produced damaging results.

The opening gun was Madle's small FAPA periodical *The Meteor*. This carried "A Reply to Donald A. Wollheim" in whose first paragraph Madle labelled Wollheim "a liar." He denied authorship of the "Pan-parade" burlesque he had been accused of writing. He indicted Woll-heim for using the "Fascist club" against Speer after he had stated at the campaign's opening that "political views of the candidates have no right to be taken into consideration," and intimated that this pronouncement had been designed by Wollheim to prevent charges of being a communist levelled at him. Madle then revealed that in the penultimate election, where twenty-two votes were counted from an eligible membership of twenty-one, English fan J. Michael Rosenblum had never voted. Further, he claimed that the one who had cast the deciding vote for vice-president was Harry Dockweiler, a friend of Wollheim's, who was not qualified to take part in the election at that time. In the same issue of *The Meteor* the new Texas fan Dale Hart also rallied to the cause, saying that he did not believe "it was right to send out the propaganda with the ballots, because the accused candidates weren't given a chance to reply in time...."

In the seventh issue of his magazine *Helios* Moskowitz accused Wollheim of deliberately placing his name on the FAPA ballot in order to split the anti-Wollheim vote.

Meanwhile, Jack Speer, with the assistance of the PSFS, composed and circulated a "Petition of Reprimand." This accused Wollheim of usurping the office of secretary-treasurer Baltadonis by mailing out ballots himself. It also objected to his sending out a campaign let-ter with the ballot as "contrary to accepted rules of order and eth-ics." Frederik Pohl was reprimanded for allegedly opening ballots and reporting on the election while it was still in progress—an act that Wilson substantiated, claiming that he had been told the names of certain individuals who had voted for him. The petition also pointed out that the constitution specifically stated that all votes had to be received by the first of July to be counted—some arriving as late as July 7 being included in results of this past contest. Wollheim's stated intention of employing irregular mailing dates was likewise protested. And, on the basis of such transgressions of procedure, signatures of protest against Wollheim and Pohl were specifically protested. Many prominent fans did not hesitate to affix theirs.

Madle, Agnew and Baltadonis also wrote a pointed *Open Letter to Donald A. Wollheim*. But this missive, due to being rephrased by Milton A. Rothman, a friend of Wollheim, ended up as a pitifully weak note that in effect asked him to behave better next time.

The very volume of opinion against him for the first time put Wollheim on the defensive. In the August, 1938, number of his *F.A.P.A.*

Fan he accused Baltadonis and Speer of attempting to destroy the club; terming them "rattlesnakes," he appealed to members to support him patiently until his opponents had "exhausted" their "venom." Fans in that day were too close to the situation, perhaps, to realize the importance of this tack. Today, in historical retrospect, we can readily see its significance: Wollheim for the first time in his career was involved in more squabbling than he could handle.

Chapter XXX

THE DEVELOPMENT OF MICHELISM

THE YEAR 1938 found the United States still in the throes of a depression serious enough to weaken the faith of many—particularly the youth of the country—in the soundness of its economic system. With few jobs available, little spending money, and no prospects for a better future, it is both excusable and understandable that young people would at least examine other forms of government on the chance that something better might be found. It is also natural to expect that some of these young people would be science fiction fans.

Perhaps John B. Michel was the first to become vocal over his researches into communism. His interest certainly led him as far as joining the Young Communist League. (Here it is essential to deviate long enough to point out that this does not necessarily mean that Michel ever became a member of, or affiliated with the party itself. The Young Communist League is an organization sponsored by the party to educate youth in the essentials of communism. From there, if desired, one might seek membership in the communist party, or, on the other hand, decide that the system had no merit and cease further investigation of it.) It was Michel who introduced Wollheim to communism, and explained to him many of its ramifications. Later Frederik Pohl evinced interest in the American Youth Congress, held by many to be a communist front organization.

We have already read of how Michel and Wollheim, at the 1937 Philadelphia convention, had generously tried to disseminate some of their newly-acquired wisdom through fan ranks by means of the "Mutation or Death" speech. Apparently believing it would be wise to give their political ideology a new name, so as to sugar-coat the pill, they decided upon "Michelism." This, of course, was in honor of Michel, who inspired the movement. Those who supported it thus became known throughout fandom as Michelists—and Michelists were for the most part located compactly in New York City and its environs. Those who agreed with or supported only a fraction of Michelism's tenets were likewise loosely—and incorrectly—referred to as Michelists. Prominent under this heading were Robert W. Lowndes, David A. Kyle, Richard Wilson, Jack Gillespie, Jack Rubinson (nom de plume: Jack Robins), Cyril Kornbluth (later writing fiction under the name S. D. Gottesman) and others who will later be mentioned. (It should be carefully noted that association with Michel and Wollheim under the banner of Michelism did not necessarily make those fans communistically inclined, though undoubtedly some had more than a speaking knowledge of the subject; yet just as certainly at least a few went along with the movement just for the sake of excitement or because interested friends did.)

The Michelists' bible was the fiery "Mutation or Death," which exhorted fans to snap out of their doldrums and use their superior mental attributes for bringing about "progress." This oft-repeated and -quoted speech was printed in a neat little red-covered pamphlet under the auspices of the Committee for the Political Advancement of

Science Fiction, a title adopted by the Michelists as being descriptive of their activities. This pamphlet was designed to be sold for five cents, but more often than not was given away to anyone who requested a copy as well as being distributed through the FAPA mailings.

In the December, 1937, issue of *Novae Terrae* (the official organ of the British Science Fiction Association) Wollheim's article "What Purpose, Science Fiction?" was featured. This article embodied much akin to that in Michel's "Mutation or Death" speech, but couched in less pyrotechnic terms. The original premise that science fiction would inspire its readers to scientific achievement was false, Wollheim contended, maintaining that those youths "who were primarily interested in science probably gave up reading science fiction after their first experimental glance at such stories." The "dreamers" were the ones who continued to read the stories, and their penchant was literary and artistic pursuit, not science. (It might be mentioned in passing that these views had been expressed by Wollheim previously, when he popularized the belief that the Gernsback idea of science fiction being educational was a delusion.) Wollheim's argument was actually in accord with the facts up until that time—but he neglected to give the adolescent science fiction fan time to grow up. It was unreasonable to suppose that science fiction would induce many already vocationally settled adults to adopt a scientific profession overnight, and it was equally unreasonable to expect the scant eleven years of science fiction's existence in magazine form to prove or disprove the "Gernsback delusion." Time had proven Wollheim to have been much in error. As he predicted, science fiction produced a great number of writers and artists—but it produced scientists as well. Dr. Thomas S. Gardner, well known gerontologist whose recent researches on longevity factors in queen bee royal jelly have been widely publicized, admits to having been stimulated to a career in science through reading fantastic fiction. Is it unreasonable to assume that others, not as well known, may have similarly been inspired to their careers? Avid science fiction fans today include mathematicians, doctors, psychiatrists, chemists, physicists, engineers, faculty members of college and university science departments; some such—David H. Keller, Robert A. Heinlein, Isaac Asimov and Eric Temple Bell ("John Taine"), to name a few—are writers as well as fans; and such prominent scientists as Drs. Muller and Oppenheimer, of Nobel Prize and atomic research fame, have been tabbed using quotations from current science fiction magazines. Current evidence seems greatly in favor of the premise that this type of literature did (and does) attract scientific man as readers as well as actually aid in producing them.

England in 1938 had begun the gradual shift toward the left that ultimately resulted in the victory of the Labor Party over Winston Churchill and his conservative government shortly after the close of World War II. This trend could be found in the opinions of young English fans, some of which saw print in *Novae Terrae*. Among these was Eric C. Williams' article "Are You a True Science Fictionist?" in the November, 1937, issue, which stated: "If there is anything worth going out for it is the introduction of sociology in science-fiction...." In the same number Albert Griffiths' article "The Future" declared dramatically that if fans put aside "Utopian dreams" and examined the world of practicability a world beyond their wildest imaginings might be attained.

Upon reading such words Donald Wollheim probably felt them to be stirrings of a credo similar to Michelism but stated in more cautious terms. He felt, too, it would seem, that this British periodical did not represent merely fertile ground, but a crop soon ready to be harvested; so, in one of the most daring, self-indicting and honest articles of his career, Wollheim pulled the cloak away from the body of Michelism and revealed it in completely positive terms as a directed instrument for recruiting fans to the communist movement. "Commentary on the November *Novae Terrae*" appeared in the January, 1938, issue of that magazine. In it Wollheim laid down his basic definitions of Michelism preceded by statements explaining why he believed that no existing government could possibly be overthrown without the use of force of some kind, but adding that he did not advocate the use of force until

> ...the present system has lost control and chaos is setting in, or when it begins to throw aside its shell of "democracy" and institute fascist crystallization of the old, then (and not before) these practical idealists united in almost military order will be the ONLY FORCE LEFT which will be able to save civilization from barbarism.... The only such force today, the most powerful force alive for the World State and the only organization that will ever achieve this result is the Communist International.

He asked fans to do him the decency to investigate communism for themselves. He pointed out that in New York a group of fans called Michelists were already working toward the enlightened end. Terming Michelism "the theory of science-fiction Action," Wollheim further defined the movement as follows:

> MICHELISM is the belief that science-fiction followers should actively work for the realization of the scientific socialist world-state as the only genuine justification for their activities and existence.
> MICHELISM believes that science-fiction is a force; a force acting through the medium of speculative and prophetic fiction on the minds of idealist youth; that logical science-fiction inevitably points to the necessity for socialism, the advance of science, and the world-state; and that these aims, created by science-fictional idealizing, can best be reached through adherence to the program of the Communist International.

Wollheim concluded his article with "SALUD, Comrades!"

In America Michelists' statements pursuant to their program were of far less outspoken character, though the inferences were quite clear. In addition to such CPASF booklets already described there was published (under other sponsorship) *The World Gone Mad,* a tract that prejudicedly summarized world conditions and ended by giving one the choice between "communism" or "chaos." The article "What is Michelism?" by Robert W. Lowndes (printed in the May, 1938, *Science Fiction Fan*) diagnosed the movement as "no more than a state of mind, a way of thinking that all alert, intelligent and progressive-minded fans *must* come to eventually, just as progressive study of mathematics leads from simple arithmetic through algebra, geometry, trigonometry, etc." Lowndes also said that "Michelists look upon the world without...colored glasses, but with the memory of...dreams, and the realization gained from stf. that these dreams are *not* impossible." These remarks, far removed from Wollheim's positive, conclusive statements in *Novae Terrae* were probably inspired by better judgement, as few fans of 1937-38 would openly espouse communism.

Jack Speer, with the damning *Novae Terrae* article at hand, composed "A Fairly Complete Case Against Michelism," which was published in the May, 1938, *Science Fiction Collector*. Speer stated that he believed everything about the movement to be wrong except the intentions of its perpetrators, which impressed him as being sincere. The *Novae Terrae* avowal of communism was referred to with surprising restraint, and used mostly to support a logical proof that many of the basic tenets of communism were false. He ended with a plea that fans reject Michelism because of "the unnecessity of revolution; the destructive communist methods; the unworthiness of Russian Communism itself."

The first (April, 1938) issue of *The Science Fiction Advance* as has already been noted, was distributed at the Newark convention of that year. Sponsored by the CPASF, it continued to appear, being devoted to the presentation of socially conscious articles connected with science fiction (a connection that was frequently very tenuous indeed) as well as that of news about Michelism's progress. New recruits were found in the greater New York area; outside of it few were to be had. Among those that were acquired, however, was the promising young fan artist, James M. Rogers, whose writings in this period led Jack Speer to nickname him "Oklahoma's gift to the Communist Party." Forrest Ackerman, a prominent name in the field at the time, gave Michelism his tacit support; he had joined the Socialist Party, a fact which Wollheim reported in his "Fanfarade" column with the remark that that group had at the time "greater revolutionary tendencies" than the communists.

Some fans supported a few of Michelism's tenets only. A good part of these were of course those whose interests lay in socialistic fields. Thus the Philadelphian Milton A. Rothman lent his qualified support. Some anti-Michelists were more disconcerting than the creed's supporters—witness Bernard E. Seufert of Rochester, New York, who, in his *Asteroid* for June, 1938, remarked that he would dearly have liked to attend the Newark convention: "I would have visited New York's little colony of Germans, Yorkville—I would have sipped a few drinks with some of the fellows—I would have Michel explain Michelism more fully—I would have had an argument with Wollheim as I am a fascist." Thankfully, there were not many like this!

Not everyone in Los Angeles acquiesced to Ackerman's tacit support of Michelism. T. Bruce Yerke, *Imagi-Nation*'s first editor, published in the April, 1938, issue of that periodical his article "A Reply to 'Michelism'." Yerke felt that Wollheim had contradicted himself in the *Novae Terrae* article by opposing the principles of a "peace pledge" folder previously distributed with that magazine and then claiming that Michelism stood for "peace, unity and freedom." Yerke felt that such general aims were all very well, but that not only were science fiction fans too scant in number to do much about them, but that it was not the destiny of science fiction to accomplish political reforms anyway. He advised Michelists to look elsewhere.

Such an article may well have been exactly what the Michelists wanted, since it provided further opportunity to restate their case in replying. In the next (May) issue of the magazine Wollheim's rebuttal, titled "In Defense of Michelism," appeared. Wollheim contended that it was enough for science fiction fans to do something—however small—to bring about world unity. He minimized contradiction of the "peace pledge" folder, which he alleged to be both "isolationist" and "purely negative" in character. Yerke and Speer were then cautioned against espousing "benevolent dictatorship," whose benevolence Wollheim emphatically denied *in toto*.

Directly across the page from this rebuttal was "A New Attack on Michelism" by "Erick Freyer," which demanded "what in the name of the *Necronomicon* science fiction had to do with Michelism." The writer's earthy philosophy was expounded and applied to fans who insisted on "being a God in a pigsty."

By this time arguments pro and con had begun to flood the editorial sanctum of *Imagination!*. Nearly all fans were interested in the question, and most wanted to get their two cents on it into print. But before debate was terminated in the July, 1938, number much more had been said. Among the longer articles were Wollheim's "In Defense of Progress," countering the Erick Freyer piece cited above, and the reply to it, "Debunking of Progress." In the latter Shroyer stated that he could not "view with alarm" Wollheim's Michelistic ultimatum that the world was at the crossroads, maintaining that the world was perpetually at a crossroads, and further that communism and progress were not compatible.

Tactics used by Michelists forced upon their opponents—particularly the younger set—a sort of guerilla warfare as a means of coping with more politically adept antagonists. This at first took the form of decided anti-Michelist views in letters to correspondents. Continually provoked, some resorted to other—often childish—devices. Two budding young Philadelphia artists, John V. Baltadonis and Jack Agnew, made a practice of drawing exceedingly unflattering pictures of Wollheim and his cohorts on the envelopes of letters mailed to fans, not forgetting to use them on letters to Wollheim himself. Since Wollheim's features readily lent themselves to caricature, this instigated not only laughter directed at him, but to some degree at Michelism as well. And it is possible that such low devices had psychological affect on the man himself. Numerous unsigned drawings, some of which were quite pornographic, were passed about from hand to hand during this period.

Eventually this form of expression—in reasonably disinfected form —came out into the open with the solicitation and publishing by Moskowitz of a legitimate political cartoon in the May-June, 1938, *Helios*. The damaging potentialities of this full-page lampoon (which Baltadonis had drawn in colors) were many: it simplified the issue in favor of the anti-Michelists; it aroused fandom at large to laugh at their opponents; it appealed to the emotions rather than to the intellect; and it utilized satire as an effective weapon.

(It should be remarked parenthetically at this point that anti-Michelists had employed satire earlier as well. In the *Helios* "As Others See Us" column Moskowitz had bitingly referred to his opponents' alcoholic partialities, and a regular feature of the magazine had been humorous parodies on items their magazines printed. Chester

L. Sprague de Camp

Fletcher Pratt

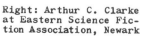

Dr. David H. Keller
delivers a blast
against Dianetics
at New York in 1949

Right: Arthur C. Clarke
at Eastern Science Fic-
tion Association, Newark

Edd Cartier

Below, l to r: Milton A. Rothman, Sam Moskowitz, Benson Dooling, Charles Lucas, Dr. Thomas S. Gardner, John Nitka, Isaac Asimov, John Wasso, Jr., Samuel Loveman, George O. Smith, L. Sprague de Camp, L. A. Eshbach and Oswald Train at the Philadelphia Conference in 1946

Robert Arthur, pro-
ducer of *Escape, the
Mysterious Traveller*

Willy Ley

Sam Merwin, Jr., then editor of *Thrilling Wonder* and *Startling
Stories,* shakes hands with Hugo Gernsback at the March 5, 1950,
meeting of the Eastern Science Fiction Association

Edd Cartier, Hannes Bok, Theodore Sturgeon

Cyril M. Kornbluth   Isaac Asimov

Fein had also written satires on the subject, of which one—titled
"The Life of Wollheim"—was too barbed for even a fan editor to
print. It passed from one to another for over two years encountering
no one foolhardy enough to publish it.)

When Wollheim used Moskowitz's lack of support and enthusiasm for
Michelism as an excuse for attacking him (as outlined in Chapter XXV)
he also made it inevitable that in any prolonged battle Moskowitz
would shift the attack from Wollheim to Michelism itself. Wollheim
did not fear this, however, feeling that once his opponent began to
attempt to disprove its tenets he could be brought to heel through
utilization of reason. Wollheim doubtless felt that he could produce
more arguments in favor of the movement than Moskowitz could conceivably marshall against it. But the nature of Moskowitz's counter-
action (partially inspired by the counsel of William Sykora) proved
as unexpected as it was effective.

For Moskowitz metamorphosed from a person with few and vague
political views into a candidate for the world's premier eighteen-
year-old red-baiter. He seized it with a vigor that left an odor
permeating the vicinity. Under no circumstance would he even consider
discussion of the movement. His view was that it was a political
idology and therefore had no place in science fiction whatsoever;
that even to discuss it was to forward its tenets. Thus, in
replying to Wollheim's complaint anent his poor reporting of the
"Mutation or Death" speech, Moskowitz branded both the speech and
its author as communistic. When *Imagination!* banned Michelistic
material Moskowitz wrote the editor jubilantly, saying that "there
is no difference between Michelism and communism...Michel is a
communist and makes no bones about the fact." He also advised the
communists to use "their own journals." But the item that caused the
Michelists to lose their patience was "That's the Way It Goes," an
article published in the August, 1938, *Science Fiction Fan;* in this
Moskowitz had this to say:

> SCIENCE FICTION'S SKELETON IN THE CLOSET was the retitled
> Communist Party's Agitators in Science Fiction. This club
> headed by Wollheim and stooges received orders from the heads
> of the Communist Party to convert the fan magazines into a
> field of propaganda. If communists can obtain control of the
> free press of this country they can easily obtain their
> objectives. Wollheim's job was to obtain control, if possible,
> by fair means or foul, of the science-fiction magazines,
> twist their liberal policies to fit their propaganda, and
> again, if possible, of the World's Science Fiction Convention
> to be used as a means of furthering communist propaganda.
> Communists' gaining control of fandom is not as fantastic as
> it sounds if the inroads of Michelism are any indication....

Wollheim's plan of long-range action to combat this "indiscretion"
will be dealt with in a later chapter for the sake of more effective
continuity. He replied to the charges immediately, however, in his
"Fanfarade" column of *The Science Fiction Fan* (September, 1938). He
termed all of them "fiction," the "chief of which was that made up
out of whole cloth about the Communist Party and its 'orders' to me!
Needless to say if the strength of that great American organization
was behind me, I'd have several first rate printed fantasy publications going and the fan field would have developed to greater
heights than dreamed of."

Another important article appearing at this time was a reply to Speer's "Fairly Complete Case Against Michelism" and appeared in the August-September, 1938, *Science Fiction Collector;* it was titled "A Better Case Against Michelism," and was written by Robert W. Lowndes. All one had to do to be labelled a Michelist by the fan press, complained Lowndes, was to do something to further the progress of the world. Concerning the Michelists he further remarked:

> I may toy with the idea that eventually, with knowledge, they will turn to Communism, but that does not alter the fact. If it *is* a fact that Communism, as I believe, is *the* way out, then this belief or conscious ignoring of it will not alter the fact; if, as you think, it is *not* true, then my belief will not change it.... I speak as a Michelist whose Michelism takes the form of Communism...*not*...merely as a Michelist. ...call me a red Michelist if you like, but the adjective, while applicable to me, is not necessarily applicable to all Michelists.

Lowndes went on to list several mistakes which he felt had been made in advancing the creed: Naming the movement Michelism, since the average fan would associate the name Michel with communism; the attempt of the "red Michelists" to make this a definite road to a clear-cut goal; too intense propaganda; the failure to "fraternize" rather than "organize" such Michelists as the New York group knew. "Thus we (at least I) bid farewell to the term 'Michelism'," Lowndes concluded, saying that he would no longer argue the subject over the keys of his typewriter. Many readers misconstrued this to mean that Michelism was being abandoned—overlooking the fact that the term, not the movement itself, had been dropped. The fan world was to hear much, much more of Michelism.

In later historical gauging of anti-Michelists' actions it is vitally important to remember that as the feud progressed communism became more and more obnoxious to them. They did not wish to associate or be catalogued with people who extolled this political ideology. This eventually made rapprochement impossible, and was a strong factor in their wanting to hold meetings and conventions and to publish magazines without coming in contact with their opponents.

Whether or not the reader accepts or rejects communism as it was promulgated by the Michelists, it must be stated that many of their observations as to the condition of the world in 1937-38 were highly accurate. From the first they maintained that the revolution in Spain was the beginning of a great struggle between the larger forces of democracy and fascism; that the world teetered on the brink of the most disastrous war in history; that citizens should face the facts. Michel's exhortation "Awake! The future is upon us!" was as prophetic as it was dramatic. Perhaps this accurate appraisal resulted in a sense of impending doom which in turn may have brought about a feeling of desperation that would justify to the Michelists their adoption of an end-justifies-the-means philosophy which outraged fans and created a powerful opposition. In any event, the open advocacy of communism more than nullified, as far as fans were concerned, whatever logic Michelism utilized.

Chapter XXXI

THE GREATER NEW YORK SCIENCE FICTION LEAGUE

UNDER HUGO Gernsback's aegis the Science Fiction League had been a vigorous, forward-driving organization that went out of its way to encourage creation and growth of local chapters and their activities. The column devoted to the organization in *Wonder Stories* up to the very end of the Gernsback regime had increased in size and importance. When Standard Publications purchased and rechristened the magazine, and solicited a grade of fiction that would appeal to a lower mental average than that catered to by the former owner, it apparently regarded the League as an annoying appendage to its business bargain. For reasons of prestige and good will the firm could scarcely drop the organization—but on the other hand no planned campaign to encourage expansion would be initiated.

The six-months' interregnum in 1936 preceding change of the magazine s ownership had in itself dealt a fatal blow to the weaker chapters in the Science Fiction League. Still, the more stable units, such as those in Los Angeles and Philadelphia, clung tenaciously to their League affiliations since these offered them their only means of advertising activities and recruiting new members. For the very same reason occasional new groups continued to arise and request charters despite the near-moribund state of the parent organization.

The long and fantastically chamber-of-commerce-like minutes of the Los Angeles chapter and the more infrequent and respectable Philadelphia SFL reports were additional incentive for fans to found new locals. Most of these were abortive attempts, however, There was a Maryland Intra-City chapter launched by Willis Conover. A Yonkers chapter was announced by O. Davidson, but that, too, ignominiously expired. Oliver E. Saari began a Minneapolis chapter of the League, and reported an apparently successful initial meeting with the well-known fantasy authors Donald Wandrei and Carl Jacobi in attendance; but this first official communication from them was also the last. A Columbus, Ohio, group headed by John Van Rooyan got no further than a good try, nor did J. Chapman Miske's Cleveland unit.

The League was also helpless to cope with such ruses as that of Frederik Pohl, who in December, 1936, applied for and received a charter for a chapter in Brooklyn, New York. This included on its roster such names as Elton V. Andrews, Henry De Costa and Allen Zweig—all of which were pseudonyms of Pohl himself. Two of the members, Walter Kubilius and Harry Dockweiler, were live fans, but it is extremely doubtful if they were guilty of anything more official than paying Pohl an occasional friendly visit. Pohl successfully continued his hoax, sending reports of the club's "progress" to headquarters at irregular intervals for several years, and even announcing a change in name to "The Greater New York Chapter" in order to "embrace more territory."

The Science Fiction League column in the August, 1937, issue of *Thrilling Wonder Stories* announced that James V. Taurasi had formed a chapter in Flushing, New York. Taurasi announced that a July meeting had been held with Robert G. Thompson, Richard Wilson and Abraham Oshinsky in attendance. The club appeared thus to be following the lead of Frederik Pohl's—for actually only Taurasi and Thompson were present, and no regular meeting had been held at all!

The appearance of such new fans as Taurasi, Wilson, Thompson and Gillespie in the New York area made it almost inevitable that a lasting science fiction club would eventually be formed there. This indeed proved to be the case. In October, 1937, Sykora, Thompson, Wilson and Mario Racic, Jr., assembled at the home of director Taurasi and joined the Queens chapter of the SFL. The second meeting held November 7, saw the planning of a hektographed club organ titled *Jeddara* (the Martian word for "queen" in Edgar Rice Burroughs' novels). The first issue was bound in with Taurasi's *Cosmic Tales Quarterly*, but two later numbers, also hektographed, were distributed independently. At the same meeting the club decided to send a delegate to visit the newly formed Washington Heights SFL, informing them of the Queens group and the presence of other fans in the New York area. One of the results of this visit, made by Richard Wilson, was to recruit to the Queens banner three important names from the Washington Heights club: Cyril Kornbluth, Chester Fein and David Charney.

The Queens chapter worked up an interesting correspondence with John W. Campbell, Jr., newly appointed editor of *Astounding Stories,* who adopted a friendly attitude toward visits from members to his office and was kept informed of their progress. Another correspondent of the club was Thomas S. Gardner, well known in those days for contributions to *Wonder Stories,* who evinced the desire eventually to meet the membership. (Both of these events proved later to be quite important.) The chapter's January, 1938, meeting was attended by Moskowitz, who found the members congenial and who offered them suggestions and help. It was at this time that he definitely resolved to work with Sykora toward holding the First National Science Fiction Convention in Newark that year.

Superficially the Queens SFL appeared to be an innocuous type of organization, bumbling happily along a slightly juvenile course and professing no world-shaking ideals or purposes. It did have a by-law, though, which stated that a recruit could not join if objected to by two members. The presence of Sykora thus made it almost certain that Wollheim and his followers would have difficulty becoming members. But motivated either by chance or by excellent sources of information, Wollheim and three of his friends—Michel, Goudket and Pohl—attended the March, 1938, meeting at which Sykora was not present. When they asked to join there was no one to cast a vote against them or rally others to do so, since no member there had ever had any serious altercation with them. The only thing standing in their way was a League ruling that no individual could belong to two chapters at the same time. To circumvent this, Pohl resigned from his Greater New York chapter, and his pen-name Elton V. Andrews ascended to its chairmanship.

And so it happened that Sykora returned to the April meeting a greatly saddened fan. His only chance of undoing these past events lay in the interpretation of a club by-law which read: "All proposed members must receive a unanimous vote of the society in order to enter. Did this mean all members in the chapter—or merely all those present at the voting? This question was brought onto the floor, and the club voted for the latter interpretation. At the same meeting it passed another ruling, one of much later significance to itself and to Sykora in particular: "A member, after three consecutive absenses, may be informed that, unless he appears at the next meeting, or gives a good reason for not doing so, be automatically dropped from the rolls."

The Queens chapter expanded gradually in size, so that at the time of the May, 1938, meeting it had thirteen active members. Many of these felt that further growth would best be promoted by retitling the chapter so as to encourage interest of fans in the entire city of New York rather than simply those living in the borough of Queens. By a majority vote the name was then changed to the Greater New York Chapter of the Science Fiction League, and an official charter was duly obtained for the new name. This change apparently was well-advised, for the June 5, 1938, meeting, the first under this new policy, was the most successful to date. Sixteen fans were present, including the newly-acquired trio from the Washington Heights chapter. Two amateur artists, John Giunta and Daniel C. Burford, were added to the roster, as was the old-timer Jack Rubinson. The third issue of *Jeddara* was distributed. Plans were made to cooperate with Herbert Goudket in producing *Sotentt-Photo,* a fan magazine composed largely of photographs. A regular talk was delivered by William Sykora, and the group seemed well on its way toward continued growth and achievement.

However, though they were not publicized, ominous undertones of dissension existed—and it was not long before these came to the surface. The group of Michelists and Michelist sympathizers continued to build up strength. One of them, Frederik Pohl, proposed at a meeting that the chapter send a delegate to the leftist American Youth Congress and/or support it with a contribution of ten cents per member. Director Taurasi, always an easy-going fellow amenable to reason, balked completely at this, refusing to allow a vote on the motion on the grounds that it was political and therefore had no place on the agenda of a science fiction organization. Accusing him of dictatorship, Michelists began impeachment proceedings against Taurasi. These were to culminate at the June meeting, but the banner attendance and presence of new members made the whole affair appear unseemly, so the matter was discreetly dropped. However, it is significant to note that Michelist-sympathizer Richard Wilson, secretary of the club during this period, included no mention of the incident whatsoever in the official minutes, which your historian has read.

Taurasi had never been partisan in previous fan dissensions, and consequently had never joined or aligned himself with any clique. but now, forced on the defensive and finding himself alone, he appealed to Sam Moskowitz to visit the chapter and give him moral support. Thus Moskowitz, accompanied by another Newark fan, Alex Osheroff, was present at the club's meeting in July. At the appropriate time he expressed the desire of Osheroff and himself to join as regular dues-paying members. The question as to whether he could attend regularly was then submitted, and both replied in the affirmative. Since they were residents of another state, however, it would be necessary to amend the club by-laws in order to permit the two to join. A motion permitting out-of-state fans to become members provided they attended regularly was then passed by a majority of the fans present. But when the membership of Moskowitz and Osheroff was balloted on, four "no" votes were cast. Moskowitz was startled by this turn of events. He rose and stated that in his opinion the banning from membership in the only local club in the area of an active, interested fan was disgraceful. Further, he said, any prejudice a few fans might have against him need not also have been directed against Osheroff. Pohl then pointedly reminded Moskowitz that he was not a member of the group, and that if he insisted on giving vent to his opinions he would have to leave. (At this point it should also be noted that the complete minutes of this July meeting had been removed from the records secretary Wilson passed on to his successor, and to date have not been recovered.)

With such controversial factions present, it was obvious that the club could not hope to present a united front much longer. And when Moskowitz presented opinions to this effect in an article published in *The Science Fiction Fan* Wollheim promptly seized upon them as evidence proving him guilty of subversive action in regard to that organization.

Because of the volume of his opposition, Sykora absented himself from the chapter meetings for some time. Michelists at this point seized upon a by-law stating that a member could be expelled for non-attendance and non-payment of dues for three or more meetings, and insisted on his expulsion. Taurasi refused to consider such action on the grounds that chapter by-laws stated that a member to be expelled must be present to defend himself. The Michelists considered this inapplicable, and Taurasi sidetracked a showdown on the point by insisting that it first be proved conclusively that Sykora had absented himself from three or more consecutive meetings. Concrete proof was lacking, for secretary Wilson did not regularly include in the minutes names of all those attending meetings. Taurasi then refused to recognize any expulsion proceedings.

Nothing daunted, the Michelists next began impeachment action against Taurasi. Before these could terminate Taurasi resigned the directorship. The meeting continued without him, and Sykora was expelled from the chapter. Taurasi announced his refusal to remain in the chapter, and stated that the cellar of his home, theretofore used as its meeting place, would no longer be available. He further wrote Leo Margulies, director of the Science Fiction League, explaining the situation. Margulies likewise received reports from Michelist members of the club. The letter he wrote in reply to Taurasi is important enough to quote from extensively. It was dated September 14, 1938, and read as follows:

> I was greatly distressed by your report concerning recent meetings of the GNYSFL. I am familiar with the differences of opinions between Messrs. Sykora and Wollheim and have made several efforts to reconcile them. But evidently their acrimonious relations have gone too far this time.
> It is impossible for *Thrilling Wonder Stories* to ascertain which group is in the right, mainly because of the colored versions that come to our attention from the principals concerned. Regardless, after serious consideration, we have decided to dissolve the Greater New York Chapter. As far as our magazine is concerned, as of this date, the Greater New

York Chapter does not exist.

While this is quite a drastic action, we have discussed the matter in great detail right here in the office, and we suggest a rather favorable alternative for your group.

Briefly, here's the plan: Let Mr. Sykora form his own branch of the SFL—that is, after he secures at least ten members. Let him be careful in organizing his chapter, as to whom he includes for membership. There is no reason why New York City can't have several individual chapters, each headed by an enthusiastic follower of science fiction, each composed of a group of individuals whose interests and relations are both mutual and compatible.

Similarly, we suggest that Mr. Wollheim round up his own chapter with ten followers; let him be careful that his members are all friendly, that no internal dissension will rise again to destroy the organization.

And thus perished the Greater New York Chapter of the Science Fiction League, and not unnaturally neither faction was satisfied with the turn events had taken. In retrospect, however, we can see that it was inevitable. Equally inevitable was an even more important corollary to the break-up. By their own deliberate actions the Michelists had not only made a new enemy, but had caused him to join forces with two old ones. And the combination of Sykora's long experience, Moskowitz's widespread contacts and penchant for article-writing, and Taurasi's publishing abilities was a formidable one indeed. This triumvirate not only outlasted Michelism itself, but lived to wield great power in future fandom.

Chapter XXXII

FANTASY NEWS AND NEW FANDOM

UNTIL LATE JUNE, 1938, Richard Wilson's *Science Fiction News-Letter* was the only weekly fan journal in the field. Begun December 4, 1937, it encountered no competition whatsoever for a full seven months. Though its very existence marked the beginning of the end for extensive inter-fan correspondence, it was by no means unreservedly popular. In the first place, its hektographed columns were all too often too lightly printed to be read easily. Again, there was its price—five cents for a single letter-sized sheet; for the same sum, other magazines provided up to ten times as much reading-matter as the *News-Letter*. Further, the *News-Letter* failed to serve the needs of fandom at the time. To discern trends of the period from a file of this journal would be impossible—despite the fact that it called itself a "news-latter." The bulk of its space was devoted to reviews of movies, plays and books, radio notes, fantasy cartoon data and similar minor irrelevancies—all the more inexcusable when one reflects on the history being made in the field at the time and the fact that the average fan hungered for more information about it.

Wilson's periodical specialized in trivial anecdotes instead of meaty news stories. We have already learned how it treated the first national convention: failing to impart to its clientele a single sentence about the affair itself. Naturally this left the *News-Letter* open to criticism and competition. Surprisingly enough, the latter appeared first.

On June 26, 1938, Taurasi brought out the first issue of *Fantasy News*. The initial purpose of this new weekly was to fill out unexpired subscriptions to Taurasi's *Cosmic Tales,* the title which Robert G. Thompson had inherited and found himself incapable of continuing. The grammar and spelling in *Fantasy News* were atrocious, and it, too, was only a single sheet of two pages. But it was mimeographed—and we have already noted that this, in a hektographing era, was provocative of respect. Further, *Fantasy News* sold at three numbers for a dime. It was set up in approved newspaper style with headlines, and its special departments were clearly separated from actual news. It even boasted an editorial staff whose members were individually responsible for radio, cinema and fan magazine reviews. Such specializations made for a better paper.

Fantasy News' initial modest success irritated Richard Wilson. From the first he reprinted in the *News-Letter's* "snicker department" the worst grammatical and spelling errors he could excerpt from Taurasi's sheet. Then a more damaging phase of his antipathy began. Taurasi was using a mimeograph machine borrowed from the defunct Phantasy Legion by permission of David Kyle. Wilson convinced Kyle that the machine could be put to better use on his more literate *Science Fiction News-Letter,* and one day the two descended upon Flushing Flats and emancipated it from the weekly slavery imposed by Taurasi. In a single stroke Wilson felt he had eliminated his competition.

In desperation, Taurasi contacted Sykora and begged permission to use his mimeograph. Sykora was willing; and so Taurasi and Mario Racic (an important behind-the-scenes worker in fandom) continued to pay Sunday visits to Sykora's house and *Fantasy News* continued to appear.

It will be remembered that at the Newark convention in May much maneuvering and counter-maneuvering marked the choice of a committee to take charge of the 1939 world convention. Sykora had been authorized by attendees to appoint a group, and he maintained that their majority abrogated the authority of a previous committee named for the same purpose at the New York convention of February, 1937. Friends of Wollheim—chairman of the old committee—prepared and circulated at the Newark convention a petition protesting this, as we have previously stated (Chapter XXVIII). Wollheim himself refused to recognize the new committee or to relinquish his chairmanship in the old one. This action received support when the Michelist-dominated Greater New York SFL chapter, at its July meeting, passed a motion accepting responsibility for being the handling committee of the 1939 convention. Two active, competing committees now existed.

Sykora called a meeting of his group, which was composed of Moskowitz, Goudket, Fein and Kubilius. Only Moskowitz appeared. Since the weather was inclement, a second set of invitations for a later date were mailed. Again only Moskowitz responded, and without a quorum the committee obviously could not hope to function. Why did the others fail to appear? Lacking definite information, we can only speculate that since all three had or had acquired friendly inclinations towards Michelism, they may have stayed away purposely to please Wollheim.

Meanwhile the Michelists had shown their petition to the science fiction magazine editors Margulies and Campbell, who decided to make an attempt at reconciling both factions, since a successful science fiction convention would aid their own interests. Early in July, therefore, Campbell, Margulies, Sykora and Wollheim met in solemn conclave in a New York restaurant. Margulies acted as interrogator, alternately questioning Sykora and Wollheim to ascertain just what their ideas and opinions were. It soon became evident that it would be impossible to reconcile their diametrically opposed views. That left but one alternative: a choice must be made between the two, predicated upon evidence as to which showed better ability to present a successful convention.

Wollheim named the Committee for the Political Advancement of Science Fiction as the logical group to sponsor the convention, and cited its support by the Greater New York SFL chapter. Sykora had nothing comparable to call upon, and it appeared the nod would go to Wollheim. And as a last resort he attempted to turn the odds by a bluff. Pooh-poohing the strength of Wollheim's supporters, he declared (with a nonchalant wave of his hand) that in a few months' time he could produce an organization twice as powerful as the CPASF. As capable a publishing executive as Leo Margulies could not be duped by such a show of mock bravado, however. If Sykora could produce something concrete, he said, he would be willing to reconsider; but in the absence of anything more substantial than boasts, he would string along at least temporarily with Wollheim. Picking up the check, he led the group from the restaurent. Campbell had taken

little active part in the proceedings, but his silence plainly
indicated that he seconded his fellow editor's stand.

When he entered the discussion, Wollheim probably felt that the
cards were stacked against him, that the discussion was preordained
to be in Sykora's favor. But as it proceeded, he was easily able to
make the better impression in the face of his opponent's weak logic.
After leaving the restaurent he accosted Sykora on a near-by corner
and offered his hand. But Sykora disdained it, feeling that to shake
hands would be to admit his own crushing defeat.

To Sykora this conference was a final set-back in an interminably
galling feud that had begun over a year before. Only at the Newark
convention had he gained a temporary victory; elsewhere he had always emerged the loser. Always he had played a lone game, enlisting
the help of others—Madle, Goudket, Taurasi, Moskowitz and others—
on occasion, but never informing them of the underlying strategy of
his campaigns.

Not surprisingly, Moskowitz had been most bewildered at the dynamic
developments at and following what he expected naively to be an
orderly convention with no determining motif save the advancement of
science fiction. Sykora had not taken him into his confidence, and
the dislike of Wollheim by both had never resulted in any mutually
planned operations against him. But when the two next met, Sykora
finally unburdened himself to Moskowitz—a bit guardedly, yet with
reasonable honesty—of the political maneuverings during the recent
convention and of the result of the recent conference with the editors (of which last Moskowitz had not even heard). He was not asking
for help, he said, since only displaying to Margulies and Campbell a
large, well-knit organization willing abd able to put on the convention would be effective—and he knew well there was no prospect of
whipping into shape any such group within a month or two.

Far from being discouraged by the prospects, Moskowitz became self-
assured, jubilant and cocky. A month seemed to him ample time in
which to produce a sizeable organization. In fact, the organization
itself was no problem at all. Instead, he wondered whether the
necessary club publication could be mimeographed or if he would have
to depend on his own worn-out hektograph outfit, and whether his
spending money of a dollar a week could do the work of the five
needed by the organization. Sykora, feeling ready to go along for a
laugh, made it plain to the neophyte that he would go as high as ten.
That being the case, Moskowitz gave his money-back guarantee that he
would produce the world's largest science fiction organization
within a month. But to do so he would need the help of Taurasi's
Fantasy News, and he asked that a meeting of the three be arranged.

This meeting was held on July 17, 1938, at Sykora's home. A more
self-assured, domineering and conceited youngster than Sam Moskowitz
was that Sunday has rarely been seen in fandom. He was barely out of
high school, and had but a few weeks past attained the pontifical
elevation of eighteen years—yet he systematically vetoed and overrode every suggestion of Sykora and Taurasi, insisting that the new
club would be run his way or not at all. Sykora, for example, wanted
a strong science motif dominent, as in the old ISA. He was told that
if the official magazine published one science article in three
issues he could consider himself lucky. Taurasi felt that the club
organ should use fiction. He was bluntly informed that nothing but

articles and columns on science fiction would be used—that there never would be any fiction there. Sykora wanted the club to use the name of the ISA again, while Taurasi favored that of the abortive American Fantasy Association, which had been stillborn two weeks before. Moskowitz unceremoniously replied that the club was to be called New Fandom (a name he had gleaned from a recent series of articles by Jack Speer, "Annals of New Fandom") and he positively refused to consider any compromise. He believed, perhaps correctly, that the word "new" bespoke the freshness of a clean slate, another start, and would attract fans to membership. Despite strong objections, he insisted that the magazine also be titled *New Fandom* and further that it be mimeographed and have silk-screen covers like the old *International Observer*.

Both Sykora and Taurasi were at the nadir of their fan careers, and had no bargaining points. Moskowitz, on the other hand, had the backing of not only the Philadelphia faction (second most influential in fandom at the time) but of the many fan publishers dependent on his manuscript bureau as well. Consequently he had his own way completely. Sykora went along because there was nothing else for him to do, but Taurasi displayed more enthusiasm when Moskowitz told him, as an incidental aside, that *Fantasy News* would have to be made the leading newspaper of fandom in both popularity and circulation. It was his intention, said Moskowitz, to perform the tasks of creating New Fandom and energizing *Fantasy News* concurrently. Probably the only thing more irritating than a braggart is a braggart who proves his point. This Moskowitz proceeded to do in as unusual a series of coincidences and political jockeyings as fandom had ever seen.

The basis of Moskowitz's self-confidence was a letter from Raymond Van Houten, director of the Science Fiction Advancement Association, dated April 22, 1938. In this Van Houten offered to turn over the organization to Moskowitz in its entirety, since he—Van Houten—was no longer able to carry it. Here fate played a hand. Before Moskowitz could write his acceptance of the dormant SFAA, *Fantasy News* published Van Houten's resignation from the organization, and the news of his appointment of Roy A. Squires as temporary managing secretary. It now appeared that he would have to deal with Squires, an old-time fan residing in Glendale, California. But gambling on the premise that Squires might not want the job, Moskowitz promptly wrote Van Houten, requesting the organization and outlining his plan to have it form the nucleus of a powerful new group whose purpose would be presenting a science fiction convention the next year.

On August 6 Van Houten replied as follows:

> Your plans to take over the S.F.A.A. are just what I've been looking for. I wanted to sponsor the 1939 convention but I didn't have the funds. You are hereby appointed Manager-Secretary; I will remain Chairman of the board of Trustees in an advisory capacity. The Mg.-Sec. runs the show, trustees notwithstanding. Will forward membership lists and other data later. Suffice it to say that the organization is in your hands.

Two days later he dispatched a follow-up letter, restating the same terms more fully, but adding the reservations that the names of the club and the official organ must be maintained. The latter clause called for immediate ironing out, for under no circumstances was

Moskowitz willing to depart from his preconceived plans as already outlined. He therefore arranged a meeting for August 14, to be attended by Van Houten, Sykora and himself, for the express purpose of bringing Van Houten around to his view. But before speaking of this further, we must backtrack for a few moments to develop other threads of the narrative.

The first official announcement of New Fandom appeared in the August 7 number of *Fantasy News*. Under Moskowitz's byline the following modest statement appeared:

> Watch for science-fiction's greatest organization! New Fandom! To form a new base for fan activities missing since the death of *Fantasy Magazine*. Backed by Sam Moskowitz and Will Sykora this is a sure-fire organization that will *start* with fifty members. Official organ out in a month.... Details in future issues of *Fantasy News*.

And beneath this announcement was a small, apparently unrelated news note to the effect that *The Science Fiction Critic* was delayed because of publisher Claire P. Beck's visit to his brother Clyde in Reno.

During the week of August 7, 1938, a strapping, red-headed young man, over six feet tall, knocked at the door of Moskowitz's Newark home and announced his name: Claire Beck. It developed that he had tired of fruit-picking in Lakeport, California, and had decided to visit his brother in San Francisco (not Reno, as *Fantasy News* erroneously reported). After leaving there he travelled east, passing en route to visit Clark Ashton Smith, R. H. Barlow, C. L. Moore and others, and arriving nineteen days later at the home of William Miller, Jr., one of his old-time correspondents, in East Orange, New Jersey. As Miller had dropped out of fandom at that time, Beck was able to spend two full weeks at his home without fandom learning he was in the East.

Beck paid Moskowitz a second visit a few days later, and asked if he could be put up for the night, since he was unable to stay longer with Miller. As this was impossible, Moskowitz suggested that he speak to Richard Wilson, who in the past had been able to accomodate visiting fans.

When the Michelists got wind of his arrival in Richmond Hill there was much excitement, for Beck's hitch-hiking feat was the first of its type by a famous fan, and represented the actual accomplishment of what many fans had dreamed of doing but had never dared to try—namely, travelling about the country, visiting well-known fans and fantasy authors, with lack of finances no serious handicap. Jubilantly, Richard Wilson mapped plans to scoop his competitor with the most sensational news story of the year. In fandom, Beck's hitch-hiking trip had a news-value comparable to that of Lindbergh's flight in the world press.

On the evening of August 13, 1938, Wilson (accompanied by Beck) visited Taurasi to gloat over his supposed scoop. He was stunned to learn that not only had Taurasi received the news from Moskowitz earlier in the week, but with it sufficient copy to fill four pages. In addition to the feature story there were associational items and an editorial by Moskowitz on the significance of the event. Further, these pages had been mimeographed, assembled and mailed.

Wilson attempted to belittle his competitor's account by having Beck point out a few minor errors in it, and publishing these in his *News-Letter* for August 20. But the prestige of the *Science Fiction News-Letter* was so badly shaken by the combined scoop and doubling in size of *Fantasy News* that it never recovered. Never again able to challenge its competitor, it dwindled on for almost eight months and then suspended publication.

On August 14, as scheduled, Van Houten, Taurasi, Sykora and Moskowitz met at the latter's home to iron out the SFAA-New Fandom merger. After some discussion, Van Houten agreed to have the personality of his organization completely dominated by the newer group. Moskowitz gained his point by pointing out that the SFAA had the reputation of a "do-nothing" group, that it was essentially dictatorial in make-up and that the best way of overcoming such faults would be to start anew with a clean slate. Arrangements were then made for Van Houten to play an important part in initiating success for New Fandom. He was first to write an editorial outlining the beneficial effects of the merger on SFAA members, and to type half of the stencils for the official magazine regularly. These negotiations had scarcely been completed when the doorbell rang.

On the threshold was Claire Beck, and behind him could be seen faces of the opposition—Wilson, Michel and Pohl. The visitors entered, and the two factions sat in comparative silence and discomfiture glaring at each other across the big living room table. The incident was later described by Van Houten (then a neutral in the dispute) in the August 20, 1938, issue of his carbon-copied magazine of commentary *Van Houten Says* as follows:

> ...I was very much amused when I was present at a meeting between (or among) Will Sykora, Sam Moskowitz, John B. Michel, Richard Wilson, and a fellow whose name I forget.... Quietude was rampant, to say the least. And the Hon. C. P. Beck was there, with a puzzled look flitting across his red-topped face every now and then. There seems to be a magnitudinous amount of bad blood someplace. Maybe I've been missing something.

The published reactions of neutrals Beck and Van Houten were clear indications as to the extent of deterioration of relations between both factions. The two groups were silent, each knowing that to broach unsubtly the bones of contention might precipitate an immediate scene.

Had Sykora, Moskowitz and Taurasi been themselves unbiased, they might have paused to consider the reason for the Michelists' visit. It could, after all, have had a conciliatory motivation. But the triumvirate had quickly reached the point where they regarded every Michelist action as aimed, directly or indirectly, at their own interests. Even a friendly Michelist move they promptly would construe to be designed to harm them. They were utterly convinced of their being victims of injustices. And, since the Michelists never bothered to explain their actions, in print or otherwise, the triumvirate's attitude is easy to understand.

Despite the Michelists' silence, and despite the fact that as competent a historian as Jack Speer considered their actions at the time "wholly indefensible," it behooves us for the sake of accurate perspective to examine their motives. When Wilson moved to deprive

Taurasi of his mimeograph he may have been morally wrong, but not
technically so. He was a member of the Phantasy Legion as well as
Taurasi, and certainly had as much right to the machine. Today, one
wonders why the two made no compromise: certainly both could have
used it without friction. When the Michelists impeached Taurasi,
they were technically correct in their procedure, and he should have
allowed a majority to make a decision. Similarly, Wollheim, in arguing for the chairmanship of the committee to sponsor the 1939 convention, had a legitimate point. If the Greater New York SFL members
voted against letting Osheroff and Moskowitz join the chapter, it
was Sykora's own sponsorship of the by-law making it possible that
put that by-law on the club books; and he had sponsored it with the
conjectural possibility of invoking it to exclude the Michelists.
Obviously, then, the Michelists could justify their actions on technical grounds. And equally obviously the triumvirate was pushing its
case on the grounds of moral and unwritten laws, the rules which in
human society frequently outweigh in importance those actually in
print.

On August 21 Moskowitz received two letters that filled him with
dire forebodings. One, from Beck, asked that a meeting be arranged
for the next afternoon to discuss a matter of extreme importance.
The other, from Van Houten, revealed what the matter was. On August
15 Beck had visited Van Houten, and had told him that he disliked
seeing the SFAA die out in name; citing a sentimental attachment to
the organization of long standing (Beck had been an early member
when Bloomer had held sway, and once before almost acquired leadership of the club) he asked Van Houten to turn the SFAA over to him.
Van Houten then stated that he approved of such a plan, and requested
Moskowitz to turn the Managing-Secretaryship back to Beck.

Moskowitz replied to neither letter, and did not go to meet Beck
at the time and place suggested. Beck then wrote once more announcing:

> I am now Managing-Secretary of the SFAA, and when I get
> back from New England I will get the membership and
> subscription list.... Meanwhile I expect New Fandom to be
> launched and started, and I am sure that you can manage it....

Beck further wrote that Moskowitz could use the SFAA mailing list,
and that he need not feel obligated to fill out membership; thus the
arrangement would be advantageous to him.

However, it was evident that without the SFAA, New Fandom could
not be launched in a month's time, and that the bid of Sykora's convention committee would therefore be lost. Moreover, Moskowitz firmly
believed that the Michelists had deliberately influenced Beck to
persuade Van Houten to renege his previous decision to merge the
SFAA with New Fandom. Psychologically he was incapable of deducing
anything else from the facts he had. As a corollary, Beck became his
enemy. And having settled this in his mind, Moskowitz took swift
steps to succor his dream of New Fandom.

The August 21, 1938, issue of *Fantasy News* followed its Claire P.
Beck scoop with another, equally newsworthy. Black headlines
announced to fandom the merging of the SFAA, *Heltos, Tesseract,
Fantasy Review* and the Moskowitz Manuscript Bureau into a single
unit: New Fandom. Moskowitz's strategy was obvious: by maximum publicity he hoped to give the new organization such momentum that no

reneging on the part of Van Houten or objection on that of Beck could effectively block submergence of the SFAA and its members therein. At the same time *Fantasy News* announced Van Houten's name as co-founder.

Close upon the heels of this, the next week's issue circulated a four-page, hektographed supplement published by Moskowitz, *Current Fantasy*. This reprinted Van Houten's letter giving to Moskowitz all rights to the SFAA. In it Moskowitz also outlined New Fandom's aims, among which were:

1) New Fandom is to attempt to establish a new base for fandom, missing since the death of *Fantasy Magazine*.
2) Our immediate aim is to sponsor the World's Fair Science Fiction Convention in 1939.
3) We are to publish the official organ of the club, which shall be for the present 20 large-size, mimeographed pages, fine material, with a special silk-screen cover.

Moskowitz then wrote to Van Houten directly, chiding him diplomatically for falling for a "Michelist scheme" that, he averred, was designed to destroy the SFAA. By the end of August Van Houten had not only abandoned any other plans for the SFAA he might have nurtured, but was actively doing his promised share of stencilling for *New Fandom*.

By the alchemical process of the above mergings, New Fandom gained as automatic members all active and inactive participants in the SFAA and subscribers to *Tesseract, Heltos* and *Fantasy Review* as well. The total came to approximately 125—a staggering total for an organization in those days. Ironically, too, it included Wollheim and Wilson (unbeknownst to themselves), arch-enemies of New Fandom's founders.

All that now remained was to issue the first number of *New Fandom* with as much speed as possible. To help finance it the founders levied a full year's dues upon themselves, dunned members of their families (!) and high-pressured all fan acquaintances in the greater New York area. Material originally intended for *Tesseract* and *Heltos* was reworked for *New Fandom* presentation. As managing-secretary, Moskowitz planned its every detail, and overrode any dissents of his associates as dictatorially and blithely as he had earlier when the organization itself had been planned.

Fortunately Moskowitz was a person who practised extreme economy, and his relationship with New Fandom showed this facet of his personality plainly. The cheapest wax stencils were used for mimeographing, and for these (as well as all other purchases) Moskowitz insisted on itemized bills before withdrawals from the club treasury could be made—and made his associates foot the difference on an overpaid bill from their own pockets besides. The result was a magazine produced for a figure far lower than its size and thickness indicated.

New Fandom contained no fiction, but only articles and columns—a radical innovation in the field at that time. Its neatly silk-screened cover was reminiscent of the old *International Observer's*. The magazine ran to twenty mimeographed pages. About two hundred copies of the initial number were mailed to members and to likely prospects. By 1938 standards the results were sensational. Renewals of membership poured in; over two dozen recruits joined, including old-time fans not then active in the field, professional authors, and a surprising percentage of names previously unheard of. Though some (like Ackerman) were not particularly enamored of the new club, most comments on it and the publication carried unqualified praise. Fans active and casual, old and new, all found some responsive chord struck within them.

Nothing succeeds like success, and the very appearance of *New Fandom* was one of success. Moreover, the forthright assertion that the organization would sponsor a banner world convention and was militantly working for that purpose with a nation-wide enrollment removed all air of sectionalism that New Fandom might otherwise have had to cope with. When such names as John W. Campbell, Jr., Eando Binder, L. Sprague de Camp, Willy Ley, Frank R. Paul, J. Harvey Haggard, John D. Clark, Thomas S. Gardner, H. C. Koenig, Roy A. Squires, Harry Warner, Dale Hart and Peter Duncan were associated with the magazine, fans had to sit up and take notice.

But for all this the organization might never have been successful had it not been for the continual publicity it received in Taurasi's *Fantasy News*. The latter was fast supplanting Wilson's *Science Fiction News-Letter* as the leading news weekly in the field. Its policies, format, size and scoops rocketed it quickly to prestige over a fading competitor. And, since *Fantasy News* had become a sounding board for New Fandom, success for one meant success for the other. It became axiomatic, for a time, that if Taurasi gained a dozen new subscribers in one month, *New Fandom* would get the same dozen the next. And later we shall see that even as both publications rose and prospered together, so would they fall together.

Chapter XXXIII

NEW FANDOM'S RISE TO POWER

LEO MARGULIES' letter of September 14, 1938, which had formally dissolved the Greater New York SFL chapter, had left New York City, proposed site of the first world science fiction convention, without an official working organization to assume local responsibility for the affair. It was evident that the first group that could organize itself into a strong club would have a clear-cut superiority in pressing claim for the coveted post of convention sponsors. And it was equally evident that the Michelists and the New Fandomites would be the two competing rivals.

New Fandom founders lost little time in making preparations. Under the stimulating aegis of Sykora, Taurasi called a meeting of fans at his home on October 2, 1938. Ten persons attended. This group agreed to organize a SFL chapter in Queens. Application for a charter was made to *Thrilling Wonder Stories,* and this was received within a week. Within the same space of time New Fandom had appointed the Queens SFL chapter the official sponsoring committee of the New York convention.

The Michelists, however, had lost even less time. On September 18 they formed the Futurian Science Literary Society (later humorously referred to by them as "a popular front blind for the CPASF") a title that usage abbreviated into simply "Futurians." The latter designation became so popular, by the way, that it eventually supplanted the term "Michelists" entirely. Among those present at this formative meeting were many names well known in science fiction circles: Frederik Pohl, John Michel, Donald Wollheim, Walter Kubilius, Jack Gillespie, Isaac Asimov, Cyril Kornbluth, Jack Rubinson, Herman Leventman and Robert W. Lowndes who had recently migrated to New York City from New England, and who (as we have seen) had come into the Futurian orbit.

The Science Fiction News-Letter soon became the general propaganda organ of the Futurians, much as *Fantasy News* was for New Fandom. In an effort to offer stiffer competition to *Fantasy News,* the *News-Letter* added Pohl to its staff as reporter, and with the September 1, 1938, issue assumed a mimeographed format. However, the fantastic speed (in fan circles, at least) with which *New Fandom* had been created and was printed and distributed—and then, most paralyzing blow of all, accepted—proved a major setback. Even that might not have proved insurmountable had it not been for another development, equally swift and disconcerting.

John W. Campbell, Jr., editor of *Astounding Stories,* had been sent a complimentary copy of *New Fandom,* and his reaction was enthusiastic indeed. In a letter he complimented the magazine highly, and went on to say:

> As I understand it, one of the main efforts of New Fandom
> will be directed toward the success of the World Science
> Fiction Convention. At the recent Newark Convention, I
> expressed my desire to help both fandom magazines and the

World Convention idea as much as possible. If you'll send
me a letter describing—in not more than 250 words—the New
Fandom magazine, giving data, aims, and how to get in touch,
I'll try to run it promptly in "Brass Tacks."

Campbell went on to urge the New Fandom heads to visit his office
and talk over the situation. This invitation was accepted, and the
resulting interview led to his support of the organization. The
October 2, 1938, *Fantasy News* spread this news throughout fandom;
and when everyone learned that Street & Smith would give the convention publicity and donate contributions for its auction, and that
Mr. Campbell himself would be present, the organization's prestige
accelerated anew. All that there remained for New Fandom to do was
gain a vote of confidence at the Philadelphia Conference. This, if
obtained—and the prospects were decidedly favorable—would squelch
permanently any Futurian hopes for sponsorship.

The gospel of New Fandom, meanwhile, was being effectively disseminated in yet another way. Taurasi's *Fantasy News,* a Cosmic
Publication, was not the only journal appearing under that banner.
Cosmic Tales was revived as a Cosmic Publication under the aegis of
Louis and Gertrude Kuslan, two serious-minded fans living in Connecticut. The first issue, dated September, 1938, proved very popular
throughout fandom. Kuslan, receiving support both from Taurasi and
the Moskowitz Manuscript Bureau (which now operated as a New Fandom
unit) was naturally generous in "plugging" the organization. Similar
plugs appeared in *The Planeteer,* now being issued by Taurasi after
it had been dropped by Blish. And New Fandom's biggest boost came
when Olon F. Wiggins, noted as a strong-minded individual not easily
swayed to any loose cause, joined Cosmic and dropped his Galactic
Publications masthead. The only remaining publishing house of importance was Philadelphia's Comet group, and all of the fans there—
with the exception of Milton A. Rothman—were inveterate anti-
Michelists and anti-Wollheimists, and so would scarcely be against
New Fandom. The remaining independant fan journals either were
neutrals or were in such moribund condition as to make them of no
importance. The sole exception, *Scienti-Snaps,* though technically
neutral did not hesitate to donate free publicity to New Fandom.

The Futurians realized that time was running out and that they
still lacked a promising rallying-point. Professionals and fans
alike were falling into line behind their rivals. Theoretically, the
Philadelphia Conference should give them an opportunity to meet them
on even terms—but in actuality, since the conference was being
sponsored by the antagonistic Comet group, the Futurians could not
count on even this. Furthermore, with a sizeable delegation from the
Queens SFL and such other visiting enemies as Jack Speer present,
they were sure to lack numbers as well as voice. The Futurians knew
these facts, and realized that a complete debacle could be avoided
only by drastic methods.

Their plan of action was unprecedented. Headlined in the *News-
Letter* for September 3, 1938, (and here we must digress to keep in
mind that the relationship between the date on the journal and the
date subscribers received it was frequently tenuous, for at this
time the *News-Letter* began a series of delayed appearances) predicted
a "Convention War" in October, and the text which followed read:

...in New York City John B. Michel and Mr. Wollheim, powers
in the field, have decided to toss a lethal monkey wrench
into the machinery by announcing a Fifth Eastern Science
Fiction Convention to be held in their city *on the same date*
as the Philadelphia affair. They reason that more fans will
attend the New York gathering than its rival....

Consternation was the order of the day in Philadelphia when this
news circulated there. New York fans would constitute the bulk of
conference attendees, and a local affair there would prove stiff
competition indeed. There was also the ever-present danger that a
larger New York group could vote an endorsement of a Futurian-
sponsored convention. Frantic correspondence between Moskowitz and
the Philadelphia fans followed, and despair dominated it at first.
Out of this gloomy crucible, however, a plan took form.

This plan might appear ridiculous but for the fact that we have
previously seen (Chapter XXVIII) an application of the psychology
underlying it. Fans in those days were avid collectors of their own
amateur journals; even feuds seldom reached the stage where opponents would cancel one another's magazine subscriptions. The worst
tragedy that could befall an active fan was to miss getting a copy
of some fan journal. Remembering this, and banking on the fact that
Fantasy News had a larger and more effective circulation than did
The Science Fiction News-Letter, announcement of the plan was run in
the former. Headlines there announced "Special Booklets to be Issued
for the Philadelphia Science Fiction Conference!" And the accompanying details emphasized that these would be obtainable nowhere else.
If you couldn't get there—well that was your hard luck. Better
attend!

Abruptly, just a week before the conference was to take place, the
News-Letter revealed that the Futurians were calling off their
counter-convention and would be in Philadelphia in full force—provided "Lowndes is permitted to make a 30-minute speech on the aims
of the group."

Though it would probably be exaggerating to credit the plan for
distributing booklets with full responsibility here, its influence
should not be underestimated. The Futurian decision was undoubtedly
influenced by rumors that began circulation at the time to the
effect that Mort Weisinger, editor of *Thrilling Wonder Stories* magazine would attend the Philadelphia meeting accompanied by several
professional authors. This would mean that Standard Publications was
following the lead of Street & Smith in throwing its weight behind
New Fandom, and that the Futurian cause was indeed lost.

The Futurians never admitted this, of course, though their actions
did. They claimed that their announced convention was a joke
instigated by David Kyle and simultaneously attacked New Fandom for
having "sold out to the pros." These statements, together with the
fact that no denial was issued until the last moment by either
Michel or Wollheim, lend credence to the belief that if a competing
affair had not been planned, then at least harm to the Philadelphia
Conference through distracting notices had been.

Near-perfect fall weather greeted attendees on Sunday, October 16,
at the City of Brotherly Love. A little over two dozen fans were
present, and almost without exception they were individuals of note
in the field. The New Fandom delegation of Sykora, Taurasi, Gardner,

Thompson and Moskowitz made up the earlier arrivals. The better-known members of the PSFS were also present—John Baltadonis, Robert Madle, Jack Agnew, Milton Rothman, Jack Johnson, Helen Cloukey, Milton Asquith, Lee Blatt, Thomas Whiteside and Oswald Train. William Perlman had arrived from Baltimore, and Jack Speer from Washington. Authors John D. Clark, Otto Binder, David Vern (pen name: David V. Reed) had come, the latter in company with Mort Weisinger of *Thrilling Wonder Stories*. No Futurians appeared.

Four conference booklets were distributed: Moskowitz's second number of the hektographed *Different,* Taurasi's mimeographed, four-paged leaflet *Space,* a special issue of the *PSFS News* and Speer's *Chronotron.* The *PSFS News* had been published (with the aid of Moskowitz) just before the call to order. *Chronotron* was a fan curiosity, an *hourly* magazine, hektographed in Washington one day between 10 a.m. and 3 p.m. (A second set was alleged to have been prepared during the conference, with hourly news there included, but historian has not seen this.)

The first business to come before the conference was that of New Fandom. Rothman opened it by announcing that the organization's preeminence seemed unchallenged, and introduced Sykora as one of the heads of the committee. Sykora pointed out that at this early date few concrete promises could be made, but if fans and professionals alike extended their help New Fandom would present a gathering to be proud of. Moskowitz next spoke at considerable length about the general set-up of New Fandom. At the moment, he admitted, it was dictatorial—and this came about necessarily in the early stages of any organization because no one save the creators cared to do any of the ground work. He felt that this dictatorial essence was to a large extent mitigated, however, comparing New Fandom to the professional magazines: these were run by single individuals for profit, yet they were democratic in the sense that their success depended on how well they followed the wishes of the majority. New Fandom was also bound by that law. Moskowitz intimated that once the organization had successfully staged the world convention steps would be taken to adopt a constitution and hold elections. He humorously mentioned the accusation of New Fandom having "sold out" to the professionals, and stated his belief that science fiction could not advance unless all concerned parties worked together; that cooperation was an imperative necessity since neither the fans nor the professionals were independant of one another. One of the aims of the organization, indeed, was to bring the two groups into the close cooperation that had existed during the era of *Fantasy Magazine.*

Discussion by the conferees followed. Finally Jack Speer suggested, and then himself framed, a motion recognizing New Fandom as the official sponsor of the 1939 convention and stating that the Philadelphia Conference went on record as supporting it. This motion was passed without dissent, though not unanimously, and New Fandom breathed a sigh of relief.

The next item on the program was a round-table discussion on the purpose of science fiction. In the process of his contribution to this, Weisinger revealed that his company would very shortly issue a new science fiction magazine called *Startling Stories,* and the first issue, in addition to carrying a new novel by Stanley G. Weinbaum, "The Black Flame," would initiate a unique department of interest to fans, "Review of the Fan Magazines." Complete addresses as well as prices would be included with these reviews. This amounted to an official announcement that the barrier between the fans and the publishers was broken, and was vitally important in what it portended. For the first time in many years an efficient method was being set up by a mass-circulation magazine to funnel new faces into fandom, and the field was bound to be changed by this influx. Weisinger went on to state that the purpose of science fiction—as far as professionals were concerned—was to make money, an assertion that did not shock the assembly. (Fandom was indeed growing up!) Neither did John Clark's speech, which concluded that it was an escape from reality for readers. Thomas Gardner backed up in part Sykora s long-standing opinion that science fiction could inspire one to pursue a career in science; he went on to state that he also believed the development of rocket-power or practical atomic energy would arouse intense public interest in science fiction—a prediction that has recently proved highly accurate. Both Robert Thompson and Milton Rothman felt that stories in the field offered inspiration to scientific workers, and William Perlman cited an example he had personally observed that lent credence to this view.

At this point in the proceedings a 700-word telegram arrived. It was from John W. Campbell, Jr., who was unable to attend, and gave his ideas on the topic of the round-table discussion. His strongest point was that science fiction was able to point a road or issue a warning more effectively than any other type of fiction, but he stressed that its message would not be read if it were not presented in an entertaining human fashion. It is generally believed that Will Sykora had been given this speech by Campbell in New York, and that just before leaving the city he had telegraphed it ahead in order to create an effect at the conference favorable to New Fandom; it turned out, of course, that an added boost such as this was unnecessary. In any event, the attendees telegraphed a reply to Campbell in the name of chairman Rothman, in which they expressed the hope of seeing him at the 1939 convention.

The dinner that followed the more formal part of the meeting was a joyous occasion of grand ·good fellowship, and bantering tomfoolery was the order of the day. The climax came when the toast was offered: "Gentlemen, down with Wollheim!"—and most drank to it. The ceaseless feuds had taken their toll, had built up a tremendous opposition, had virtually shattered the once commanding-position held by Donald A. Wollheim. They had brought, too, a general feeling that feuds were to be avoided. On Sykora's advice the New Fandom leaders capitalized upon this, letting it be known that thenceforth none of them would engage in feuding, regardless of what heights of vituperation their opponents rose to. This stand proved popular with fandom as a whole, though there were a few die-hard dissenters—such as Speer and a few Philadelphians—who felt that the initial anti-Wollheim and -Futurian advantage should be pressed until the opposition had been reduced to helplessness for all time. Some of these, indeed, continued their open campaign. Most fan journals, however, were quick to adopt the no-controversy policy. The result was that almost all means of propaganda other than that self-published became closed to the Futurians.

New Fandom s string of quick victories nevertheless resulted in several unusual and totally unexpected actions by the Futurians, as we shall eventually see.

Chapter XXXIV

THE OPPOSITION CRUMBLES

THE INFLUENCE and popularity of any general movement is usually determined by the ability of its leaders to express its aims and ideals; and the personal beliefs or views expressed by those leaders on related subjects are, rightly or wrongly, attributed to the organizations they head or are influentially connected with. Therefore in the fan world of 1938 when two powerful groups, the Futurians and New Fandom, wrestled for supremacy, their strength and ability to recruit new members could adequately be measured by the readiness of their leading writers to compose propaganda about the organization and communicate their own ideas about science fiction itself to interested fans.

Because of a deliberate and wearing campaign by his opposition, Donald A. Wollheim, while a leader of the Futurians and a competent writer whose knowledge of fantasy was generally respected, had but little influence on the field. His right hand man, John B. Michel, was not particularly active in fandom, and his writings were confined to a few flaming manifestos such as the notorious *Mutation or Death* document. Richard Wilson, on the other hand, was one of the Futurians' stronger aids, liberally publicizing the cause in a generally favorable manner in his *Science Fiction News-Letter;* he was well liked throughout the field, and was noted for an ability to turn cynically biting phrases of wit.

In the New Fandom group, William S. Sykora had long been the victim of a systematic campaign to discredit him, and though an able writer found his ideas being discarded in much the same way that his own friends discarded Wollheim's. James V. Taurasi was a good editor but did not express himself well. Raymond Van Houten could give a fine account of himself with a typewriter, but was, like Michel, not sufficiently active in the field and in comparison even less influential. Robert A. Madle, live-wire Philadelphia fan and editor of *Fantascience Digest,* was of outstanding aid to the movement through his publications. And Jack Speer, who had won considerable respect through his IPO polls, was writing more often and also rapidly becoming one of the Futurians' most potent foes, setting forth his arguments with a precision and care for detail that presaged his later entrance into the legal profession.

The most influential writers, however—the ones that placed the philosophies of their groups before the largest audiences most often—were Robert W. Lowndes and Sam Moskowitz. A nation-wide fan poll, the results of which appeared in the September, 1938, *Science Fiction Fan,* bore this out: in the science fiction fan author category, Lowndes garnered 46 points to Moskowitz's 45 for the two top places.

Robert W. Lowndes wrote creditable fiction and poetry of exceptional merit, But it was through articles and essays that his influence was most strongly felt. Lowndes' forte was the air of sophistication and the appearance of objectivity in phraseology that characterized most of his pieces. Also characteristic was his habit of reworking provocative ideas or styles that had caught his fancy with an eye to improving upon them and/or approaching them from a different angle. This was apparent in his fiction and poetry as well as in his factual writings. His poems showed at various times the strong influence of Poe, Lovecraft, and C. A. Smith, utilizing often similar themes and meters, and always showing pronounced ability. In his fiction he tended to adopt the heavy, deliberate style of Lovecraft, but showed also versatility in handling dialogue. The desire to cast another's ideas into his own mold was evidenced, for example, in his story "The Gourmet" (published in the December, 1939, *Polaris*), whose theme and handling bespoke kinship to Robert Bloch's powerful tale "The Feast in the Abbey," printed in *Weird Tales* almost five years before. In articles—particularly when engaged in a feud—this imitativeness was probably deliberate. If an opponent gave a summary of the best fantasies of the year, Lowndes was apt to write one himself. Should an opponent compose a critical essay on fan philosophy or some phase of a professional's writings, Lowndes would follow with a use of the same theme for an article of his own, probably attempting to show superior qualifications or analytical ability—sometimes successfully. A number of contributions to *The Science Fiction Fan* in late 1937 and early 1938 on fan philosophy, several articles on Stanley G. Weinbaum and critical summaries of fantasy periodicals, in addition to forthright pieces of Michelistic propaganda, helped establish his reputation.

Sam Moskowitz, at first, wrote a negligible amount of fiction and poetry. His reputation as a science fiction writer stemmed almost entirely from articles and essays. The majority of these in this period were characterized by dominating elements of sentimentality and nostalgia. He often strove for beautiful phrasing. On the other hand, many of his critiques of professional fantasy magazines were coldly bitter and cynical. Called upon endlessly to fill the pages of fan magazines as he was, his productions were extremely voluminous. He wrote articles by the hundreds, often using thousands of words to describe a single fan gathering, and thought nothing of devoting two entire pages to reviewing a single issue of a fan journal. As contributing editor of *Fantasy News*, he regularly filled from 25% to 100% of each number. As a duty, he mailed every month from 1,000 to 5,000 words to Wiggins' *Fantasy Fan*. Moskowitz's work appeared under such pseudonyms as Robert Bahr, Robert Sanders Shaw, William Weiner and others, most of which were well known at the time. He wrote a long series of essays on fan philosophy that proved extremely popular. He was obsessed with the concept of fan history, and wrote many articles on this subject. Another of his favorite themes was collecting fantasy, and this likewise brought forth a series of articles. In fiction, he created the "science fiction fan story," a sort of hybrid between an article and a tale that utilized fans, their journals, backgrounds in the field and so on, as themes and settings. Such "fan stories" as "Grand Old Fan," "The Road Back," "Requiem" and "The Last Fan" were vital bulwarks in the continuing popularity of his writings. Moskowitz very often made careless typographical and grammatical errors, and these his publishers reproduced sacredly intact. Yet the criticisms he received were not for these so much as for his provocative habit of making positive statements, assuming his readers were as well aware of their justification

in fact as he. These criticisms were answered either by time or by
his own documentations. As a result, he paradoxically gained a
reputation for prognostication which irritated his critics. As time
went on they became increasingly cautious about nibbling at statements, however, since these occasionally had been designed as bait,
and Moskowitz had the aid of Speer when pulling in the hook.

To both factions the problem was clearly one of discrediting or
silencing the leading spokesman of the opposing group. A powerful
effort in this direction came from the Futurians as a result of
Moskowitz's article in the August, 1938, *Science Fiction Fan,* which
stated that their parent organization, the CPASF, had received
orders from the Communist Party to utilize fan journals as a field
for disseminating propaganda. There are conflicting stories as to
how the ensuing event came about, but the bare facts are as follows.
In the next number of *The Science Fiction Fan,* editor Wiggins made
a simple, direct statement that was greatly surprising to readers at
the time: "Beginning with this issue there will be no more material
by Sam Moskowitz in the pages of the *Fan.*" He went on to explain
that he had long considered this ouster, carrying Moskowitz only
because "the readers wanted him"; that it seemed unfair to him to
print diametrically opposed views by both Moskowitz and Wollheim;
and that Moskowitz was being dropped because he, Wiggins, personally
favored the contributions of Wollheim.

Moskowitz himself was stunned by the ingratitude and callousness
of Wiggins' decision. Naturally, too, he suspected that it had been
motivated by more than a simple protest from his opponent. His only
consolation was the relief he felt on being released from the onerous
chore of submitting regular contributions to *The Science Fiction
Fan.*

Shortly thereafter Wiggins announced that since only two subscribers
had cancelled their subscriptions, events proved his action had
not been misguided. Counter-action by the New Fandom group was
quickly forthcoming. This amounted to Wiggins' expulsion from Cosmic
Publications for behavior unbecoming a member. Most parties favoring
the New Fandomites interpreted Wiggins' action as placing him automatically in the Futurian orbit, moreover, and he soon found himself
completely and helplessly dependent upon Futurian support for *Fan*
material.

Yet even these happenings might not alone have been fatal blows to
Wiggins' prestige had it not been for simultaneous developments in
the Fantasy Amateur Press Association. Once a defeated candidate for
the post, Wiggins still coveted its presidency. Currently, as we
have already seen (Chapter XXIX) Futurians held all but one of the
FAPA offices—Michel, Lowndes and Wollheim being respectively president, vice-president and official editor. Within a short time after
appearance of the September, 1938, *Science Fiction Fan,* FAPA members
received a special issue of the organization's official organ, *The
Fantasy Amateur.* It carried sensational news. Lowndes had resigned
his post, and his resignation had been accepted by Michel. Michel
appointed Wiggins vice-president, an action that was within his
official rights. Then Michel resigned, automatically elevating
Wiggins to president. Finally Wollheim resigned, suggesting his
friend Milton Rothman for official editor, an appointment Wiggins
promptly made. Wiggins also appointed Marconette vice-president. In

his first presidential message after this amazing ascent to power
Wiggins stated his position in the December, 1938, *Fantasy Amateur*
as follows:

> You might correctly term me as anything from a communist to
> a technocrat. A rigid foe of Fascism and allied beliefs.
> You are probably wondering if this makes me an ally of the
> Michelist faction—only in belief. I have never come out
> openly for any faction. But if it ever comes to a showdown
> you would more than likely find me backing the Michel fac-
> tion.

New Fandom leaders immediately raised the cry that Wiggins had
sold out to the Futurian camp in exchange for the FAPA presidency. His
actions had indeed built up a powerful circumstantial case against
him, and this Jack Speer did his best to convert into a coffin in
his *Cosmic Tales* column, "Thots from Exile." The issue having once
been raised spread like wildfire through fan circles, and Wiggins'
sagging reputation dropped several notches lower.

Included with the Moskowitz ouster in the September, 1938, *Science
Fiction Fan* was yet another Futurian effort to discredit him. This
was a mock essay "How to Write a Moskowitz Article" by Sham Marko-
witz as told to Braxton Wells (a pseudonym of Wollheim). The essay
poked fun at the length, amount of detail and personal eccentricities of style typical of Moskowitz's compositions. Because this
issue also began another series of articles it was dubbed by one
British journal "the official organ of the society for the mutual
admiration of Wollheim." This was in reference to such flowery eulogies written about Futurians by Futurians as Lowndes' "Wollheim: the
Most Fan," Michel's "My Comrade, Doc Lowndes," Lowndes' "Glance at
Michel," and so on.

As time went on, many excellent items did appear in the *Fan*,
particularly in the realm of the critical essay and material slanted
at collectors, and even the fan of today will find many rewarding
pages in the magazine. Most of this improvement was due to the
efforts of the veteran fan Paul J. Searles, now well-known as book
reviewer for the New York *Herald-Tribune*. Searles (who is not related
to the editor of *Fantasy Commentator*) took over the combined task
of editing and publishing *The Science Fiction Fan* with the August,
1939, issue. He held the title of associate editor, Wiggins still
retaining the editor's position, but Searles actually did nearly all
the work. Under his aegis the quality of the material, reproduction,
and illustrating all took a remarkable upward turn. Long a follower
of fan journals and professional fantasy fiction, Searles' only previous activity was contribution of a book review and a short story
to Hornig's *Fantasy Fan* and an occasional article under his pen name
of "Autolycus" appearing elsewhere. He will also be remembered as a
winner of the *Marvel Science Stories* prize contest at this time.
When the Wollheim-Moskowitz feud was at its height in the *Fan*,
Searles had contributed anonymously a four-paged supplement appealing for reason. As a mature individual, Searles doubtless felt a
certain reticence about involving himself deeply in activities that
were only too often juvenile in nature, but like H. C. Koenig and
others, found the lure irresistible at the time. He continued to edit
and publish the magazine through its January, 1941, issue. With the

February, 1941, number he relinquished the task to a young Denver fan, Lew Martin, and accepted the honorary post of assistant editor. Martin mimeographed but a single issue of the magazine (#55), and with that it ceased publication and was never again heard from.

Despite Searles' best efforts, however, *The Science Fiction Fan* never attained its previous position of importance or influence in the field. The chief reason was its policies, which remained lop-sidedly in favor of the Futurian faction from August, 1938, on. Even under Searles' editorship many articles printed were either forth-rightly or subtly propagandizing efforts that mirrored the Communist Party line. It seems probable that this policy was insisted upon by Wiggins and tolerated by Searles as a gesture of liberality, for he put himself on record in several articles as opposing the red viewpoint that the Second World War was just another imperialistic adventure, and called upon fans to work in the best interests of the nation.

It can be seen, then, that these Futurian tactics, far from injuring Moskowitz, actually lent him the role of a martyr; and it also almost completely destroyed the prestige of *The Science Fiction Fan* and Olon F. Wiggins. Pressure of fan opinion became so great against the Futurian circle that, even before the FAPA episode, the *Science Fiction News-Letter*'s October 22, 1938, number printed a news item to the effect that plans were afoot to "liberalize and decommunize the Futurian Literary Society." The next (October 29) issue carried the further information that four Futurians—Wollheim, Michel, Lowndes and Pohl—would resign from all offices in science fiction organizations other than their own, and in other ways reduce activity. On every side, ordinarily neutral fans, such as Litterio Farsaci and Louis Kuslan, were openly putting into print long articles against Michelism. Despite this trend of opinion, Wollheim's article "Retreat" (*The Science Fiction Fan*, December, 1938) came as a bomb-shell. In that work he pointed to his long-standing interest in the field, his outstanding collection of fantasy magazines, books and fan journals, his dozens of published articles, his attendance at innumerable fan gatherings, and personal associations with countless fantasy enthusiasts to attest his sincerity and his authority in the field. Through acquaintance with science fiction fans he had come to note, he asserted, that they were mentally different, that they seemed to be searching for certain logics and truths. The search for these had led him and his friends to find out that they "were close-ly parallel to communism. That is to say to the intellectual aspect of communism as it affects literature, science, culture." The scope of Marxism very closely approached, in their opinion, the goals of the fans. "Accordingly," said Wollheim, "We came out openly for communism." Its immediate acceptance had not been expected, but the overwhelming, "vicious" nature of the opposition had taken the Futu-rians by surprise. "What intelligent fans there were failed to stand up firmly, we were deluged by a mass of stupid and vicious hate. This slop pile grew in quantity and intensity. Actual violence was threatened. And through lies, the editors of the magazines were enlisted into the campaign against us." At the same time, Wollheim maintained, the standard of the material in fan magazines and the activities of the fans themselves had sunk to a hopeless low. "To remain further active in stf fandom while it is in its present condition would be to lower myself to its level. I, and my friends, fought as best we could against those overwhelming odds. My purse and my health do not permit me to carry on such a one-sided fight. There comes a time when it becomes necessary to withdraw for a while and recuperate." Fan activities, concluded Wollheim, would forever remain puerile until they accepted the basic tenets of Michelism.

Donald A. Wollheim, scarred veteran of fan feuds, had for the first time publicly admitted defeat. The campaign that had begun so gloriously a year before with Michel's fiery "Mutation or Death" speech at the memorable Philadelphia convention had run its course. The very vigor with which it had been pressed, its callous, rough-shod ways, its uncompromising viewpoint that the end justified the means—these things had first created lethal opposition where there had been none, then strengthened that opposition, and finally gave it sufficient momentum to crush its creator.

Very few fans of that period took Wollheim's statement of retreat as being anything more than temporary disgruntlement over continued setbacks. Least of all his opponents! Even though Wollheim meant what he said, New Fandom leaders were by no means sure the Futurians would be content to sit back and lick their wounds. Later events showed their suspicions were justified, but equally they showed that the Futurians no longer had the support or contacts to wage anything more than a harrassing delaying action. The fight had long since resolved itself into the question of whether the fan world was willing to accept communism as the price of peace with the Futurians—and the answer was definitely no.

Realizing that the attempt to communize the field had been a fail-ure, Lowndes' "Open Letter to Louis Kuslan" (published in the Janu-ary, 1939, *Science Fiction Fan*) tried to convince fans that they had been misled by the personal beliefs of Michel into thinking that Michelism and communism were identical. Michelism had never had as its purpose the converting of fans to the Communist Party, asserted Lowndes, and one might be a good Michelist without being a communist.

The reply to this was more membership in New Fandom, more new subscriptions to *Fantasy News*.

But an era was coming to a close, an old order was changing. The day of the hektograph and the close-unit corollary of fifty active fans was already a thing of the past. Of the two formerly leading journals in the field, *The Science Fiction Fan* was discredited and *The Science Fiction Collector* had just suspended publication—iron-ically enough with an issue carrying an article by Moskowitz that showed current trends pointed to the end of an era. New names were entering the field; and old names, some of which had been driven into inactivity by disagreement with Wollheim, were returning. The complexions of the professional fantasy magazines themselves were completely altered, and new titles were appearing. For the first time in many years most of fandom was united in seeking a common goal: a world science fiction convention to be held in conjunction with the 1939 World's Fair. The past, since 1937, had been an era of turmoil, ceaseless feuding, shattered plans and abortive dreams. The immediate future, at least, looked better. And as 1938 drew to a close, the keynote of science fiction fandom was optimism.

Chapter XXXV

THE NEW FANTASY MAGAZINES AND THEIR INFLUENCE ON FANDOM

THE NEW FANDOM group had as its objective the creation of a larger and more cooperative fandom, and aiding the realization of this objective were the economic factors then molding the science fiction field.

From prosperous beginnings in the late twenties, professional fantasy magazines had suffered a series of set-backs that left them almost prostrate as the depression met its depths in 1933. By then there were but four titles being published, and these changed size and lapsed into irregular appearance occasionally in an effort to maintain themselves.

With the disappearance of its rival *Ghost Stories* in early 1932 and by dint of appealing to other readers through publishing science fiction stories in its columns, *Weird Tales,* the lone purveyor of the supernatural, managed to keep its appearance of equilibrium best of all.

Wonder Stories, as we have noted earlier, continued to hold on after changing ownership, editors and policy in mid-1936.

When Clayton Publications was sold to Street & Smith in 1933, *Astounding Stories* reappeared after a six-month hiatus under the editorship of F. Orlin Tremaine, whose reputation at that time was at an all-time high. A science fiction fan himself, Tremaine managed within two years time to rocket *Astounding* to the leading position among fantasy pulps, printing such a highly popular quality of fiction that his two competitors were almost forced out of the running.

With the April, 1938, issue, Teck Publications gave up the ghost of *Amazing Stories,* selling that title, along with the rest of their chain of periodicals, to the Ziff-Davis Company of Chicago. And through the intervention of Ralph Milne Farley, old-time fan Raymond A. Palmer obtained the job of editing the rejuvenated *Amazing.*

Palmer's progress was watched by the entire field with great interest. The type of story formerly printed in the magazine was discarded entirely. The covers and interior illustrations were enlivened. In short, *Amazing Stories* was made over into a pulp magazine in the usual sense of that phrase, every legitimate type of appeal being utilized to attract the largest possible group of readers. Though occasional stories of superior merit did appear, Palmer concentrated on stories that veteran fans considered "written down" and far too elementary and stereotyped in concept. But despite disappointing the old guard, the magazine's circulation rose in substantial jumps with every issue. Thus science fiction, for the first time in many years, began to reach an expanding instead of a diminishing audience. Moreover, Palmer, probably remembering his own fan days, was liberal in publishing free notices of various fan events and publications.

The brief 1937-38 recession experienced by the country managed, paradoxically enough, to stimulate fantasy publishing. Because even such standbys as detective and western story magazines showed slumps in sales, pulp chain executives were more than willing to investigate any medium showing possibilities of profit. The double precedent of Standard and Ziff-Davis entering the field and *Astounding*'s circulation nosing over the 80,000 mark gave Red Circle Publications the incentive to launch a fantasy magazine of their own. The first issue of the magazine, *Marvel Science Stories,* was dated August, 1938, and appeared in May. It featured Arthur J. Burks' "Survival," a complete novel considered by fans as one of the finest science fiction stories of the year. *Marvel* also brought back to the field the artwork of Frank R. Paul, whose popular illustrations had not been seen since *Wonder Stories* changed hands over two years previously. As an added and probably experimental attraction, the publishers cagily included a couple of stories featuring the sex element in a crude and obvious fashion. This first issue sold in excess of 60,000 copies—considered very good for that time.

The flood was now on; an orgy of science fiction publishing which refused to abate was under way.

Elated by their own success, Red circle publications cheerfully let it be known that they were issuing a companion to *Marvel* entitled *Dynamic Science Stories,* whose first number would feature a new novel by Stanton Coblentz.

Standard Magazines, which had long hinted at a companion magazine to *Thrilling Wonder,* now announced that the first issue of *Startling Stories,* featuring a previously unpublished novel by the late Stanley G. Weinbaum called "The Black Flame" would appear late in November and bear the date January, 1939.

Almost simultaneously Ziff-Davis announced that not only was *Amazing Stories* going to appear monthly (instead of bimonthly) as a result of its success, but that it, too, would have a companion named *Fantastic Adventures.* As an added attraction this was to be large-sized, like the earlier *Amazings* and *Wonders.*

Not to be outdone, Blue Ribbon Magazines hired Charles Hornig, the ex-editor of *Wonder Stories,* to direct their new pulp *Science Fiction.*

Finally, two new titles competing more or less directly with the hoary *Weird Tales* came into being. These were *Strange Stories,* put out by Standard, and *Unknown,* which John W. Campbell declared was being put out be Street & Smith solely because receipt of a sensational novel by Eric Frank Russell called for creation of an entirely new type of fantasy magazine. Both of these periodicals hit the newsstands early in 1939.

And as though fate had intended it that way, on Sunday, October 30, 1938, Orson Welles presented his memorable radio adaptation of Wells' *War of the Worlds,* which sent Americans screaming and scurrying into the streets, their heads wrapped in wet towels to protect them against Martian heat-rays. This was all that was needed to focus public attention openly on science fiction, in which most people had long believed anyway.

The nerve center disseminating all these reports was Taurasi's weekly *Fantasy News,* which, by the aid of reporters Racic and Moskowitz, easily scooped its rival *The Science Fiction News-Letter* and continued to gain prestige and circulation. Professional publishers were appreciative of the liberal space and bold headlines with which their ventures were publicized throughout fandom, and were in turn generous with their own help whenever it was solicited. As a result

New Fandom, through *Fantasy News,* made good its promise to promote a more harmonious relationship between the fan field and the professionals. Doubtless this was in part responsible for the fact that almost without exception every new magazine featured numerous departments of chief interest to the fans themselves, printing letters and announcements with complete addresses. The most influential of these were the fan magazine review column in *Startling Stories* and what amounted to a miniature fan magazine in every number of Hornig's *Science Fiction.*

It was inevitable that as a result of this cooperation there would be a great influx of new names into the fan field, and this indeed did come to pass. And New Fandom, which had set itself up as representing fans everywhere, found itself working towards the First World Science Fiction Convention with steadily mounting membership, the wholehearted cooperation of almost all onlookers, and the complete good will of every publisher, who, without exception, promised help without stint—all in vivid contrast to the antagonism that had marked the condition of the field a year previously.

Chapter XXXVI

THE ROLE OF THE QUEENS SFL

WHEN SYKORA and Taurasi hastily reorganized the Queens SFL chapter, it had been an action motivated by political expediency only; and certainly they, if anybody, had no illusions that the group would ever amount to anything. Indeed, it is nowhere recorded that anyone had the vision to predict a rosy future for the chapter. But destiny had rolled the dice—and in the space of a few months the Queens SFL was to emerge as a power to be reckoned with in the field, and earn for itself an important seat in the roster of the great fan clubs.

The first meeting, as we have seen, took place on October 2, 1938, in Taurasi's home. A charter was applied for and received from League headquarters.

At the second meeting, held the following month, all those present signed the charter. The attendance was double that previously, and included no other special guest than Mortimer Weisinger, editor of *Thrilling Wonder Stories*.

Julius Schwartz, well known veteran fan and literary agent, was a guest at the December meeting, which again boasted an attendance of twenty.

These meetings were described in chamber of commerce style by Sam Moskowitz, whose glowing, multi-paged accounts made the club seem unquestionably on the road to success. Thus aided, the news quickly spread about that the Queens SFL was *the* place to spend the first Sunday of every month, and when the first meeting of 1939 found twenty-five enthusiasts cramming into Taurasi's home, members began to think in terms of more spacious quarters. It was at this meeting, with delegations from New England and Philadelphia on hand to hear guests Willy Ley and Charles Hornig, that the chapter gained its slogan of "a miniature convention at every meeting"—which, all press-agentry aside, was a fairly accurate description of what went on. Authors, editors and other leading lights in the field were either actual members or such frequent attendees that they might just as well have been. The average number of people at each gathering was over thirty, and included leading lights like John W. Campbell, Jr., Eando Binder, Thomas S. Gardner, John D. Clark, Eric Frank Russell, Jack Williamson, Willy Ley, C. H. Ruppert, Charles D. Hornig and many others.

The casual onlooker would scarcely have realized the political importance the Queens SFL was assuming because of the great whirl of celebrities and orgy of science fiction discussion present, but it played a vital role. It was there that New Fandom wooed and won the support of the professionals of the field to its cause. A professional would be extended the most cordial possible invitation to attend a meeting, with travel instructions carefully detailed. At the meeting itself he would be treated with the greatest respect, feted as a celebrity; his words would be listened to carefully, he would be flooded with questions, his autograph would be solicited. If an editor, an issue of his magazine would be scheduled for oral review story by story, illustration by illustration, department by department. If at all possible, a friend of his would be invited to the same meeting so that he would have a companion and feel completely at home. If he were an author, a science fiction quiz on the program would be sure to include questions alluding to some of his stories; if an artist, a key topic for discussion might be similarly slanted. A few days after the meeting, the celebrity would be thanked for his interest and asked to attend some future meeting. Within a week, while the memory was still pleasantly warm in his mind, an issue of *Fantasy News* would appear in his letter-box bearing his name in headlines and an account of his statements at the gathering. Shortly thereafter he would receive a letter from Sam Moskowitz telling him that his talk at the Queens meeting had been so popular it would be little less than a crime not to publish its text in *New Fandom* for dissemination to the fan world. In *New Fandom* it would be presented in dignified tone, and often other articles of comment by professionals would be solicited and/or received regarding it.

In this fashion, though even many of its members scarcely realized the fact, the Queens SFL became an essential member, with New Fandom and *Fantasy News,* of a powerful trinity that was dominating and setting a tone for all of science fiction fandom. Here was being created the good will that resulted in the wholehearted cooperation among professionals so necessary for a successful fan convention. Directly or indirectly everyone was benefited—for, even as the professionals received widespread publicity of the most favorable variety, so were the members of the Queens SFL and readers of *New Fandom* and *Fantasy News* receiving material that interested them greatly. As a result, too, fandom at large found it increasingly easy to gain access to and help from those very authors and editors who but a few months previously had been cold to every tentative advance.

It could be seen, too, that the Queens SFL would share with New Fandom the brunt of the work for putting on the convention the coming summer. All key men behind the project were members of both organizations, and every meeting of the Queens chapter (which was held in Bohemia Hall, Astoria, after January, 1939) had as part of its program a report by either Sykora or Moskowitz on progress of convention preparations.

It is hard to apportion fair credit to individuals for the early success of the Queens group for this was, in many ways, due largely to selfless cooperation. Probably Sykora, the instigator, and Taurasi, the director, deserve the lion's share of credit for management of club affairs and program presentation. A powerful aide was Mario Racic, a capable and willing worker. Julius Schwartz was instrumental in persuading many celebrities to attend, and Sam Moskowitz's familiarity with their "pedigrees" and ability to warm them to the task at hand was as useful as his later published accounts of the meetings. Hyman Tiger's comprehensive knowledge of current science fiction and contributions to the Queens library and various drives were all extremely helpful. And taken as a whole, these things, together with the group's location in the largest city of the country, made the Queens SFL as popular as it was influential.

Chapter XXXVII

AMATEUR MAGAZINES OF THE PERIOD

WE HAVE SEEN that New Fandom was to form a central hub about which all fan activities revolved. New Fandom preached the doctrine of improvement through cooperation instead of through anarchic effort. Instead of half a dozen fans publishing as many diverse titles, none of which had any great impact singly, New Fandom urged, and set by example, the consolidation of many small efforts into a few big ones. *New Fandom* magazine itself was the result of merging the major resources of six smaller journals, one large club and a manuscript bureau. *Fantasy News* became a success because several fans, each capable of gathering material for and publishing a newspaper, foreswore this course in the interest of unity and were willing to work constructively together to produce a single superior effort.

Fandom as a whole was not unaffected by the example set by New Fandom, and as a result early 1939 saw appearance of a comparatively small number of fan magazines of better quality; moreover, these magazines adopted a more serious attitude toward professional publications than they had done previously.

One of the leading amateur journals of this period was *Spaceways,* published in Hagerstown, Maryland, by Harry Warner, Jr. Warner had been a follower of science fiction since 1933, but his interest had not been aroused intensely until early 1938, when subscriptions to fan journals and a correspondence with James S. Avery, a young man living in Maine, decided him to launch into publishing his own amateur effort. A cooperative effort between the two in a hektograph medium proved abortive. But nothing daunted, Warner then went ahead on his own, producing a letter-sized mimeographed publication of twenty pages, the first issue of which was dated November, 1938. This number contained a story by the professional fantasy writer Amelia Reynolds Long, a biography of author E. E. Smith, and other material of general fan interest. *Spaceways* was begun as a bimonthly but proved so popular that Warner soon averaged an issue every six weeks.

The quality and variety of material in *Spaceways* was commendable. The early numbers carried such names as H. P. Lovecraft, Jack Williamson, Cyril Mand, Thomas P. Kelley, Ralph Milne Farley, Thomas S. Gardner, Robert W. Lowndes, Bob Tucker, Frederik Pohl, Larry B. Farsaci, F. J. Ackerman, Sam Moskowitz and many others. Two of its most popular features were "Stardust," a gossip column by "The Star Trader" (J. Chapman Miske) and "What They Are About," J. Michael Rosenblum's column of British book reviews, both of which appeared regularly. As nearly as possible Warner tried to remain outwardly neutral in fan politics and disagreements, barring from publication insofar as possible unnecessarily personal material. Though at times chided for excessive caution in this respect, he made few enemies and many friends, and rapidly assumed a popular position during that period. Warner was frequently visited by passing fans, but he himself made virtually no known excursions of importance outside his native city, thus earning the nickname "the Hermit of Hagerstown" —an appelation he richly deserved, since he frequently refused offers of free transportation to these excursions by others. His action may in part have been due to poor health, for he was alleged to suffer from painful and repetitious headaches of long duration. Whatever the motivation, however, this stay-at-home attitude was widely commented upon before fans became reconciled to it.

Robert A. Madle's *Fantascience Digest* had led an up-and-down existence until it assumed a mimeographed format with its January, 1939, number. Up until then, too, he had had the help of Willis Conover and John Baltadonis. But these two slumped into inactivity, leaving Madle only Jack Agnew. Paradoxically, such losses served only to prove that Madle was a top-ranking editor in the field. He solicited and obtained material of high reader-interest, and gathered about him such staff writers as Mark Reinsberg, Milton A. Rothman, Harry Warner, Sam Moskowitz and Fred W. Fischer, a long-standing reader of the old Munsey magazines who wrote copiously about fantasy stories published there. Other well-known names that contributed were Henry Kuttner, Ray Bradbury, Ralph Milne Farley, Donald A. Wollheim, John Giunta, Cyril Mand and Oswald Train. Like *Fantasy News, New Fandom* and *Spaceways, Fantascience Digest* had a paid circulation list of over a hundred; and it was apparent from this that in the short period of six months marked by a policy of friendly cooperation with the professionals the number of active inner circle fans had actually doubled.

Under the capable editorship of Gertrude and Louis Kuslan, *Cosmic Tales* had quietly become a neatly mimeographed publication featuring a higher, quality of fan-written fiction than had appeared in some years. In addition to stories by Taurasi, Sykora, Farsaci, Giunta, Avery, Speer, Frome and Moskowitz, the magazine managed to obtain items from such professionals as David H. Keller, Thomas S. Gardner and J. Harvey Haggard. It featured work by such British writers as J. F. Burke, Christopher Youd and David McIllwain as well, which lent an agreeable international tone to its pages. But *Cosmic Tales'* most popular feature was a regular column by Jack Speer, whose title had a curious origin. Speer, who lived in Washington, D.C., borrowed his brother's car and started out for New Haven, Connecticut, where he planned to spend a Thanksgiving week-end with the Kuslans. Only a fraction of a mile from his destination he fell asleep at the wheel and hit a telephone pole. Speer himself suffered little more than a shaking-up, but the severe damage to the car caused him expenses that forced him to cut down his fan activities drastically. Thus the appropriately titled *Cosmic Tales* column called "Thots from Exile." This was one of the earliest columns devoted to political commentary on fan feuds and similar controversial topics, and this novelty lent it wide popularity and influence.

Walter Marconette published four quarterly issues of *Scienti-Snaps* in 1938, not including the special number for the First National Science Fiction Convention. His companion publication, *Science-Fantasy Movie Review,* also appeared five times during the year. Following the trend of the times, the former title became a mimeographed journal with its February, 1939, number, and combined with the latter with the following April issue. Marconette's mimeography, like his hektography, was a paragon of neatness; and his magazine continued to increase in popularity through the first half of 1939, featuring a medley of fiction, articles and columns by well known fans of the day. In August, J. Chapman Miske was added to its staff, and he aided in producing the finest chapters of its history.

As can be seen, the day of the hektograph was virtually past; with expanded horizons before them fan editors had either to publish larger editions or keep them limited if they refused to abandon the hektograph. Thus every journal of importance was switching to the medium of the mimeograph. There were, however, a few important exceptions to the trend. One of them was *Fantasy Digest,* a title published in Fort Wayne, Indiana, by Thaddeus E. Dikty, known today as co-owner of Shasta Publishers. *Fantasy Digest* published material by many leading fans of the day, but its pride and joy was the work of its discovery, artist Bernard Maskwitz. Maskwitz's style closely resembled that of Alex Raymond, who drew the "Flash Gordon" comic strips, and was so effective that Standard Publications attempted to solicit work from him for *Thrilling Wonder Stories*. However Maskwitz, with whom drawing was but a spare-time hobby, refused on the grounds that such work would intrude on his regular vocational duties.

These, then, were the leading American fan publications of early 1939, and with the exception of *The Science Fiction News-Letter* and *The Science Fiction Fan* (whose histories have been outlined in previous chapters) they all followed in general the New Fandom policies and worked in close, harmonious accord. The field for the first time in some years was not glutted with titles, and titles that were being published appeared with commendable regularity. With increased professional publicity drawing more and more fans into activity, circulation and general quality rose steadily higher, and fan magazines once more became items that were worth collecting.

Chapter XXXVIII

MINOR DISSENSIONS

ROUGHLY THREE YEARS had passed since Arthur W. ("Bob") Tucker had perpetrated his infamous death hoax on the editor of *Astounding Stories*. In this period little or nothing had been heard out of Bloomington, Illinois. In the interim, however, F. Orlin Tremaine had left Street & Smith, and *Astounding Stories,* now retitled *Astounding Science Fiction,* came under the editorship of John W. Campbell, Jr. Even before Tremaine left, the harsh edict to abolish "Brass Tacks" (a column devoted to readers' letters) had been relaxed, and its succeeding "Science Discussions" became diluted with general comments from subscribers. The June, 1938, issue carried a letter from James S. Avery which bemoaned, among many other things, the fact that readers' letters published in *Astounding* were no longer either intelligent or clever. Whether it was pure chance that Tucker decided to reply to this point, or whether he was looking for an opportunity to return to the field and would have picked another had not this one appeared is an interesting subject for speculation. At any rate, Tucker's letter defending the current wit of readers' letters appeared in the August, 1939, *Astounding;* and like Al Jolson after a long layoff Tucker went joyously into his old song and dance, ending his communication with a humorous parody on the letters of old. Perhaps as a result Tucker recieved letters asking him to return to activity once more, as during the fall of 1938 fans began receiving letters and subscriptions from him. In any event, Bob Tucker was back in the swim of things again.

Among others, he contacted James Taurasi, and when late in 1938 Tucker issued a little four-paged hektographed leaflet titled *Science Fiction Advertiser* the legend "A Cosmic Publication" was prominently displayed on its masthead. The *Advertiser* was the earliest serious attempt at a fan magazine devoted solely to advertising, being preceded only by Moskowitz's *Science Fiction Circular* earlier that year, the latter being of purposely limited circulation. The second *Advertiser* boasted a distribution of two hundred (very high in those times), and underwent a slight change in title. The third issue of *Science & Fantasy Advertiser* was letter-sized, and carried an announcement of the forthcoming *Unknown.* Thereafter it passed into the hands of one Sully Roberds (believed by many to be Tucker under a pseudonym), and though forecasted to appear as a professionally printed publication never did.

Probably Tucker's failure to do anything with this effort can be traced to a wish to write and publish humorous works which had long been his forte. To facilitate this he first reestablished his *D'Journal,* abandoned since 1935, and followed its success with a new title, *Le Zombie.* Both were Cosmic Publications and the latter was distributed at first as a free supplement to Taurasi's *Fantasy News.* *D'Journal* featured humorous articles and squibs by Tucker and others, including "Poor Pong's Almanac," "On the Care and Feeding of Vampires," etc. *Le Zombie* carried advertising as well, and short, satirical, cynical paragraphs departmentalized in *The New Yorker* fashion like "Subtle Advertising Dept.," "Terrible Secrets Dept." and the like. An attempt was made to give such comments a homey, plain-spoken twang, and Tucker impartially sank their barbs into foe and friend alike. His humorous articles, whether signed by himself or his cognomen "Hoy Ping Pong" were generally burlesques or satires of the fantasy field. This was relatively new to science fiction fan magazines, and Tucker barred few holds in displaying his undeniable talent for it.

Sam Moskowitz, because of his intense fan activity, had been himself a favorite target for many of these quips and burlesques. Like most others he had let them pass in silence. Like others, too, he realized that such commentaries could be extremely effective weapons for attack: Tucker could ridicule what and whom he pleased, and if a victim objected he would be told everything was being offered in the spirit of good fun and that only a sorehead could not take a joke. Now Moskowitz had had an article titled "The World Changes" published in *Spaceways* for February, 1939. In this piece (which, it might be noted, had been written some time before it appeared in print) he tried to show that a new era of fandom was coming about through the influx of new professional magazines and the creation of New Fandom. He maintained that the field was almost quadruple its former size and was still growing. Past fan eras were briefly reviewed, and the article was ended on the prediction of a bright future for fans. There were few points of controversy in the article: it simply covered events that had for the most part actually happened since its composition. But it was enough to evoke from Tucker in the next *Spaceways* a parody entitled "The Moon Changes Too." "Of course history repeats itself!" he declared therein, "Moskowitz has written another ar-tikle on old times, that's history repeating itself!" He went on to burlesque the idea that Moskowitz was writing to any large new group of fans, and then presented a mock history of fan eras. "Gadzooks, but eras were thick in those days!"

Moskowitz realized that when people laughed *at* something they would no longer take it seriously; and to him, these articles on fan history were serious things indeed. Therefore he wrote a reply to Tucker for *Spaceways* in which he stated that he believed Tucker was using humor as a weapon, not merely for humor's sake alone. He maintained that Tucker was fostering an erroneous impression by belittling the fact that the fan field was made up of many new faces, and questioned his opponent's ability to take such criticisms after being so long out of touch with happenings in fandom. He pointed out that neither Tucker nor anyone else had so far found any errors of fact in "The World Changes," and intimated that the genesis of Tucker's burlesque might well be annoyance over an uncomplimentary piece printed in the November, 1938, *New Fandom*.

This last was a reference to an article by "Loki" (Peter Duncan) which was written in the belief that Tucker's "death" had been genuine and which went to vitriolic lengths to lambaste his reputation as a humorist. So strong was the adverse opinion of subscribers to this and other writings of Loki that they were thenceforth not published in the magazine. Moskowitz reminded Tucker that he had been written about the column in advance, and that no reply had been received to an offer to withdraw it. Actually, Tucker may have been irked for another reason entirely: in "The World Changes" Moskowitz had inadvertantly omitted his name and that of Robert Madle (who made specific objection to this) in listing several "old time" fans. credence for this viewpoint is lent by the fact that in a following issue of *Le Zombie* the editor remarked, "Altho Tucker (yeh, me) was *not* mentioned by Moskowitz in his *Spaceways* 'old-timer' article, he lays a few claims to being one anyway."

In the past the agile mind of Jack Speer had proved of powerful aid to Moskowitz in his clashes with the Futurians. In this case, being on friendly terms with both parties concerned, he might have made an effective mediator, but it so happened that he, too, had a bone to pick with "The World Changes," and it did not deal with accuracy of detail. Apparently Speer had been secretly writing a history of science fiction fandom which he intended to spring as a surprise on everyone when completed. He seemed to see in Moskowitz's short article an annoying anticipation of his own, and was forced to reveal his project ahead of time because of it. He gently deplored Tucker's attempt to disguise the fact that there had been distinct eras in fandom, but beyond that took no reconciliatory action.

To add fuel to the fire another Tucker article was published in *Fantasy Digest* almost concurrently with the burlesque in *Spaceways*. The content of "Procession of Yesterdays or Are You a Veteran Too?" is obvious from the title, and Moskowitz felt 'that Tucker was making undue issue out of the points he stated. He therefore wrote to Tucker about that and other matters; the tone of the reply was calculated to assure Moskowitz that everything really was being done in good fun, with no malice intended. Undoubtedly this would have smoothed over the tiff had not Tucker's "A Little Lesson in Tuckerology" (*Spaceways*, August, 1938) come out shortly thereafter. Here he took a serious, mature viewpoint, saying that he deplored people misunderstanding his purposes, which were to create a little fun and laughter. Fans took life too seriously, he felt, and denied any personal animus because of Loki's tirade in *New Fandom*. This was all very well, but when he then proceeded to refer to Moskowitz as "a big-headed little punk trying to act as if he knows what it's all about" he could scarcely be accused of attempting a rapprochement. This virtually assured fandom that regardless of what developed in the near future, Tucker and Moskowitz would not be aligned in the same camp—and that this was more important than it seems will later be shown.

Tucker was responsible for several other items in the 1938-1939 publishing field. As a FAPA member, he produced *Science Fiction Variety*, a small journal composed of odds and ends of advertising, wit and art. During early 1939 he produced *The Year Book of 1938*, which listed and cross-indexed all stories that had appeared in fantasy magazines during 1938. He repeated this publication in 1940 (for 1939 issues), and both numbers have since become valuable items in the eyes of collectors. Tucker had also struck up a friendship with James Avery as a result of answering his *Astounding* letter and the two produced several fan publications together.

Early in 1938 he organized the Vulcan Manuscript Bureau, which contributed largely to Vulcan Publications, a new publishing chain which he had organized. The pride of Vulcan Publications was a fan magazine called *Nova*. It was intended to be something entirely new in the realm of fan journalism, being five seperate and distinct

.

titles bound together. Three of these five were new: *Nova, Science Fiction Esquire* and *Science Fiction Times*. Two, *D'Journal* and *Le Zombie,* were of course regularly-appearing Tucker productions. Probably in order to keep peace with Taurasi for the loss of these two to the Vulcan fold, Tucker tactfully labelled *Nova* a Cosmic-Vulcan publication. (Of special interest in the *Science Fiction Esquire* portion was a column called "The Battleground," in which Tucker appealed to Robert Lowndes to drop the onus of "decadism" and "Marxism" featured so prominently in most of his articles, and return to the strong, undiluted science fictional flavor that had in past years made him one of the most popular of fan writers. Lowndes replied to the effect that he would try to write occasional efforts in his former vein, but that because of his newly-acquired Marxist outlook he could not be held responsible for any propaganda that inadvertantly crept into the lines.) Moskowitz predicted that because of its very nature *Nova* would probably never see a second issue. And when Tucker did indeed find it necessary to dissolve it after the initial number he made wry allusion to the prophesy of "Merlin Moskowitz," which naturally brought the two fans no closer together.

From the foregoing one can see the welter of abrupt activity that pushed Bob Tucker back into prominence in a relatively short time. As the date of the coming world science fiction convention approached, he had become a powerful figure destined to be a leader in the growth of mid-western fandom.

In Chicago, dormant since late 1936 when the city's SFL chapter had given up the ghost, there were stirrings of new activities. A new circle of fans had formed in which the leading figures were such names as Mark Reinsberg, Melvin Korshak, Richard I. Meyer and William L. Hamling. The rejuvenation of *Amazing Stories* by the local firm of Ziff-Davis was especially propitious for the growth of this circle, who found editor Raymond Palmer a source of almost every variety of help needed for forwarding their activities. Mark Reinsberg was the most active of the group, his columns in *Amazing Stories* having appeared regularly for more than a year in *Fantascience Digest*. Melvin Korshak had dabbled a bit in fantasy book dealing, being one of the first fans to garner profitable returns from their hobby.

With *Amazing*'s Julian S. Krupa as art editor, the above four collaborated to produce a new fan magazine, *Ad Astra*. Its first issue was dated May, 1939, and sported a pictorial mimeographed cover by Krupa. Generally speaking, the magazine had a sloppy appearance, but the material and editing was flashy. In addition to an interview with Raymond Palmer, the editors had managed to concentrate between their covers contributions from E. E. Smith, John W. Campbell, Hugo Gernsback, Robert Madle, Harry Warner and William Hamling. A second number appeared before convention time, material by Clifford Simak and Jack Williamson in the featured roles.

But Reinsberg, Korshak and Mayer had a misunderstanding with Hamling, whom they accused of being temperamental, and Hamling in return resorted to name calling which included anti-Semitic phrases. Chicago was thus divided into two camps, though news of the schism was kept out of circulation for many months. Even after the news leaked out, however, both factions attempted to appear to be working together.

And against this troubled background Reinsberg and Korshak planned to make a bid for a 1940 Chicago science fiction convention at the forthcoming New York affair. History was once more in the making.

Chapter XXXIX

THE GREAT DRIVE TOWARD THE CONVENTION

THE END OF 1938 found the New Fandom faction, headed by Taurasi, Sykora and Moskowitz, approaching their objectives more rapidly than in their most optimistic hopes. Older organizations and publications had been successfully amalgamated into this new one, which was receiving prompt support. Its official organ, *New Fandom,* had won the admiration of John W. Campbell, Jr., who pledged to the convention the backing of *Astounding Science Fiction, Thrilling Wonder* had just climbed on the band wagon. And of course fandom itself had endorsed convention plans by a majority vote at the Philadelphia Conference the previous autumn, an act that automatically rejected the bid by the Futurian group. The reorganized Queens SFL chapter was now one of the largest and most active fan clubs in the country, and as we have seen was serving as a base of operations for New Fandom's convention aspirations. *Fantasy News* had no near competitors, and fan periodicals generally were swinging into line behind it, the Cosmic Publications group and the manuscript bureau. Obviously, then, the machinery for a successful convention now existed. It was only up to the operators to use it properly.

It should be emphasized that although a convention on a smaller scale held in Newark the previous year had drawn over a hundred attendees, there was otherwise no precedent for what was now being attempted. Facts which everybody today accepts without question could not be taken for granted in 1939. Even the most minor aspects of the affair presented problems for debate and discussion at that time. The thought that such conventions would become annual events was given no thought whatsoever by the sponsors; this one was planned as a "one-shot," and the very year had been chosen because it coincided with that of the World's Fair, and it was hoped that out-of-town fans might be more likely to attend with such a double prospect in view. It is interesting to conjecture on how long it would have taken for a second convention to come about had the first one failed.

One can see that this initial world convention required far greater effort than did its successors, which by and large used the original pattern with comparatively few major modifications. Nothing was mere routine in 1939!

To give fandom at large a sense of solidarity and to give the event a truly national flavor, New Fandom from the outset appointed regional representatives throughout the country to solicit aid and handle convention work in their areas. Soon a cross-section of the most influential names of the day formed a network that resulted in large regional delegations to the affair.

Next, the dates set were the second, third and fourth of July, the hope being that the holiday weekend would bring in more outsiders than it would lose New Yorkers. Events justified this hope.

The problem of deciding upon a convention chairman was discussed. The idea of allowing an important personage to act as master of ceremonies for purposes of prestige was broached and discarded;

preference to any one magazine editor, for example, might discourage cooperation from the others and give a general air of partiality. Only a fan could be truly neutral. Ultimately Sam Moskowitz was decided upon as chairman, partly because he was already chairman of the sponsoring group and partly because the potential volume of his voice made microphone failures no problem.

Another question to be resolved was the locale of the affair. If held on the grounds of the World's Fair itself, officials offered a free hall, a discount of twenty to thirty percent on admission tickets if purchased in blocs of five hundred or more, and a day to be called jointly the Science Fiction and Boy Scouts of America Day. This plan was finally discarded because of the necessary daily admission charge and the fact that too many distractions would be harmful. Instead, the sponsors arranged to rent Caravan Hall, whose mid-Manhattten location (110 E. 59th St.) and low cost made it ideal.

Remembering one reason for the success of the Newark Convention, Moskowitz decided to institute here, also, the plan of having fan publishers prepare special editions of their journals for contribution to and sale at Caravan Hall. Dozens of titles were announced in short order. A drive for contributions to an auction was begun, and items soon began to pour in from fans and professionals alike. An additional burst of enthusiasm greeted the news that a copy of the famous fantasy film "Metropolis" had been obtained for showing. Arrangements were begun to make a printed souvenir program booklet available for the convention—the first time this had been attempted. This proved very important, especially since advertisements solicited for it provided a new medium of revenue. To add an element of fun to the affair, the Queens SFL organized a softball team and challenged the Philadelphia Science Fiction Society to a game for fan supremacy on the last day of the convention. Finally, Frank R. Paul, the famous fantasy artist, was chosen to be guest of honor at the convention banquet.

As these developments transpired they were individually subjected to the most intensive press-agentry possible. Routine-seeming events today, fans a decade ago eagerly scanned the black headlines with which *Fantasy News* adorned descriptions of these preparations. Right up to convention time, too, *New Fandom* featured colored, silk-screen covers that were little more than posters advertising the event, and carried behind them extensive and rabid publicity composed by Sam Moskowitz. Large announcements were printed and posted in local libraries and museums, and two sets of circulars giving all information and full travelling instructions were mailed to fans everywhere.

As promised, professional publicity was also forthcoming. *Amazing Stories, Astounding Science Fiction, Thrilling Wonder Stories* and *Science Fiction* all published announcements of varying lengths with full details. In some cases these were beautifully timed to appear just near enough to the affair to boost potential attendance.

Behind-the-scenes activity reached new peaks as the great day drew near. Meetings of the convention committee were held weekly. At every gathering of the Queens SFL chapter, without exception, vigorous and minutely detailed reports were presented. Fan typewriters clattered and pens scratched out personal letters to acquaintances and celebrities, begging them to attend. Rarely had so many worked so selflessly on any fan event.

Chapter XL

THE CHARACTER OF THE OPPOSITION

IN ORDER THAT we may comprehend fully and accurately the fateful events which transpired on the first day of the first world science fiction convention, as well as the motives inspiring them, we must outline the opposition encountered by the New Fandom convention committee.

Later national gatherings found little but good will and helping hands attending their efforts, but from the beginning those of New Fandom were marked by strife and desperate measures. The organization's struggle for recognition had aroused such widespread opinion against fan feuding that by adopting this as a plank in its platform New Fandom virtually lifted itself quite a height by its own bootstraps. So successful was the campaign urging editors to bar such fights from fan magazine pages that by the end of 1938 only the Futurian-controlled *Science Fiction Fan* and *Science Fiction News-Letter* continued to print columns of vituperation, most of which was aimed at New Fandom. For a short while it was hoped that when Wollheim sounded his famous "Retreat" (see Chapter XXXIV) the *Fan* would discontinue these efforts—but this was not to be.

Olon F. Wiggins, editor of the *Fan* and by devious politics president of the FAPA, suddenly launched an anti-convention campaign that for vicious unreasonableness had no parallel before nor any since. Its opening gun was "What's New about New Fandom?", published in the February, 1939, *Science Fiction Fan*. In this article he denied that there was anything novel about New Fandom, insisting the latter was not essential to the success of the convention.

> The real purposes of the affair have been overlooked by a majority of fans, very few there are who have fathomed the real truth of the matter. Not through ignorance, perhaps, but rather through their eagerness.... I will not go into the truth of this as I don't wish to disillusion those who haven't woke up as to what is going on. Rather shall I sit back and watch the culmination of this farce.

Wiggins doubted that New Fandom had formed a new base for fan activity, and he refused it any credit for the influx of fans into the field that had been brought about since its inception. New Fandom, he reiterated, had "failed the fans miserably."

> Are its leaders incapable of handling the affair now that they have started it? Present indications point in that direction. The New Fandom group are not the logical sponsors of the convention anyhow. The only logical committee to handle the convention is the one headed by Donald A. Wollheim.... Before it has gone too far why not put the convention back into the hands of its logical sponsors. The Wollheim-headed group. For a true stf. convention for the real fans and a return to normal.

Whatever Wiggins lost in being cryptic and ungrammatical, he gained in forcefulness: there was no doubt where his sympathies lay!

And this article was but the beginning. He also wrote letters to every important fantasy magazine editor urging that support be withdrawn from New Fandom. One was even published in *Amazing Stories'* letter column early in 1939. Another was brought by John Campbell to the March 5, 1939, meeting of the Queens SFL. In it Wiggins disparaged the attempt of appealing to a mass audience, saying he doubted if there were more than fifty true fans in existence, and stating that authors, editors and artists of fantasy had no place in such an audience. A rebuttal of these remarks (together with the text of the letter itself) appeared in the March 12, 1939, issue of *Fantasy News*. Wiggins replied to the rebuttal in April, 1939, *Technocrat* (which was distributed with his *Fan*). This reply was more an outburst of temper than a logical answer. Moskowitz and Taurasi were accused of lacking "the necessary intelligence" to write such a rebuttal. Campbell (who refused to withdraw his allegiance to New Fandom) was labelled "either ignorant or not aware of the full facts of the case." Wiggins doubted that the professionals would contribute much of anything to the convention, and then insisted that they were backing it, but because of selfish motives. New Fandom, he intimated, had "sold out" to the pros. Fans would rue the day they ever supported such an affair.

At this point Wiggins appeared ready to drop the debate. But the Futurians were not. The March, 1939, *Science Fiction Fan* found R. W. Lowndes pitching the same brand of ball in an article that bore the same title as Wiggins' original one. He opened with a broadside against Leo Margulies and Standard Magazines, maintaining that Margulies had promised the Michelists that they would receive representation on the convention committee; New Fandom having not given them notice, he accused Campbell, Margulies and Weisinger of having made "no effort to follow their pledges. In the face of double-crossing by Sykora they have remained silent and continue to support one they know to be dishonest." The convention was in incompetent hands, he maintained, but the weight of numbers probably would make it a success. Indeed, he hoped it would not fail, for if it did New Fandom would certainly attribute such an outcome to the "terrible machinations of the Michelists, the reds, the stooges from Moscow who disrupted the proceedings because they could not run them themselves." Lowndes concluded by accusing the editors of "welching," and describing New Fandom as "crooked."

Early in December, 1938, Lowndes had begun issuing from Springdale, Connecticut, a weekly sheet entitled *Le Vombiteur*. This hektographed publication ran to two to four pages; its contents made no attempt at being topical, but were rather devoted to whatever struck the writer's fancy. There were exchanges with August Derleth and Jack Speer on fan matters and politics, and a poll of fans' favorite stories. *Le Vombiteur* was not outstanding and had but small influence upon important fan events of the day, but it did serve the function of directing anti-New Fandom propaganda to whatever readers came its way. More important, it showed that the apparent resignation of the Futurians from activity was nothing more than the veriest camouflage.

As far back as September, 1938, regular meetings of the Futurian Society were being held at the homes of its members. Though small, the society by 1939 was a loyal, well-knit group including Donald

Wollheim, Frederik Pohl, Robert W. Lowndes, Cyril Kornbluth, Richard Wilson and the up-and-coming author Isaac Asimov, who served as secretary. The Futurians were the active core of opposition to New Fandom and the allied *Fantasy News* and Queens SFL. This opposition appeared unified and well-planned. In addition to material in *Le Vombiteur,* it manifested itself in other ways.

Early in April, 1939, Frederik Pohl announced the formation of the Futurian Federation of the World. This organization, sponsored by the New York Futurians, announced it would publish regularly *The Futurian Review* and devote itself to correcting past "mistakes" of such groups as the ISA and New Fandom. Advertising for recruits began, and attempts were made to siphon prospective members from the ranks of New Fandom. This "world" federation received luke-warm support from some young fans (such as James S. Avery and Harry Warner, Jr.), but managed to publish only one issue of their *Review* before convention time, thereafter completely dropping from sight. These facts lend the distinct impression that the organization was merely one more device trying to reduce the effectiveness of New Fandom and the convention.

When New Fandom announced acquisition of a print of "Metropolis," the Futurian Society immediately circulated an open letter demanding to know if money for the film had been sent to Nazi Germany. They based their demand on a statement in the May, 1939, issue of Sykora's *Scientifilmaker* which said that he (Sykora) was "carrying on negotiations for the rental of this film from the original makers." As it had been originally made by UFA in 1926, he was of course implying dealings with a German firm. But the nature and wide distribution of this open letter branded it an obvious device to lower the prestige of the convention committee. Actually "Metropolis" had been obtained on loan from the files of the New York Museum of Modern Art, which owned the print outright.

At the April 2, 1939, meeting of the Queens SFL two Futurians, Richard Wilson and Cyril Kornbluth, were present, and tendered an official offer from the Futurian Society that the two organizations hold a joint meeting for the purpose of promoting harmony. Because of the long-standing differences between the two groups, Queens director Taurasi viewed this attempt at conciliation with suspicion, particularly in the light of the "Metropolis" episode, then but a few weeks old. He feared it might be a trick of the Futurians to infiltrate and disrupt the Queens SFL, having good reason to remember the former's abilities along such lines when he recalled how they engineered his own impeachment back in the days of the Greater New York SFL chapter. Further, since many Futurians were admitted communists and communist-sympathizers, he felt that association with them would be detrimental to his club. He therefore fell back on the Margulies stipulation that Wollheim and Sykora and their followers could not be active in the same SFL chapter, and on this basis requested Kornbluth and Wilson to leave the hall. But the latter two requested the decision on the question to be put to the membership present. Taurasi then ruled that to decide otherwise than he had would involve changing the chapter charter in the light of Margulies' stipulation in granting it; and that initiating such a change would be possible (if at all) only through request of a member present. And neither Kornbluth nor Wilson, of course, were Queens SFL members.

No member spoke; everyone was willing to let the decision Taurasi had voiced stand.

Sam Moskowitz stopped Wilson before he left and asked him point-blank if he favored New Fandom sponsorship of the convention. It was an especially pertinent question , since Wilson was at once a New Fandom member and a Futurian. When he replied in the affirmative Moskowitz asked him to print a statement to that effect in his *News Letter* to clarify his stand to outsiders. As a result the April 8, 1939, *Science Fiction News Letter* carried the following remarks by Wilson:

> Sam Moskowitz has asked us to state publicly that we favor New Fandom's sponsorship of the World Science Fiction Convention this July, if we so thought, in order, presumably, to banish any doubt in people's minds. Consider it stated.... New Fandom also wishes it known that the film "Metropolis," which will be shown at the affair, was obtained from an American firm...and that not one pfennig will go to der Vaterland for its rental.... The Marxist Manhattenites, incidentally, are sniggering happily to themselves at NF's move in this direction since "Metropolis" was made in Socialist Germany by a bunch of red-hot Communists and fairly oozes propaganda.

This statement proved of great significance, for from its tone and from the editorial "we" casual readers got the impression that Wilson was speaking for the Futurians in general rather than for himself alone. Many therefore felt the two rival groups were working together.

In later years the Futurians claimed that they had gone out of their way to be neutral, had kept their hands off the convention and allowed New Fandom the utmost leeway—and this despite their feeling the group was unqualified to handle the affair and that they themselves were unjustly treated. Existing evidence shows this claim to be utterly false. Wilson's statement did not check the constant barrage of Futurian anti-New Fandom propaganda, which continued unabated up to the very date of the convention.

In the May, 1939, *Science Fiction Fan* which was distributed two months after the appearance of the above-quoted Wilson statement (ample time for its withdrawal from publication had its author so desired) Donald Wollheim's column "Fanfarade" launched yet another attack on the convention and its leaders. After plugging the Futurian Federation of the World Wollheim declared the New Fandom meeting was merely an "advertising convention." Completely ignoring the statements clarifying the status of the "Metropolis" film, he re-hashed the issue from the standpoint of the Futurian open letter and quoted Sykora's remarks again as proof positive that the film print was being rented from German sources. Then, forgetting that he had just claimed there would be no motions allowed from the floor at the New Fandom convention, Wollheim contradicted himself by predicting that Sykora would railroad through a motion changing the name of New Fandom to the International Scientific Association, the older group of which he had once been president.

Yet throughout all these attacks New Fandom had hewed closely to their no-feud policy, confining themselves merely to formal explanations of the facts behind the "Metropolis" rental and Wiggins' letter to Campbell. However, the continuous barrage was worrying. New Fandom sponsors were, in effect, pioneers. They were tackling what up to then was the biggest fan job ever attempted. They needed every bit of help they could get, and felt it reasonable to suppose that if some, such as the Futurians, were unwilling to help, they at least would not go out of their way to harm the affair. But the facts show clearly that New Fandom was subjected to a most trying ordeal, and that the nature of the opposition was definitely calculated to be damaging. This should be carefully borne in mind when appraising the situation soon to follow.

Chapter XLI

THE FIRST WORLD SCIENCE FICTION CONVENTION

JULY 2, 1939, the first day of the convention, was a fair day with the temperature in the mid-eighties. At 10:00 a.m. the hall, located on the fourth floor of the building, was opened so that the growing groups of fans in the street below might have a comfortable place to congregate and converse before the program got under way. A refreshment stand selling soft drinks and pie at a nickel per portion was also opened.

Among the things first impressing a fan arrival were the striking modernity of the newly decorated hall; the original colored paintings for covers of fantasy magazines, loaned especially for the occasion, and including a colored Paul original never before published; and the official souvenir booklet with its shining gold cover. The latter, it should be noted, had been printed by the old time fan Conrad Ruppert. It featured original decorations by Frank R. Paul and two pages of photographs of such well known professionals as Stanley G. Weinbaum, Henry Kuttner, David H. Keller, Otis A. Kline and others.

From the earliest hours it could easily be seen that the convention had been successful in bringing distant fans together. There was a California delegation composed of Forrest Ackerman, Morojo and Ray Bradbury. From Texas had come Dale Hart, Julius Pohl, Allen R. Charpentier and Albert S. Johnston. New and old Chicago fans were represented in Erle Korshak, Mark Reinsberg, William Dillenback and Jack Darrow. A photograph of Darrow and Ackerman, most famous of the letter writers to fantasy magazines, was of course taken for posterity. Several Canadian names lent an international flavor to the convention. Others, too, had travelled long distances to attend. There was Jack Williamson from New Mexico; Ross Rocklynne from Cincinnati; Nelson Bond from Virginia. Among other authors in attendance were Harl Vincent, Ray Cummings, Manly Wade Wellman, Edmond Hamilton, L. Sprague de Camp, Isaac Asimov, Norman L. Knight, Eando Binder, John Victor Peterson, Frederick C. Painton and Malcolm Jameson. In addition to Frank R. Paul, artist Charles Schneeman was in attendance, and the professional fantasy magazine editors were represented by Campbell, Margulies, Weisinger, Hornig, and Farnsworth Wright of *Weird Tales,* who unfortunately arrived after the main sessions had been concluded. Many of the authors, editors and artists brought wives and children with them. Present also were such well-known fantasy fans as David V. Reed, L. A. Eshbach, John D. Clark, David C. Cooke, R. D. Swisher, Milton A. Rothman, Oswald Train, Kenneth Sterling, Charles F. Ksanda, Robert A. Young, Scott Feldman, Julius Schwartz, Vida Jameson, John V. Baltadonis, Walter Sullivan, Gertrude and Louis Kuslan, David A. Kyle, Robert A. Madle, John Giunta, Julius Unger, Richard Wilson, Herbert Goudket, Robert G. Thompson, A. Langley Searles, Arthus Widner and Leon Burg.

Fifteen special convention publications had been issued for the occasion. In addition to the program booklet there were Jack Speer's

justly famous *Up To Now,* a 20,000-word account of fan history to
date, the first serious attempt along such lines; Louis Kuslan's
Cosmic Tales Special; Morojo's *Stephen the Stfan,* a booklet contain-
ing facsimile signatures of famous science fictionists as well as
blank pages for attendees to solicit autographs of others present;
Metropolis, contributed by Ackerman; Wilson's *Escape; The Fantasy
Collector* of Farsaci; Mario Racic's *Fantasy in Opera; Van Houten
Says; Le Zombie,* published by Bob Tucker; Sully Roberd's *Science
Fiction Abbatoir, The Grab Bag,* by Ted Dikty; Bob Formanek's *Fanta-
verse; We Have A Rendezvous,* a technocratic propaganda issued by
Russell J. Hodgkins; and Daniel McPhail's *Stf. and Nonesense.* The
wide variety of publications was ample evidence of the interest
fandom took in the proceedings.

Of the three New Fandom leaders only one was present at the hall
during the initial morning session. Moskowitz was arranging last-
minute details at his Newark home, and Sykora was likewise at home,
busily engaged in binding enough copies of the July *New Fandom* for
convention distribution. So it happened that when the main body of
the Futurian group—Wollheim, Lowndes, Pohl, Kornbluth and Gillespie
—stepped from the elevator and headed toward the hall Taurasi alone
was on hand to confront them and question their right to enter in
view of their flagrant anti-convention activities.

Now, prior to the convention the New Fandom heads had discussed
what course should be taken if a Futurian delegation did put in an
appearance. They felt, first of all, that in view of the Futurians'
slurs they might not come at all. But if they did, then the triumvirate felt serious consideration should be given to excluding them.
Taurasi, Sykora and Moskowitz reached no definite decision, however,
other than that the Futurian group was not to enter the hall unless
it first satisfied the convention heads as to its good intentions.

So in the absense of any consultant Taurasi felt it would be
wisest to refuse entrance to these Futurians until his confreres
arrived. And when Moskowitz made his appearance Taurasi was still
arguing with the would-be attendees, none of whom had yet gotten
more than ten feet from the elevator door. Wollheim promptly
appealed to Moskowitz, maintaining that he had not carried out any
strong action against the convention (!), that he had come without
propaganda of any sort to distribute, and that the intentions of
himself and of his group were merely to mingle with others present
and have a good time. Moskowitz then decided to permit the quintet
to enter, conditional to his first speaking to Sykora as a matter of
courtesy.

(At this point it might be asked why the much larger Futurian
group did not simply brush past Taurasi and Moskowitz since, as they
later stated, they debated the ethical grounds on which they were
being kept out. Aside from the wish to enter properly, readers
should be reminded that both Taurasi and Moskowitz weighed close to
200 pounds, and next to science fiction Moskowitz's greatest
enthusiasm was boxing.)

It was at this juncture that fate played its peculiar hand. Sykora,
it so happened, was not destined to arrive until considerably later,
and in the normal course of events Moskowitz and Taurasi would simply have waited a reasonable time and then permitted the Futurians to
enter. But the next group of fans leaving the elevator included

Louis Kuslan, the well-known Connecticut fan. He carried in his hand
a little yellow pamphlet titled *A Warning!*. "Look what John Michel
gave me downstairs before," he said as he handed the pamphlet to
Moskowitz. Michel, who had joined the other Futurians awaiting entry,
said nothing.

The pamphlet was dated July 2, 1939, and its cover also bore the
heading "IMPORTANT! Read This Immediately!" It contained four pages
of text, and when Moskowitz opened it he found himself reading the
following:

BEWARE OF THE DICTATORSHIP

YOU, who are reading this pamphlet, have come to attend the
World's Science Fiction Convention. You are to be praised
for your attendance and complimented on the type of fiction
in which you are interested. But, TODAY BE AWARE OF ANY
MOVEMENT TO COERCE OR BULLY YOU INTO SUBMISSION! Remember,
this is YOUR convention, for YOU! Be on the alert, lest
certain well-organized minorities use you to ratify their
carefully conceived plans.

WHY THIS WARNING?

This warning is being given to you by a group of sincere
science fiction fans. The reasons for this warning are
numerous; THEY ARE BASED UPON EVENTS OF THE PAST—particularly events which took place at the Newark Convention of
1937. At that time the gathering of fans and interested
readers was pounded into obedience by the controlling
clique. The Newark Convention set up, dictatorially, the
machinery for the convention which you are now attending.
THE NEWARK CONVENTION MUST NOT BE PERMITTED TO REPEAT
ITSELF! It remains in your power to see that this convention today will be an example of perfect democracy.

STARTLING FACTS

The Queens Science Fiction League was formed by the Newark
clique, after that convention, in order to make the necessary local organization upon which the dictatorial convention committee could base itself.... The editors and those
dependant on them for a living, the authors, have made it a
duty to attend Queens S.F.L. meetings regularly in order to
keep it going and to keep the 1939 convention in hand. At
the elections held last meeting, held openly so as to detect
any possible opposition, the three dictators were re-elected
unanimously in perfect un-democratic harmony.

HIGH HANDED TACTICS

At the same time that the Queens S.F.L. was established, a
large number of New York City fans formed the Futurian Society of New York. Contrary to much propaganda, the Futurian
Society is not confined to communists, michelists, or other
radical elements; it is a democratic club, run in a democratic way, and reflecting science fiction fan activity....

A LOADED WEAPON

The World's Science Fiction Convention of 1939 in the hands
of such heretofore ruthless scoundrels is a loaded weapon in
the hands of such men. This weapon can be aimed at their
critics or can be used to blast all fandom. But YOU, the
readers of this short article, are the ammunition. It is
for YOU to decide whether you shall bow before unfair
tactics and endorse the carefully arranged plans of the
Convention Committee. Beware of any crafty speeches or sly
appeals. BE ON YOUR GUARD!

The booklet ended after a few more paragraphs of a similar nature, and was signed "The Association for Democracy in Science Fiction Fandom."

Actually the pamphlet had been composed and printed by Futurian David Kyle on the presses of his brother's Monticello, New York, newspaper. But this, of course, was not known to Moskowitz until considerably later. At the time, the charge that New Fandom was a puppet in the hands of the professionals, the kind words for the Futurian Society, the cry of dictatorship—these appeared but a repetition of the clichés that had been hurled against convention backers for the past year. And it seemed to Moskowitz, as it probably would have to any reasonable man in his place, that the Futurians had come prepared to agitate against and possibly disrupt the proceedings.

Moskowitz turned to Wollheim and said, "I thought you just stated that you would do nothing to hurt the convention." Wollheim shrugged his shoulders and eyed the pamphlet. "I didn't print them." "But his group was passing them out," Louis Kuslan quickly added.

Now thoroughly worried by the turn of events, Moskowitz went downstairs to see if Sykora had arrived as yet. Failing to find him, he returned barely in time to intercept the building superintendant, Maurice J. Meisler, who informed him that he was wanted by policemen waiting on the street level. It appeared that Taurasi, before Moskowitz's arrival, had anticipated difficulty in restraining the Futurians and had called upon official assistance. Moskowitz explained the situation to the officers, saying he believed he could handle it, but asking the police to stop back in an hour or so to check, which they agreed to do.

As he concluded this conversation, his eye was caught by bright colors beneath a near-by radiator. Investigation showed that here were cached several hundred copies of booklets printed by the Futurian Society of New York. In the press of circumstances, with no opportunity to read them carefully, Moskowitz assumed from their origin, authorship and surreptitious concealment that they were further anti-convention propaganda.

(Later examination showed the booklets to be recruiting fodder for the cause of Michelism, their common denominator being more pro-Marx than anti-New Fandom. There were five different titles, as follows: *An Amazing Story,* by Robert Lowndes, a bitter, five-paged condemnation of editor Raymond A. Palmer because he published anti-Russian and anti-communist stories; *Dead End 1938,* also written by Lowndes, which discussed whether the dreams expressed in fantastic fiction could ever be broken by economic, social or psychological disaster from a Marxist viewpoint; John Michel's *Foundation of the CPASF* (a reprint from the April, 1938, *Science Fiction Advance*); a reprint from *New Masses* of Upton Sinclair's article, *Science Fiction Turns to Life,* which is a review of two social satires, *Show and Side Show* by Joshua Rosett and E. C. Large's *Sugar in the Air;* and *The Purpose of Science Fiction,* in which British fan Douglas W. F. Mayer expressed the opinion that science fiction broadened a fan's horizon, and even if it did not lead him to take up a scientific career, if it could but influence him to follow political movements promoting social reform (such as, of course, the Futurians) it would be accomplishing its purpose.)

It seemed to Moskowitz at this juncture that the Futurians intended to deluge the convention with unfavorable material. At the same
time he still hoped, for the sake of harmony, that this difficulty
could be resolved smoothly. When he returned upstairs, therefore, he
approached Wollheim and asked: "If we let you in will you promise on
your word of honor that you will do nothing in any way to disturb
the progress of the convention?" "If we do anything to disturb the
convention you can kick us out," Wollheim replied. "We don't want to
kick you out," said Moskowitz. "We simply want your honored promise
not to harm the convention." But this promise Wollheim adamantly
refused to give. Later he claimed he could make no such promise
because Moskowitz intended it to be binding on his friends as well
as himself. This allegation is untrue, for Moskowitz then spoke to
each Futurian member, offering to admit anyone who would guarantee
his own conduct by so promising. On this basis several were admitted,
Richard Wilson, Jack Rubinson, Leslie Perri, Isaac Asimov and David
Kyle among them. But the core of the group—Wollheim, Lowndes, Pohl,
Kornbluth and Gillespie—chose to remain without. And when Sykora
arrived somewhat later he thoroughly concurred with the action that
Moskowitz and Taurasi had taken, declaring that it would be the
height of folly to admit any fan who would refuse to promise not to
cause trouble.

It is possible that the Futurians refused admittance would have
behaved in orderly fashion in the hall and, aside from voicing
indignation at their reception, would have entered into the spirit
of the gathering. It is conceivable also that the refusal of
Wollheim and others to promise good behavior can be laid to personal
pride. But to New Fandom leaders, in the light of past experiences,
refusal to promise not to cause trouble meant one thing: that this
was precisely what the Futurians were going to cause. Sykora,
Taurasi and Moskowitz remembered the expulsion of Sykora from the
Greater New York SFL; the refusal to admit to membership Osheroff
and Moskowitz to the same organization; the subterfuge employed in
soliciting signatures to a petition of reprimand regarding the operation of the 1938 Newark convention, as well as the communist propaganda distributed at that convention; the steady bombardment of
abuse that preparations for the 1939 gathering had elicited; and
they remembered, too, that all these things had been engineered by
Futurians or friends of Futurians. At the convention hall they found
the Futurians distributing plainly disruptive literature in advance
of the meeting, and apparently armed with a reserve stock of similar
material. Faced with these facts, and with a group of fans refusing
a simple promise not to cause trouble, what conclusion were they to
come to?

In retrospect, we can see their dilemma more clearly. Looking at
the circumstances in the most pessimistic light, we can see that the
Futurians had everything to gain and nothing to lose. If allowed to
enter, they could have disrupted proceedings, and thus proved their
prior claim that New Fandom was incompetent to run a successful convention; if not allowed to enter, they could point to another prior
claim of New Fandom's being essentially dictatorial as proved.
Indeed, Futurian strategy may have been devised with these possibilities foremost in mind. Whether it was or not, Futurians stood to
gain public sympathy as a result of the convention if they played
their cards properly no matter what stand New Fandom took.

It is of course impossible to say, even now, if New Fandom's decision was the wisest that could be made. It can still be argued pro and con. At least we can see how it came to be made, and should understand that Moskowitz, Taurasi and Sykora felt themselves to be acting for the good of the greatest number present, and therefore to be adopting the morally right course. It was a course that violated the principles of accepted convention harmony inevitably, however, and as we shall later see one which brought both condemnation and personal difficulties to the formulators.

At later times the excluded Futurians made several attempts to enter the hall, usually in pairs, but were stopped by Taurasi or the attendant Meisler, who had orders not to permit them entrance. Inside the hall, meanwhile, Futurians and their friends who had been admitted circulated about and did their best to rally support for those outside. The ladies present, particularly Morojo and Frances Swisher, attempted every method of reason with the triumvirate, though to no effect. Leslie Perri persuaded Jack Williamson to approach Moskowitz on the matter, and others present subjected Taurasi and Sykora to similar pressure. David Kyle passed about the room, distributing circulars announcing that the Futurians would hold a conference of their own the day after the convention. Debate on the action of New Fandom leaders grew in tempo until by two o'clock, when the convention was scheduled to be called to order, the task seemed an impossible one. The entire attendance was milling about and discussion was rife. Would the convention break up before it had even begun?

At this point Maurice Meisler, the attendant, nudged Moskowitz, who had paused irresolute. "Call the convention to order," he said. "They'll have to come to a decision on whether they stay or go. But if you let things go any further as they are you won't have a convention at all." Moskowitz looked dubious. "Go ahead," urged Meisler. "I've seen this sort of thing happen before. Call it to order and your troubles are over."

Moskowitz ascended the platform and walked to the podium. There, disdaining the microphone, he bellowed: "In the name of New Fandom I call this, the first world science fiction convention, to order!"

The conversation and controversy subdued, and New Fandom workers on the convention committee started for their seats or for positions of assignment. The editors and authors, who had generally remained aloof from the difficulties that had already transpired, took their seats also, and were followed in this action by those who were attending the convention for the first time and those who had been introduced to fantasy by the event. With the great majority seated, debating fans had little choice but to follow suit or withdraw from the hall. They also took their seats, as did finally Futurian Society members and their friends, most of whom were now in the hall. The crisis was past.

Sam Moskowitz opened the program with an address of welcome. Said he in part:

> You know, it's really a soul-inspiring sight to a lover of science fiction to stand on this platform and gaze down at an assembly of two hundred or more kindred souls. Five years ago I might have said that such an assembly was impossible (in fact a few of my colleagues were reading my thoughts

back to me only a few hours ago). But now, one glance
assures me that the event is a success! The World Science
Fiction Convention, probably the greatest gathering science
fiction has ever known, is at this moment recording its
name indelibly on the record of history.

This was indeed a vital moment in the lives of the convention
committee; all its members felt that a great progressive step forward had been taken in the face of continuous turmoil and strife. In
future days world conventions might surpass this one; they would
undoubtedly be held in a more harmonious setting; but this was the
first—and its effect was to be profound.

After the customary eulogies and acknowledgements, Moskowitz went
on to differentiate the active fantasy fan from the entire group of
fiction readers as a class unique, unparalleled in interest and
enthusiasm for his literary choice. He pointed out that science fiction was on the threshold of vast expansion and greater popularity,
and that an effort must be made to plot its course and guide its
development. He asked attendees to weigh their words carefully at
this convention, for they could be exceptionally influential at a
time when every important name in the field was either present or
eagerly awaiting report of events.

Moskowitz reviewed the highlights of the 1938 national convention
held in Newark, wishing to maintain the continuity of conventions by
presenting what amounted to the minutes of the previous one. In
order to aid the continuity still further he asked for a volunteer
from the audience to act as secretary for this gathering. Raymond
Van Houten offered his services, which were accepted.

The first speaker introduced was William Sykora. The title of his
address was "Science Fiction and New Fandom." He offered the presentation of this convention as proof that fans were not escapists;
escapists, he maintained, could never have pushed through so massive
an affair, any more than they could have created New Fandom, the
Queens SFL or the many amateur journals in existence. Escapists
might exist, but they were a tiny minority. He concluded by saying:

> My message, then, to you delegates from far and near to
> this great gathering is this: Whether we believe that sci-
> ence fiction justifies its existence as pure entertainment
> or not, let us not permit ourselves to be labelled as "save
> the world" crackpots; let us rather take the messages of
> the authors of science fiction, and working together, hand
> in hand with progressive New Fandom, strive to make the
> fancies of science fiction become reality.

Leo Margulies, editorial director of Standard Magazines, was
introduced and said, "I didn't think you fellows could be so damn'
sincere. I've just discussed plans with my editor Mort Weisinger for
a new idea in fantasy magazines...that will interest you." He did
not state what the idea was at the time, possibly to preclude
competitors' using it, but the idea developed to be a character
fantasy magazine titled *Captain Future*.

Next Kenneth Sterling, remembered for his stories in *Wonder Stories*
in previous years, asked for permission to read an announcement of a
proposed memorial volume to H. P. Lovecraft to be published by
August Derleth and Donald Wandrei. The book was to be entitled *The
Outsider and Others,* and he begged attendees to rally to its support
by sending in $3.50, the special advance price.

Then followed the introduction of the feature speaker, Frank R. Paul, whose many illustrations in fantasy magazines had brought him wide fame and great popularity. Though his hair had turned gray and a trace of Austrian accent had not left his speech, he was in manner and statement typical of the average science fiction lover. His talk was titled "Science Fiction, the Spirit of Youth." Said he in part:

> Two thousand years ago a meeting such as this, with all these rebellious, adventuresome minds, would have been looked upon as a very serious psychological phenomenon, and the leaders would have been put in chains or at least burned at the stake. But today it may well be considered the healthiest sign of youthful, wide-awake minds—to discuss subjects beyond the range of the average provincial mind.
> The science fiction fan may well be called the advance guard of progress... [he] is intensely interested in everything going on around him, differing radically from his critic. His critic is hemmed in by a small provincial horizon of accepted orthodoxy and humdrum realities and either does not dare or is too lazy to reach beyond that horizon.
> Once in a while we also find eminent scientists throwing cold water on our enthusiasm; for instance the other day Dr. Robert Millikan said we should stop dreaming about atomic power and solar power. We.., as much as we love the doctor as one of the foremost scientists of the day, because he cannot see its realization or gets tired of research is no reason to give up hope that some scientist of the future might not attack the problem and ride it. What seems utterly impossible today may be commonplace tomorrow.

Thus did Frank R. Paul prophesy, offering as a model Dr. Arthur Compton, "...who sees all kinds of forces in nature...which are waiting for discovery or exploitation." He finished with the statement, "...in the future we will have bigger and better science fiction with the accent on science." The ovation that listeners gave Paul's talk was tremendous, as had been that which greeted his earlier introduction.

Ray Cummings, well known author of "The Girl in the Golden Atom," was introduced from the floor, and was greeted by an exceptional display of enthusiasm, which was perhaps surprising, for his recent stories had received adverse criticism in magazines' readers' columns.

A brief intermission was then called while the projector and screen were set up for the showing of the film "Metropolis." Its story concerned the slavery in a future age of most of the people, who were dictatorially controlled by their government, and in portions was so melodramatic as to become a comedy. A city master is considering changing his human workers for tireless robots. He has a scientist construct for him a robot in the form of a beautiful woman; this is to be used for inciting riots and sabotage among the workers, thereby providing an excuse for mass layoffs, and the shift to robot control. The subterfuge succeeds—but in the ensuing violence the inventor of the robots is killed and his secret lost. The master is then forced to make peace with the workers on the most favorable terms he can get. Despite the crudities of acting, "Metropolis" is memorable for its vividly imaginative future scenes.

After another recess of considerable conviviality the convention reconvened. John Campbell of *Astounding* spoke next on "The Changing Science Fiction." He pointed to "Metropolis" as an example to show

how science fiction was advancing. He compared the crude description accompanying the early science fiction character Hawk Carse with that utilized in present-day stories. Campbell stated that science fiction must continually advance, and that there must be no halt in the development of plot and story; and his magazine, he declared, was dedicated to presenting "modern" types of science fiction and keeping abreast of the times.

Mortimer Weisinger then spoke on "Man and Science Fiction." This talk was devoted to entertaining anecdotes concerning such well-known figures in the field as Stanley Weinbaum, T. O'Conor Sloane, Eando Binder, David Keller, etc.

Following this, Sam Moskowitz turned the gavel over to William Sykora, who continued in the role of master of ceremonies, introducing most notables present, including Charles Hornig, who spoke at some length expounding his ideas on the development and future of science fiction.

The convention then adjourned to the auction, in which original cover and interior drawings from fantasy magazines, hundreds of the magazines themselves (including some complete sets), numerous manuscripts by famous authors and rare fan magazines in almost limitless amounts were offered. A complete catalog of all material sold was never compiled, since the majority of it had been brought in by attendees at the last minute. The quantity was so great, however, that two full evenings were required for its disposal. All of it went for bargain prices, too—original cover drawings no higher than eight dollars, original Finlays no more than two, story manuscripts (including an autographed Merritt) at a quarter or so. Yet so deep was America in the recession at that time that attendees considered these prices moderately high, and the auctioneers (Moskowitz, Taurasi and Giunta) were complimented on their salesmanship.

As can be seen, the charged atmosphere resulting from earlier friction with the Futurians had been largely dispelled. The only potential source of further trouble came while Sykora was introducing the notables present. At that time David Kyle rose and attempted to make a motion that the six barred fans be allowed to enter the hall. Sykora, however, declined to recognize the motion, pointing to the previous decision that motions were not to be considered. Later, after nearly everyone had left the hall, a telegram signed "Exiles" arrived for David Kyle, requesting him to announce the "Futurian Meeting" and offering regards "to the tyrannous trio." The committee regarded this as a delayed signal for Kyle to create a disturbance at the gathering. This interpretation, of course, was alleged to be false by the Futurians.

The second day of the convention, July 3rd, was to be devoted largely to science, and the two o'clock call to order found less than a hundred people in attendance, though many new faces were in evidence.

Moskowitz spoke first, on the effect of scientific advance on the fan world of the future. He envisioned a day when such gatherings would be truly international because of greatly accelerated transportation devices, and expressed the opinion that science fiction would have to race to keep ahead of science.

Next Sykora spoke on "Science and Science Fiction." Science, he stated, had a definite place on the agenda of any convention such as

this: "Speculative discussion as to what may be our future civilization, how science may improve living conditions, possible super-
scientific inventions and discoveries are not out of place by any
means." He felt that those who were inspired to become scientists
through science fiction should not be discouraged.

Ruroy Sibley, the well known astronomical lecturer, was the
feature speaker on the program. His talk, a complete outline of
present-day astronomical knowledge, was illustrated by the film
"Seeing the Universe." Mr. Sibley then answered questions posed from
the floor, and upon completion of this discussion period there was a
short recess.

The auction was completed when the group reconvened, and afterwards
the high spot of the convention occurred. This was the first science
fiction banquet and was held at the Hotel Wyndham in honor of Frank
R. Paul. Only thirty-two fans were able to afford the dollar asked
for the meal (a figure that seems ridiculously cheap today), but
those who did will never forget it, not so much for the food (which
was scarcely exceptional) but for the luxurious compactness of the
private dining room, the lively conversation and the after-dinner
talks, of which Willy Ley's was particularly excellent. It was one
a.m. before the group left.

The third day of the convention was devoted to a softball game
between the Queens SFL and the philadelphia SFS, though player-
selections did not adhere rigidly to this dividing-line. The Queens
Cometeers, captained by Sam Moskowitz, trounced the Philadelphia
Panthers, captained by Baltadonis, by 23 to 11 in a 9-inning game.
A. Langley Searles, the Queens pitcher, hurled three innings of
scoreless ball. In the fourth, however, he strained his wrist and
was replaced by John Giunta, who, though hit hard, managed to retain
the lead given him and finish the game. Searles was shifted to the
outfield, and further distinguished himself by getting five hits in
six times at bat. Moskowitz and Taurasi each got six-for-six at the
plate, and Korshak and Unger capably played their short field and
catching assignments. Hero of the Panthers was Art Widner, who made
a "home run" by the aid of three errors. Sykora was batted out of
the box early, but redeemed himself with a solid double later in the
game. Though such Panthers as Madle, Agnew, Train and Reinsberg got
hits frequently, they were unable to bunch them effectively. Moving
pictures of the game were taken by Sykora, and have often been shown
at fan gatherings. Among the audience were Ray Bradbury, Ross
Rocklynne and Charles Hornig.

The evening of this last convention day was spent at the nearby
World's Fair grounds.

The July 7th issue of *Time* magazine gave the convention a two-
column illustrated write-up, which unfortunately emphasized the
juvenile aspects. Later accounts appeared in *The New Yorker, Writers'
Digest, Thrilling Wonder Stories, Amazing Stories, Science Fiction*
and other periodicals. That in *Thrilling Wonder* featured photographs
of the convention committee.

Thrilling Wonder Stories also played dinner host to the convention
committee as well as to the more distant out-of-towners as Ackerman,
Morojo, Reinsberg, Korshak and Rocklynne.

The sixth issue of *New Fandom* was devoted almost entirely to the
convention; reprints of (or from) most of the speeches, review of

convention magazines, a partial list of auctioned items and an itemized expense account were included. It is interesting to contrast
this latter with expense accounts of later conventions, and amusing
to remember how the 1939 fan press sarcastically challenged such an
item as Mario Racic's three-dollar carfare, incurred during nearly a
year's time. Although the total income of the convention ($306.00)
was given as topping expenses by $36.06, this "profit" had actually
been used to buy the makings of free lunches for attendees. Officially, then, the convention broke even, though actually money was lost
in those miscellaneous, unlisted expenditures that always accompany
preparations for such an event. It might be noted at this point that
the cost of the gathering was almost equally divided between the
fans and the professionals.

Of special interest also was Julius Unger's *Illustrated Nycon Review*, which in addition to summarizing the main points of interest,
contained over two dozen pertinent photographs, and briefly reviewed
previous smaller conventions in the field. *Fantasy News* devoted
three issues (#55-57) to the gathering. The Futurian viewpoint was
covered in two numbers of *Looking Ahead*, which appeared as a supplement to Robert Lowndes' *Science Fiction Weekly*. Finally, there was
Erle Korshak's "Memoirs of a New York Trip," published in the June-
July, 1939, issue of *Fantasy Digest*, which gave good coverage of the
event.

An appraisal of the far-reaching effects of the first world convention can be made more clearly and accurately now, over a decade later,
than it could have been shortly after the event. First of all, the
convention widened the potential recruiting area for new readers by
attaining publicity in well known, nationally circulated periodicals.
This was publicity that the professional fantasy publishers could
never themselves have obtained because it would appear too commercial—but a show put on by two hundred fans to extol their choice of
reading matter was definitely printable news. Moreover, breaking
this ice made subsequent write-ups easier to obtain, so that by now
such general publicity is not at all uncommon.

As a corollary to attracting a larger audience was the attraction
of a number of new writers to fantasy's cause; and as an indirect
result of the convention a number of outstanding new names thus
began to appear in the magazines.

Secondly, the convention brought about a change in relations
between fans and professionals. Previously, general aid from the
latter to the former was confined exclusively to those few fans who
knew an open sesame to the portals, and all the rest found themselves held coldly at arm's length. Now, however, both fans and
publishers were awakened to the fact that it was of mutual benefit
to cooperate. The old axiom that fans were fans and pros were pros,
and never were the twain to meet was discarded. Henceforth such magazine features as reviews of fan journals and fan clubs became regular.

Thirdly—feuds and bickerings aside—the New York Convention presented substantial evidence that fandom was rising to a more mature
level; and it was through the mature efforts of Julius Schwartz and
Conrad Ruppert, indeed, that a large measure of the event's success
was obtained.

Finally, the very success of the convention insured that it would
be an annual affair thenceforward. With the exception of the war

years, there has been a world science fiction convention every year, its site alternately moved to and fro across the country to favor different groups. Each of these conventions has proved newsworthy, and the cumulative publicity has done much for the field.

The basic ideas used in the New York Convention have also been continued. All others (save the Pacificon) have maintained a three-day schedule. A guest of honor has always been chosen. There have been auctions to help pay expenses, and after the other events a banquet. Some form of general entertainment in which many could participate has become the rule—first a ball game, later a masquerade ball, finally an amateur show. Some improvements have been made, too—chiefly the plan of holding the convention in a hotel where visiting fans can meet in smoke-filled rooms in minor sub-conventions of their own. But the important structural framework of these events has remained almost unchanged.

Seeing all these things as clearly as we do today, one would certainly expect that the First World Science Fiction Convention would have reaped little but praise. But though credit was duly given unstintingly in the general and professional publications, the convention committee was to find fandom's attitude far, far different.

Chapter XLII

OPINION RALLIES

ON JULY 4, 1939, the day that the convention was winding up with a softball game at Flushing Flats, the Futurian Society held an open meeting attended by some two dozen people, including Morojo and Ackerman of the California delegation. An open forum on science fiction and fandom was held, such topics as Michelism, actions at the convention just concluded and the site of the next convention being discussed. It was decided to back the bid of Chicago for the 1940 gathering. Mark Reinsberg, spokesman for the Chicago delegation, had approached Moskowitz repeatedly in an effort to gain New Fandom's support for this, mentioning several times in the course of the conversations that no one should take seriously any derogatory reports about him coming from W. Lawrence Hamling, whom he described as the leader of a Chicago faction opposing him. Not wishing to involve either himself or New Fandom in any developing fan feud, however, Moskowitz cautiously had asked Reinsberg to wait until New Fandom leaders had had an opportunity to discuss the question at greater length; and at the same time he had ventured the personal opinion that holding major conventions only a year apart might result in an annual farce where the time at each convention would largely be spent fighting over the site of the next. Reinsberg was of course dissatisfied with this wait-and-see attitude. He needed something concrete, such as a New Fandom or convention vote of approval, to take back to Chicago in order to give his proposal officiality. He considered Moskowitz's stand uncooperative, and felt embittered over it. Quite naturally, then, he was inclined to view the Futurians in a good light when they voiced support of his plan.

A prompt indication that fan strife would continue well after the convention was a brief, hastily-mimeographed pamphlet *In Your Teeth, "Gentlemen": Convention Sketches,* distributed outside the dining-room where Standard Magazines played host to the convention committee and far-travelled fans on July 7, three days later. This pamphlet consisted of two pages of derogatory text and four of cartoons, the latter bearing such titles as "Tyrannous Unholy Trio" and "We Are the Exiles." The text of the pamphlet read in part as follows:

Our objection [to Taurasi, Moskowitz and Sykora] is not directed by personal motives but rather by a feeling of extreme distaste for the stench of overpowering imbecility. We regret the fact that the TRIO were either so senile or so ridiculously blind as to believe that we, Frederik Pohl, John B. Michel, Donald A. Wollheim, Robert W. Lowndes, Cyril Kornbluth, Jack Gillespie and the writer had no intentions other than the feeling of complete friendship and the desire to welcome all out of town convention-goers as warmly as was proven by our activities in regard to meeting various members as they arrived in New York and even in some cases, providing rooms for them to stay. We have our own very good reasons for detesting the stupidity and crass unsportsmanshiplike attitude as was displayed by the by-now

225

famous "exclusion Act".... For Mr. Taurasi, Mr. Moskowitz and Mr. Sykora...WE MEAN TO FINISH YOU IN THE INTEREST OF JUST- ICE WHICH CANNOT EXIST UNTIL YOUR STRONG ARM TACTICS ARE DISCLOSED TO WORLD SCIENCE FICTION.

The pamphlet went on to demand that every fan who thought the exclusion wrong say so publicly. A page was also devoted to an open letter to Sykora, condemning him for his part in the affair, and branding him guiltiest of all.

Moskowitz read this pamphlet aloud in entirety to a group which included Ackerman, Morojo, Korshak, Taurasi, Racic and Sykora. Every- one laughed about it, and spoke with great conviviality on the street for some time, parting on good terms and with expressions that could reasonably have been construed to mean that the convention difficul- ty with the Futurians was unfortunate but past and forgotten as far as those immediately present were concerned.

The first major account of the convention, run serially in three issues of *Fantasy News,* contained no mention of the difficulty with the Futurians. Attendees returning home presented their stories as they saw them. Futurian publications, like *Science Fiction Progress* and the aforementioned *In Your Teeth, "Gentlemen"* not only carried the expected heated accounts of their version of the incident, but were larded with bitter similes, insults and some outrightly inaccur- ate statements like "New Fandom would not cooperate with their [Chi- cago] convention unless they promised to bar the Futurians...." Included also were some very pertinent observations by Donald Wollheim. From the Futurian standpoint he felt the results of the convention were particularly fortunate. The Philadelphia fans were now largely neutral instead of antagonistic toward them, and the Los Angeles delegation perhaps even favorably inclined. The affair, he said, was a great moral victory for the Futurians, and their forward progress was inevitable.

The first mention of the Futurian incident in an accredited fan magazine of general circulation published by an unimplicated party appeared in Ted Dikty's *Fantasy Digest* for June-July, 1939. This consisted of a single sentence in Korshak's "Memoirs of a New York Trip": "Some unpleasantness was caused when Don Wollheim and his brother Futurians were not allowed in the Convention Hall." Bob Tucker, who had been involved in several brisk spats with Moskowitz, editorialized on this statement in the first subscription number (August 5, 1939) of his *Le Zombie.* Under the heading "A Little Unpleasantness Dept.," he said of it, "If true (and all reports seem to indicate it is) makes us a little ashamed of being a member of New Fandom which evidently is responsible for the happening. It seems to us that Wollheim and Co., regardless of political *or* person- al differences, should have been allowed into the convention hall.... For one group to bar another group's entrance, because of politics or personal causes is...well, unmanly to be mild. It's grossly unfair, and considered so not only by the Wollheim faction, *but* by every fair minded fan as well! New Fandom, we spank your hands!"

A blow to the New Fandom group and a boost to Futurian morale came when Philadelphians Baltadonis and Train, long anti-Futurian in convictions, stated in their revived *Science Fiction Collector* that they felt the excluded six should have been permitted to enter, even acknowledging their past actions.

In the absense of a single word of rebuttal from the convention committee and in view of the accusations from apparently neutral attendees, fans at large had little alternative but to believe that New Fandom had indeed been guilty of spiteful action prompted merely by personal animosity. Opinion began to harden against the committee and all they stood for as well—New Fandom, *Fantasy News* and the Queens SFL chapter. Memberships to New Fandom no longer flowed in with previous speed and subscriptions to *Fantasy News* were not always renewed. Two of the strongest props in the New Fandom stronghold were seriously weakening. This change of fan opinion came with lightning speed, and every positive aspect of convention success was being overshadowed. In this History readers have the advantage of knowing the inside story just as it transpired, while fans around the country then of course did not.

As a result of these events, the "Retreat" Wollheim had sounded in the December, 1938, *Science Fiction Fan* came to an end, and the Futurians planned to set up apartment headquarters in New York, replete with three mimeographs, and renew in earnest the activities they had in fact never completely terminated. By personal contact, too, their side of the story was spread far and wide. A questioned Futurian would speak to an individual fan at great length. Moreover, Michel, Wollheim and Wilson had toured the Northeast in May, 1939, just before the convention; they had made it a point to visit most leading fans of the area, had put their best foot forward to make new friends, had settled old enmities, and had become human beings instead of merely names on printed pages to many prominent fans in the field. The fact that the Futurians had been the only welcoming party to out-of-towners, and the only group to pal about with during and after the convention (Moskowitz, Taurasi and Sykora not being easily accessible even when not up to the ears in convention preparations) also contributed heavily.

The first report in some fashion justifying New Fandom's actions came in "Speer's Scribblings," a regular column devoted to commentary on fan political activity that appeared in Louis Kuslan's *Cosmic Tales*. The Summer, 1939, number, which appeared in August, 1939, contained his observation that there had been no suppression of sociological matter at the convention, Hodgkins' technocrat publication *We Have A Rendezvous* having been given the same distribution advantages as the other journals there. Of the "Warning" pamphlet distributed by Futurians he said: "It is filled to the ears with half truths, one-sided statements, and bald inaccuracies. If the dissenters had ammunition like that ready, what might they have planned to do if they were admitted to the hall?" He concluded: "More and more it came to me, as matters progressed, that this, counting out the undercover dissension, was in general the way a convention should be run. Such an event shouldn't be, isn't, in the case of other organizations, a deliberate assembly; there are many present not interested, or ill-informed, and people can usually think better from behind typewriters, anyway."

Despite everything, including systematic Futurian propaganda and suspicious silence by the convention committee, the entire matter might have quickly blown over, if only for lack of leadership in outlining a plan of action to be taken—but then leadership dramatically resolved itself. This leadership came from the Los Angeles SFL

chapter, which wielded the most fanwide influence of any in the
country. It had held over a hundred meetings, published a number of
fan magazines, and had sent three delegates across the country to
the convention and back. *The Voice of the Imagination,* a letter
'zine published by Morojo and Ackerman, usually carried chapter news
and announcements, and enjoyed a wide circulation; the first page of
its September, 1939, issue was emblazoned with the following:

OUR REACTION TO THE *"EXCLUSION ACT"*

From the full and adjured-unprejudiced report of three
delegates to the convention——reports orally discussed
during five consecutive meetings of the LASFL——and from
published accounts and correspondence with concerned parties; it is the considered opinion of the Los Angeles chapter of the Science Fiction League, as of September 7, 1939,
that the action on the part of William S. Sykora, Sam
Moskowitz and James V. Taurasi, sponsors of the "First
World Science Fiction Convention," in arbitrarily barring
from the proceedings advertised as "open to the public" six
persons—known to all fandom as science fiction fans—was
discriminatory and dictatorial, premeditated and openly
contrary to the mass-will of the conventioneers, in irrecon-
cilible conflict with the distinctly democratic ideals of
sincere science fiction. In brief, it is believed that a
matter of personal animosity—a local feud—was allowed to
run away with reason on the part of the promulgators of the
convention. Our attitude is one of severe censure of a
shameful occurrence, a reprehensible happening which we
feel we reflect all fair-minded fans in stating: *Must never
be repeated!* Our sentiments scarcely can be too strong in
plainly criticizing this egregious error, in outrightly
condemning this—outrage.

As the oldest and leading chapter of the league the LASFL
had felt it its responsibility to make public this, the
decision of its majority of members, as arrived at as
described foregoing, and as of the date recorded. Signed
Russell J. Hodgkins, Director; T. Bruce Yerke, Secretary.

This statement could not be ignored. It was a clarion call for
fans to rally against an alleged outrage. It meant that the New Fandom convention committee had either to fight the combined ranks of
the LASFL, the Futurians and in a sense the Midwest group which was
shortly to fall under the leadership of Tucker, also outspokenly
against it, or ignominiously be forced out of active fandom by the
strength of its opposition. If it elected to fight, it not only
would be forced to discard its theretofore successful "no-feuding"
policy, but would enter the conflict with its former ally, the
Philadelphia SFS, now a neutral observer. The committee could coun
on little help from New Fandom members at large, and would have t
seek fan magazines to publish their arguments intact or else prin
them itself alone. For three months no word was forthcoming from th
trio. If they did not speak out soon the entire edifice of Ne
Fandom must inevitably collapse. Those "in the know" felt it alread
too late, that the committee had indeed marked time too long. It
fate seemed inexorably sealed.

Chapter XLIII

BREASTING THE UNDERTOW

THE QUESTION is certainly apropos—why had the committee made no reply to the charges brought publicly against them for three months
after the convention? And what were its thoughts and impressions of
the gathering storm? The answers are as human as they are valid.

First of all, the committee members anticipated no reaction
approaching in vigor that which actually transpired. They were of
course prepared for all manner of indignant ravings from the Futurians, but expected these to be for the most part ignored on the basis
of the Futurians' past record. Wollheim, leader of the group, had
been perpetually involved in fan disagreements for several years
prior to the convention. He was more a notorious than a popular
figure at the time, and his exclusion from the New York gathering
was not expected to arouse any widespread sympathy. Futurian tactics
at the 1938 Newark convention (as detailed in Chapter XXVIII of this
History) varied from acts of bad taste to some of outright dishonesty,
and taken in concert were a deliberate attempt to interfere with its
functioning to a point where it might actually be disrupted. It was
not unreasonable to expect fandom to remember these actions.

It was expected that fandom would also remember the Futurian
blackball votes that barred Moskowitz and Osheroff from membership
in · the Greater New York SFL chapter for no reason that could
sufficiently be considered honest and impartial. There was also the
Futurian-sponsored impeachment of director Taurasi of that organization because of his refusal to recognize a motion to contribute to a
communist-front organization from the group's treasury. Could the
Futurian attempt to wreck the 1938 Philadelphia Conference by
scheduling another meeting at the identical time have passed this
soon from fan memories? Had fans also forgotten the political
maneuvering that transparently catapulted Olon F. Wiggins into the
APA directorship after Wiggins had closed his *Science Fiction Fan*
to all but pro-Futurian material and written letters to professional
editors asking them to withdraw support from the New York Convention?

All available evidence showed that the Futurians were unfavorably
disposed toward the affair. The *Science Fiction Fan* carried anti-
convention material up to the very date of the gathering; the Futurians attempted to prove that the film to be shown, "Metropolis," was
obtained from Nazi sources; they distributed anti-convention material
to attendees at the very doors of the hall; and with them they had
for later distribution a set of inflammatory and pro-communist
booklets.

Moreover, this list of inimical actions, long as it may appear,
represents (as readers of this History know) but a fraction of those
that might be cited in documented detail to convince any unbiased
individual that there was more than sufficient reason to bar from the
convention a group that refused even a promise not to cause trouble
here.

Secondly, the convention committee anticipated no later opposition

from Los Angeles and Chicago, for their representatives had departed
from the city with a manner that plainly indicated a belief that
excluding the Futurians was a regrettable small blemish on the
affair's success not to be pressed further. The strong action from
these sectors was shocking because it was so completely unexpected—
and, in the minds of the committee, hypocritical as well.

Thirdly, preparations for a gathering on the scale of the "Nycon"
(as it has come to be called) necessitated so much labor that it
left the chief workers in a state of mental and physical exhaustion
for a considerable time. Other fans who have put on major conventions
will attest to the fact that on their conclusion they felt not the
slightest inclination to tackle a major fannish task again. It will
be remembered, too, that the heat of the 1939 summer was enough to
accentuate this feeling considerably.

Finally, three of the major workers for New Fandom—Taurasi, Sykora
and Racic—had almost simultaneously at this time begun serious
courtships of fair young maidens, and were more in a mood for
butterflies and roses than for waging a sordid fan feud.

Moskowitz, who was fully aware of the situation, was unemployed,
and found it no mean matter to raise even a few cents for postage
stamps. He did, however, frantically attempt to arouse his co-workers
to some activity, arranging for them all to meet at his Newark home
to frame a plan of action. Sykora's view that it was advisable to
continue the "no feud" policy by not rebutting any of the accusations
and slanders prevailed. A second meeting, a short time later, found
Sykora more alarmed at the intensity of the opposition rallying
against New Fandom, but now convinced that the situation had been
permitted to progress too far, and in favor of slipping out of the
difficulty by whatever means seemed expedient—even to the point of
admitting that his own judgement at the convention had been at fault
But Moskowitz, whose every fan action had been tinged with a sort of
fanatical sincerity, was deeply hurt by the unjust attitude many had
taken toward them, and angrily determined to force all ill-considered
accusations down the throats of their makers. He persuaded Sykora
and Taurasi that the situation was not impossible, and voiced a plan
which he hoped would turn the tide. New Fandom had been run openly
and honestly in the manner of a benevolent dictatorship. The most
damaging charge brought against it, contended Moskowitz, was that i
could not truly represent fandom since members could not vote demo
cratically on its policies or its officers. Therefore he proposed
that a liberal democratic constitution be prepared for ratificatio
by the membership. In view of past achievements—and despite recen
developments—most of the present leaders would probably be retained
in any general election. It was then agreed that Sykora, who had ha
considerable experience in such matters, was the one best suited t
compose such a document.

Moskowitz visualized the framing of a constitution as but one
phase in an overall strategy calculated to restore New Fandom an
its leaders to a place of respect. The special convention issue of
New Fandom, now long delayed, was to be issued as soon as possibl
so that members at large could read details of the convention'
success and its implications. Raymond Van Houten worked in a print
ing shop, and claimed that he could get the magazine professionall
printed at a price within reach of the New Fandom treasury, and o

the strength of this an imposing line-up for the issue was prepared. (In 1939, appearance of a printed fan magazine was news of first importance, and announcements of it amounted in themselves to worthwhile progress.) Finally, the "no feuding" policy was to be discarded as harmful, and Moskowitz was given a free hand to stem and counteract unfavorable publicity wherever and whenever he could.

The facts of the matter were that there was still a great deal of material to work with, if the cards were played properly. Though weakened by the aftermath of the Nycon, New Fandom and its allied *Fantasy News* and Queens SFL chapter still formed formidable bases of power. These remaining assets must now be manipulated not only defensively to restore prestige and influence, but offensively to strike the opposition a crippling blow at the same time.

The Queens SFL had been affected least of all—in fact it was prospering better in late 1939 than it ever had before. The September meeting broke all chapter attendance records, and boasted such visiting celebrities as Charles Hornig, Malcolm Jameson, John D. Clark and Willy Ley. The October meeting enrolled artist Frank R. Paul and author Eando Binder as members. At this time, too, a show of hands revealed that nineteen Queens SFL members planned to travel to the Philadelphia Conference of science fiction fans scheduled for October 29th, at which the newly-written New Fandom constitution was to be read publicly.

Meanwhile attempts were being made to inject new vigor into *Fantasy News,* which had been steadily sinking in quality and influence. With its August 5 issue *Le Zombie* had become a biweekly subscription news-sheet, and was not only offering new, direct competition, but championing New Fandom opposition as well. After voicing its protests, support in the form of news submissions and subscriptions came immediately from the Futurians and (at the direct expense of *Fantasy News*) from the Los Angeles and Chicago groups. *Le Zombie* presented news informally, with considerable editorial slanting along the lines of Tucker's personal prejudices. Since Tucker had a marked penchant for sarcastic wit, his newscasting was highly amusing and found considerable fan favor. A preferred target for many of these barbed rejoinders was *Fantasy News* itself, and Taurasi was badly outclassed when it came to a clever reply. The competition was easily the most damaging *Fantasy News* had ever received, the ironic part being that *Le Zombie* was guilty of every fault (discounting grammar) it found in *Fantasy News*. Thus constantly harrassed, with some of his best news sources gone, Taurasi needed yeoman work indeed from his remaining reporters if he hoped to stay in the running. From September onwards he did receive this, but though scoops came in thick and fast his paper no longer presented as comprehensive coverage of the fan world as it had previously.

As nearly all outside journals were either avowedly of the opposition or following the disastrous "no feuding" policy, solid, detailed rebuttals to attacks on New Fandom simply could not be placed in them. If such replies were altered to become "non-controversial," they were of course gleefully pounced upon and ripped to shreds. In addition, the opposition had many mimeographs and many hands to turn the cranks, making possible the publication of all manner of small leaflets; New Fandom had small facilities and too few workers to produce any comparable barrage.

In an effort to find a general outlet for his counter-attack, Moskowitz turned to *The Science Fiction Collector*. John Baltadonis had kept the *Collector* appearing monthly since its revival in March, 1939, and had received considerable aid from Moskowitz for his third anniversary number. Surely Baltadonis would not exclude controversial material from an old friend! So Moskowitz threw himself into preparation of an article which he hoped would be strong enough to reverse the trend of prevailing opinion. Realizing that many new fans did not read the magazine, he calculatingly dispatched a letter to *Le Zombie* announcing his heartrending loss of faith in fandom, and revealing that his side of the story would soon appear in the *Collector*. Moskowitz hoped also that his vague phrasing would draw fire from his opponents, misdirect their attention, and make his forthcoming remarks all the more effective.

Both hopes were realized. Tucker printed the letter in *Le Zombie,* and Baltadonis recieved over two dozen new subscriptions for the *Collector* as a result. At the same time Russell Hodgkins, director of the Los Angeles SFL, rose to the bait, and in a letter which appeared in the next *Le Zombie* tore into Moskowitz's statements. Everything was progressing according to plan, and the plan named the Philadelphia Conference as the climactic site. Here the opposing forces would group for the showdown. The Futurians had announced that they would be on hand—*en masse*. A Chicago delegation was to include Tucker and Walter Marconette. Jack Speer was driving in from Washington, D.C. The Queens SFL was to be well represented. Baltadonis promised Moskowitz that the issue of the *Collector* containing his article would be ready for distribution by that time. And behind the scenes, at the same time that New Fandom was whipping its proposed constitution into final shape, Milton Rothman and David Kyle were readying proposals for a new national fan organization to replace it. The fuse steadily burned its way towards the powder keg.

Chapter XLIV

THE SECOND PHILADELPHIA CONFERENCE

THE CONFERENCE was to have been held in the large back room of the tavern owned by Baltadonis' father, where the first such conference had been so successfully and convivially held the previous October. However, it had since been learned that a local ordinance forbade holding a public meeting in the premises on Sundays. Baltadonis, Madle and Agnew had nevertheless managed to secure a hall in downtown Philadelphia by dint of hasty footwork at the last minute. To help pay for the unexpected added cost a donation of ten cents was accepted from each attendee, and to aid the cause of refreshments the Queens SFL gave ten dollars from its treasury. Despite the last-minute site-change the conference was called to order by chairman Baltadonis precisely at 3:00 p.m. as scheduled.

First on the agenda was a discussion and vote as to whether the Fantasy Amateur Press Association election just past should be repudiated or permitted to stand. What had happened was as follows: Rothman, who had been elected editor and mailing manager, had appointed Robert Madle to assume his duties for the duration of his term because of the pressure of personal affairs. It developed that Rothman had constitutional right to do no more than resign, and that it was the duty of the FAPA president to appoint a successor. This the president had not done. The secretary-treasurer, Taurasi, was supposed to obtain an official list of active members from the editor before elections, and send ballots to them only. Taurasi wrote to Madle for this list, but received no reply; whereupon he mailed ballots to all members he knew of—which of course included some who previously had been dropped from the organization rolls, and who were therefore not eligible to vote. Should this election, which was technically illegal, be accepted? As nearly two dozen attendees at the conference were FAPA members, a discussion of the situation was held and a vote taken. The majority favored letting the election results stand as the simplest solution.

(Subsequent events rendered this vote useless, however. Wollheim in the meantime had submitted the entire matter to Walter Marconette, who as FAPA vice-president was empowered to rule on all such questions. Marconette ruled that Rothman's appointment of Madle was invalid, and that since Rothman had not submitted any resignation he was officially editor up to election time. Marconette also ruled the election illegal, and ordered another. As a result of the second election Rothman succeeded Wiggins as president, Speer became vice-president, Madle the secretary-treasurer, and Marconette official editor. But this did not end FAPA's troubles. Immediately thereafter Marconette resigned, claiming that his name had been placed on the ballot without his knowledge, and president Rothman appointed Jack Agnew to fill his place. Taurasi, meanwhile, doubting the legitimacy of the second election, balked at turning over FAPA records and monies; and it became necessary for Rothman to travel from Philadelphia to New York and personally persuade Taurasi to do so. Thus passed into history the FAPA's gravest crisis, which for a time actually threatened to destroy the organization.)

The Philadelphia Conference now turned to the question of a national fan organization. The first speaker on the subject was Rothman. He felt that New Fandom was dictatorial in management, and that a brand new organization with a democratic framework should be contemplated. "It's too much work to build up an entirely new organization, so we'll simply take over the New Fandom membership, treasury and other resources and mold it to suit the fans," he said, adding hastily, "With the consent of New Fandom's dictators, of course." Speer, the second speaker, felt like Rothman that New Fandom with a change of name and a new constitution would make an excellent fan organization. He had come prepared with a suggested sample, and passed around copies of his constitution for consideration. David Kyle then spoke, suggesting a sort of federation or congress of local groups each of which would have a single vote in the federation. Speer took immediate exception to this plan, pointing out that it was unfair for clubs having unequal memberships to have the same vote, that nothing had been said about overlapping memberships, which would mean that nothing could stop a given clique from forming numberless "front" groups, each of which would be able to vote.

Moskowitz was the next speaker. Tense silence prevailed as he stepped forward, for everyone realized he probably had strong views on the statements of his predecessors. His speech was comparatively brief, and began by outlining the history of New Fandom in the past year. He defended its semi-dictatorial set-up on the grounds that circumstances freely and publicly discussed had made a benevolent dictatorship initially necessary, and that the First Philadelphia Conference had voted unanimous support of the organization after hearing this. Moskowitz reminded the assembly that at the Nycon banquet he had announced that New Fandom was planning a constitution based on democratic principles for approval of its membership, and that in the ensuing three months such a document had actually been prepared. It embodied the ideas of several, including Van Houten, Speer and Sykora, and had been cast into its final form by the latter. A copy, together with a large diagram that outlined its major tenets simply, had been brought along to the conference, and New Fandom officials were ready to present and explain it to the assemblage.

This move apparently took the opposition—as represented by Rothman and the Futurians—completely by surprise. And in what appeared to be a time-consuming delaying action they began a marathon debate over taking New Fandom's assets as the groundwork for another major fan organization. This was well on the way to become a filibuster when Lloyd Eshbach, exasperated by the proceedings, made a strong plea for sanity and a sensible settlement of problems. Moskowitz took advantage of the lull following this plea to ask the chair that Sykora be permitted to read New Fandom's constitution aloud. Baltadonis granted permission, but it was some time before this could be done for Futurians Kyle, Wollheim, Kornbluth and Pohl alternately challenged and debated with the chair on points of procedure for half an hour.

Finally Sykora was permitted to erect a large chart diagramming the document, to which he referred constantly. A copy of the consti tution is unfortunately no longer available to this historian, so the details which follow are necessarily drawn from memory. Briefly, membership in New Fandom was divided into an outer circle and an inner circle of fans; only those in the outer circle could join the inner, and only those in the inner circle could vote or hold office. Admission to both divisions was to be directed by a committee created for that specific purpose. The reason for the two groups was to allow the more active fans, the publishers of magazines and sponsors of public events, to do the work of organization and guide its policies, while providing a definite place also for the newcomers and the general readers whose interest did not go beyond joining the organization for milder participation in its activities. Members of course could gravitate from one circle to another as time strengthened or weakened their interest in fandom.

With prize-fighters there are nights when they reach their peak, when they will never reach greater heights; with artists there comes the day when they have completed their finest painting; with authors, the completion of their masterpiece. October 29, 1939, was William Sykora's day. Rarely has a man done such justice to a document. Despite the unceasing chatter of heckling Futurians he sold his product to the audience. On completion of the reading majority acceptance seemed almost a foregone conclusion. Now there were questions and discussion with Sykora replying in careful detail to all questions asked.

Futurian Leslie Perri called the document "magnificent," but queried as to whether there might be present some concealed legal device for barring her group. The Futurians themselves were impressed by the constitution, but appeared suspicious of its length and what they construed as evasiveness in some of Sykora's remarks. Their heckling had by this time grown to extreme intensity, and Sykora had borne all of it with incredible patience, wisely realizing his doing so would strengthen New Fandom's cause and render Futurian conduct the more unsportsmanlike. Probably this forbearance alone prevented an explosion in the charged atmosphere pervading the conference.

But fate was not to be denied. During the course of one of Sykora's explanations Wollheim shouted, "That's a lie!" Had this exclamation been made by any other Futurian it might not have touched off the explosion—but coming from Wollheim, who had inflicted many a fannish hurt upon Sykora in the past, it was the straw that broke the camel's back. Sykora's face reddened, his fists clenched. "Nobody can call me a liar and get away with it," he said audibly, and determinably advanced to the front row where his opponent sat a scant ten feet away. As Wollheim pressed against the back of his chair tiny Jack Gillespie, who weighed scarcely a hundred pounds, sprang in front of him to intervene. Sykora brushed him aside with one hand and confronted his opponent. As the whole Futurian contingent were sitting together, there were eleven men for Sykora to deal with, not merely Wollheim alone. Shocked into realization of Sykora's danger by Gillespie's action, Moskowitz headed down one aisle toward the group and Taurasi hastened down the other. Speaking for most of the Philadelphians, Madle shouted to Moskowitz, "we're here if you need any help!"

It was the diplomacy of chairman John V. Baltadonis that deserves the laurels for avoiding a clash. He dissuaded Sykora from any further action, convinced Moskowitz and Taurasi that Sykora was safe enough so they could resume their seats, and quieted members of his own Philadelphia group that were itching for a fracas.

Wollheim then arose and asked that Sykora, Taurasi and Moskowitz be made to apologize to the assembly for their actions or leave the hall. Moskowitz arose and with great assumption of indignation asked that the Futurians be forced to apologize for their heckling or leave the hall. The alternatives, both groups intimated, being that they themselves would walk out if their demands were not met. Again, chairman Baltadonis with commendable diplomacy persuaded both factions to waive their motions and stay.

Moskowitz then phrased a motion to the effect that the Philadelphia Conference go on record as approving New Fandom's constitution. The motion was seconded and a vote called for, but the Futurians seized upon the wording of the motion and delayed the vote for forty-five minutes while Taurasi rephrased the motion more concisely. The motion was passed 21 to 12 and the New Fandom group had scored one of the most amazing come backs in fan annals.

New Fandom had earned the right to live, but it had to renew the confidence of the science fiction fans in its organization if it expected to get the new memberships necessary to insure its existence, and this could not be done unless it could clear itself or at least minimize the accusation of "Exclusion Act" when it had acted to prevent six Futurian members from entering the hall the first day of the Nycon.

John V. Baltadonis had promised Moskowitz that his article of explanation and rebuttal titled "There *Are* Two Sides" would appear in time to be distributed at the Conference. This promise he kept, but in his rush to do so his usually superb hektographing was light and indistinct. The issue of the *Science Fiction Collector* containing that article was dated July-August, 1939. The article opened by completely reprinting the Los Angeles Science Fiction League's statement regarding its disapproval and condemnation of the "exclusion act" and then rebutting with the following arguments: it called the LASFL members liars because they claimed to have heard all sides of the story, and yet had never even written any member of the New Fandom group asking his view of the question, forming their complete judgement without attempting to do so. Secondly it pointed to the statement maintaining that Ackerman and Morojo's testimony was "unprejudiced" and then showed published articles by Ackerman and Morojo which stated sympathy for the Michelism sponsored by the Futurians. It accused fandom of permitting an admittedly communist front movement, the Michelists, to insist that their opponents hew to their notion of "democracy," while the Michelists barred no holds in their own tactics. Moskowitz stated: "...And because they have raised a din of "undemocratic," you, who are so afraid for democracy, follow their falsely accusing voices and like a puppet on a string, accomplish what they are not strong enough to do themselves." He further demanded to know why no fans had uttered a word of disapproval when the Michelist group had barred himself and Alex Osheroff from membership in the Greater New York SFL, without any stated grounds whatsoever; he asked where was the chorus of protest when Olon F. Wiggins had banned him from the pages of *The Science Fiction Fan?* He then termed the LASFL "Democratically minded hypocrites" for their failure to act on those points. In conclusion, Moskowitz maintained that the Futurians had planned to be barred from the convention; that they deliberately frustrated every attempt made by him to get them into the hall. He claimed that they hoped to regain the position of power they had lost through being previously discredited by making an issue of being kept out of the hall, and in his view the fans had been taken in by this ruse. To strengthen his hypothesis he gave a point by point breakdown of what transpired that fateful Sunday afternoon in July, when the First World Science Fiction Convention was almost shattered by Futurian action.

The wording of his article was so fiery and acridly bitter, that few denied its honesty and sincerity.

At the close of the Philadelphia Conference Moskowitz began to make the rounds of out-of-town fans and ask them if they had read his article in the *Collector* and if their opinion of the "exclusion act" had been altered by it. Appearing as it did at a time when the Futurian group had put on a reprehensible heckling and delaying campaign, which was still fresh in the minds of the attendees, virtually all who had read the article at the time of the query stated that their opinion had altered toward New Fandom's side of the story.

The overnight change of fortune in the New Fandom group's lot, was expressed by the write-up on the conference in the November 5, 1939, issue of *Fantasy News*. This one-sided write-up written by Moskowitz was highly editorialized and pulled no punches. To make it worse, Taurasi, editor of *Fantasy News*, wherever he felt that Moskowitz had been too impartial or not sufficiently vehement, "edited" and wrote into the story such expletives, exaggerations and insults as would, in his opinion, improve the forcefulness of its tone. This added insult (literally) to injury. The Los Angeles group was thunderstruck when they read the news. They found particularly hard to believe Moskowitz's statement regarding the "exclusion act" that: "all fans contacted completely absolved New Fandom of any blame in the matter." They dispatched air-mail letters to various fans they knew had attended the convention and asked them if this was true. Bob Tucker, Erle Korshak and Mark Reinsberg replied that Moskowitz had not contacted them and that they had made no statement to him. Immediately the LASFL took this information, mimeographed it in green ink and mailed it far and wide in fandom. When Moskowitz saw this it was his turn to be thunderstruck, because he clearly remembered his talks with the individuals in question. He quickly wrote them. Tucker grudgingly admitted that Moskowitz *had* contacted him after all and that he had not yet read Moskowitz's article so was unable to give an opinion at the time. He maintained that while wrong in fact he was right in principle, since Moskowitz had alleged that "*all* fans contacted completely absolved New Fandom of any blame in the matter." However, Moskowitz obtained from Reinsberg and Korshak signed statements saying that they had forgotten the incident but they had been contacted and had given Moskowitz statements which could have been construed as absolving New Fandom of blame in the "exclusion act." Moskowitz's letter containing this information was publicly printed in the January-February, 1940, issue of *The Fantascience Digest*.

Chapter XLV

THE ILLINI FANTASY FICTIONEERS

IN THE FEVER of excitement resulting from the attempt of New Fandom to obtain approval for their new constitution and the dramatic interlude between Wollheim and Sykora, the Chicago delegation's bid for the next world convention had come perilously close to never reaching the floor of the conference. Important as it was in the long view, it did not receive the attention either at the conference or afterward to which, as a move which established the continuity of world science fiction conventions as an annual event, it was rightly entitled.

The Chicago delegation had suffered through much to give the appearance of unity and competence. At the First World Science Fiction Convention, it was already common knowledge that there was a split on the matter of how the second World Convention should be bid upon and held. There were two factions. One was headed by Mark Reinsberg, a very serious-minded young man of sixteen years. An intelligent boy his activities were marked by great intensity and single-mindedness. The preparation of a convention was of world-shaking importance to him and he seemed almost incapable of even tolerating a humorous aside that in any fashion detracted from the master-work. While always willing to talk compromise, he never did in actual practice more than minutely deviate from his preconceived ideas. His two best friends and invaluable aids were Erle Korshak and Richard I. Meyer. The latter was a pleasant youth who aided the convention on the local scene and acted as associate editor of *Ad Astra* but was rarely heard of otherwise. The former became a well-known figure in the science fiction fan world. Though only fifteen at the time, Erle Korshak already had formulated certain personality traits that are recognizable to this day. In word and action he always played the role of the super salesman, and to do his methods justice the word *super* should really be underlined. From his earliest days of activity he organized and carried on a little side business of buying and selling science fiction magazines and books. For a long period he maintained this business under the aegis of one *Melvin* Korshak, who he said was his brother, but the years eventually washed out the truth of the matter, the Melvin was but Erle's middle name. In activities and business Korshak's attempts to sell himself and his product was on the surface driving, ingenious and ostensibly mercenary. But Korshak had a weakness as a salesman. Despite the fact that some of his methods were legendary, it was possible to turn the tables abruptly on him by utilizing an appropriate sob story. The veneer would swiftly melt and Erle Korshak would stand revealed in the generosity and kindness that was his basic nature.

William Lawrence Hamling, himself little more than eighteen, was the leader of the opposition to Reinsberg's group, and his actions gave the appearance of great temperament, often giving away to wild, unreasonable actions when aroused. He was accused by his detractors of entertaining a superiority complex, but he proved by achievement that he was an individual of above-average capability as we can see when we later appraise *Stardust,* the semi-pro fantasy magazine which he edited and published. He had precedent for this, having served as editor-in-chief of *The Lane Tech Prep,* the largest slick prep publication in the world, boasting a circulation of 10,000. In many respects he was extremely cooperative, more, so, in point of fact than his opposition.

Before the idea of bidding for Chicago as a science fiction convention site had been conceived, the leaders of the two factions, Mark Reinsberg and W. Lawrence Hamling, had been on excellent terms, even collaborating upon a science fiction story "War with Jupiter" which appeared in the May, 1939, issue of *Amazing Stories.* If Reinsberg had been able to get an endorsement from the First World Science Fiction Convention, it would have given him the upper hand in the situation, but failing in this he found himself in double trouble. W. Lawrence Hamling had hastily re-formed the Chicago chapter of the SFL, with himself elected as director, Jack Darrow (next to Forrest J. Ackerman the most famous letter-writer to the science fiction magazines), as assistant director and Neil de Jack as secretary. In addition, such well known Chicagoans as Henry Bott, Howard Funk and Chester S. Geir were also members. Not only did Hamling have the only organization in the city, but if it came to a count of heads he had more names on his side than did Reinsberg. This being the case Hamling made the point that perhaps he was better qualified to present a World Convention in Chicago than Reinsberg. To lend credence to this claim, Hamling sent out printed postcards October 2, 1939, announcing a printed, semi-professional fan magazine to be titled *Stardust,* which magazine was to be large—eight by eleven inch—size and contain line and half-tone illustrations. Announcing a printed fan magazine in those times was comparable to *Colliers* announcing today that starting with the next issue it would continue as an all-science fiction publication. The prestige of the editor of a well-printed fan journal could not help but be considerable.

Up to this time, the group headed by Reinsberg had not been too worried about Hamling's activities, for they had previously pulled off a coup of their own. On August 30 and 31, Reinsberg and Korshak journied to Bloomington, Illinois, for a meeting at Bob Tucker's home. Also present were fans Sully Roberds, Fleming and Lakewizc. According to *Le Zombie,* September 16, 1939, which carried the story, William Lawrence Hamling had been invited but had not been able to make it. There is some question in this historian's mind as to whether or not too much pressure was exerted on Hamling, for the proceedings could scarcely have gone as smoothly had he been present. An organization called the Illini Fantasy Fictioneers was formed to sponsor the convention. There was no great intent of continuing the organization beyond the date of the planned convention. It was decided to mimeograph a club organ to be titled the *Fantasy Fictioneer.* Officers of the organization were to be Richard Meyer as corresponding secretary and treasurer, Sully Roberds as publicity director, Erle Korshak as executive advisor, Mark Reinsberg as convention committee chairman, but the crowning scoop was electing Bob Tucker as director of the Illini Fantasy Fictioneers. Tucker was at the time one of the best known and best liked fans in the country. He was more mature than the Chicago fans and could receive more confidence from editors, authors and fans. He was an excellent "front" and advisor for the youngsters, and he published the popular bi-weekly fan magazine of news and chit-chat, *Le Zombie*.

Now, however, since Hamling had gotten big-name fan-letter-writer Jack Darrow on his team, organized a club which composed a majority of Chicago fans and contemplated an elaborately printed semi-professional publication, he represented no inconsiderable barrier to the plans of the Illini Fantasy Fictioneers which had allocated no place in the governing committee for Hamling, though they did find themselves able to give an important post to Richard I. Meyer who did not even attend the organizational meeting. If Hamling made enough noise, the Illini Fantasy Fictioneers could never get a vote of approval at the Philadelphia Conference for their plans to hold the Second World Science Fiction Convention in Chicago.

Hamling wasted little time in expressing his violent disapproval of the Bloomington meeting at which the Illini Fantasy Fictioneers was formed. In a letter to Bob Tucker which was dated September 6, 1939, and was later published in part in the November, 1943, issue of *Le Zombie,* he stated: "Just a line to let you know that I found out about the election in Bloomington last week, from Meyer. I don't mind telling you that any election for Secretary-Treasurer, or for Chairman of the Convention Committee are null and void as far as I am concerned....

"...I know that I can count on you Bob to see that justice is done...." His letter to Tucker and a similar one to Wollheim descended in the intensity of anger to slurs on the background of his opponents which he must have been ashamed of as he looked back on them from a maturer aspect.

Something had to be done to placate Hamling and give the fan world the impression that all was harmonious in Chicago. Mark Reinsberg showed up at the October 8, 1939, meeting of the Chicago SFL. At this meeting he assured the assembly of the honest intentions of himself and the Illini Fantasy Fictioneers. As a compromise measure he promised he would appoint a City Committee of the convention, giving posts to other important Chicago fans including members of the Chicago SFL; and that the Chicago SFL would be eligible to work on an equal, cooperative basis with the Illini Fantasy Fictioneers on the presentation of the convention.

In exchange the Chicago SFL agreed to support the Illini Fantasy Fictioneers on the convention project and approved the officers already appointed for that organization. Some details of the meeting remained cloaked in secrecy but a dispatch was released in time to be published in the October 15, 1939, issue of *Fantasy News* announcing: "CHICAGO FEUD ENDS!" This was timed to appear before the Philadelphia Conference, paving the way for approval of the convention bid by the Chicago group.

In order to reach the Philadelphia Conference the Chicago group made a great trek. Reinsberg, Korshak and Meyer hitch-hiked to Bloomington, Illinois, where Bob Tucker had an auto to ride them all on a share-the-expense basis, Tucker's wife accompanying the group. At Dayton, Ohio, the young giant fan, Walter E. Marconette, publisher of the meticulous fan magazine *Sctentt-Snaps* joined the group and the auto journey was considered a newsworthy trip of that period.

In order to favorably impress the audience the group produced for the Philadelphia Conference the first, November-December, 1939, issue of *The Fantasy Fictioneer,* which contained the club constitution, a progress report from Mark Reinsberg which among other things announced the tentative date for the Chicago Convention as the Labor-day weekend, September 1, 1940, and also that Edward E. Smith might be the guest of honor. There were messages and reports from Tucker, Korshak and Roberds and a bit of humor by Hoy Ping Pong. Reinsberg and Meyer had produced the fourth issue of *Ad Astra* with outstanding material by Edward E. Smith, Ph. D., John W. Campbell, Jr., J. Harvey Haggard, Donald A. Wollheim and Forrest Ackerman and artwork by Julian Krupa, but its format and production were as carelessly sloppy as was that of all other issues of the magazine. Bob Tucker had a special souvenir Philadelphia Conference issue of *Le Zombie,* which magazine was now openly bucking *Fantasy News* for sovereignty in the field of newsgathering and dispensing.

Mark Reinsberg, head of the Chicago delegation, was originally scheduled to speak after Sam Moskowitz on the Philadelphia Conference program. He had asked, however, that the assembly permit Bob Tucker to substitute for him since Tucker was more familiar with the inner workings of the Illini Fantasy Fictioneers than he was. David A. Kyle wanted the entire matter postponed until later in the program, since it was out of context with the debate on fan organizations then ensuing, but by putting the matter to a vote of the assembly it was decided to permit Tucker to speak at that point. Bob Tucker had a vitally important statement to make. He said, in effect, that the Illini Fantasy Fictioneers had no intention of incorporating with any national fan organization decided upon at this convention or elsewhere and that it intended to present the Chicago Convention under its own auspices. Further, since it desired to remain neutral in the fan battles raging at present, it had no immediate intention of aligning itself in any fashion, cooperative or otherwise, with New Fandom or the Futurians, the two warring clubs.

Mark Reinsberg added to Tucker's talk by giving a brief breakdown of the constitutional set-up of the Illini Fantasy Fictioneers. Yet, strangely, none of the Illinois delegation suggested a vote be taken approving their sponsorship of the Chicago affair. They seemed to accept the good-will prevalent about them as an indication of approval. The meeting wore on, New Fandom's constitution was approved, and the Chicago delegation seemed to have been hypnotized by the proceedings. The conference was drawing to a close and they had overlooked the very thing they had come to Philadelphia to pro-cure, a vote of approval from fandom as represented by this confer-ence on their sponsorship of the Chicago Convention. Moskowitz went over to Reinsberg and spoke urgently to him on the necessity of presenting such a motion. He had a political motive for this, since now that the New Fandom constitution had been accepted, he could follow Reinsberg's motion with a magnanimous offer of aid, which the Chicago group might find embarrassing to refuse, and which would show that New Fandom intended to exert its utmost to help every worthwhile fan project and was therefore deserving of its vote of confidence.

The closing gavel was virtually ready to fall when Reinsberg, with acoustical aid from Moskowitz, managed to get the attention of director John V. Baltadonis.

Mark Reinsberg then moved that this conference give a vote of recognition to the Illini Fantasy Fictioneers as the only committee authorized to present the Second World Science Fiction Convention in Chicago. He gave as reasons priority and accomplished work. This motion was passed by a large majority. Again it must be emphatically pointed out that this was the only official authorization ever obtained by the Illini Fantasy Fictioneers for the presentation of their affair, and that no vote at all was taken on it at the Nycon. Now Moskowitz arose and said he was personally behind the affair and would urge full support by New Fandom.

When the Chicago delegation left Philadelphia, they left as powers in science fiction fandom. They had superficially unified all of midwest fandom behind the idea of the Second World Science Fiction Convention, the Illini Fantasy Fictioneers to sponsor that event and produced one issue of an official organ for that organization titled *The Fantasy Fictioneer*. In addition they had received a vote of approval as authorized sponsors of the convention from as representative a group of fans as could be assembled at that time. Significantly, Moskowitz's announcement of personal support of the affair, inferring as it did official support by New Fandom was not even acknowledged. The Chicago boys felt they no longer needed either Moskowitz's or New Fandom's help to put across their project. They were perfectly capable of carrying through the event themselves, and they understandably felt the fewer in the act the better.

Chapter XLVI

THE FUTURIAN COMEBACK

TO THE FUTURIAN Society of New York, the events that terminated in six of their members not being permitted to attend any of the sessions of the First World Science Fiction Convention was a political wind-fall of great consequence. If, as Sam Moskowitz had attempted to reason, through a chain of inductive logic in his bitter article "There *Are* Two Sides," the situation had been planned that way by the Futurian Society mentors, the strategy could be termed no less than brilliant. If, as the Futurians stoutly maintained, it was caused by a chain of coincidences, nothing more providential had ever befallen them. Previous to the convention, New Fandom and its leaders had succeeded in thoroughly discrediting most of the Futurian Society's leadership, and with the aid of the Futurian leaders' own published statements attached the red label to the Futurian Society, the political implications of Michelism and the leading Futurian figures' own personal political beliefs. The Futurian influence had dwindled to their local New York meetings and the pages of Olon F. Wiggins' *Science Fiction Fan.* Even in the Fantasy Amateur Press Association they were no longer all-powerful. Their only major source of dispensing news, *The Science Fiction News-Letter,* had been driven out of the race and at one point they had dipped to a low-point of despondency where Donald A. Wollheim wrote what at the time appeared to be his swan-song in fandom, "Retreat," which appeared in the December, 1938, issue of *The Science Fiction Fan.*

Even before the convention was many hours old the Futurians had grasped the value of playing the "exclusion" angle for all it was worth. Outside the hall they halted and spoke with prominent science fiction delegates from many points of the country. They influenced Jack Williamson from New Mexico to temporarily take the stand that if his "friends" were not admitted he would not stay either. Women attendees such as Frances N. Swisher, wife of R. D. Swisher, Ph. D., and Myrtle R. Douglas, better known at the time as Morojo, were particularly active in the Futurians' behalf, urging almost unceasingly that the barriers be dropped and that the Futurians be permitted to enter the hall without pledging good behavior. Dale Hart from Texas, a well-known and active fan of the period, made considerable effort for the Futurians. There was no denying then that the Futurian group had gained tremendous sympathy from that part of the science fiction world that they had been able to contact. Knowledge of this catapulted them into action. Before the sessions of the convention were over the Futurians were distributing to delegates entering or leaving the hall a hastily mimeographed circular which announced an open meeting of the Futurian Society of New York to be held Tuesday, July 4, 1939, 2:00 p.m. at 224 Flatbush Avenue, Brooklyn, New York. On the agenda were placed the following topics: 1) The future of science fiction organizations. 2) The Fantasy Amateur Press Association crisis. 3) Conventions in coming years. 4) Estimates of the convention just past. An open forum was promised on all questions.

The last-minute preparation of the affair, and the inability of the Futurian Society to offer more of a program than one of general discussion necessarily limited the attendance. Seventeen were present at this meeting. Ten of them—Wollheim, Michel, Lowndes, Pohl, Kornbluth, Gillespie, Wilson, Kyle and Isaac Asimov—were members of the Futurian Society, one other was Asimov's sister. Significantly, while only six non-Futurians attended this gathering, most of them were people of considerable influence in the science fiction fan world. They included Forrest J. Ackerman and Myrtle R. Douglas of California, Milton A. Rothman of Philadelphia, Mark Reinsberg of Chicago, and Kenneth Sterling, a New York area fan who was noted for several short stories he had sold to Charles D. Hornig's *Wonder Stories*. While the Futurian "Conference," as it was later referred to by its sponsors, was a dismal failure from the viewpoint of attendance and presentation of a particularly interesting program, it was a considerable political success inasmuch as *all* of the important science fiction figures named above swung toward the Futurian viewpoint to the extent that in action, in print or in speech they turned emphatically against New Fandom.

Cyril Kornbluth was the chairman of this special Futurian meeting. As a youth, Kornbluth was blocky and rotund in appearance, possessing a voice of stentorian depth. He was described by his Futurian friends as "faustian, ribald, puckish." He was a master of the cynical and bitter retort and maintained a facial expression that led one to believe that he was repressing a sneer by the excercise of prodigious restraint. Beyond the immediate New York circle he was seldom active, and therefore, nationally, but little known. His fiction and verse had appeared in Louis Kuslan's *Cosmic Tales* and Robert W. Lowndes' *Le Vombiteur*. Small though his published output was, it did, even then, show some talent. He entered fandom through the Washington Heights SFL chapter run by Chester Fein (see Chapter XXVI) and first made the acquaintance of the Futurians when Richard Wilson and Jack Gillespie visited the Washington Heights SFL in January, 1938. He gradually became an accepted and important member of the Futurian Spciety's inner-circle, but his value to that group was shown to better effect in his literary production as will eventually be shown.

Chairman Kornbluth and Futurians Wollheim, Lowndes, Michel and Pohl were titled as an Answering Committee to clarify all questions relative to science fiction fandom put to them by the visitors. Under press of the visitors, the Futurians agreed to seriously consider a change in the name of their fan political dogma known as Michelism, inasmuch as it was felt that the name had only had an egotistical connotation, being named after its originator John B. Michel, but was hopelessly stuck with the communist label pinned on it by its opponents. John B. Michel headed the committee to investigate a possible change in name.

It was decided that David A. Kyle would continue to head the Association for Democracy in Science Fiction Fandom, under whose aegis had been distributed the yellow leaflet *A Warning* at.the First World Science Fiction Convention.

Mark Reinsberg announced the intention of his group of holding a world convention the following year in Chicago, Illinois, and the Futurian Society of New York pledged its support at that time.

Neither Reinsberg nor the Illini Fantasy Fictioneers afterward acknowledged publicly that support.

The Futurians considered their "conference" a triumph for democracy and free discussion as compared to the First World Science Fiction Convention, but as previously pointed out, were it not for its obvious influence on the future fan attitudes of important out-of-town delegates, it would rate scarcely a footnote under the pitiless scrutiny of historical perspective.

In their attempts to pose as true Marxists, bohemians, apostles of the decadent in art and literature and the pursuit of journalistic or artistic careers, the members of the Futurian Society, a minority of them of voting age and most of them living with their parents, had chaffed under the restraints placed upon them by these ties. They yearned for independence of a sort, an independence which would make it possible for them to pursue their goals and desires to the limits of their capabilities without being hamstrung by kin. Even their holy crusade against New Fandom and its acolytes often suffered because home limitations curtailed their ingenuity, therefore they set forth in search of a dwelling which would house as a single community all Futurian members who wished to live there on a share-the-expense basis.

Originally, Fred Pohl, Leslie Perri (Doris Baumgardt, then affianced to Fred Pohl), Donald A. Wollheim, Harry Dockweiler (who subsequently became better known under the pseudonym of Dirk Wylie), John B. Michel and Richard Wilson were to have permitted their genius to be nurtured jointly in an eight room house in Kensington, Brooklyn, but at the last moment Fred Pohl and Leslie Perri found it expedient to withdraw. However, Pohl being over twenty-one magnanimously agreed to sign the lease which would permit the others to move in, which move they accomplished sometime in August, 1939. They were not to be doomed to lonesomeness or boredom, for George R. Hahn, up-state New York fan, whose major claim to fame was the publication of a story in *Weird Tales* Magazine, "The Fifth Candle," under the pen-name of Cyril Mand, descended upon the newly christened Futurian House and took up residence there, borrowing enough money from its inhabitants and visitors to live on, writing fiction until 4:30 in the morning at which time Harry Dockweiler got up to go to work, and Hahn would appropriate his bed and catch up on his sleep. Some of George Hahn's professional prestige slipped when a fellow visitor from Buffalo, New York, Richard Levin dropped in and took up non-contributing residence at the Futurian House. It developed that Levin had done at least half the work on the lone Cyril Mand story which had been professionally sold, but Hahn had neglected to inform anyone of this fact. Other visitors who were present so frequently as to practically be inhabitants were Cyril Kornbluth and David A. Kyle, with an occasional look-in from Julius Unger, a fan who disappeared from sight after being active with the Scienceers in 1930 (see Chapter III), had since married and was once again evincing an interest in the field. According to Richard Wilson, who once wrote an account of the Futurian residence in Futurian House, they were, on at least two occasions, engaged in scuffles with the local constabulary. Two police officers dropped in on one occasion and questioned Wilson, Kornbluth and Hahn about the place, having received strong complaints from the neighbors about classical record-

ings played at peak volume during ungodly hours of the night and of
"fencing exhibitions on the side walk." On another occasion George
Hahn and Richard Levin were allegedly awakened from their sleep at
two o'clock in the afternoon to be accosted by three men with
revolvers. These men explained they were treasury agents and that
the neighbors had reported that there was little furniture in the
apartment but a plethora of printing presses and mimeograph machines
and that the group was suspected of being counterfeiters. A thorough
search of the premises from cellar to roof ensued, the agents not
leaving until they were convinced that no illegal activities were
being carried on by this bizarre menagerie of bohemianized science
fiction fans.

Eventually, it developed that the owner of the house had been
unable to keep up payments and that the property was being foreclosed
upon. The Futurians were given notice to move by the new owners and
it now became imperative that the four primary contributors to the
cause find new housing. This had to be accomplished by September 15,
1939.

Harry Dockweiler, John B. Michel, Donald A. Wollheim and Richard
Wilson were still the four primary members in the act. They secured
a new residence at 2574 Bedford Avenue, Brooklyn, New York, running
into difficulty when John B. Michel, the only member of their group
over twenty-one was taken ill and hospitalized and couldn't sign
the lease. Harry Dockweiler, who lacked a few months of being of
legal age, bluffed it through and signed the lease. At this time
Dockweiler was the only man of the group with a job.

The new residence was promptly dubbed the Ivory Tower, due to the
fact that the fourth floor apartment occupied by the Futurians had
been painted in ivory, and this new apartment became the Futurian
pentagon for the war against New Fandom and against editorial
obstinacy that up to this time had refused to recognize the brilliant
character of their ringing prose.

From the bastions of the Futurian House and the Ivory Tower the
Futurian brain trust launched a better coordinated attack against
New Fandom and its followers than they had previously been capable
of. They were less than reluctant to correspond with fans anywhere
in the world as to the justice of their cause, and they made many
converts in this grass-roots fashion. In order to keep in the good
graces of the Illinois group, they carried on a constant series of
plugs in all their publications for the forthcoming Chicago convention, but more than that they enlisted, one and all, as tried and
true reporters of the science fiction world for the news and views
magazine, *Le Zombie,* published by Bob Tucker. This served a two-fold
purpose, for mixed in among the news they found it possible to
insert many cracks at New Fandom and bits of propaganda for their
cause. Bob Tucker proved far from reluctant to accept their help,
for their choice bits and scoops helped build *Le Zombie* into a news
organ which all but scuttled the strait-laced *Fantasy News*. Tucker,
further, never let up on New Fandom and its leaders, Moskowitz,
Sykora and Taurasi, on his own, giving them the literary needle
frequently and with scant mercy.

The Science Fiction Fan, whose policies were almost completely
controlled by the Futurians, continued to print pointed columns and
articles by Donald A. Wollheim and Robert W. Lowndes directed
against the New Fandom faction.

No group was too humble to be a fallow ground for Futurian propaganda. In Maine, active fan James S. Avery, who had been one of the co-editors of the first contemplated issue of *Spaceways,* and who had issued the humor magazine *Funtasy,* which later continued as a part of Bob Tucker's *Nova,* was striving mightily to organize the science fiction fans of Maine. In September, 1939, there appeared the first number of the *Maine Scientifiction Association Bulletin* or *MSA Bulletin.* Concurrently with this appeared a hektographed publication, titled *Special Bulletin* also dated September, 1939. This later was published as a supplement to the *MSA Bulletin* (which was mimeographed), and was intended to carry news of primary interest to MSA members only, and its circulation largely limited to members. The first elections held the first week in October found Gerald Clarke president and James S. Avery executive-secretary. Other members of the organization were Norman F. Stanley, Carl Paradis, Laurence Dube, Phil Gilbert and Gerald Meader. Local and little known science fiction fans continued to add to the roster. Norman F. Stanley, who owned the largest collection of the group, offered to loan any of his seventy bound volumes of professional science fiction magazines to any member who wished to read them, with few takers.

From the first issue of the *MSA Bulletin,* the Futurians managed to get their material against New Fandom into print. Donald A. Wollheim had therein an article titled "'New Fandom' versus True Fandom" in which he charged New Fandom with being fascist, juvenile and a menace to the field. The primary importance of this article is that it invented a new term, in use, perforce usually smilingly, to this day, when he called Sam Moskowitz a "fake fan." Old time fans, sometimes active and interested for decades, when accused by new-comers of being too cynical and lacking interest are wont to make a wry face and retort: "I guess I'm nothing but a fake fan."

They also carried a two-part article by Richard Wilson on the misadventures of the Futurian House and news items relating to the Futurians. On one occasion they lashed out at Taurasi and *Fantasy News* which in printing a story of a farewell dinner given to Louis Kuslan of New Haven, Connecticut, who was breaking off activity in science fiction fandom to enter college, had eulogized Kuslan by saying: "Mayhap that Gertrude (his sister) will fill the New England vacancy, which yawns now, wider than ever before." The Maine group regarded this as an affront which in effect denied them any importance or role in the fan world. The facts are plainly that the *Fantasy News* story was datelined September 14, 1939, and the first issue of the *MSA Bulletin* was stenciled on September 15, 1939. Previous to that date *Le Zombie* for September 2, 1939, had published news of an "attempt," and a not-too-successful one, since only three individuals were contacted, to organize a Maine group. Kicking New Fandom and its affiliates had become a popular vogue, since for a long period there was no apparent retaliation. Peculiarly, though fully indoctrinated, James S. Avery suffered from an embarrassing fondness for Moskowitz's articles. It became a common thing in the readers' columns of fan magazines to have Avery apologize fore and aft for enjoying an article by Moskowitz: "Regardless of what I may think of the man and his methods," he would say, "he's still one of the best of the many good fan writers." Later, other fans, convinced by Futurian logic that New Fandomites could do no good, but with

their real heart one with Moskowitz's youthfully enthusiastic single-.
centered purist notions that the most important thing to discuss and
write about in science fiction fandom was science fiction, began to
similarly praise Moskowitz's articles with appropriate qualifications.
Yet they refused to admit the truth to themselves, that since Moskowitz's writings could not help but fully reflect his ideas as to
what composed ideal science fiction activities, liking his articles
meant that they approved of his ideas and ideals. It was a hard and
lack-luster task that the Futurians had insisted this group of fan
teen-agers assume. First to drive out "the fascists in fandom" and
then to work with the communists for the achievement of a world-
state.

In a pamphlet written by Robert W. Lowndes titled "The Futurians
and New Fandom," Lowndes had set the key-note of the new, reinstated
Futurian drive against New Fandom. He offered the fact that the
Futurians and New Fandom basically were working for the same things,
and in point of fact, he asserted that New Fandom had accomplished
much more in the field than the Futurians, but he asked science fiction fandom to unite against the New Fandom leaders for New Fandom
represented to his eyes dictatorship and the Futurians democracy. He
dramatically presented incidents to illustrate his point, and ended
to the effect that the Futurians were united and strong and would
never relent or give up in their battle until this matter was decided
and their opponents crushed. This pamphlet was prepared in October,
1939, shortly before the Philadelphia Conference and distributed
there with a long poem by Lowndes on a single sheet with the self-
explanatory title *Moskowitz's Farewell to his Greatness*.

In the special issue sixteen of Bob Tucker's *Le Zombie,* also distributed at the Philadelphia Conference, Lowndes had a letter expressing his thanks and happiness at the manner in which science fiction
fandom, particularly "top" fans, had rallied to the Futurian side
after the fiasco at the First World Science Fiction Convention.

This apparently indicated a real softening of the strong Michelist
line previously taken, for immediately beneath it, Tucker published
in "Our Annual Eyebrow Lifter Dept.," a statement from a Futurian
whose name he withheld which read: "...the line adopted since the
Futurian Conference is to take politics out of fandom without
excluding such aspects as sociology, which really do have a place in
science fiction fan discussions. In other words: we Communists will
confine our propaganda to personal correspondence in fandom. We will
also refrain from leftist attacks upon other fans and their viewpoints *so long as they tolerate us and our viewpoints."*

Even as he wrote of the unconquerable resolve of the Futurians to
crush their foes, and of their own invulnerability, Robert W. Lowndes
excercised more perspicacity than many of his followers. In "The
Futurians and New Fandom" he seemed to sense the possibility of a
set-back at the Philadelphia Conference, was suspicious of the over-
long silence of the New Fandom parties. He wrote: "We are not seers
and prophets. We can not say precisely what events will occur; we
have been defeated in the past. We cannot say precisely what line of
attack the dictators and their followers will use; they had succeeded
in hypocritically presenting themselves as the saviors of democracy
in the past, even while they denied simple democratic rights to
their own members."

In the past, the Futurians had made a great show of obtaining an open platform with the New Fandomites. They maintained that New Fandom heads had deliberately kept business the floor of the convention to muzzle them. They repeated and reiterated that the New Fandomites were afraid to meet them in open debate. That New Fandom was fearful of letting the truth be known. At Philadelphia the Futurians had their opportunity. There was no limit to the amount of time their speakers could have had, if the desire to speak had been made known. There were strong representatives from many segments of fandom to rally to their defense if they did not get a fair hearing. Opinion was already strongly against New Fandom, and former powerful allies like Jack Speer were working against, not for, New Fandom. Outstanding figures like Milton A. Rothman and Bob Tucker made strong statements in their speeches which literarily punished New Fandom. Yet before the conference was over the Futurians were a confused group. New Fandom, the organization that was purportedly undemocratic, had arrived on the scene with a prepared constitution and an illustrative chart pointing out its salient features. More, they agreed to mail for consideration to their members the constitution of any other individual who would mimeograph sufficient copies to cover the entire membership. That the Futurians had been more than just confused, but were thoroughly beaten, was illustrated by their tactics which consisted of the most continuous and insulting mass heckling ever witnessed at a science fiction conference or convention in the entire recorded histories of these events. Where before they had accused New Fandom of attaining its ends through parliamentary trickery, now they desperately utilized every device they were able to contrive in this line to forestall even a *vote* for or against New Fandom's constitution. When the conference had ended, the entire Philadelphia faction with the exception of Milton A. Rothman had swung strongly back in with New Fandom. Moskowitz's claim that the Futurians had forced politics and feuds upon them and deliberately practiced communistic techniques in the form of leftist attacks now seemed dramatically credible in view of the poor behavior of the Futurians at the Philadelphia Conference, the explanation in the article "There *Are* Two Sides" and the simultaneous appearance in Tucker's *Le Zombie* of an anonymous letter from a Futurian substantially admitting the same thing!

Again Robert W. Lowndes covered the affair in his pamphlet "Storm over Philadelphia," written November, 1939, at 1197th Co., CCC, Portland, Maine, and published by the Futurian Society in December, 1939, in an account which he openly admitted: "...with the exception of direct quotations (statements in quotation marks), I have not tried to reproduce exact wordings of either speeches or statements. Thus the reader is warned that some details will be inaccurate. The general tone of this report is, as those who were there can testify, accurate." In this pamphlet he gave a highly fictionalized and colored account of the Philadelphia Conference, particularly stressing the doubts that the Futurians had about the constitution, but unable to show that Futurians had not had an equal chance to attend, debate and vote on their points against the New Fandomites. They had lost, as groups lose points at political conventions, in a manner which does not make the winners 100 percent right or the losers 100 percent wrong. He attempted to intimate that possibly there had been collusion between the New Fandomites and the PSFS's. Considered as evidence of this was the fact that the New Fandomites, through the auspices of the Queens SFL, contributed $10.00 for liquid refreshments for the entire convention, which refreshments were consumed by the Futurians with no particular prejudice. Yet, the actions of chairman John V. Baltadonis in averting a clash between Sykora and Wollheim was universally praised as was the adroit manner in which he pacified both factions and prevented a threatened walk-out. If there were any collusion, it could certainly have not been with the chairman.

the same month Robert W. Lowndes wrote and had published by the Futurian Society another mimeographed pamphlet entitled "Unity, Democracy, Peace," which was an attempt to counteract the effect of Moskowitz's article "There *Are* Two Sides." Again Lowndes proved that he was the wisest politician on the Futurian side. He recognized that Moskowitz's letter in Tucker's convention issue of *Le Zombie,* expressing his loss of faith in fandom and asking readers to buy *The Science Fiction Collector* for the true facts about the case was but a feint to divert and mislead. He pointed out techniques Moskowitz had used to defeat the opposition and win his point. Previously the Futurian method had been to satirize their opponents, search for spelling and grammatical errors which could be offered as indications of lack of intelligence, to malign and tease their opponents but never, under any circumstances, give them credit for good intentions or intelligence. Lowndes changed all that with his series of bulletins. He took a new tack. First he claimed that the New Fandom intentions were fine but their methods, which were "those of fascists," made it necessary to fight them. Now he admitted that there was intelligence, design and artfulness in the methods of his opponents which he contended proved the insincerity of their statements. He particularly deplored the fact that the communist label was used to "frighten" fans and turn them against the Futurian group. He said: "Their cry is: a communist cannot be a science fiction fan. When they have persuaded fandom as a whole that this absurdity is true, then they intend to raise the same cry against others who oppose them or with whom they disagree."

The same pamphlet went on to urge fans to stay completely neutral so far as the war in Europe, which had broken out in September, 1939, was concerned. They urged immediate anti-war activity. They wanted anti-war stickers printed and pasted on all envelopes. "We must explain to new fans, and to oldtimers who may not understand, precisely why the entrance of the USA into war would mean the end of stf and fandom here." This was diametrically opposed to their previous promise to keep politics out of fandom. Shortly later, when Germany attacked Russia, the viewpoint against the United States entering the war altered radically.

EPILOGUE

IT WAS ORIGINALLY the intention of this historian to utilize this Epilogue to very briefly outline the major events and trends that immediately follow the preceding chapter and in synoptic form bring the History up to America's entry into the war. It was while doing an outline and research on this period that I realized that this History could not be carried forward in that manner, and what is more, *should* not. The actual events and occurrences themselves are so minute on a national scale, that if individual personalities, aims, ambitions, emotional motivations are not taken into consideration, this History loses all meaning and impact.

This History should be carried further. Carried forward with the same detail, research and thoroughness which has characterized it to this point. There must be no important omissions that might cause knowledgeable parties to question its authenticity or careless errors that might be seized upon to discredit the entire work. There are so many fascinating aspects to the field, so many events filled with interest and purport.

It is my hope and desire to someday have the time to carry this History forward in *detatl* at least to *Pearl Harbor,* and possibly beyond. Carried that far, it will be seen that the events in the science fiction field that follow will, in widening circles, be merely history repeating itself. Then, even if the History is never carried further, it will be a complete unit, for the problems and difficulties faced by the science fiction fans and professionals today are unquestionably the same as those of yesterday. The play remains the same, only the costumes and scenery have been changed.

As it stands, this History may be said to be complete up to November, 1939, as far as the American fans are concerned. With sections needed to bring the professional magazines and British fandom up to that same point. Summarily, the situation in the science fiction world when this work terminates was as follows:

In England, the high-promise of British fan and professional activity continued strongly in upward spirals of achievement through 1938 and into 1939. *Novae Terrae,* the official organ of the Science Fiction Association continued a roughly monthly publication until January, 1939, maintaining an increasingly high standard of interest in their articles and columns, after which it was carried forth under the title of *New Worlds* under the capable editorship of Edward J. (Ted) Carnell, who raised the quality of interest and reproduction still higher, counting among his contributors Arthur C. Clarke, Ray Bradbury, Sam Moskowitz, Donald A. Wollheim and Robert W. Lowndes. Other important British fan journals were John F. Burkes and David McIlwain's *The Satellite,* begun as the official organ of the Liverpool SFA; C. S. Youd's *The Fantast* which leaned predominantly toward fiction with lengthy, somewhat callow letters from readers on various phases of communism and socialism, with digressions for appropriate pseudo-intellectual discussions, and J. Michael Rosenblum's *The Futurian* continuing as a nicely printed publication. Undoubtedly the banner publishing accomplishment of the

British fans was *Tomorrow,* which had seen four issues as a mimeographed publication and then combined with Walter Gillings' *Scientifiction,* metamorphosing into a handsomely printed, 16 paged, letter-sized publication with a quality of material and presentation far too good for the times. Douglas Mayer capably edited the three issues of this publication during 1938, after which it was suspended because of the expense.

Professionally, Walter Gillings' *Tales of Wonder* continued quarterly publication, featuring selected reprints from American science fiction magazines plus some new material by British authors. Its average quality was as high as any of the American science fiction magazines. In 1938, a second professional British science fiction magazine titled *Fantasy* was placed into circulation by George Newnes, Limited, publishers of *Wide World,* and the same company which Walter Gillings had unsuccessfully attempted to persuade to publish a science fiction magazine previous to beginning *Tales of Wonder* with the Worlds Work people. Edited by T. Stanhope Sprigg, this magazine was an excellent job for the times, with a few exceptions featuring new material by leading writers comparable in quality to magazine science fiction being published anywhere in the world. So it was that despite the depression England was showing steady building and accomplishment in science fiction.

In the United States the fights and feuds continued, the petty struggles for power parallelling on their microcosmic scale the major events of world history. The Futurians gradually moved into the professional ranks, controlling at one time five professional newstand publications. To the consternation of the Futurian group, the leaders of New Fandom (which organization gradually died a slow painless death due to inertia and lack of funds) also moved into the professional field and the feud of the fan magazines continued unabated in the professional magazines. The leaders of both factions were fully cognizant of the dangerous potentialities of this situation, so much so that Donald A. Wollheim, writing with a touch of contemplative fear said in his article "The Final Feud" published in the March-April, 1940, issue of *Fantasy Digest*: "What will be the outcome of this I dare not predict. This is something that has never happened before in science fiction. This is indeed the final feud..."

Sam Moskowitz also understood the dangers of the situation and split with Sykora and Taurasi as to a matter of procedure and policy, even meeting with Frederik Pohl of the Futurian group to attempt to arrange a truce, but his associates were implacable and most of the members of the Futurian group too undiplomatic to permit a dignified "cease fire."

As a back-drop loomed the threat of another World War as Germany began a systematic annexation of nearby countries and provinces in Europe and France and England came to grips with her. The culmination came on December 7, 1941, when the Japanese bombed Pearl Harbor. Things would never again be quite the same in science fiction or science fiction fandom.

tution is unfortunately no longer available to this historian, so the details which follow are necessarily drawn from memory. Briefly, membership in New Fandom was divided into an outer circle and an inner circle of fans; only those in the outer circle could join the inner, and only those in the inner circle could vote or hold office. Admission to both divisions was to be directed by a committee created for that specific purpose. The reason for the two groups was to allow the more active fans, the publishers of magazines and sponsors of public events, to do the work of organization and guide its policies, while providing a definite place also for the newcomers and the general readers whose interest did not go beyond joining the organization for milder participation in its activities. Members of course could gravitate from one circle to another as time strengthened or weakened their interest in fandom.

With prize-fighters there are nights when they reach their peak, when they will never reach greater heights; with artists there comes the day when they have completed their finest painting; with authors, the completion of their masterpiece. October 29, 1939, was William Sykora's day. Rarely has a man done such justice to a document. Despite the unceasing chatter of heckling Futurians he sold his product to the audience. On completion of the reading majority acceptance seemed almost a foregone conclusion. Now there were questions and discussion with Sykora replying in careful detail to all questions asked.

Futurian Leslie Perri called the document "magnificent," but queried as to whether there might be present some concealed legal device for barring her group. The Futurians themselves were impressed by the constitution, but appeared suspicious of its length and what they construed as evasiveness in some of Sykora's remarks. Their heckling had by this time grown to extreme intensity, and Sykora had borne all of it with incredible patience, wisely realizing his doing so would strengthen New Fandom's cause and render Futurian conduct the more unsportsmanlike. Probably this forbearance alone prevented an explosion in the charged atmosphere pervading the conference.

But fate was not to be denied. During the course of one of Sykora's explanations Wollheim shouted, "That's a lie!" Had this exclamation been made by any other Futurian it might not have touched off the explosion—but coming from Wollheim, who had inflicted many a fannish hurt upon Sykora in the past, it was the straw that broke the camel's back. Sykora's face reddened, his fists clenched. "Nobody can call me a liar and get away with it," he said audibly, and determinably advanced to the front row where his opponent sat a scant ten feet away. As Wollheim pressed against the back of his chair tiny Jack Gillespie, who weighed scarcely a hundred pounds, sprang in front of him to intervene. Sykora brushed him aside with one hand and confronted his opponent. As the whole Futurian contingent were sitting together, there were eleven men for Sykora to deal with, not merely Wollheim alone. Shocked into realization of Sykora's danger by Gillespie's action, Moskowitz headed down one aisle toward the group and Taurasi hastened down the other. Speaking for most of the Philadelphians, Madle shouted to Moskowitz, "we're here if you need any help!"

It was the diplomacy of chairman John V. Baltadonis that deserves the laurels for avoiding a clash. He dissuaded Sykora from any further action, convinced Moskowitz and Taurasi that Sykora was safe enough so they could resume their seats, and quieted members of his own Philadelphia group that were itching for a fracas.

Wollheim then arose and asked that Sykora, Taurasi and Moskowitz be made to apologize to the assembly for their actions or leave the hall. Moskowitz arose and with great assumption of indignation asked that the Futurians be forced to apologize for their heckling or leave the hall. The alternatives, both groups intimated, being that they themselves would walk out if their demands were not met. Again, chairman Baltadonis with commendable diplomacy persuaded both factions to waive their motions and stay.

Moskowitz then phrased a motion to the effect that the Philadelphia Conference go on record as approving New Fandom's constitution. The motion was seconded and a vote called for, but the Futurians seized upon the wording of the motion and delayed the vote for forty-five minutes while Taurasi rephrased the motion more concisely. The motion was passed 21 to 12 and the New Fandom group had scored one of the most amazing come backs in fan annals.

New Fandom had earned the right to live, but it had to renew the confidence of the science fiction fans in its organization if it expected to get the new memberships necessary to insure its exist-ence, and this could not be done unless it could clear itself or at least minimize the accusation of "Exclusion Act" when it had acted to prevent six Futurian members from entering the hall the first day of the Nycon.

John V. Baltadonis had promised Moskowitz that his article of explanation and rebuttal titled "There *Are* Two Sides" would appear in time to be distributed at the Conference. This promise he kept, but in his rush to do so his usually superb hektographing was light and indistinct. The issue of the *Science Fiction Collector* contain-ing that article was dated July-August, 1939. The article opened by completely reprinting the Los Angeles Science Fiction League's state-ment regarding its disapproval and condemnation of the "exclusion act" and then rebutting with the following arguments: it called the LASFL members liars because they claimed to have heard all sides of the story, and yet had never even written any member of the New Fandom group asking his view of the question, forming their complete judgement without attempting to do so. Secondly it pointed to the statement maintaining that Ackerman and Morojo's testimony was "unprejudiced" and then showed published articles by Ackerman and Morojo which stated sympathy for the Michelism sponsored by the Futurians. It accused fandom of permitting an admittedly communist front movement, the Michelists, to insist that their opponents hew to their notion of "democracy," while the Michelists barred no holds in their own tactics. Moskowitz stated: "...And because they have raised a din of "undemocratic," you, who are so afraid for democracy, follow their falsely accusing voices and like a puppet on a string, accomplish what they are not strong enough to do themselves." He further demanded to know why no fans had uttered a word of disapproval when the Michelist group had barred himself and Alex Osheroff from membership in the Greater New York SFL, without any stated grounds whatsoever; he asked where was the chorus of protest when Olon F. Wiggins had banned him from the pages of *The Science Fiction Fan?* He then termed the LASFL "Democratically minded hypocrites" for their

INDEX

NOTE.—Amateur titles are underscored. Professional titles appear in italics.